RELIGION AND STATE
IN THE
AMERICAN JEWISH
EXPERIENCE

Jonathan D. Sarna
and
David G. Dalin

The University of Notre Dame Press

© 1997 by
University of Notre Dame Press
Notre Dame, Indiana 46556
All Rights Reserved

Manufactured in the United States of America

Book design by Paul K. Wilson
Set in 10/12 Stone Print by Books International
Printed and bound by Braun-Brumfield, Inc.

Library of Congress Cataloging-in-Publication Data
Religion and state in the American Jewish experience / Jonathan D. Sarna and
David G. Dalin.
    p.   cm.
    Includes bibliographical references and index.
    ISBN 0-268-01654-2 (alk. paper)
    1. Jews—United States—History—Sources.   2. Jews—Legal status, laws,
etc.—United States—History—Sources.   3. Freedom of religion—United
States—History—Sources.   4. Church and state—United States—History—
Sources.   5. United States—Ethic relations—Sources.   I. Sarna, Jonathan D.
II. Dalin, David G.
E184.J5R43   1997
322'.1'089924073—dc20   96-27119
                                         CIP

∞ *The paper used in this publication meets the minimum requirements of the*
American National Standard for Information Sciences—Permanence
of Paper for Printed Library Materials,
ANSI Z39.48-1984

For our children

Aaron Yehuda Sarna

Leah Livia Sarna

Simona Sara Dalin

Barry Simcha Dalin

Contents

Preface

W hile American Jews have written a great deal on the subject of church and state, almost every word has been issue-oriented, supporting or opposing some particular practice or innovation. Dispassionate scholarly literature on the subject has been far more rare, and reliable historical inquiries, aside from a recent work by Naomi W. Cohen, almost nonexistent. Much of what passes for fact in the field (e.g., "American Jewry's longstanding historic embrace of separationism") turns out upon careful examination to consist of half-truths, and sometimes pure fantasy.

Religion and State in the American Jewish Experience seeks to remedy this sorry situation by making available for the first time critical documents that have shaped debates over religion and state issues throughout the course of American Jewish history. Following a comprehensive historical introduction, we present a wide range of primary source materials representing different positions on both general and specific church-state topics as they affected Jews from colonial times to the present. Chapters proceed chronologically to offer a sense of change over time, and each chapter is subdivided into discrete themes to enhance conceptual clarity. Quite deliberately, we have sought in this volume to recover *divergent* voices and opinions from days gone by. Indeed, what we have discovered in our research is that American Jewish views on religion and state issues have never in the past been monolithic, just as they are not monolithic now.

* * *

The Reverend Richard John Neuhaus, currently president of the Institute on Religion and Public Life and editor-in-chief of *First Things,* stimulated this volume. Back in 1985, he invited Jonathan Sarna to prepare a paper on religion and state for a small scholarly gathering convened at Temple Emanu-El in New York on the subject of Jews and Judaism in American public life. The paper, entitled "Christian America or Secular America? The Church-State Dilemma of American Jews," was subsequently published in *Jews in Unsecular America* (Eerdmans, 1987), a volume that Neuhaus edited. Sarna soon returned to this subject in a much more comprehensive way at the invitation of the American Jewish Committee. His monograph entitled *American Jews and Church-State Relations: The Search for "Equal Footing"* was published by the Committee in 1989, and in a slightly modified and updated form is republished here as the introduction. We are grateful to the American Jewish Committee, and especially to Dr. Steven Bayme, director of its Jewish communal affairs department, for permitting this republication.

Meanwhile, David Dalin had simultaneously been working on twentieth-century Jewish attitudes towards church-state issues as part of his research on the American Jewish thinker, Will Herberg. Dalin's article in the July 1988 issue of *Commentary* entitled "Will Herberg in Retrospect," followed by his *From Marxism to Judaism: Collected Essays of Will Herberg* (Markus Wiener, 1989) brought to light a minority Jewish viewpoint on religion and state issues that diverged markedly from the mainstream, and belied the supposed "Jewish consensus" that dominates most writing on the subject. At Neuhaus's suggestion, Sarna and Dalin agreed to join forces to extend their research and to produce the present work. Sarna assumed primary responsibility for the preface, introduction, and chapters 1–6; Dalin drafted chapters 7–11 and the "Suggestions for Further Reading." In the end, of course, the work demanded collaboration. Each author benefited from the criticisms of the other.

* * *

During the course of this research we have accumulated more scholarly debts than it is possible to acknowledge here. The American Jewish Archives, the American Jewish Historical Society, and the libraries of the American Jewish Committee, Hebrew Union College–Jewish Institute of Religion, the Jewish Theological Seminary of America, and our home institutions, Brandeis University and the University of Hartford, have all been extraordinarily helpful to us, and we thank the staffs of these institutions for locating documents that would otherwise have eluded us. Of the many individuals we consulted, we especially thank Jerome A. Chanes, Nathan Lewin, David Novak, and Marc Stern. All took time out from their own enormously busy schedules to locate documents that we required and to answer pertinent questions. We alone, of course, bear responsibility for the interpretation offered and for any errors that remain. Finally, we express our gratitude to Mr. Richard Gilder and the Gilder Foundation, as well as to the Institute on Religion and Public Life for their material support of this project. We appreciate both their forbearance and their faith.

Jonathan D. Sarna and David G. Dalin
April 19, 1996 / Rosh Hodesh Iyar 5756

American Jews and Church-State Relations

The Search for "Equal Footing"

Jonathan D. Sarna

◆   ◆◆◆   ◆

The Constitutional Convention meeting in Philadelphia in 1787 received exactly one petition on the subject of religious liberty. The petitioner was Jonas Phillips, a German Jewish immigrant merchant, and what he requested—a change in the Pennsylvania state constitution to eliminate a Christological test oath—was outside of the convention's purview. But the sentiments expressed in the petition contain one of the earliest known American Jewish statements on religious liberty. "The Israelites," it declares, "will think themself happy to live under a government where all Religious societies are on an Equal footing."[1]

Eighteen days before Phillips penned his September 7 petition, the Constitutional Convention, meeting behind closed doors, accepted the provisions of Article VI: "no religious test shall ever be required as a qualification to any office or public trust under the United States." Two years later, under pressure from six different states,[2] Congress passed a much more explicit guarantee of religious liberty as part of the First Amendment (ratified on December 15, 1791): "Congress shall make no law respecting an establishment of religion, or prohibiting the free exercise thereof." For Jews, however, these Constitutional provisions did not immediately translate into the kind of "Equal footing" that Jonas Phillips had sought. Indeed, the whole question of what equal footing means and how

1

best to achieve it would continue to occupy American Jewish leaders for two full centuries.

The Colonial Experience

In the colonial period, Jews never expected to achieve complete
religious equality. Given the right to settle, travel, trade, buy land,
gain citizenship, and "exercise in all quietness their religion," they
put up with blasphemy laws, Sunday laws, Christian oaths, church
taxes, and restrictions on their franchise and right to hold public office. "They had not come to North America to acquire political rights," Jacob Marcus reminds us, and besides, as late as the
1760s "there was not one American colony which offered political
equality to all Christians."[3]

Actually, dissenting Christians gained increasing equality as time
went on. Recent scholarship has demonstrated that in colony after
colony traditional religious establishments, in the European sense
of "a single church or religion enjoying formal, legal, official, mo-
nopolistic privilege through a union with the government of the
state," eventually gave way to "multiple establishments." Dissenters, so long as they were Protestant, could arrange to have their
taxes remitted to the church of their choice. Jews and other non-
Christians, however, did not benefit from these arrangements, and
for the most part neither did Catholics. Although many states enacted new liberal constitutions after the Declaration of Independence, religious tests and other restrictive measures remained in
force. North Carolina's new (December 16, 1776) constitution, for
example, promised inhabitants the "natural and unalienable right
to worship Almighty God according to the dictates of their own
consciences," yet also decreed that "no person who shall deny the
being of God or the truth of the Protestant religion . . . shall be
capable of holding any office or place of trust or profit in the civil
department within the state." Similar provisions found in other
state constitutions make clear that most Americans in 1776 spoke
the language of religious liberty but had not yet come to terms with
its implications. While in theory they supported equality and freedom of conscience, as a practical matter they still believed that
Christianity was essential to civil order and peace, and that the
state should be ruled only by God-fearing Protestants.[4]

The New Nation

The first decade and a half of American independence saw the pa-
rameters of religious liberty in the new nation steadily widen. New

York, one of the most religiously pluralistic of the states, became in 1777 the first to extend the boundaries of "free exercise and enjoyment of religious profession and worship" to "all mankind," whether Christian or not (although it retained a limited anti-Catholic naturalization oath). Virginia, in its 1785 Act for Religious Freedom (originally proposed by Thomas Jefferson in 1779), went even further with a ringing declaration "that no man shall be compelled to frequent or support any religious worship, place or ministry whatsoever . . . but that all men shall be free to profess and by argument to maintain, their opinions in matters of religion, and that the same shall in no wise diminish, enlarge or affect their civil capacities." The Northwest Ordinance, adopted by the Continental Congress in 1787, extended freedom of worship and belief into the territories north of the Ohio River. Finally, under the Constitution and the First Amendment, "no establishment" and "free exercise" became fundamental principles of federal law.[5]

America's two thousand or so Jews played no significant role in bringing these developments about. They received their rights on the federal level along with everybody else, not, as so often the case in Europe, as part of a special privilege or "Jew Bill." Religious liberty developed from de facto religious pluralism and a complex web of other social, ideological, political, and economic factors affecting the nation as a whole. For this reason, Jews were always able to couch their demands for religious equality in patriotic terms. In seeking rights for themselves on the state level, they appealed to principles shared by Americans of all faiths.[6]

Initial Jewish Efforts to Attain Equal Rights

The first half-century following the adoption of the Constitution and First Amendment saw America's small Jewish communities engaged in a wide variety of local campaigns to achieve equal rights in the states. First Amendment guarantees, until the Supreme Court ruled otherwise in 1940, affected congressional legislation only; states remained free to engage in religious discrimination. There was no Jewish communal defense agency, and much depended on the work of concerned individuals, often working in concert with sympathetic Gentiles. Typically, Jews pointed up contradictions between their rights under the Constitution and their rights under state law, pleaded for religious equality on the basis of liberty and reason, and then legitimated their claims by trumpeting their contributions to the war effort against Britain.[7]

More often than not, Jews found that their boldness in defense of Jewish rights eventually paid off. In 1783, for example, a delegation of prominent Philadelphia Jews petitioned against a Christological state religious test. They argued that it deprived them "of the most eminent rights of freemen," and was particularly unfair since they had "distinguishedly suffered" for their attachment to the Revolution. Seven years later, when a new state bill of rights was passed, the problem was remedied.[8] In 1809, when several legislators sought to deny Jacob Henry his seat in the North Carolina House of Commons for refusing to subscribe to a Christian test oath, he too refused to concede. Instead, he wrote a celebrated address defending his "natural and unalienable right" to worship according to the dictates of his own conscience, and won his place. In this case, however, the offensive test oath remained on the books, apparently unenforced, until a new constitution was promulgated in 1868.[9]

The most widely publicized of all religious-liberty cases took place in Maryland. According to that state's constitution, anyone assuming an "office of trust or profit" (including lawyers and jurors) was required to execute a "declaration of belief in the Christian religion" before being certified. Solomon Etting, one of the first Jewish merchants in Baltimore, petitioned in 1797 and 1802 to have this law changed, "praying to be placed on the same footing as other good citizens," but to no avail.[10] It took thirty years, a great deal of help from non-Jewish lawmakers, particularly Thomas Kennedy, and a state political realignment before the bill permitting Jews to subscribe to an alternate oath won final passage in 1826 by a narrow margin.[11]

Christian America or Religious America?

By 1840 Jews had won formal political equality in twenty-one of the twenty-six states. In the others, legal disabilities would shortly disappear, or would remain largely unenforced.[12] Yet, full equality still proved elusive, for church-state separation, the principle upon which Jews hinged so many of their hopes, turned out to mean different things to different people. Many Americans, especially in the wake of the Second Great Awakening, the religious revival that overtook the country in the early nineteenth century, had come to understand religious liberty in pan-Christian terms, as if the Constitution aimed only to place all Protestant denominations on an equal footing. Christianity, according to this argument, formed the basis of American society and was implicitly endorsed by the Constitution, even if not mentioned explicitly.[13] The legal case for this school of interpretation was made by Justice Joseph Story writing about the First Amendment in his famous *Commentaries on the Constitution:*

> The real object of the amendment was, not to countenance, much less to advance Mahometanism, or Judaism, or infidelity, by prostrating Christianity; but to exclude all rivalry among Christian sects, and to prevent any national ecclesiastical establishment, which should give to an hierarchy the exclusive patronage of the national government.[14]

This understanding of America as an essentially "Christian nation" carried wide appeal. Leading judges and lawyers, including James Kent of New York and Theophilus Parsons and Daniel Webster of Massachusetts, endorsed it, and it accorded with British precedent that recognized "the Christian religion . . . as constituting a part of the common law."[15] This same view led South Carolina governor James H. Hammond, in an 1844 Thanksgiving Day proclamation, to urge citizens of his state "to offer up their devotions to God the Creator, and his Son Jesus Christ, the redeemer of the world." In the face of Jewish protests, he refused to relent. "Whatever may be the language . . . of [the] Constitution," he wrote, "I know that the civilization of the age is derived from Christianity, that the institutions of this country are instinct with the same spirit, and that it pervades the laws of the State as it does the manners and I trust the hearts of our people."[16]

American Jews naturally opposed this "Christian America" interpretation of the First Amendment, and denied that Christianity formed part of the common law. They called instead for "equal footing" to all religions, Judaism included. Philadelphia Jews thus petitioned for the "rights of freemen, solemnly ascertained to all men who are not professed Atheists." Jacob Henry argued that "if a man fulfills the duties of that religion which his education or his Conscience has pointed to him as the true one; no person . . . has the right to arraign him at the bar of any inquisition." Mordecai Noah, perhaps the leading American Jew of his day, defined religious liberty as "a mere abolition of all religious disabilities." "You are free," he explained, "to worship God in any manner you please; and this liberty of conscience cannot be violated."[17]

This sense of America as a broadly inclusive religious nation, while understandable as a response to "Christian America," was quite different from the theory of religion and state espoused by Thomas Jefferson and James Madison. Jefferson believed that religion was a personal matter not subject to government jurisdiction at all; we owe to him the famous interpretation of the First

Amendment as "a wall of separation between church and state."
Madison called in a similar vein for the "entire abstinence of the
Government from any interference [with religion] in any way whatever."[18] The view that government should in a nondiscriminatory
way support religion did, however, have firm roots in American tradition. The Northwest Ordinance of 1787 grouped religion with
morality and knowledge as things "necessary to good government
and the happiness of mankind." When the First Amendment was
adopted, Samuel Huntington of Connecticut, speaking in Congress,
quite explicitly sought "to secure the rights of conscience, and free
exercise of the rights of religion, but not to patronize those who
professed no religion at all." Several state constitutions and the writings of men like Benjamin Franklin all reinforced the same idea:
that religion, defined in its broadest sense, benefits society and
government alike.[19]

The fact that early American Jews embraced this tradition explains why, as a community, they never linked their rights to those
of nonbelievers. Nor did they protest when several states, including Pennsylvania and Maryland, accorded Jews rights that non-
believers were denied. Indeed, in one unusual petition in 1813,
the Trustees of New York's Congregation Shearith Israel, seeking a
share of the state's school fund, attacked the appropriation made
to the New York Free School because it "encourage[d] parents in
habits of indifference to their duties of religion." Siding with Presbyterians, Roman Catholics, Baptists, and Methodists against the
school, they praised religious education as "the greatest foundation
of social happiness," and argued on the basis of "the liberal spirit
of our constitution," that funds should be made available to religiously sponsored charity schools as well.[20]

Defenders of American Jewish Rights

By the middle decades of the nineteenth century, thanks to immigrants from Germany and Poland, the American Jewish population had grown substantially, reaching 15,000 in 1840 and almost
150,000 twenty years later. Jews now formed a sizable and self-con-
scious minority community, complete with its own institutions and
leaders. Jews also had their first regular periodicals—the *Occident*
(1843–69), the *Asmonean* (1849–58), and the *Israelite* (1854–)—to
keep them informed, to help them maintain ties with one another,
and to promote vigilance in defense of Jewish rights. Where before,
church-state violations (except in unusual cases such as the Maryland bill) had usually been matters of local Jewish concern, now
thanks to these newspapers they were trumpeted far and wide.[21]

Jews during this period looked to the First Amendment as a guarantor of Jewish rights and used it to legitimate their claims to equality. "The laws of the country," explained Isaac Leeser, editor of the *Occident* and the foremost traditionalist Jewish religious leader of his day, "know nothing of any religious profession, and leave every man to pursue whatever religion he pleases." He insisted that neither Christianity, nor Judaism, nor "infidelity and atheism" was the law of the land, but that "there is here freedom for all, and rights and protection for all."[22]

Religious liberty, to Leeser and most of his fellow Jews, meant "the right to worship God after the dictates of our own hearts." Nathaniel Levin, one of the leading Jewish citizens of Charleston, went out of his way to underscore this point when he delivered a public toast to religious liberty in 1859. "Separate man from religion in any of the duties of life," he declared, "and you degrade him to the level of the brute." Religious liberty, as he defined it, meant "liberty of conscience," and "freedom of thought" within a religious context.[23] Having defined religious liberty in this way, mid-nineteenth-century Jews saw no need to protest that Congress and most state legislatures began their sessions with religious invocations. They simply insisted that Jews be invited to deliver such prayers as well—and in at least three cases rabbis were invited to do so. Similarly, when in 1861 Jews learned that only "regularly ordained minister[s] of some Christian denomination" could legally serve as regimental chaplains in the Union army, most did not object to the chaplaincy itself, although on its face it violated principles of strict church-state separation. Instead, they campaigned to have the law broadened to include rabbis, which, thanks to support from President Lincoln, it eventually was.[24]

From a Jewish point of view, church-state violations were no different from anti-Jewish defamations and Christian missionizing. All alike, Jews thought, aimed to deprive them of their equal status in American society.[25] Thanksgiving Day proclamations that excluded Jews by referring to Christianity, references to Americans as a "Christian people," discriminatory laws and practices, anti-Jewish slurs and stereotypes, conversionist sallies, efforts to write Christianity into the Constitution—these and similar instances of thoughtlessness, maliciousness, and prejudice seemed to Jews not just wrong but distinctly un-American, a violation of the Constitution as they understood it.[26] They usually responded forcefully, for as Isaac Leeser explained, Jewish rights had jealously to be guarded:

> Though a captious fault-finding and a constant nervousness to take offense should never be manifested by Israelites, as unbecoming

and unmanly, at the same time, no public insult either of omission or commission should be passed over in silence; for we ought to take good care of our rights and never allow them to be tacitly violated.[27]

Rabbi Isaac Mayer Wise of Cincinnati, America's leading Reform rabbi and editor of the *American Israelite,* was even more vehement in defense of Jewish rights. He saw Jews engaged in a political war not only to safeguard their own hard-won equality, but American liberty as well. "Not because we profess Judaism do we oppose the attempt to crush religious liberty," he wrote in 1865, "we do it because we love liberty and justice, and hold them in esteem infinitely higher than all earthly gifts." By explicitly linking the safeguarding of Jewish rights to the safeguarding of American liberties, he raised Jewish vigilance on church-state issues to the level of a patriotic duty—which is what many Jews have considered it ever since. No wonder, then, that Wise was so proud of the fact that on these issues he had fought to the last. Looking back late in his life, he claimed, according to his biographer, that he had never shirked his "duty" on the issue of civil and religious rights, whatever the cost.[28]

Beginning in 1859, individual rabbis no longer had to fight church-state battles on their own. The Board of Delegates of American Israelites, founded that year, made defense of Jewish rights one of its central objects, and although it was never truly representative of the American Jewish community, on these issues it spoke for a broad constituency. It thus repeatedly objected to efforts by the National Reform Association to rewrite the preamble to the Constitution to include references to "Almighty God," "the Lord Jesus Christ," and "Christian government." It likewise protested provisions of the 1866 Reconstruction Act providing that Southerners' mandatory oath of allegiance be administered upon the "Holy Evangelists," and was instrumental in having the form of oath modified.[29] That same year it published an address to "the friends of Religious Liberty in the State of North Carolina" attacking an article in the state's proposed new constitution that would have barred from government office those who "deny . . . the divine authority of both the Old and New Testaments." "Do not enact a Constitution which denies the equality of citizens whatever their religious profession," the Board implored, reprising Jonas Phillips's "equal footing" demand of eighty years before. Significantly, the Board did not speak out against *all* religious tests, only those that denied equality to "good citizens because they worship God in accordance with their conscientious convictions."[30]

Sunday Laws

The issue that most occupied nineteenth-century Jews, and that remained a central church-state issue well into the twentieth century, involved the emotional question of Sunday ("blue") laws, regulations that required everyone to close down on the Christian Sabbath, thereby making it economically difficult for Jews to rest on their own Sabbath, observed on Saturday. Explicit discrimination was not the issue here; in theory, if not in effect, Sunday laws treated Jews and Christians alike. Indeed, proponents proudly pointed out that limiting the work week to six days benefited *all* workers, made it possible for Christians to have a day off to go to church, and ensured that rich and poor alike would have an equal chance to keep Sunday holy without facing economic hardship. But what seemed to many Christians to be a legitimate means of assuring religious "free exercise" was in Jewish eyes an effort to "establish" Christianity as the national religion. Jews found laws requiring observance of the Christian Sabbath to be religiously coercive, blamed such laws for lax observance by Jews of their own Sabbath (when most Jews had to work), and insisted that forcing observant Jews to keep two days of rest, their own and the state's, amounted to economic discrimination, for it required Jews to suffer monetary losses on account of their faith. The question tested the meaning and limits of church-state separation, and raised anew the problem of majority rule versus minority rights.[31]

To be sure, American Christians were by no means of one mind regarding the "Sunday question." Laws and practices varied from state to state, immigrants from different lands brought divergent Sabbath traditions with them, and Protestant denominations differed among themselves not only over how the Sabbath should be observed, but whether it should be observed on Sunday at all. Seventh Day Baptists, for example, advocated a return to the biblical Sabbath. Still, all of the states enacted Sunday laws of some form or other in the nineteenth century, and over the years religious leaders mounted recurrent campaigns to revitalize Sabbath observance, both by enacting new laws and by promoting enforcement of those already on the books. Especially when strictly enforced, such laws caused Jews a great deal of hardship.[32]

Jewish responses to Sunday laws covered a broad and revealing spectrum. There were, first of all, a small number of Jewish leaders who took it for granted that the Christian majority could exercise some power in shaping the nation's character, and therefore found Sunday laws unobjectionable. Mordecai Noah, for example, felt that the laws had "nothing to do with liberty of conscience at all," but were a "mere local or police regulation." Believing that Jews would enforce similar laws regarding Saturday if they "possessed a government of their own," he advised Jews to keep quiet. "Respect to the laws of the land we live in," he warned, "is the first duty of good citizens. . . ."[33] Half a century later, Rabbi Emil Hirsch of Chicago offered Jews similar advice, albeit for different reasons. As an exponent of social justice, Hirsch believed that the state had to be "the guardian of the community's interest, to be the protector of the weaker in the community." Sunday laws, to his mind, were a form of security for working people. Without them, he feared "that for six days' hire seven days work will be exacted from all." In his own temple, he shifted the Sabbath day to Sunday in conformity with American norms.[34]

At the opposite extreme stood Jews who considered all Sunday laws to be illegal, a violation of strict church-state separation. Isaac Leeser, perhaps the best known exponent of this view, characterized Sunday legislation as a whole as "tyrannical and unconstitutional." He argued on the basis of "freedom of conscience" that Sabbath observance should be left up to the "conviction of individuals," and considered it the "natural right" of all human beings to work whenever and for however long they pleased without state interference. Indeed, he believed that the Christian Sabbath would have a "stronger hold on the affections" if it were observed voluntarily, as the Jewish Sabbath was, rather than under coercion.[35]

This argument, resting on basic American principles, was thoroughly egalitarian; it did not demand exceptions for those who observed the Sabbath on another day. In 1889, Rabbi David Philipson made a similar case in opposing Ohio's Sabbath law, and parallel ideas were expressed as late as 1958 in a bold address by Rabbi Harold Silver. Yet the claim, as expressed by Silver, that the Sabbath is entirely a matter of "private religious conscience" and that "in a democracy like ours, a man has the right to work or rest seven days a week or none" never won widespread support. It not only alienated many workers who thought otherwise, it also logically required Jews to oppose other forms of labor legislation, including the minimum wage and the forty-hour week. Moreover, it ran afoul of the courts, which generally declared that states *could* legally enact blue laws on the basis of their well-accepted right to regulate trade.[36]

The strategy that succeeded better and enlisted more widespread support was a live-and-let-live attitude toward Sunday blue laws, a middle-ground position. It saw Jews acquiesce to the laws on the basis of their social and religious benefits, while insisting upon exemptions for those, like themselves, who observed the Sabbath on the seventh day of the week. As early as 1817, a Jewish lawyer named Zalegman Phillips, the son of Jonas Phillips, argued in this vein, seeking to persuade a Philadelphia judge that "those who profess the Jewish religion and others who keep the seventh day" should be exempted from blue laws on freedom of religion grounds. Without contesting the application of the laws to others, he declared that the Decalogue, according to Jewish tradition, not only commanded rest on the seventh day, but also labor on the previous six, and that Jews should therefore not be obliged to close their businesses on both Saturday and Sunday.[37] Phillips lost his case, but his argument—that Jews and others who observed Sabbath on Saturday should be exempt from Sunday legislation—won considerable popular support. Leading early-nineteenth-century proponents of Sunday legislation, faced with charges that blue laws violated freedom of conscience, advocated exemptions for all who conscientiously observed the Sabbath on Saturday, and in time several states (twenty-four by 1908) enacted them into law. Following the model of New York's 1860 statute, however, most only permitted adherents of the Saturday Sabbath to labor in private where others would not be disturbed; stores and other businesses operating in public had to remain closed.[38]

Many Jews nevertheless applauded this approach to the Sunday law problem as a sensible compromise. In 1838, a group of Pennsylvania Jews (writing in a memorial that was composed but apparently never sent) thus expressed a willingness "to yield any outdoor occupations which might be offensive to the community at large on the First day of the week," as well as indoor labors that might disturb Christians "in their public or domestic devotions," in exchange for a limited exemption permitting Saturday Sabbath observers (such as themselves) to labor in private on Sunday. A half-century later, Rabbi Isaac Mayer Wise lauded a similar accommodationist approach to Sunday laws as "sensible and constitutional in harmony with the idea of personal liberty." The Union of American Hebrew Congregations, founded in 1873, agreed. Its resolutions did not oppose Sunday laws as a whole, but only "unjust and oppressive" ones. It sought equality for Jews, the right for them to keep their Sabbath and still be able to work six days like everybody else, nothing more.[39]

Louis Marshall, the foremost American Jewish leader of the early twentieth century, also backed this approach. He urged the New York State legislature to agree that:

> No person who observes the seventh day of the week as the Sabbath, and actually refrains from secular business and labor on that day, or from sundown on Friday to sundown on Saturday, shall be liable to prosecution for carrying on secular business or performing labor on Sunday, provided public worship is not thereby disturbed.

He claimed to have support for his bill from Orthodox and Liberal Jews, as well as from the membership of the American Jewish Committee.[40]

By supporting exemptions, rather than opposing Sunday laws entirely, Jews were able to project a proreligion, pro-Sabbath attitude, even as they spoke of religious freedom and sought to advance their own goals. The very names assumed by twentieth-century Jewish anti–blue-law organizations—"Upholders of the Sabbath" and the "Jewish Sabbath Alliance" (the Jewish answer to the Christian "Lord's Day Alliance")—underscored this point. Similarly, in advocating exemptions for Jews, Louis Marshall first defended Sunday laws, and then explained that he sought to extend the same Sabbath benefits without accompanying disabilities to the minority that rested on a different day of the week. "Every right-thinking man must favor one day of rest in seven," he agreed, "but no right-thinking man should compel another to observe two days in seven."[41]

In the final analysis, of course, it was not the policy of granting Jews exceptions that won the day so much as the advance of the five-day work week that made the whole problem increasingly moot. Supported by Jews and Christians alike for social and economic as well as religious reasons, the five-day week created, in effect, two possible days of rest. This, plus changing consumer habits, the decline of small merchant ("mom and pop") businesses, and pressure from department stores seeking to remain open seven days a week, led many states in the 1970s and 1980s to modify their blue laws; some abandoned them altogether. Still, the lesson of the long battle over Sunday laws remains instructive. On this issue, the bulk of the Jewish community pragmatically supported a proreligion, live-and-let-live stance that took Jews' own special needs into account.[42]

The Shift to Separationism

The last third of the nineteenth century witnessed a momentous change in American Jewish attitudes toward issues of religion and state. Where before, as we have seen, the community generally adhered to a proreligion stance, supporting impartial government aid to *all* religions so long as Judaism was treated equally, now an increasing number of Jews spoke out unequivocally for a government free of *any* religious influence whatsoever, a secular state. To some extent this reflected the changing spirit of the times. In the post–Civil War decades, James Turner has shown, agnosticism emerged as a respectable alternative to traditional religion: "Disbelief in God was, for the first time, plausible enough to grow beyond a rare eccentricity and to stake out a sizable permanent niche in American culture." Even more important, however, is the fact that Jews during this period found to their dismay that calls for religious equality fell more and more on deaf ears. The spiritual crisis and internal divisions that plagued Protestant America during this era—one that confronted all American religious groups with the staggering implications of Darwinism and biblical criticism—drove Evangelicals and liberals alike to renew their particularistic calls for a "Christian America." Evangelical leaders championed antimodernist legislation to protect the "Christian Sabbath," to institute "Christian temperance," to reintroduce Christianity into the schoolroom, and to write Christian morality into American law codes. Liberal Christians may have been somewhat more circumspect, but as Robert Handy indicates, their goal too was "in many respects a spiritualized and idealized restatement of the search for a specifically Christian society in an age of freedom and progress."[43] The implication, spelled out in 1867 by a writer in the *American Presbyterian and Theological Review,* was that non-Protestants could *never* win full acceptance as equals:

> This is a Christian Republic, our Christianity being of the Protestant type. People who are not Christians, and people called Christians, but who are not Protestants dwell among us, but they did not build this house. We have never shut our doors against them, but if they come, they must take up with such accommodations as we have. . . . If any one, coming among us finds that this arrangement is uncomfortable, perhaps he will do well to try some other country. The world is wide; there is more land to be possessed; let him go and make a beginning for himself as our fathers did for us; as for this land, we have taken possession of it in the name of the Lord Jesus Christ; and if he will give us grace to do it, we mean to hold it for him till he comes.[44]

A proposed "Christian Amendment" designed to write "the Lord Jesus Christ" and the "Christian" basis of national life into the text of the Constitution attempted to ensure that these aims would be speedily realized. Then, in 1892, the Supreme Court in *Church of the Holy Trinity v. United States* declared that the United States actually was a "Christian Nation." The justice who wrote this decision, David Brewer, the son of a missionary, subsequently added insult to injury by defending his views in a published lecture, *The United States—A Christian Nation* (1905), where he relegated Judaism to the level of a tolerated creed.[45]

As Naomi W. Cohen has observed, Jews took little immediate public notice of the 1892 Supreme Court decision.[46] Only one substantive reply, by Louis Marshall, was published, and it appeared in 1896, four years after the ruling. The publication of Justice Brewer's 1905 lecture, by contrast, elicited considerable Jewish attention. The most thoroughgoing critique and refutation came in a pamphlet by Isaac Hassler (excerpted below in chapter 7), in which he forcefully rebutted Brewer's contentions. His critique, Cohen observes, "closely corresponded with the case for equality that American Jewish leaders had been building since the Revolutionary era."[47]

In spite of Hassler's efforts, Jews, all too familiar with the anti-Jewish rhetoric of Christian romantics in Europe, became alarmed. As in the Old World so in the New, they thought, proponents of religion were allying themselves with the forces of reaction. "The Protestants come now and say defiantly that this is a Protestant country," Rabbi Max Lilienthal warned in a celebrated public address in 1870. "When I left Europe I came to this country because I believed it to be free." In search of a safe haven, many Jews now settled down firmly in the freethinking liberal camp; it seemed far more hospitable to Jewish interests. They also turned increasingly toward a more vehement response to "Christian America" claims—the doctrine of strict separation.[48]

Strict church-state separation was, of course, an old idea in America; its roots lay deeply embedded in colonial and European thought. As we have seen, the idea had been embraced by Thomas Jefferson and James Madison, who believed that the state should be utterly secular, religion being purely a matter of personal preference. While certainly not hostile to religion, they believed that religious divisions were salutary and that religious truth would be most likely to flourish in a completely noncoercive atmosphere. "Whilst we assert for ourselves a freedom to embrace, to profess, and to observe the religion which we believe to be of divine origin," Madison wrote in his *Memorial and Remonstrance* (1785), "we cannot deny an equal freedom to those whose minds have not yet yielded to the evidence which has convinced us." Jefferson refused to proclaim so much as a Thanksgiving Day lest he "indirectly assume to the United States an authority over religious exercises."[49] However, theirs was a decidedly minority view that fell into disfavor with the revival of national religious fervor early in the nineteenth century. It was only now, in the post–Civil War era and as a response to "Christian America" agitation, that strict separation attracted a school of new adherents.

Jews became particularly ardent supporters of the Jefferson-Madison position. Alarmed by the tenor of public debate, they began to participate in such groups as the Free Religion Association and the National Liberty League, both dedicated to complete church-state separation. Notable Reform Jewish leaders, including Rabbis Isaac Mayer Wise, Bernhard Felsenthal, and Max Schlesinger, as well as the Jewish lay leader Moritz Ellinger, embraced the separationist agenda spelled out in *The Index*, edited by Francis Abbot. "The issue of church-state relations," observes Professor Benny Kraut, "precipitated a natural, pragmatic alliance uniting Jews, liberal Christians, religious freethinkers, and secularists in common bond, their religious and theological differences notwithstanding."[50] Thus in 1868, Rabbi Max Lilienthal elevated complete church-state separation to one of the central tenets of American Judaism:

> [W]e are going to lay our cornerstone with the sublime motto, "Eternal separation of state and church!" For this reason we shall never favor or ask any support for our various benevolent institutions by the state; and if offered, we should not only refuse, but reject it with scorn and indignation, for those measures are the first sophistical, well-premeditated steps for a future union of church and state. Sectarian institutions must be supported by their sectarian followers; the public purse and treasury dares not be filled, taxed and emptied for sectarian purposes.[51]

Lilienthal's Cincinnati colleague, Rabbi Isaac Mayer Wise, proclaimed a year later that "the State has no religion. Having no religion, it cannot impose any religious instruction on the citizen, adult or child."[52] This soon became the predominant American Jewish position on church-state questions, seconded by one Jewish organization after another. During the latter decades of the nineteenth century, they opposed "religious legislation" in any form, and applauded liberal efforts to "secularize the State completely."[53]

To be sure, as Shlomith Yahalom has shown, Jewish advocates of church-state separation stopped short of supporting the blatantly anti-religious planks advocated by some separationist organizations. Calls by the Liberal League, the American Association for the Advancement of Atheism, and others for taxation of church property, elimination of chaplains from the public payrolls, abolition of court and inaugural oaths, and removal of the phrase "In God We Trust" from the currency never won serious Jewish support, even from those who seconded their larger objectives.[54] Indeed, the Central Conference of American Rabbis, in attacking religious legislation in 1892, went out of its way to recognize at the same time "the value of religious sentiment." Similarly, Rabbi David Philipson, a champion of strict separation, (naively) records his "amazement" at finding that the American Secular Union, which he had been invited to address on church-state separation, "was practically an irreligious organization." One speaker, he writes, so outraged him, "that . . . I cast my manuscript aside" and spoke instead "on religion and the Bible."[55] Eager to foster voluntary adherence to religion, even as they sought to combat any form of state religion, American Jews steered a middle course. They embraced separationism in theory as the best and most legitimate defense against a Christian-dominated state, but as a practical matter they were much more circumspect and pragmatic, generally keeping in mind other competing considerations and speaking up only in those instances when they believed Jewish interests to be genuinely at risk.

The Battle over Religion in the Public Schools

The issue that stood at the heart of church-state debates in late nineteenth- and twentieth-century America and affected American Jews significantly concerned the emotional question of religion in the public schools. Open to rich and poor children alike, organized on a uniform and systematic basis, largely tax-supported, and dedicated to moral education and good citizenship, these schools emerged in America during the three decades prior to the Civil War.[56] Whatever their claims to the contrary, the schools then were culturally Protestant: "They associated Protestant Christianity with republicanism, with economic progress, and with virtue."[57] Curricula and textbooks were, consequently, rife with material that Catholics and Jews found offensive. As early as the 1840s, New York Jews are known to have protested the use of such textbooks in the public schools, but to no avail; the board of education, controlled by Protestants, refused to declare stories about the "Son of God" or readings from the New Testament out of bounds. As a result, Jews who could afford to do so sent their children to Jewish schools—which flourished not only in New York but in every major city where Jews lived.[58]

But not for long. As public schools, under pressure from Catholics and others, became more religiously sensitive, Jews flocked to them for they were free, convenient, often educationally superior, and usually far more commodious than their Jewish counterparts. Furthermore, public schools had in a short time become symbols of American democracy: "temples of liberty," Julius Freiberg of Cincinnati once called them, where "children of the high and low, rich and poor, Protestants, Catholics and Jews, mingle together, play together, and are taught that we are a free people, striving to elevate mankind, and to respect one another."[59] As such, the schools came to have an insurmountable advantage over "sectarian" schools; Jews perceived them as an entree to America itself and supported them as a patriotic duty. By the mid-1870s, most Jewish day schools had closed, replaced by Sabbath, Sunday, and afternoon supplementary schools.

By the 1870s and 1880s, then, a growing number of Jewish leaders had begun to espouse the ideal of nonsectarian, religiously-neutral public school education. To attend public schools and to guard them from sectarianism became not just a matter of Jewish communal interest, but a patriotic obligation as well. In carrying out this "obligation," however, Jews frequently came into conflict with their Protestant and Catholic neighbors. Many schools, for example, began the day with morning religious exercises "usually including, in whole or in part, reading of the King James version of the Bible, reciting of some form of prayer, and singing of hymns." In several states such devotions were even mandated by state law, on the theory that public schools should not be "godless," and that while "sectarianism" was constitutionally enjoined, religion (which usually meant Protestantism) was not.[60] A Texas court, in a 1908 opinion, upheld this view, and defended it with an argument that many at the time found convincing:

> Christianity is so interwoven with the web and woof of the state government that to sustain the contention that the Constitution prohibits reading of the Bible, offering prayers, or singing songs of a religious character in any public building of the government would produce a condition bordering upon moral anarchy.[61]

The problem faced by American Jews was how to dissent from this approach without embracing the very "godlessness" that so many devout Christians sought to preclude. Since the public school symbolized American ideals, Jews wanted their children to be treated in accordance with what they believed those ideals demanded. They wanted the public schools to make their children "Americans," not Christians. It was not enough, then, that most states, particularly in the twentieth century, made provisions for students who wished to be excused from religious exercises, for coercion was not the major issue.[62] Instead, as so often before, the issue was one of religious equality. Jews sought to have schools and other public institutions that would be "undisturbed," in the words of Rabbi Max Lilienthal, "by sectarian strife and bigoted narrow-mindedness."[63]

How to achieve this goal proved a most difficult problem. Rabbi Isaac Mayer Wise sought to make religion a private affair: "Parents, guardians and especially clergymen must make it their business to teach religion," he wrote in 1869, "the public school can not do it."[64] Later that year, when the Cincinnati school board in an effort to placate the city's Catholics resolved to dispense with the reading of the Bible in the public schools, he was pleased. Indeed, he along with Max Lilienthal was among those who loudly supported the board's decision when it was challenged in court by outraged Protestants. Denouncing both Catholic and Protestant leaders as religious fanatics, the former for seeking to destroy the public schools in favor of Catholic ones and the latter for seeking to make the schools Protestant, Lilienthal, in a celebrated address, firmly aligned him-self with "the Americans"—those who favored, as he did, religious liberty and freedom of conscience.[65] This strategy—to associate the position claimed by Jews with the patriotic position on church and state—was widely emulated. "Opposition to sectarianism," explained one Jewish pamphleteer in 1906, "is not an indication of hostility to Christianity but of devotion to American ideals."[66]

Much as they opposed sectarianism in the public schools, many Jews in this period sympathized with Christian fears that schools devoid of religion might become secular and "godless." They searched, therefore, for some way of reconciling their belief in church-state separation with their conviction that education needed to be (in Max Lilienthal's words) "thoroughly . . . preeminently and essentially Godful." Lilienthal himself urged educators to stress the importance of "good deeds and actions." Teach young people "to cling to that sacred covenant of mutual love, mutual good will, and forbearance . . . ," he wrote, "and you will make our schools Godful and truly religious in the noblest sense of the word."[67] Rabbi Bernhard Felsenthal, a Reform rabbi in Chicago, called for "instruction in unsectarian ethics."[68] This, however, did not satisfy the more Orthodox editors of the *American Hebrew*. Calling it "absurd to ask that the State should support schools and identify them with agnosticism," they called on government to teach not just bland ethics but:

> the three great religious facts upon the verity of which all religions are united, viz:
> 1. The existence of God,
> 2. The responsibility of man to his Maker,
> 3. The immortality of the soul.

These principles did not, to their mind, conflict with church-state separation for they were "nonsectarian" and represented a religious consensus. Foreshadowing arguments that would be widely heard a century later, they warned that it would be "just as wrong to associate the schools with implied agnosticism as with any sectarianism."[69]

The twentieth century brought with it no resolution to the public school problem. Fueled in part by mainstream Protestants who saw public schools as a vehicle for Americanizing the immigrants and stemming their own movement's decline, pressure to strengthen the religious component of state-sponsored education heightened. Jewish pupils suffered particularly acutely, for both prayers and Bible readings tended to be cast in a Protestant mold; in some cases, they even included New Testament passages that doomed Jews to eternal damnation. Determined to protect Jewish children, the Reform Movement's Central Conference of American Rabbis (CCAR), in 1906, established a standing committee on church and state to collect information and work for Jewish rights.[70]

Initially, the committee focused all its attention on battling "sectarianism in the public schools." It marshaled evidence to prove that "morning religious exercises" in most public schools involved "Protestant religious worship," and argued that, as such, the exercises were both offensive and un-American. As the documents in chapter 8 illustrate, however, unity dissolved when the question turned to what function the public schools *should* play in the realm of religion and ethics. Indeed, the issue became the subject of spirited debate at the Central Conference's annual convention in 1911.[71]

The same kind of debate took place over the so-called Gary Plan, initiated in Gary, Indiana in 1913, permitting released time during the school day for moral and religious instruction outside of school property. Many rabbis were opposed to the plan, despite its nation-wide popularity, fearing that once the wall between church and state was breached "the religion of the majority will receive general sanction." One rabbi went so far as to urge his colleagues to line up with the Free Thinking Society and fight the Gary Plan tooth and nail. Other rabbis, such as Samuel Schulman of New York, a selection from whose 1916 address on the subject is included in chapter 8, voiced support for the plan, with certain changes. The CCAR, he proclaimed, "should not content itself merely with the negative attitude of insisting upon the complete separation of church and state, but should, wherever it can, constructively and helpfully meet all efforts made for the improvement of ethical and religious education in the nation."[72]

As one of the leading American rabbis of his day, Schulman actually sought to change the whole tenor of church-state thinking within the American Jewish community. In a private letter to Samson Benderly, director of New York's Bureau of Jewish Education, he explained why:

> In America, we have a unique and therefore, very delicate problem. We, of course, want to keep religion, Bible reading, hymn singing out of the public schools. At the same time we know that there is not enough efficient moral and religious education in the country. . . . Jews make a mistake in thinking only of themselves and assuming always a negative and critical attitude. They must supplemement that negative attitude with a constructive policy. Otherwise, they will soon be classed in the minds of the Christian men and women in this country with the free-thinkers and with those who have no interest in the religious education of the youth. That, of course, is undesirable both because it is contrary to our genius as Jews and also contrary to the real spirit of Americanism, which while not ecclesiastical, and separates Church from State, has always been religious.[73]

Many of the leading figures in Reform Judaism, including Rabbi Julian Morgenstern, came to agree with Schulman, and in 1926, in a highly significant and much disputed policy departure, the Dismissal Plan, a modified version of the Gary Plan that called on schools to "reduce their time schedule by . . . one hour or more at the end of the school day," won CCAR approval, in the hope that parents would devote the time gained to their children's religious education. Related plans were endorsed by the Conservative movement's United Synagogue of America and by the Commission on Jewish Education of the (Reform) Union of American Hebrew Congregations.[74] Louis Marshall was prepared to go even further. He believed that released time *during* the school day was constitutional and "highly commendable," and urged his fellow Jews to support the idea, fearing that "unless something of this sort is done, we shall have a Godless community."[75]

Fears of godlessness, however, were soon drowned out by renewed fears of Christianization, as evidence mounted that released-time programs were being abused. "Practices employed by over-enthusiastic religious groups in many communities," the *American Jewish Year Book* reported in 1947, "not only involve the public schools as a co-partner in the enforcement of their own sectarian instruction, but employ public school facilities. . . ." Teachers in some communities pressured students to attend religious classes; in others, Jewish students were taunted for studying apart from everybody else. In one unhappy incident, public school children were asked to pledge allegiance to a "Christian flag" as a mark of their "respect for the Christian religion."[76] The dilemma that American Jews faced, especially in the 1940s, was whether, given these abuses, released-time programs should be opposed everywhere, even at the risk of seeming "godless," or whether in the interests of Jewish education, as well as goodwill and interfaith harmony, only the abuses themselves should be attacked, not the program as a whole. Rabbis themselves were divided on the issue: in one memorable case, the Northern California Board of Rabbis opposed a released-time bill, while the Southern California Board supported it! Conservative and Orthodox rabbis tended to be more sympathetic to such plans than Reform rabbis, although the Conservative Rabbinical Assembly went on record in 1946 against any form of religion in the public schools, released time included. And even in Reform congregations, the issue sometimes pitted rabbis opposed to released time on principle against congregants who pragmatically sought to make the plan work, if only for the sake "of good public relations."[77]

The Supreme Court decision in *McCollum v. Board of Education* (1948), declaring unconstitutional released-time plans that used public-school classrooms for religious instruction during regular school hours, strengthened the hands of those in the Jewish community who favored a high wall of separation between church and state. The Synagogue Council of America (representing Orthodox, Conservative, and Reform rabbinic and congregational associations) as well as the organizations associated with the National Community Relations Advisory Council (NCRAC), founded in 1944 as the national coordinating body in the field of Jewish community relations (representing the American Jewish Committee, the American Jewish Congress, the Anti-Defamation League of B'nai B'rith, the Jewish Labor Committee and the Jewish War Veterans), had all filed *amicus curiae* (friends of the court) briefs in the case supporting the McCollums. This raised some eyebrows since the McCollums were atheists, but most Jewish organizations felt that Jews had a compelling interest in the case, especially given the abuses that released-time programs entailed. When the Supreme Court declared that "both religion and government can best work to achieve their lofty aims if each is left free from the other within its respective sphere," the organizations felt vindicated.[78] A month after the decision, the Synagogue Council of America and NCRAC, allied in a Joint Committee on Religion and the Public Schools (later the Joint Advisory Committee on Religion and the State), issued an important statement of principles embodying the new spirit that *McCollum* had unloosed. "The maintenance and furtherance of religion are the responsibility of the synagogue, the church and the home," the statement declared. It proceeded to condemn not only religious education and sectarian observances in the public schools, but also all government aid (other than lunches, medical, and dental services) to denominational schools.[79]

Major Jewish organizations scarcely deviated from this position in the ensuing decades; indeed, it represented somewhat of a Jewish consensus for over a generation. During these years, the Supreme Court became increasingly involved in church-state problems—a consequence of *Cantwell v. Connecticut* (1940) that applied "the liberties guaranteed by the First Amendment" to the states under terms of the Fourteenth Amendment—and Jewish organizational activities, as a result, shifted ever more toward the legal arena. The American Jewish Committee, the Anti-Defamation League of B'nai B'rith, and the American Jewish Congress became particularly active in this realm—especially the latter, whose Commission on Law and Social Action, directed for many years by attorney Leo Pfeffer, maintained "an absolutist approach to the First Amendment." Pfeffer's view that "complete separation of church and state is best for the church and best for the state, and secures freedom for both" seemed to most Jews to be both logically consistent and historically convincing.[80]

The Supreme Court appeared increasingly to agree. In a critical decision, *Engel v. Vitale* (1962), it outlawed state-composed prayers as constituting an impermissible establishment of religion. The particular prayer involved was a nondenominational one composed by the New York Board of Regents and actually approved by several rabbis, including Rabbi Menachem Schneerson, the Lubavitcher Rebbe, who argued that "it is necessary to engrave upon the child's mind the idea that any wrongdoing is an offense against the divine authority and order."[81] But the overwhelming majority of American Jews, along with many liberal Christians, applauded the decision, notwithstanding the firestorm of protest from Evangelicals, and hailed it "as an affirmation of the position they had long espoused." The same kind of reactions greeted the Court's complementary decision a year later, in *Abington Township School District v. Schempp* (1963), outlawing all devotional reading of the Bible in the public schools, including the practice of reciting the Lord's Prayer.[82] In the case of *Lee v. Weisman,* decided in 1992, the Court extended this principle to hold that a state may not sponsor prayers at public school graduation ceremonies either.[83]

With these decisions, the long agonizing battle over the character of America's public schools—a battle that, as we have seen, really reflected divergent views over the character of the nation as a whole—largely came to an end. Jewish organizations continued to keep a vigilant watch lest religion reenter classrooms through the back door via mandated teaching of "creationism" or other devices, and the Supreme Court on several occasions found it necessary to reiterate, as it did in *Wallace v. Jaffree* (1985), that state encouragement of school prayer was unconstitutional.[84] But the central focus of church-state controversy now shifted from the public schools to public funding of religious schools. And on this issue Jews found themselves seriously divided.

State Aid to Parochial Schools

Unlike other church-state issues that aroused Jewish concern, state aid to parochial schools did not involve the question of Jewish equality. Where Sunday closing laws and prayer in the public schools clearly disadvantaged Jews and could be fought on the basis of Jewish group interests as well as minority rights, state aid to parochial schools was offered to Christian and Jewish schools alike. The issue, then, was not the "equal footing" demand insisted upon since the days of Jonas Phillips, but rather the "wall of separation" axiom upon which Jews had built so much of their twentieth-century church-state philosophy. The debate, which began in earnest in the 1960s, pitted advocates of principle, who felt that any breach in the "wall of separation" would affect America and its Jews adversely, against proponents of pragmatism, who argued for an accommodationist policy benefiting Jewish day schools, interfaith relations, and American education as a whole.

In early America, before the modern public school system existed, Jews readily supported state aid to parochial schools, and at least in New York City received funds on the same basis as Protestants and Catholics.[85] With the rise of the "nonsectarian" public school and the developing view that parochial (especially Catholic) schools were separatist, if not indeed un-American, most church schools lost state funding, and, as we have seen, most Jewish day schools closed down. In 1927 there were no more than twelve Jewish parochial schools in the whole United States.[86] Consequently, the issue of state aid to parochial schools scarcely arose in Jewish circles during this period. In one case, *Pierce v. Society of the Sisters of the Holy Names of Jesus and Mary* (1925), the Supreme Court ruled unconstitutional a Ku Klux Klan–sponsored anti-Catholic Oregon law that sought to require all parents to send their children to public schools. In another case, *Cochran v. Louisiana State Board of Education* (1930), the Court permitted the State of Louisiana to lend secular textbooks to schoolchildren who attended parochial schools. Neither case, however, affected the great majority of Jews directly. Yet Louis Marshall, representing the American Jewish Committee in an *amicus curiae* brief opposing Oregon's public-school law, did enunciate a basic principle—the right of parents to control the education of their children and to send them to private schools—that made all subsequent debate possible. Attacking as "an invasion of liberty" any effort to make public schools "the only medium of education in this country," Marshall pointed out that private schools could in many cases accomplish what public schools could not—including "religious instruction, the importance of which cannot be minimized."[87]

The growth of parochial schools, Catholic and Jewish alike, during the 1940s, coupled with heightened national concern over the quality of primary education, led to renewed pressure on behalf of state and federal measures to grant limited assistance to parochial schools on the basis of the "child benefit theory," the idea, supported by the Supreme Court, that state aid could be extended to parochial-school children so long as "the school children and the state alone are the beneficiaries."[88] As early as 1945, the Central Conference of American Rabbis had expressed concern over this development. In the wake of *Everson v. Board of Education of Ewing Township* (1947), an important case that permitted states to fund the cost of transporting students to parochial schools, this concern turned into real alarm. "The wall of separation between the church and state is surely being breached," Rabbi Joseph Fink, chairman of the Committee on Church and State, exclaimed. He called on his colleagues to do all that they could to uphold the status quo. For a time, leading Jewish organizations and religious bodies, including the Orthodox, united behind the 1948 Synagogue Council–NCRAC statement broadly opposing *all* government aid to parochial schools. Beginning in the 1950s, however, demands for a reevaluation of this policy sounded from a variety of quarters.[89]

In 1952, Will Herberg, author of *Judaism and Modern Man* and considered at the time "a fresh voice in the world of modern religious thought," published in *Commentary* magazine a widely-read article urging Americans of all faiths to rethink their views on the problem of church and state given the new pluralistic realities of American life. Herberg was especially harsh on his fellow Jews. "Judging by their public expressions," he wrote, "they seem to share the basic secularist presupposition that religion is a 'private matter'—in the minimizing sense of 'merely private'—and therefore peripheral to the vital areas of social life and culture." He urged Jews to "rid themselves of the[ir] narrow and crippling minority-group defensiveness," called for interreligious harmony, and insisted that Jews had little to fear from proposals to extend limited federal aid to parochial schools.[90]

Six years later, Rabbi Arthur Gilbert reiterated some of these same concerns in an address to the annual Convention of the Central Conference of American Rabbis, in which he challenged his rabbinic colleagues to rethink their knee-jerk commitment to strict separationism, and the secular bias upon which it was predicated. "Our record is stuck in its groove," he warned, and he specifically attacked Reform opposition to the use of public funds to pay for the transportation of parochial-school children. Drawing from his own experience at the Anti-Defamation League of B'nai B'rith, he called for policy positions "that appear to be more realistic and respond in a more sophisticated fashion to the temper and needs of today's society."[91]

While still highly unusual in the 1950s, by the 1960s these views were gaining a more respectful hearing. For one thing, advocates of Jewish day schools found themselves increasingly in sympathy with their Catholic counterparts; like them they complained that on account of their religious beliefs they were unfairly required to pay twice for education. Moreover, public education itself was under widespread attack. Some turned to parochial schools looking for higher-quality education; others, shocked by Russia's success in launching the Sputnik satellite, advocated enhanced federal aid to *all* schools in America, public and parochial alike. Thus, in 1962, the *American Jewish Year Book,* reviewing the events of the previous year, noticed for the first time that "unexpectedly strong support for the Catholic position [favoring state aid to parochial schools] appeared within the Jewish community, especially among the Orthodox." Rabbi Moshe Sherer, executive vice president of Agudath Israel of America, had testified before Congress in support of federal aid to private and parochial schools, arguing that Jewish day schools faced "extremely difficult financial circumstances." He was soon joined by representatives of the National Council of Young Israel and the Jewish day-school organization, Torah Umesorah. Even more surprisingly, aid to parochial schools was simultaneously endorsed by a leading Conservative Jewish layman, Charles H. Silver, who was also at the time president of the New York board of education.[92]

In the years that followed, calls for change sounded in more and more circles. Professors Jakob J. Petuchowski of Hebrew Union College and Seymour Siegel of the Jewish Theological Seminary spoke out in support of state aid to parochial schools and advocated abandonment of the whole separationist agenda in favor of a more proreligious, "equal-footing" stance. Siegel, attacking defenders of the "non-existent wall of separation" who "brain-washed" the Jewish community, charged that a secular state and "desacralized" society were alien to both Americanism and Judaism. Echoing Will Herberg, he described Supreme Court rulings banning Bible reading and prayer from the public schools as bad law and bad public policy.[93] Immanuel Jakobovitz, then the rabbi of the prestigious Fifth Avenue Synagogue in New York and later Chief Rabbi of the British Empire, came to similar conclusions from an Orthodox perspective. In a stinging dissent, he attacked the New York Board of Rabbis for its support of the Supreme Court's decision in *Engel,* and expressed his "dismay at the alliance between teachers of Judaism and the spokesmen of secularism and atheism."[94]

Writing in *Commentary* in 1966, Milton Himmelfarb, another critic of separationism as well as a staunch advocate of state aid to parochial schools, posed a more pragmatic argument for change:

> It is time we actually weighed the utility and cost of education against the utility and cost of separationism. All the evidence in America points to education, more than anything else, influencing adherence to democracy and egalitarianism. All the evidence points

to Catholic parochial education having the same influence. . . . Something that nurtures a humane, liberal democracy is rather more important to Jews than twenty-four-karat separationism.[95]

Orthodox leaders fully agreed, insisting that aid to parochial schools was "good for Torah," "good for the Jews," and "good for America." It was, they argued, "both constitutional and equitable" for the government to share the cost of secular programs, since the government required such programs, set standards for what they should contain, and derived benefit from the well-educated citizens they produced.[96]

In 1965, when Congress debated the Elementary and Secondary Education Act that included "child benefit" money earmarked for special educational services in parochial and private schools, intra-Jewish divisions came out into the open. Jewish spokesmen testified on both sides of the issue, and as a result of the debate the National Jewish Commission on Law and Public Affairs (COLPA) was formed to support aid to parochial schools and to promote the rights and interests of the "observant Jewish community."[97]

Since then, the Jewish community has consistently spoken with two voices on programs to assist secular education in parochial schools. Most Jewish organizations continue to condemn the programs on "no establishment" grounds. Any breach in the "wall of separation between church and state," they fear, will ultimately work to the detriment of Jews and America as a whole. A minority of Jewish organizations, meanwhile, staunchly defend such programs on pragmatic and "free exercise" grounds. The tangible benefits that would result from federal aid to parochial education, they insist, would more than compensate for any potential problems.

"Overhauling our Priorities"

The creation of COLPA and the attendant calls for a new American Jewish policy on church-state questions carried implications that went far beyond the issue of aid to parochial schools. A growing minority came to agree with Rabbi Walter Wurzberger, a leading Modern Orthodox rabbi and onetime president of the Synagogue Council, that the time had come for a "thorough overhauling" of Jewish priorities on *all* church-state issues. In place of what Wurzberger spoke of as "obsessive preoccupation with the Establishment Clause," they called for far greater attention to "free exercise" claims. They especially sought support for initiatives that could make it easier for Jews to observe their religious traditions.[98]

Surprisingly, the religious tradition that most frequently found its way into the courts concerned public displays of the menorah (candelabrum), symbol of the relatively minor Jewish holiday of Chanukah usually celebrated in December. The issue as popularly understood involved a basic question: should government property be devoid of *any* religious symbols, or should it be open to *all* religious symbols? What made the issue complex was the widespread public celebration of Christmas, the only American legal holiday from which Jews, as non-Christians, felt emotionally excluded. Jews had long protested sectarian celebrations of Christmas, especially in public schools, and in more recent years they had also fought to remove such Christmas symbols as the cross and the creche from public property, arguing (as opponents of menorah displays also did) that these amounted to an impermissible establishment of religion. The Supreme Court in the controversial case of *Lynch v. Donnelly* (1984) partially overruled this objection, declaring that the creche, at least in the company of other "secular" Christmas symbols, was constitutionally unobjectionable. The question, then, was whether the menorah too was unobjectionable and whether, if so, Jews should ask for it to be placed on public property alongside the permissible symbols of Christmas.[99]

Most Jewish organizations, unhappy with the *Lynch* decision, continued to believe that religious symbols of any sort should be kept off public property on First Amendment grounds. Some Orthodox groups, however, and particularly the Chabad (Lubavitch) organization, took an opposite stance. They insisted that menorahs *should* be placed on public property both as a Jewish response to Christmas and as a symbol of religious pride.[100] In *Allegheny County v. ACLU of Pittsburgh* (1989), the Supreme Court partially vindicated this view, upholding the placement of a menorah on public property, next to a Christmas tree, on the grounds that "both Christmas and Chanukah are part of the same winter-holiday season, which has attained secular status in our society."

Within the Jewish community, however, debate continued focusing on a much deeper issue. Supporters of the publicly displayed menorah argued that the public square should be filled with a multitude of religious symbols. These, they believed, would foster respect for religion, stimulate Jewish observance, and help fight assimilation. Opponents, meanwhile, feared that displays of religious symbols on government property would foster fanaticism and intolerance. Confining such symbols to private property, they felt, was the best guarantee of church-state separation and the rights of religious minorities.

Similar debates have swirled around other Jewish attempts to reorder church-state priorities. In one celebrated case, *Goldman v. Weinberger* (1986), an Orthodox Jewish Air Force officer named Simcha Goldman contested the military's uniform dress requirements that barred him from wearing a yarmulke while serving on duty. The Supreme Court ultimately ruled against Goldman, but the fact that his case was supported on "free exercise" grounds by COLPA, the American Jewish Committee, and other Jewish organizations pointed to a renewed emphasis on freedom *for* religious practices.[101] Related "free exercise" cases, most of them confined to lower courts, have involved everything from issues of Sabbath and holiday observance, to the religious rights of Jews incarcerated in prison, to divorce-law protection for women whose husbands refused to issue them a traditional Jewish divorce (Get).[102] No matter how different the circumstances in each case, however, the ultimate goal has generally been the same: "to remove the obstacles which face adherents of minority religions in the exercise of their religious rights."[103]

Conclusion

In the two hundred years since Jonas Phillips pleaded with the Constitutional Convention for religious freedom, the condition of Jews in America has improved dramatically. They have won full legal equality under federal law and in each of the states; they face few if any hardships from Christian Sunday laws; and their children, at least in most places, can attend state-sponsored public schools without fear of intimidation on religious grounds. Most of these improvements derive, directly or indirectly, from the principles set forth in the Constitution itself, particularly the "no establishment" and "free exercise" clauses of the First Amendment. What these clauses mean, however, has remained a subject of continuing controversy. Does the First Amendment imply that America is a Christian nation (as some Evangelicals claim), a religious nation, or a secular nation? Does it envisage a government guaranteeing equality to *all* religions, one divided by a high wall from *any* religion, or one occupying some middle ground? And what happens when the "no establishment" and "free exercise" clauses conflict with one another? Which takes precedence?

American Jews have never been of one mind on these questions. While quite generally opposed to those who would Christianize the country or discriminate on religious grounds, they have been far less certain about what their communal priorities should be: religion in American life or governmental secularism? Accommodation to religion or separation from it? Historically, as the documents in this book demonstrate, American Jews have supported a wide range of positions on church-state relations; indeed, over the long span of American Jewish history there has been far less communal consensus on the subject than generally assumed. Fearing the persecutory potential of the Christian state, on the one hand, and the possible antireligious animus of the secular state, on the other, many American Jews have sought a middle ground, a quest that has thus far proved elusive. But if there has been no community-wide consensus on specific policies and approaches, there has, at least, been a common vision, one that links Jonas Phillips with his modern-day counterparts. It is the search for "equal footing," the conviction that America should be a land where people of all faiths are treated alike.

Notes

An earlier version of this essay was published as a pamphlet by the American Jewish Committee, which graciously permitted me to revise it for this volume.

Abbreviations

AJH - American Jewish History
AJYB - American Jewish Year Book
CCARYB - Central Conference of American Rabbis Yearbook
PAJHS - Publications of the American Jewish Historical Society

1. Reprinted in Morris U. Schappes, ed., *A Documentary History of the Jews in the United States, 1654–1875* (New York, 1971), 68–69, and with minor differences in Bernard Schwartz, *The Roots of the Bill of Rights* (New York, 1980), 439–440.

2. The states were Pennsylvania, New Hampshire, New York, Virginia, North Carolina, and Maryland (minority position); see Schwartz, *Roots of the Bill of Rights,* 1167.

3. Jacob R. Marcus, *The Colonial American Jew* (Detroit, 1970), 226, 511–512; see also Abram Vossen Goodman, *American Overture: Jewish Rights in Colonial Times* (Philadelphia, 1947).

4. The colonial situation has recently been reexamined in two related books: Thomas J. Curry, *The First Freedoms: Church and State in America to the Passage of the First Amendment* (New York, 1986); and Leonard W. Levy, *The Establishment Clause: Religion and the First Amendment* (New York, 1986); see also Mark V. Tushnet, "Book Review: The Origins of the Establishment Clause," *The Georgetown Law Journal* 75 (April 1987): 1509–1517. Important older studies include William G. McLoughlin, "Isaac Backus and the Separation of Church and State in America," *American Historical Review* 73 (June 1968), esp. 1402–1403; and the classic study, Anson Phelps Stokes, *Church and State in the United States*, 3 vols. (New York, 1950). For the North Carolina constitution, see Jonathan D. Sarna, Benny Kraut, and Samuel K. Joseph, *Jews and the Founding of the Republic* (New York, 1985), 93; see the similar situation in Pennsylvania's constitution reprinted in Schwartz, *Roots of the Bill of Rights*, 264–266 (articles II, XVI).

5. Stanley F. Chyet, "The Political Rights of the Jews in the United States: 1776–1840," *American Jewish Archives* 10 (1958): 14–75; Oscar and Mary Handlin, "The Acquisition of Political and Social Rights by the Jews in the United States," *AJYB* 56 (1955): 43–98; Conrad H. Moehlman, *The American Constitutions and Religion* (Berne, Ind., 1938); many of these documents are reprinted in Sarna, Kraut, and Joseph, *Jews and the Founding of the Republic*, 85–102.

6. Jonathan D. Sarna, "The Impact of the American Revolution on American Jews," *Modern Judaism* 1 (September 1981): 149–160.

7. In addition to items cited in nn. 4–6 above, see Morton Borden, *Jews, Turks, and Infidels* (Chapel Hill, N.C., 1984). The Rosenbach Foundation Library in Philadelphia owns a volume entitled *The Constitutions of the Several Independent States of America* (Philadelphia, 1781) with handwritten notes detailing the rights and limitations of Jews under each state's laws. Whether the notes were written, as alleged, by the Sephardic Jewish minister Gershom M. Seixas has been questioned; the fact that the volume exists at all, however, is highly revealing. See Edwin Wolf 2nd and Maxwell Whiteman, *The History of the Jews of Philadelphia* (Philadelphia, 1956, 1975), 147; Jacob R. Marcus, *The Handsome Young Priest in the Black Gown: The Personal World of Gershom Seixas* (Cincinnati, 1970), 16–17.

8. Schappes, *Documentary History of the Jews in the United States*, 61–63; Wolf and Whiteman, *History of the Jews of Philadelphia*, 146–151.

9. Joseph L. Blau and Salo W. Baron, *The Jews of the United States, 1790–1840: A Documentary History* (New York, 1963), 1:28–32.

10. Quoted in Isaac M. Fein, *The Making of an American Jewish Community* (Philadelphia, 1971), 26.

11. See E. Milton Altfeld, *The Jew's Struggle for Religious and Civil Liberty in Maryland* (Baltimore, 1924) and Edward Eitches, "Maryland's Jew Bill," *American Jewish Historical Quarterly* 60 (March 1971): 258–279.

12. Chyet, "Political Rights of the Jews in the United States," 80.

13. Robert T. Handy, *A Christian America* (New York, 1971); Borden, *Jews, Turks, and Infidels*, 53–74; see also James R. Rohrer, "Sunday Mails and the Church-State Theme in Jacksonian America," *Journal of the Early Republic* 7 (Spring 1987): 60.

14. Joseph Story, *Commentaries on the Constitution of the United States* (Boston, 1833) as reprinted in John F. Wilson and Donald L. Drakeman, *Church and State in American History* (Boston, 1987), 92–93; for a modern view, see Leonard W. Levy, "The Original Meaning of the Establishment Clause of the First Amendment," in *Religion and the State: Essays in Honor of Leo Pfeffer*, ed. James E. Wood, Jr. (Waco, Tex. 1985), 43–83.

15. On Kent, see *People v. Ruggles*, 8 Johns Rep. (N.Y.) 294 (1811), and John Webb Pratt, *Religion, Politics, and Diversity: The Church-State Theme in New York History* (Ithaca, N.Y., 1967), 138. On Parsons see Nathan Dane, *A General Abridgement and Digest of American Law* (Boston, 1823–29), 2:337 as quoted in Borden, *Jews, Turks, and Infidels*, 12. On Webster, see *Vidal v. Girard's Executors*, 2 How. 127 (1844), and Jonathan D. Sarna, "The Church-State Dilemma of American Jews," in *Jews in Unsecular America*, ed. Richard John Neuhaus (Grand Rapids, Mich., 1987), 10–11. For British precedent, see *Shover v. The State*, 5 Eng. 259 as quoted by Bernard J. Meislin, "Jewish Law in America," in *Jewish Law in Legal History and the Modern World*, ed. Bernard S. Jackson (Leiden, 1980), 159.

16. Schappes, *Documentary History of the Jews in the United States*, 235–246.

17. Schappes, *Documentary History of the Jews in the United States*, 64, 122; Jonathan D. Sarna, *Jacksonian Jew: The Two Worlds of Mordecai Noah* (New York, 1981), 132–135.

18. See Jefferson's letter to the Danbury Baptists (1802) and Madison's letter to Rev. Jasper Adams (1832), reprinted in Wilson and Drakeman, *Church and State in American History*, 78–81. For the background to Jefferson's letter, see Constance B. Schulz, "'Of Bigotry in Politics and Religion': Jefferson's Religion, the Federalist Press, and the Syllabus," *Virginia Magazine of History and Biography* 91 (January 1983): 73–91, esp. 85.

19. *Annals of the Congress of the United States*, compiled by Joseph S. Gales, Sr. (1834) as reprinted in Wilson and Drakeman, *Church and State in American History*, 76; Sarna, "Church-State Dilemma of American Jews," 11.

20. The petition is reprinted in *PAJHS* 27 (1920): 92–95.

21. Naomi W. Cohen, "Pioneers of American Jewish Defense," *American Jewish Archives* 19 (November 1977): 116–150.

22. *Occident* 7 (1850): 564–566.

23. *Occident* 16 (1859): 580. See Naomi W. Cohen, *Encounter With Emancipation: The German Jews in the United States, 1830–1914* (Philadelphia, 1984), 77: "The Jewish pioneers for religious equality generally asked for government neutrality on matters of religion . . . a neutral-to-all-religions rather than a divorced-from-religion state."

24. Bertram W. Korn, *Eventful Years and Experiences* (Cincinnati, 1954), 98–124; idem, *American Jewry and the Civil War* (New York, 1970), 56–97.

25. Cohen, "Pioneers of American Jewish Defense," 120. As late as 1913, the Committee on Church and State of the Central Conference of American Rabbis was concerned not only with infringements on church-state separation, but also with "any ridicule of the Jew on the stage . . . and any pre-judicial statement in our public press." See Joseph L. Fink, *Summary of C.C.A.R. Opinion on Church and State as Embodied in Resolutions Adopted at Conferences Through the Years* (Philadelphia, 1948), 6.

26. See Borden, *Jews, Turks, and Infidels*, 97–129.

27. *Occident* 7 (1850): 525.

28. *American Israelite*, March 3, 1865; James G. Heller, *Isaac M. Wise: His Life, Work and Thought* (New York, 1965), 621.

29. Allan Tarshish, "The Board of Delegates of American Israelites (1859–1878)," *PAJHS* 49 (1959): 23; Borden, *Jews, Turks, and Infidels*, 63; *PAJHS* 29 (1925): 105.

30. *PAJHS* 29 (1925): 81–82, 105.

31. For the general theme, see James R. Rohrer, "Sunday Mails and the Church-State Theme in Jacksonian America," *Journal of the Early Republic* 7 (Spring 1987): 53–74; Leo Pfeffer, *Church, State, and Freedom* (Boston, 1967), 270–286; and for Jewish attitudes, Shlomith Yahalom, "American Judaism and the Question of Separation Between Church and State" (Ph.D. diss. in Hebrew, Hebrew University of Jerusalem, 1981), 100–134; and Borden, *Jews, Turks, and Infidels*, 103–129.

32. See William A. Blakely, *American State Papers Bearing on Sunday Legislation* (New York and Washington, 1891); Albert M. Friedenberg, "Jews and the American Sunday Laws," *PAJHS* 11 (1903): 101–115; idem, "Sunday Laws of the United States and Leading Judicial Decisions Having Special Reference to the Jews," *AJYB* 10 (1908–1909): 152–189; and Jacob Ben Lightman, "The Status of Jews in American Sunday Laws," *Jewish Social Service Quarterly* 11 (1934–1935): 223–228, 269–276.

33. Schappes, *Documentary History of the Jews in the United States*, 279–281; Sarna, *Jacksonian Jew*, 134.

34. Emil G. Hirsch, *Sunday Law, Liberty and License: A Discourse Before the Sinai Congregation, December 16, 1888* (Chicago, [1888?]); see Kerry M. Olitzky, "Sundays at Chicago Sinai Congregation: Paradigm for a Movement," *AJH* 74 (June 1985): 356–368.

35. *Occident* 4 (March 1847): 565; 16 (September 1858): 274; see p. 275 for evidence that Leeser was echoing arguments by proponents of Sunday mails.

36. David Philipson, *Sabbath Legislation and Personal Liberty: A Lecture Delivered Before Congregation B'ne Israel* (Cincinnati, 1889); Harold Silver, *What Is Wrong With the Sunday Blue Laws: Address Delivered . . . at Temple Emanuel of South Hills, Pittsburgh, Pa.* (Pittsburgh, 1958). For Supreme Court decisions

on Sunday closing cases, see Robert T. Miller and Ronald B. Flowers, *Toward Benevolent Neutrality: Church, State, and the Supreme Court* (Waco, Tex., 1987), 289–322.

37. Blau and Baron, *Jews of the United States,* 22–24.

38. Rohrer, "Sunday Mails and the Church-State Theme in Jacksonian America," 68; *AJYB* 10 (1908–1909): 169.

39. Isaac Leeser, *The Claims of the Jews to an Equality of Rights* (Philadelphia, 1841), 90; *American Israelite,* February 28, 1887; *Where We Stand: Social Action Resolutions Adopted by the Union of American Hebrew Congregations* (New York, 1960), 66.

40. Charles Reznikoff, ed., *Louis Marshall, Champion of Liberty: Selected Papers and Addresses* (Philadelphia, 1957), 2:923–928.

41. Ibid., 929; cf. Benjamin Kline Hunnicutt, "The Jewish Sabbath Movement in the Early Twentieth Century," *AJH* 69 (December 1979): 196–225.

42. Bernard Drachman, *The Unfailing Light: Memoirs of an American Rabbi* (New York, 1948), 233; Richard Cohen, *Sunday in the Sixties,* Public Affairs Pamphlet No. 327, New York, 1962; Pfeffer, *Church, State, and Freedom,* 287.

43. James Turner, *Without God, Without Creed: The Origins of Unbelief in America* (Baltimore, 1985), 171; Robert Handy, *A Christian America* (New York, 1971), 101; see also Ferenc M. Szasz, "Protestantism and the Search for Stability: Liberal and Conservative Quests for a Christian America, 1875–1925," in *Building the Organizational Society,* ed. Jerry Israel (New York, 1972), 88–102; Paul A. Carter, *The Spiritual Crisis of the Gilded Age* (DeKalb, Ill., 1971); and Jackson Lears, *No Place of Grace: Antimodernism and the Transformation of American Culture, 1880–1920* (New York, 1981).

44. *American Presbyterian and Theological Review* 5 (July 1867): 390–391.

45. Borden, *Jews, Turks, and Infidels,* 62–74; Cohen, *Encounter With Emancipation,* 98–100, 254–256.

46. Naomi W. Cohen, *Jews in Christian America: The Pursuit of Religious Equality* (New York, 1992), 101.

47. Ibid., 103

48. David Philipson, *Max Lilienthal* (New York, 1915), 121; the above paragraphs are adapted from Sarna, "Church-State Dilemma of American Jews," 13–14.

49. James Madison, *A Memorial and Remonstrance to the Honorable the General Assembly of the Commonwealth of Virginia* (1785), and Thomas Jefferson to the Rev. Mr. Millar (1808), both reprinted in Wilson and Drakeman, *Church and State in American History,* 69, 79; see Robert M. Healey, "Jefferson on Judaism and the Jews: 'Divided We Stand, United, We Fall!'" *AJH* 73 (June 1984): 359–374, and more broadly, William Lee Miller, *The First Liberty: Religion and the American Republic* (New York, 1986), 5–150.

50. Benny Kraut, "Frances E. Abbot: Perceptions of a Nineteenth Century Religious Radical on Jews and Judaism," in J. R. Marcus and A. J. Peck, *Studies in the American Jewish Experience* (Cincinnati, 1981), 99–101.

51. Reprinted in Philipson, *Max Lilienthal*, 456–457, cf. 109–125.

52. Quoted in Heller, *Isaac M. Wise*, 620.

53. "Commending the 'Congress of Liberals,'" reprinted in *Where We Stand*, 14–15.

54. Yahalom, "American Judaism and the Question of Separation Between Church and State," esp. 257–264; Stokes, *Church and State in the United States* 3:592–595.

55. *CCARYB* 3 (1893): 45; David Philipson, *My Life As An American Jew* (Cincinnati, 1941), 76.

56. Carl F. Kaestle, *Pillars of the Republic* (New York, 1983); Lawrence A. Cremin, *American Education: The National Experience, 1783–1876* (New York, 1980).

57. Kaestle, *Pillars of the Republic*, 93; Lloyd P. Gartner, "Temples of Liberty Unpolluted: American Jews and Public Schools, 1840–1875," in *A Bicentennial Festschrift for Jacob Rader Marcus*, ed. B. W. Korn (Waltham, Mass. and New York, 1976), 161; see Robert Michaelson, *Piety in the Public School* (New York, 1970).

58. Hyman B. Grinstein, *The Rise of the Jewish Community of New York, 1654–1860* (Philadelphia, 1945), 235–236; Joseph R. Brandon, "A Protest Against Sectarian Texts in California Schools in 1875," *Western States Jewish History* 20 (April 1988): 233–235; Alexander M. Dushkin, *Jewish Education in New York City* (New York, 1918), 46–50. Catholics, of course, were vehement in their opposition to the Protestant character of the public schools. On this issue, the *New York Herald* noted with amusement, Jews and Catholics were united for the first time in 1,840 years; see Diane Ravitch, *The Great School Wars: New York City, 1805–1873* (New York, 1974), 53.

59. Quoted in Gartner, "Temples of Liberty Unpolluted," 180.

60. Ibid., 177, 182; William E. Griffiths, *Religion, the Courts, and the Public Schools: A Century of Litigation* (Cincinnati, 1966), 1–92.

61. *Church v. Bullock*, 104 Texas 1, 109 SW 115 (1908), quoted in Griffiths, *Religion, the Courts, and the Public Schools*, 50.

62. Griffiths, *Religion, the Courts, and the Public Schools*, 72–92; see, however, Henry Berkowitz's memoir of religious coercion in the Pittsburgh public schools quoted in Cohen, *Encounter With Emancipation*, 92.

63. Philipson, *Max Lilienthal*, 123.

64. *American Israelite*, January 8, 1869.

65. Philipson, *Max Lilienthal*, 121–122. The case, *Minor v. Board of Education of Cincinnati*, is reprinted with additional documents in *The Bible in the Public Schools* (1870; reprint, New York, 1967); see also F. Michael Perko, "The Building Up of Zion: Religion and Education in Nineteenth-

Century Cincinnati," *Cincinnati Historical Society Bulletin* 38 (Summer 1980): 97–114.

66. Ephraim Frisch, *Is the United States A Christian Nation? A Legal Study* (Pine Bluff, Ark., 1906).

67. *American Israelite*, September 19, 1873.

68. *The Nation* 34 (January 12, 1882): 34.

69. *American Hebrew*, March 2, 1888, 50, 51, 59; Cohen, *Encounter With Emancipation*, 95.

70. The committee was established on the basis of a 1904 proposal by Rabbi Joseph Krauskopf; see *CCARYB* 14 (1904): 32. Its first publication was entitled, significantly, *Why the Bible Should Not Be Read in the Public Schools* (1906). See Lance J. Sussman, "Rhetoric and Reality: The Central Conference of American Rabbis and the Church-State Debate, 1890–1940," in *In Celebration: An American Jewish Perspective on the Bicentennial of the United States Constitution*, ed. Kerry M. Olitzky (Lanham, Md., 1989), 72–100; and Eugene Lipman, "The Conference Considers Relations Between Religion and the State," in *Retrospect and Prospect*, ed. Bertram W. Korn (New York, 1965), 114–128.

71. *CCARYB* 16 (1906): 153; 21 (1911): 259, 262.

72. Nathan Schachner, "Church, State and Education," *AJYB* 49 (1947–48): 29; *CCARYB* 25 (1915): 426, 428; 35 (1925): 60.

73. Samuel Schulman to Samson Benderly, December 9, 1915, Schulman Papers 1/5, American Jewish Archives, Cincinnati, Ohio.

74. *CCARYB* 36 (1926): 84, 87; *AJYB* 29 (1927–1928): 40.

75. Reznikoff, *Louis Marshall, Champion of Liberty*, 970–971.

76. *AJYB* 49 (1947–48): 32; *CCARYB* 53 (1943): 80.

77. *CCARYB* 51 (1941): 121; 53 (1943): 75; *AJYB* 48 (1946–1947): 129.

78. *McCollum v. Board of Education*, 333 U.S. 203 at 383; Naomi W. Cohen, *Not Free to Desist: A History of the American Jewish Committee, 1906–1966* (Philadelphia, 1972), 440; *CCARYB* 58 (1948), 104–106.

79. *AJYB* 50 (1948–1949): 221–223. According to the official history of the Synagogue Council, this position could "be fairly said to represent the majority opinion, almost the official opinion of American Jewry," quoted in Murray Friedman, *The Utopian Dilemma* (Washington, D.C., 1985), 29.

80. Leo Pfeffer, "Is the First Amendment Dead?" reprinted in Naomi W. Cohen, "Schools, Religion and Government—Recent American Jewish Opinions," *Michael* 3 (1975): 373; Pfeffer, *Church, State, and Freedom*, 728; see Pfeffer's "An Autobiographical Sketch," in *Religion and the State: Essays in Honor of Leo Pfeffer*, ed. Wood, 487–533. On the Supreme Court's involvement in the question of religion and the public schools, with copies of relevant decisions, see Miller and Flowers, *Toward Benevolent Neutrality: Church, State, and the Supreme Court*, 378–452.

81. "Letter from the Lubavitcher Rabbi (1964)," quoted in Cohen, "Schools, Religion, and Government," 364; Pratt, *Religion, Politics, and Diversity: The Church-State Theme in New York History,* 290.

82. *AJYB* 64 (1962–63): 110; Cohen, "Schools, Religion, and Government," 348.

83. On *Lee v. Weisman,* see Terry Eastland, ed., *Religious Liberty in the Supreme Court: The Cases That Define the Debate Over Church and State* (Washington, D.C., 1993), 439–467; and Leonard W. Levy, *The Establishment Clause: Religion and the First Amendment,* 2d ed. (Chapel Hill, N.C., 1994), 200–204.

84. Pfeffer, *Church, State, and Freedom,* 342, 350; *Wallace v. Jaffree,* 105 S.Ct. 2479.

85. Schappes, *Documentary History of the Jews in the United States,* 126–127; Dushkin, *Jewish Education in New York,* 42–45.

86. Pfeffer, *Church, State, and Freedom,* 510.

87. The brief is reprinted in Reznikoff, *Louis Marshall, Champion of Liberty,* 957–967; for the context, see Morton Rosenstock, *Louis Marshall, Defender of Jewish Rights* (Detroit, 1965), 211–213.

88. *Cochran v. La. State Board of Education,* 281 U.S. 370 at 375.

89. *CCARYB* 55 (1945): 92; 57 (1947): 122; *AJYB* 50 (1948–1949): 222.

90. Will Herberg, "The Sectarian Conflict Over Church and State," *Commentary* 14 (November 1952): 450–462; David G. Dalin, "Will Herberg in Retrospect," *Commentary* 86 (July 1988): 38–43.

91. *CCARYB* 68 (1958): 55, 57.

92. *AJYB* 63 (1962): 176–178.

93. Seymour Siegel, "Church and State," *Conservative Judaism* 17 (Spring/Summer 1963): 1–12.

94. Cohen, *Jews in Christian America,* 177–178.

95. Milton Himmelfarb, "Church and State: How High A Wall," *Commentary* 42 (July 1966), reprinted in his *The Jews of Modernity* (New York, 1973), 171; see also Seymour Siegel, "Church and State," *Conservative Judaism* 17 (1963): 1–12; idem, "Church and State: A Reassessment," *Sh'ma* 1 (December 11, 1970), reprinted in *Listening to American Jews,* ed. Carolyn T. Oppenheim (New York, 1986), 130–134; and Jakob J. Petuchowski, "Logic and Reality," *The Jewish Spectator,* September 1962, 20.

96. Quoted in Sheldon J. Harr, "Church, State, and the Schools: A Jewish Perspective" (Rabbinic thesis, HUC-JIR, 1973), 83–84.

97. Cohen, "Schools, Religion, and Government," 378–379; *AJYB* 67 (1966): 128, 139–141.

98. Walter Wurzberger, "Separation of Church and State Revisited," *Face to Face* 8 (Fall 1981): 8; see Noah Pickus, "Before I Built A Wall—Jews, Religion and American Public Life," *This World* 15 (Fall 1986): 28–42; see also Friedman, *The Utopian Dilemma,* esp. 87–98.

99. Jonathan D. Sarna, "Is Judaism Compatible with American Civil Religion? The Problem of Christmas and the National Faith," in *Religion and the Life of the Nation*, ed. Rowland A. Sherrill (Urbana, Ill., 1990), 152–173.

100. See, for example, *American Israelite*, December–January 1987; Yosef Friedman, ed., *And There Was Light* (New York, 1988).

101. *Goldman v. Weinberger*, 106 S.Ct. 1310.

102. For examples see Bernard J. Meislin, *Jewish Law in American Tribunals* (New York, 1976) with updates in *Jewish Law Annual*, and Louis Bernstein, *Challenge and Mission: The Emergence of the English Speaking Orthodox Rabbinate* (New York, 1982), 184–210. J. David Bleich has surveyed Jewish divorce in American law in "Jewish Divorce: Judicial Misconceptions and Possible Means of Civil Enforcement," *Connecticut Law Journal* 16 (Winter 1984): 201–289.

103. Wurzberger, "Separation of Church and State Revisited," 8.

ONE

The Colonial Era

✦   ✦   ✦

While individual Jews found their way to the American colonies as early as the sixteenth century, the origins of the Jewish community in America are traditionally dated to 1654, when a ship carrying several families of Jews expelled from the colony of Recife, Brazil docked at the port of New Amsterdam (later New York), and the Jews sought permission to stay. Recife had been a Dutch colony since 1630, and the administrative rules under which it was governed guaranteed liberty to Catholics and Jews alike. "The liberty of Spaniards, Portuguese and natives, whether they be Roman Catholics or Jews, will be respected," article ten of the colony's administrative rules proclaimed. "No one will be permitted to molest them or subject them to inquiries in matters of conscience or in their private homes; and no one should dare to disquiet or disturb them or cause them any hardship." This guarantee of liberty of conscience ended when Recife was recaptured by the Portuguese in 1654. Jews, now faced with the choice of leaving within three months or living under Portugal's much more restrictive religious code (as well as the dictates of its Catholic Inquisition), departed en masse.

Religious liberty was not something that seventeenth-century Jews thought they could demand as an inalienable right. Instead, experience had taught them that governments accorded Jews "rights" as a matter of privilege, usually in exchange for some real or hoped-for benefit. Economically "useful" Jews could obtain substantial measures of equality. When Jews no longer proved "useful," these privileges were more often than not withdrawn.

As European nations developed colonies in the New World, some, led by the Calvinist state of Holland, extended special rights to Jews in their colonies as a form of incentive. By luring them to these new frontiers with the promise of rights unobtainable at home, they hoped to promote colonial economic expansion. This experiment proved to be a great success for the Dutch in Recife, and it was later emulated throughout the Caribbean. The question posed by the small group of Jews that sailed into the port of New Amsterdam was whether this policy would now be extended into North America as well.

Officially, the village of New Amsterdam, like all of New Nether-land (roughly the area of present-day New York State) and like Hol-land itself, had an established Reformed Church; the state religion was Calvinism. Most of the colony's residents were taxed to support the ministers and teachers of the Dutch church, and by a charter negotiated in 1640 it was agreed that "no other Religion shall be publicly admitted in New Netherland except the Reformed, as it is at present preached and practiced by public authority in the United Netherlands." In Holland and Brazil, however, these official poli-cies were tempered, in practice, by a great deal of religious tolerance justified by the state's interest in promoting commerce and trade. In New Amsterdam, by contrast, the governor, Peter Stuyvesant, placed "tranquility, peace and harmony" at the top of his list of pri-orities and sought to enforce religious homogeneity as a means of preserving social order. With the backing of the Reformed clergy, he resisted all efforts to extend religious liberty to non-Calvinists, be they Lutherans, Quakers, Catholics, or Jews.

Stuyvesant's efforts to stifle minority religious faiths in New Amsterdam failed. The Directors of the Dutch West India Company in Holland, who controlled the colony, felt that his uncompromis-ing policies would deter immigration and hinder economic growth. In the case of the Jews, the directors also felt a certain responsi-bility toward those who had suffered so severely in the capture of Recife. Jews were substantial shareholders in the West India Company, and they did not hesitate to make their influence felt on their co-religionists' behalf. As a result, Jews won the right to settle, trade, and worship in New Amsterdam, so long as they did so "in all quietness" and made sure that the "poor among them" did not become a burden on the larger community. While Jews were by no means granted full equality—nor, for that matter, were the Lutherans—they had, at least, achieved freedom enough for them to remain.

The experience of these first Jews in New Amsterdam set a pat-tern that came to characterize the relationship between the Jew-ish community and the state throughout the colonial period. On the one hand, no colony proved inviting to Jews. Everywhere they confronted powerful Protestant religious establishments, social opposition on the part of early settlers, and fundamental laws that explicitly linked the colonies to the practice and propagation of Christianity. On the other hand, compelling pragmatic considerations, notably the urgent need to promote immigration, development, and trade, made it difficult to exclude Jews completely. By the eighteenth century, under the British, Jews freely enjoyed the legal right to live unmolested, to trade, and to worship openly. Yet, debates over their right to acquire citizenship, vote, hold public office, bear witness, substitute for Christian oaths, employ Christian servants, and be exempted from Sunday laws and mandatory church assessments continued to flare sporadically wherever Jews lived—principally in the port cities of New York, Savannah, Charleston, Philadelphia, and Newport.

These ongoing clashes over religion, politics, and economics hint at a deeper question that underlay the issue of rights for Jews and other minority faiths in colonial America—a question that helps to explain the issue's continuing relevance. For ultimately, the debate over the rights of Jews that began in colonial America continues still: it is a debate over the social and religious character of society as a whole.

1. The Right to Settle and Trade

The approximately twenty-three Jews from Recife who landed in New Amsterdam in 1654 were Dutch subjects and had every reason to expect freedom of residence. Governor Peter Stuyvesant, however, was opposed to their settlement and wrote back to Amsterdam that "the deceitful race—such hateful enemies and blasphemers of the name of Christ—be not allowed further to infect and trouble this new colony." In response, the Jews apparently wrote to the leaders of the Portuguese Jewish community in Holland requesting their support. The result was the remarkable correspondence that follows in which "the merchants of the Portuguese Nation" in Amsterdam successfully petitioned to allow Jews to remain in New Netherland with the same rights that they would have enjoyed in the mother country.

As the documents make clear, Jews in this period were concerned not with freedom for individuals, but with corporate rights affecting the minority Jewish community as a whole. The Portuguese Jewish merchants were clearly experienced in the practice of minority group politics. Note the artful way in which they formulated their initial petition, at once pleading, persuading, and subtly threatening economic pressure, to win the coveted "apostille" (marginal annotation) which permitted the Jews of New Netherland "to reside and traffic, provided they shall not become a charge upon the deaconry or the Company."

◆   ◆   ◆

Petition to the West India Company on behalf of Jews in New Netherland, 1655

1655, JANUARY PETITION OF THE JEWISH NATION.

To the Honorable Lords, Directors of the Chartered West India Company, Chamber of the City of Amsterdam.

The merchants of the Portuguese Nation residing in this City respectfully remonstrate to your Honors that it has come to their knowledge that your Honors raise obstacles to the giving of permits or passports to the Portuguese Jews to travel and to go to reside in New Netherland, which if persisted in will result to the great disadvantage of the Jewish nation. It also can be of no advantage to the general Company but rather damaging.

Granted that they may reside and traffic, provided they shall not become a charge upon the deaconry or the Company.

There are many of the nation who have lost their possessions at Pernambuco and have arrived from there in great poverty, and part of them have been dispersed here and there. So that your petitioners had to expend large sums of money for their necessaries of life, and through lack of opportunity all cannot remain here to live. And as they cannot go to Spain or Portugal because of the Inquisition, a great part of the aforesaid people must in time be obliged to depart for other territories of their High Mightinesses the States-General and their Companies, in order there, through their labor and efforts, to be able to exist under the protection of the administrators of your Honorable Directors, observing and obeying your Honors' orders and commands.

It is well known to your Honors that the Jewish nation in Brazil have at all times been faithful and have striven to guard and maintain that place, risking for that purpose their possessions and their blood.

Yonder land is extensive and spacious. The more of loyal people that go to live there, the better it is in regard to the population of the country as in regard to the payment of various excises and taxes which may be imposed there, and in regard to the increase of trade, and also to the importation of all the necessaries that may be sent there.

Your Honors should also consider that the Honorable Lords, the Burgomasters of the City and the Honorable High Illustrious Mighty Lords, the States-General, have in political matters always protected and considered the Jewish nation as upon the same footing as all the inhabitants and burghers. Also it is conditioned in the treaty of perpetual peace with the King of Spain that the Jewish nation shall also enjoy the same liberty as all other inhabitants of these lands.

Your Honors should also please consider that many of the Jewish nation are principal shareholders in the Company. They having always striven their best for the Company, and many of their nation have lost immense and great capital in its shares and obligations.

The Company has by a general resolution consented that those who wish to populate the Colony shall enjoy certain districts of land gratis. Why should now certain subjects of this State not be allowed to travel thither and live there? The French consent that the Portuguese Jews may traffic and live in Martinique, Christopher and others of their territories, whither also some have gone from here, as your Honors know. The English also consent at the present time that the Portuguese and Jewish nation may go from London and settle at Barbados, whither also some have gone.

As foreign nations consent that the Jewish nation may go to live and trade in their territories, how can your Honors forbid the same and refuse transportation to this Portuguese nation who reside here and have been settled here well on to about sixty years, many also being born here and confirmed burghers, and this to a land that needs people for its increase?

Therefore the petitioners request, for the reasons given above (as also others which they omit to avoid prolixity), that your Honors be pleased not to exclude but to grant the Jewish nation passage to and residence in that country; otherwise this would result in a great prejudice to their reputation. Also that by an Apostille and Act the Jewish nation be permitted, together with other inhabitants, to travel, live and traffic there, and with them enjoy liberty on condition of contributing like others, &c. Which doing, &c.

✦

West India Company directive to New Netherland

We would have liked to effectuate and fulfill your wishes and request that the new territories should no more be allowed to be infected by people of the Jewish nation, for we foresee therefrom the same difficulties which you fear, but after having further weighed and considered the matter, we observe that this would be somewhat unreasonable and unfair, especially because of the considerable loss sustained by this nation, with others in the taking of Brazil, as also because of the large amount of capital which they still have invested in the shares of this company. Therefore after many deliberations we have finally decided and resolved to apostille upon a certain petition presented by said Portuguese Jews that these people may travel and trade to and in New Netherland and live and remain there, provided the poor among them shall not become a burden to the company or to the community, but be supported by their own nation. You will now govern yourself accordingly.

✦

Renewed petition to West India Company

To the Honorable Lords Directors of the West India Company, Chamber of the City of Amsterdam:

With due reverence, the merchants of the Portuguese Nation of this city state that, on the representation of the petitioners, your Honors, on the 15th of February, in the year 1655, consented and permitted the Portuguese Jews to navigate and trade near and in New Netherland, and to live and reside there, as is shown in the requests and apostilles here annexed.

In the same sense the Honorable High Mightinesses, in December of 1645, ordered and commanded the High Government in Brazil to recognize the Jewish Nation and to let it enjoy the same rights and protection in its business dealings and actions as the natives of this country.

How much more reason that the same rights should be extended in New Netherland and in all other places under the jurisdiction of the Company when we consider the great desolation suffered by this Nation and the loyalty shown by it everywhere to the state of the Company!

However, it appears that Mr. Stuyvesant, the general over there, does not permit the Jewish Nation to enjoy in quietness the exercise of its religion, at its own expense, as it may in all the places of the Company, and at present in this country. Nor does he permit them to buy and sell real estate, to employ Christians if there is no other possibility, to trade and traffic in all places of the Company, just as the Christians are permitted by the Company to trade and transport in their own ships, just like all other natives of this country, provided they support their own poor and pay their contributions together with all the other natives.

And thus Mr. Stuyvesant does not follow, in this matter, the instructions of this Chamber in accordance with the orders of Her High Mightiness. Therefore, the petitioners request your Honors kindly to order the aforesaid Stuyvesant to grant to the Portuguese Jews everything that has been agreed upon and to recognize and admit them like all other natives, and kindly to take such measures so that the Lord General will act according to your consent and orders.

So doing, etc.

◆

Company's renewed directive to New Netherland

We have here seen and learned with displeasure, that your Honors, against our apostille of the 15th of February, 1655, granted to the Jewish or Portuguese nation at their request, have forbidden them to trade at Fort Orange and South River, and also the purchase of real estate, which is allowed them here in this country without any difficulty, and we wish that this had not occurred but that your Honors had obeyed our orders which you must hereafter execute punctually and with more respect. Jews or Portuguese people, however, shall not be permitted to establish themselves as mechanics (which they are not allowed to do in this city), nor allowed to have open retail shops, but they may quietly and peacefully carry on their business as heretofore and exercise in all quietness their religion within their houses, for which end they must without doubt endeavor to build their houses close together in a convenient place on one or the other side of New Amsterdam—at their choice—as they have done here.

2. Religion and State in Colonial Law

The charters and fundamental laws of the American colonies set forth the central principles that governed church-state relationships in each community. These differed across time and place, reflecting each colony's changing circumstances, ideological stirrings, and socio-religious composition. It is well to remember that legal documents of this sort inevitably disclose more about ideals than reality; law and practice often diverged. Nevertheless, the selections that follow shed light on the evolving theory of church-state relations in the American colonies and on the improving legal position of Jews in the era preceding the American Revolution.

The earliest charter of an English settlement in America, the First Charter of Virginia (1606), granted by King James I, associated the settlement with missionary work, the "propagating of Christian religion." Connecticut's Fundamental Orders

(1639), the first to be drawn up by the colonists themselves, pledged to "maintain and preserve the liberty and purity of the gospell of our Lord Jesus which we now profess, as also the discipline of the Churches, which according to the truth of the said gospell is now practised amongst us." Maryland, in a special act concerning religion that became known as the Toleration Act (1649) owing to its pathbreaking effort to guarantee tolerance for minority Catholics, forbade blasphemy, religious epithets, and profaning of the Sabbath, and explicitly promised freedom of religion without fear of molestation or disrespect—but, again, only to those "professing to believe in Jesus Christ."

Non-Christians received greater recognition in three colonial constitutions: the 1663 Charter of Rhode Island inspired by Roger Williams, The Fundamental Constitutions of Carolina (1669) drafted by John Locke, and the Pennsylvania Charter of Privileges (1701) promulgated by William Penn. All of these fundamental laws considered religion a legitimate state interest, all of them mentioned God and promoted Divine worship, and all of them reflected majority Christian concerns. Yet in extending expanded (if not full) rights to non-Christians they also—and not necessarily consciously—opened the door to Jews. This was a critical step in guaranteeing Jews individual rights along with other Americans, rather than corporate privileges accorded to Jews as a group, and it paved the way for subsequent guarantees of religious liberty in the United States Constitution.

◆   ◆   ◆

First Charter of Virginia, 1606

James, by the Grace of God, King of England, Scotland, France and Ireland, Defender of the Faith, &c. Whereas our loving and well-disposed Subjects, Sir Thomas Gates, and Sir George Somers, Knights, Richard Hackluit, Clerk, Prebendary of Westminster, and Edward-Maria Wingfield, Thomas Hanham, and Ralegh Gilbert, Esqrs. William Parker, and George Popham, Gentlemen, and divers others of our loving Subjects, have been humble Suitors unto us, that We would vouchsafe unto them our Licence, to make Habitation, Plantation, and to deduce a colony of sundry of our People into that part of America commonly called Virginia, and other parts and Territories in America, either appertaining unto us, or which are not now actually possessed by any Christian Prince or People, situate, lying, and being all along the Sea Coasts, between four and thirty Degrees of Northerly Latitude from the Equinoctial Line, and five and forty Degrees of the same Latitude, and in the main Land between the same four and thirty and five and forty Degrees, and the Islands thereunto adjacent, or within one hundred Miles of the Coast thereof;

And to that End, and for the more speedy Accomplishment of their said intended Plantation and Habitation there, are desirous to divide themselves into two several Colonies and Companies; the one consisting of certain Knights, Gentlemen, Merchants, and other Adventurers, of our City of London and elsewhere, which are, and from time to time shall be, joined unto them, which do desire to begin their Plantation and Habitation in some fit and convenient Place, between four and thirty and one and forty Degrees of the said Latitude, alongst the Coasts of Virginia, and the Coasts of America aforesaid: And the other consisting of sundry Knights, Gentlemen, Merchants, and other Adventurers, of our Cities of Bristol and Exeter, and of our Town of Plimouth, and of other Places, which do join themselves unto that Colony, which do desire to begin their Plantation and Habitation in some fit and convenient Place, between eight and thirty Degrees and five and forty Degrees of the said Latitude, all alongst the said Coasts of Virginia and America, as that Coast lyeth:

We, greatly commending, and graciously accepting of, their Desires for the Furtherance of so noble a Work, which may, by the Providence of Almighty God, hereafter tend to the Glory of his Divine Majesty, in propagating of Christian Religion to such People, as yet live in Darkness and miserable Ignorance of the true Knowledge and Worship of God, and may in time bring the Infidels and Savages, living in those parts, to human Civility, and to a settled and quiet Government: Do, by these our Letters Patents, graciously accept of, and agree to, their humble and well-intended Desires. . . .

✦

Fundamental Orders of Connecticut, 1639

Forasmuch as it hath pleased the Allmighty God by the wise disposition of his diuyne pruidence so to Order and dispose of things that we the Inhabitants and Residents of Windsor, Harteford and Wethersfield are now cohabiting and dwelling in and vppon the River of Conectecotee and the Lands thereunto adoiyneing; And well knowing where a people are gathered togather the word of God requires that to mayntayne the peace and vnion of such a people there should be an orderly and decent Gouerment established according to God, to order and dispose of the affayres of the people at all seasons as occation shall require; doe therefore assotiate and conioyne our selues to be as one Publike State or Comonwelth; and doe, for our selues and our Successors and such as shall be adioyned to vs att any tyme hereafter, enter into Combination and Confederation togather, to mayntayne and prsearue the liberty and purity of the gospell of our Lord Jesus wch we now prfesse, as also the disciplyne of the Churches, wch according to the truth of the said gospell is now practised amongst vs; As also in or Ciuell Affaires to be guided and gouerned according to such Lawes, Rules, Orders and decrees as shall be made, ordered & decreed. . . .

◆

Maryland Act concerning Religion, 1649

Afforasmuch as in a well governed and Xpian Comon Weath matters concerning Religion and the honor of God ought in the first place to bee taken, into serious consideracon and endeavoured to bee settled. Be it therefore ordered and enacted by the Right Hoble Cecilius Lord Baron of Baltemore absolute Lord and Proprietary of this Province with the advise and consent of this Generall Assembly. That whatsoever pson or psons within this Province and the Islands thereunto belonging shall from henceforth blaspheme God, that is Curse him, or deny our Saviour Jesus Christ to bee the sonne of God, or shall deny the holy Trinity the ffather sonne and holy Ghost, or the God-head of any of the said Three psons of the Trinity or the Vnity of the Godhead, or shall use or utter any reproachfull Speeches, words or language concerning the said Holy Trinity, or any of the said three psons thereof, shalbe punished with death and confiscaton or forfeiture of all his or her lands and goods to the Lord Proprietary and his heires, And bee it also Enacted by the Authority and with the advise and assent aforesaid. That whatsoever pson or psons shall from henceforth use or utter any reproachfull words or Speeches concerning the blessed Virgin Mary the Mother of our Saviour or the holy Apostles or Evangelists or any of them shall in such case for the first offense forfeit to the said Lord Proprietary and his heirs Lords and Proprietaries of this Province the sume of ffive pound Sterling or the value thereof to be Levyed on the goods and chattells of every such pson soe offending, but in case such Offender or Offenders, shall not then have goods and chattells sufficient for the satisfyeing of such forfeiture, or that the same bee not otherwise speedily satisfyed that then such Offender or Offenders shalbe publiquely whipt and bee ymprisoned during the pleasure of the Lord Proprietary or the Leivet or cheife Governor of this Province for the time being. And that every such Offender or Offenders for every second offence shall forfeit tenne pound sterling or the value thereof to bee levyed as aforesaid, or in case such offender or Offenders shall not then haue goods and chattells within this Province sufficient for that purpose then to bee publiquely and severely whipt and imprisoned as before is expressed. And that every pson or psons before mentioned offending herein the third time, shall for such third Offence forfeit all his lands and Goods and bee for ever banished and expelled out of this Province. And be it also further Enacted by the same authority advise and assent that whatsoever pson or psons shall from henceforth vppon any occasion of Offence or otherwise in a reproachful manner or Way declare call or denominate any pson or psons whatsoever inhabiting residing traffiqueing trading or comerceing within this Province or within any the Ports, Harbors, Creeks or Havens to the same belonging an heritick, Scismatick, Idolator, puritan, Independant, Prespiterian popish prest, Jesuite, Jesuited papist, Lutheran, Calvenist, Anabaptist, Brownist, Antinomian, Barrowist, Roundhead, Sepatist, or any other name or terme in a reproachfull manner relating to matter of Religion shall for every such Offence forfeit and loose the some or terne shillings sterling or the value thereof to bee levyed on the goods and chattells of every such Offender and Offenders, the one half thereof to be forfeited and paid unto the person and persons of whom such reproachfull words are or shalbe spoken or vttered, and the other half thereof to the Lord Proprietary and his heires Lords and Proprietaries of this Province, But if such pson or psons who shall at any time vtter or speake any such reproachfull words or Language shall not have Goods or Chattells sufficient and overt within this Province to bee taken to satisfie the penalty aforesaid or that the same bee not otherwise speedily satisfyed, that then the pson or persons soe offending shalbe publickly whipt, and shall suffer imprisonmt without baile or maineprise vntill hee shee or they respectively shall satisfy the party soe offended or greived by such reproachfull Language by asking him or her respectively forgivenes publiquely for such his Offence before the Magistrate or cheife Officer or Officers of the Towne or place where such Offence shalbe given. And be it further likewise Enacted by the Authority and consent aforesaid That every person and persons within this Province that shall at any time hereafter pphane the Sabbath or Lords day called Sunday by frequent swearing, drunkennes or by any uncivill or disorderly recreacon, or by working on that day when absolute necessity doth not require it shall for every such first offence forfeit 2s. 6d sterling or the value thereof, and for the second offence 5s sterling or the value thereof, and for the third offence and soe for every time he shall offend in like manner afterwards 10s sterling or the value thereof. And in case such offender and offenders shall not have sufficient goods or chattells within this Province to satisfy any of the said Penalties respectively hereby imposed for prophaning the Sabbath or Lords day called Sunday as aforesaid, That in Every such case the ptie soe offending shall for the first and second offence in that kinde be imprisoned till hee or shee shall publickly in open Court before the cheife Commander Judge or Magistrate, of that County Towne or precinct where such offence shalbe committed acknowledg the Scandall and offence he hath in that respect given against God and the good and civill Governemt of this Province And for the third offence and for every time after shall also bee publickly whipt. And whereas the inforceing of the conscience in matters of Religion hath frequently fallen out to be of dangerous Consequence in those commonwealthes where it hath been practised, And for the more quiett and peaceable governemt of this Province, and the better to pserve mutuall Love and amity amongst the Inhabitants thereof. Be it Therefore also by the Lo: Proprietary with the advise and consent of this Assembly Ordeyned & enacted (except as in this psent Act is before Declared and sett forth) that noe person or psons whatsoever within this Province, or the Islands, Ports, Harbors, Creekes, or havens thereunto belonging professing to beleive in Jesus Christ, shall from henceforth bee any waies troubled, Molested or discountenanced for or in respect of his or her religion nor in the free exercise thereof within this Province or the Islands thereunto belonging nor any way compelled to the beleife or exercise of any other Religion against his or her consent, soe as they be not unfaithfull to the Lord Proprietary, or molest or conspire against the civill Governemt established or to bee established in this Province vnder him or his heires. And that all & every pson and psons that shall presume Contrary to this Act and the true intent and meaning thereof directly or indirectly either in person or estate willfully to wrong disturbe trouble or molest any person whatsoever within this Province professing to beleive in Jesus Christ for or in respect of his or her religion or the free exercise thereof within this Province other than is provided for in this Act that such pson or psons soe offending, shalbe compelled to pay trebble damages to the party soe wronged or molested, and for every such offence shall also forfeit 20s sterling in money or the value thereof, half thereof for the vse of the Lo: Proprietary, and his heires Lords and Proprietaries of this Province, and the other half for the vse of the party soe wronged or molested as aforesaid, Or if the ptie soe offending as aforesaid shall refuse or bee vnable to recompense the party soe wronged, or to satisfy such ffyne or forfeiture, then such Offender shalbe severely punished by publick whipping & imprisonmt during the pleasure of the Lord Proprietary, or his Leivetenat or cheife Governor of this Province for the tyme being without baile or maineprise And bee it further alsoe Enacted by the authority and consent aforesaid That the Sheriff or other Officer or Officers from time to time to bee appointed & authorized for that purpose, of the County Towne or precinct where every particular offence in this psent Act conteyned shall happen at any time to bee comitted and wherevppon there is hereby a fforfeiture ffyne or penalty imposed shall from time to time distraine and seise the goods and estate of every such pson soe offending as aforesaid against this psent Act or any pt thereof, and sell the same or any part thereof for the full satisfaccon of such forfeiture, ffine, or penalty as aforesaid, Restoring vnto the ptie soe offending the Remainder or overplus of the said goods or estate after such satisfaccon soe made as aforesaid

The ffreemen haue assented. Tho: Hatton
Enacted by the Governor Willm Stone

❖

Charter of Rhode Island and Providence Plantations, 1663

... Now know yee, that wee beinge willinge to encourage the hopefull under-takeinge of oure sayd loyall and loveinge subjects, and to secure them in the free exercise and enjoyment of all theire civill and religious rights, appertaining to them, as our loveing subjects; and to preserve unto them that libertye, in the true Christian ffaith and worshipp of God, which they have sought with soe much travaill, and with peaceable myndes, and loyall subjectione to our royall progenitors and ourselves, to enjoye; and because some of the people and inhabitants of the same colonie cannot, in theire private opinions, conforme to the publique exercise of religion, according to the litturgy, formes and cere-monyes of the Church of England, or take or subscribe the oaths and arti-cles made and established in that behalfe; and for that the same, by reason of the remote distances of those places, will (as wee hope) bee noe breach of the unitie and unifformitie established in this nation: Have therefore thought ffit, and doe hereby publish, graunt, ordeyne and declare, That our royall will and pleasure is, that noe person within the sayd colonye, at any tyme hereafter, shall bee any wise molested, punished, disquieted, or called in question, for any differences in opinione in matters of religion, and doe not actually disturb the civill peace of our sayd colony; but that all and everye person and persons may, from tyme to tyme, and at all tymes hereafter, freelye and fullye have and enjoye his and theire owne judgments and consciences, in matter of reli-gious concernments, throughout the tract of lande hereafter mentioned; they behaving themselves peaceablie and quietlie, and not useing this libertie to lycentiousnesse and profanenesse, nor to the civill injurye or outward dis-turbeance of others; any lawe, statute, or clause, therein contayned, or to bee contayned, usage or custome of this realme, to the contrary hereof, in any wise, notwithstanding. And that they may bee in the better capacity to defend them-selves, in theire just rights and libertyes against all the enemies of the Chris-tian ffaith, and others, in all respects, wee have further thought fit, and at the humble petition of the persons afosesayd are gratiously pleased to declare, That they shall have and enjoye the benefitt of our late act of indempnity and ffree pardon, as the rest of our subjects in other our dominions and territoryes have; and to create and make them a bodye politique or corporate, with the powers and priviledges hereinafter mentioned. ...

◆

Fundamental Constitutions of Carolina, 1669

Ninety-five: No man shall be permitted to be a freeman of Carolina, or to have any estate or habitation within it, that doth not acknowledge a God; and that God is publicly and solemnly to be worshipped. . . .

Ninety-seven: But since the natives of that place, who will be concerned in our plantation, are utterly strangers to Christianity, whose idolatry, ignorance, or mistake gives us no right to expel or use them ill; and those who remove from other parts to plant there will unavoidably be of different opinions concerning matters of religion, the liberty whereof they will expect to have allowed them, and it will not be reasonable for us, on this account, to keep them out, that civil peace may be maintained amidst diversity of opinions, and our agreement and compact with all men may be duly and faithfully observed; the violation whereof, upon what pretence soever, cannot be without great offence to Almighty God, and great scandal to the true religion which we profess; and also that Jews, heathens, and other dissenters from the purity of Christian religion may not be scared and kept at a distance from it, but, by having an opportunity of acquainting themselves with the truth and reasonableness of its doctrines, and the peaceableness and inoffensiveness of its professors, may, by good usage and persuasion, and all those convincing methods of gentleness and meekness, suitable to the rules and design of the gospel, be won ever to embrace and unfeignedly receive the truth; therefore, any seven or more persons agreeing in any religion, shall constitute a church or profession, to which they shall give some name, to distinguish it from others. . . .

One hundred and nine: No person whatsoever shall disturb, molest, or persecute another for his speculative opinions in religion, or his way of worship.

◆

Pennsylvania Charter of Privileges, 1701

I

Because no People can be truly happy, though under the greatest Enjoyment of Civil Liberties, if abridged of the Freedom of their Consciences, as to their Religious Profession and Worship: And Almighty God being the only Lord of Conscience, Father of Lights and Spirits; and the Author as well as Object of all divine Knowledge, Faith and Worship, who only doth enlighten the Minds, and persuade and convince the Understandings of People, I do hereby grant and declare, That no Person or Persons, inhabiting in this Province or Territories, who shall confess and acknowledge One almighty God, the Creator, Upholder and Ruler of the World; and profess him or themselves obliged to live quietly under the Civil Government, shall be in any Case molested or prejudiced, in his or their Person or Estate, because of his or their conscientious Persuasion or Practice, nor be compelled to frequent or maintain any religious Worship, Place or Ministry, contrary to his or their Mind, or to do or suffer any other Act or Thing, contrary to their religious Persuasion.

And that all Persons who also profess to believe in Jesus Christ, the Saviour of the World, shall be capable (notwithstanding their other Persuasions and Practices in Point of Conscience and Religion) to serve this Government in any Capacity, both legislatively and executively, he or they solemnly promising, when lawfully required, Allegiance to the King as Sovereign, and Fidelity to the Proprietary and Governor, and taking the Attests as now established by the Law made at New-Castle, in the Year One Thousand and Seven Hundred, entitled, An Act directing the Attests of several Officers and Ministers, as now amended and confirmed this present Assembly.

3. Naturalization

Under British law, aliens could not engage in British commerce without severe penalty. Although not always enforced in the colonies, the law made it advantageous for immigrants to the American colonies to gain naturalization, if possible, or at least denization, a lower legal status lacking many of the property and inheritance rights that naturalized and native-born citizens enjoyed. In England, naturalization generally required both a profession of Christian belief and proof that an individual had taken the Sacrament in a Protestant church. As a result, most Jews had to be satisfied with denization—and even that was expensive. As part of their effort to encourage commerce and trade, however, the colonies granted naturalization on much easier terms; between 1718 and 1739, for example, at least thirteen Jews were naturalized in New York. These local grants of naturalizations were not always recognized elsewhere.

The 1740 Naturalization Act, also known as the Plantation Act, sought to regularize and systematize naturalization procedures while encouraging immigration to the American colonies. The act imposed a seven-year residence requirement, simplified operating procedures, and reduced costs. Most important of all, from a Jewish point of view, it specifically exempted Jews from the Protestant Sacrament and it deleted the words "upon the true Faith of a Christian" from the oath that they were required to swear—both exemptions added to the bill at the last minute, after it had already been reported from committee and amended. No similar exemption was offered to Catholics.

With the bill's passage, Jews had a far easier time obtaining naturalization in the colonies than back in England. The English "Jew Bill" of 1753 attempted to end this anomaly, but it was defeated. For a variety of reasons, only a comparatively small number of Jews in the North American colonies actually took advantage of the Naturalization Act; it had a much more important impact on the Jewish community of Jamaica. The act's symbolic significance, however, was considerable, for it marked an important step on the Jewish road to full legal equality.

◆   ◆   ◆

British Naturalization Act, 1740

An Act for naturalizing such foreign Protestants, and others therein mentioned, as are settled or shall settle, in any of his Majesty's Colonies in America. Anno 13 Geo. II [1740], Cap. VII

Whereas the Increase of People is a Means of advancing the Wealth and Strength of any Nation or Country; And whereas many Foreigners and Strangers from the Lenity of our Government, the Purity of our Religion, the Benefit of our Laws, the Advantages of our Trade, and the Security of our Property, might be induced to come and settle in some of His Majesty's Colonies in America, if they were made Partakers of the Advantages and Privileges which the natural born Subjects of this Realm do enjoy; Be it therefore enacted by the King's Most Excellent Majesty, by and with the Advice and Consent of the Lords Spiritual and Temporal, and Commons, in this present Parliament assembled, and by the Authority of the same That from and after the first Day of June in the Year of our Lord One thousand seven hundred and forty, all persons born out of the Legiance of His Majesty, His Heirs or Successors, who have inhabited and resided, or shall inhabit or reside for the Space of seven Years or more, in any of His Majesty's Colonies in America, and shall not have been absent out of some of the said Colonies for a longer Space than two Months at any one time during the said seven Years, and shall take and subscribe the Oaths, and make, repeat and subscribe the Declaration appointed by an Act made in the first Year of the Reign of His late Majesty King George the First, intituled, An act for the further Security of His Majesty's Person and Government, and the Succession of the Crown in the Heirs of the late Princess Sophia, being Protestants; and for extinguishing the Hopes of the pretended Prince of Wales, his open and secret Abettors; or, being of the People called Quakers, shall make and subscribe the Declaration of Fidelity, and take and affirm the Effect of the Abjuration Oath, appointed and prescribed by an Act made in the eighth Year of the Reign of His said late Majesty, intituled, An Act for granting the People called Quakers, such Forms of Affirmation or Declaration, as may remove the Difficulties which many of them lie under; and also make and subscribe the Profession of his Christian Belief, appointed and subscribed by an Act made in the first Year of the Reign of their late Majesties King William and Queen Mary, intituled, An Act for exempting Their Majesties Protestant Subjects from the Penalties of certain Laws; before the Chief Judge, or other Judge of the Colony wherein such Persons respectively have so inhabited and resided, or shall so inhabit and reside, shall be deemed, adjudged and taken to be His Majesty's natural born Subjects of this Kingdom, to all Intents, Constructions and Purposes, as if they and every of them had been or were born within this Kingdom; which said Oath or Affirmation and Subscription of the said Declarations respectively, the Chief Judge or other Judge of every of the said Colonies is hereby enabled and impowered to administer and take; and the taking and subscribing of every such Oath or Affirmation, and the making, repeating and subscribing of every such Declaration, shall be before such Chief Judge or other Judge, in open Court, between the Hours of nine and twelve in the Forenoon; and shall be entered in the same Court, and also in the Secretary's Office of the Colony wherein such Person shall so inhabit and reside; and every Chief Judge or other Judges of every respective Colony, before whom such Oaths or Affirmation shall be taken and every such Declaration shall be made, repeated and subscribed as aforesaid, is hereby required to make a due and proper entry thereof in a Book to be kept for that Purpose in the said Court; for the doing whereof two Shillings and no more shall be paid at each respective place, under the Penalty and Forfeiture of ten Pounds of lawful Money of Great Britain for every Neglect or Omission: and in like manner every Secretary of the Colony wherein any Person shall so take the said Oaths or Affirmation, and make, repeat and subscribe the said Declarations respectively, as aforesaid, is hereby required to make a due and proper Entry thereof in a Book to be kept for that Purpose in his Office, upon Notification thereof to him by the Chief Judge or other Judges of the same Colony, under the like Penalty and Forfeiture for every such Neglect or Omission.

II. Provided always and be it enacted by the Authority aforesaid, That no Person, of what Quality, Condition or Place soever, other than and except such of the People called Quakers as shall qualify themselves and be naturalized by the ways and means hereinbefore mentioned, or such who profess the Jewish

Religion, shall be naturalized by virtue of this Act, unless such persons shall have received the Sacrament of the Lord's Supper in some Protestant and Reformed Congregation within this Kingdom of Great Britain, or within some of the said Colonies in America, within three Months next before his taking and subscribing the said Oaths, and making, repeating and subscribing the said Declaration; and shall, at the time of his taking and subscribing the said Oaths, and making, repeating, and subscribing the said Declaration, produce a Certificate signed by the Person administering the said Sacrament, and attested by two credible Witnesses, whereof an Entry shall be made in the Secretary's Office of the Colony, wherein such Person shall so inhabit and reside, as also in the Court where the said Oaths shall be so taken as aforesaid, without any Fee or Reward.

III. And whereas the following Words are contained in the latter Part of the Oath of Abjuration, *videlicet*, (upon the true Faith of a Christian): And whereas the People professing the Jewish Religion may thereby be prevented from receiving the Benefit of this Act: Be it further enacted by the Authority aforesaid, That whenever any Person professing the Jewish Religion shall present himself to take the said Oath of Abjuration in pursuance of this Act, the said Words (upon the true Faith of a Christian) shall be omitted out of the said Oath in administering the same to such Person, and the taking and subscribing the said Oath by such Person, professing the Jewish Religion, without the Words aforesaid, and the other Oaths appointed by the said Act in like manner as Jews were permitted to take the Oath of Abjuration, by an Act made in the tenth Year of Reign of His late Majesty King George the First, intituled, An Act for explaining and amending an Act of the last Session of Parliament, intituled, An Act to oblige all Persons, being Papists, in that part of Great Britain called Scotland, and all persons in Great Britain, refusing or neglecting to take the Oaths appointed for the Security of His Majesty's Person and Government, by several Acts herein mentioned, to register their Names and real Estates; and for enlarging the time for taking the said Oaths, and making such Registers, and for allowing further time for the Inrolment of Deeds or Wills made by Papists, which have been omitted to be inrolled pursuant to an Act of the third Year of His Majesty's Reign; and also for giving Relief to Protestant Lessees shall be deemed a sufficient taking of the said Oaths, in order to intitle such Person to the Benefit of being naturalized by virtue of this Act.

IV. And be it further enacted by the Authority aforesaid, That a Testimonial or Certificate under the Seal of any of the said Colonies, of any Persons having resided and inhabited for the Space of seven Years or more as aforesaid within the said Colonies or some of them, to be specified in such Certificate, together with the particular time of Residence in each of such respective Colonies (whereof the Colony under the Seal of which such Certificate shall be given to be one) and of his having taken and subscribed the said Oaths, and of his having made, repeated and subscribed the said Declaration, and in case of a

Quaker of his having made and subscribed the Declaration of Fidelity, and of his having taken and affirmed the Effect of the Abjuration Oath as aforesaid, and in case of a Person professing the Jewish Religion, of his having taken the Oath of abjuration as aforesaid, within the same Colony, under the Seal whereof such Certificate shall be given as aforesaid, shall be deemed and taken to be a sufficient Testimony and Proof thereof, and of his being a natural born Subject of Great Britain, to all Intents and Purposes whatsoever, and as such shall be allowed in every Court within the Kingdoms of Great Britain and Ireland, and also in the said Colonies in America. (Extended, 20 G. 2, c. 44, Sec. I.)

V. And be it further enacted by the Authority aforesaid, That every Secretary of the said respective Colonies for the time being, shall and is hereby directed and required at the End of every Year, to be computed from the said first Day of June in the Year of Our Lord One thousand seven hundred and forty, to transmit and send over to the Office of the Commissioners for Trade and Plantations kept in the City of London or Westminster, a true and perfect List of the Names of all and every Person and Persons who have in that Year intitled themselves to the Benefit of this Act, under the Penalty and Forfeiture of fifty Pounds of lawful Money of Great Britain for every Neglect or Omission: All which said lists to [sic] transmitted and sent over, shall, from Year to Year, be duly and regularly entered by the said Commissioners, in a Book or Books to be had and kept for that Purpose in the said Office, for publick View and Inspection as Occasion shall require.

VI. Provided always, and it is hereby further enacted, That no Person who shall become a natural born Subject of this Kingdom by virtue of this Act, shall be of the Privy Council, or a Member of either House of Parliament, or capable of taking, having or enjoying any Office or Place of Trust within the Kingdoms of Great Britain or Ireland, either civil or military, or of having, accepting or taking any Grant from the Crown to himself, or to any other in trust for him, of any Lands, Tenements or Hereditaments within the Kingdoms of Great Britain or Ireland; any Thing hereinbefore contained to the contrary thereof in any wise notwithstanding. (Extended, 20 G. 2, c. 44. Persons naturalized by this Act capable of Offices, etc., civil and military, 13 G. 3, c. 25.)

4. The Lopez-Elizer Incident

The chasm between principle and practice in religion-state issues is well illustrated in the following documents concerning the unsuccessful petition of two significant Newport merchants, Aaron Lopez and Isaac Elizer (spelled Elizar in the documents), to obtain naturalization under English law. Not-withstanding Rhode Island's liberal constitution and tradition of tolerance, the economic clout of the Jewish community of Newport, and the clear terms of the 1740 Naturalization Act, their petition was rejected. The court claimed that the Natu-ralization Act only applied to underpopulated settlements, which Rhode Island was not, and that local law limited citi-zenship to believing Christians; both claims were dubious. Some believe that the court's real concern was that Lopez sup-ported a political faction led by Stephen Hopkins that op-posed the influential Samuel Ward, who controlled the court and the upper house. Whatever the case, Lopez and Elizer soon arranged to be naturalized elsewhere (Lopez in Massa-chusetts and Elizer in New York). The incident, which appar-ently received some publicity, demonstrated that Jews, as non-Christians, remained second-class citizens even in places where laws seemed to protect them. This foreboded—at least so Newport's famous minister Ezra Stiles believed—"that the Jews will never become incorporated with the p[eo]ple of America, any more than in Europe, Asia and Africa."

◆　　◆　　◆

Petition of Jews for naturalization, 1762

Newport, ss.

To the Honorable Superior Court of Judicature held at Newport in & for the County of Newport the first Tuesday of March AD 1762.

Aaron Lopez & Isaac Elizar Persons professing the Jewish Religion between the hours of Nine and twelve in the Forenoon being present in said Court do give the said Court to understand and be informed that they were born out of the Liegiance of his Majesty the King of Great Britain but have resided in the Colony of Rhode Island upwards of Seven Years without being absent at any one time two months and therefore they pray that they may have Leave to take the Oaths of Allegiance &c & to conform themselves to the Directions of an Act of Parliament of the 13th Year of his late Majesty George the Second intitled an Act "for Naturalizing such foreign Protestants &c as are settled or shall settle in any of his Majestys Colonies of America, and as in Duty bound they will ever pray &c.

AARON LOPEZ
ISAAC ELIZAR

◆

Petition dismissed by Rhode Island Court

The petition of Messrs. Aron Lopez & Isaac Elizar, Persons professing the Jewish Religion, praying that they may be naturalized on an Act of Parliament made in the thirteenth Year of his late Majesty's Reign, George the Second, having been duly considered, and also the act of Parliament therein referr'd to; this Court are unanimously of Opinion that the said Act of Parliament was wisely designed for increasing the number of Inhabitants in the plantations, but this Colony being already so full of People that many of his Majesty's good Subjects, born within the same have removed & settled in Nova Scotia & other Places, cannot come within the Intention of the said act. Farther by the Charter granted to this Colony it appears that the free & quiet Enjoyment of the Christian Religion and a Desire of propagating the same were the principal Views with which this Colony was settled, & by a Law made & passed in the year 1663, no Person who does not profess the Christian Religion can be admitted free of this Colony. This Court, therefore, unanimously dismiss the said Petition as absolutely inconsistent with the first principles upon which the Colony was founded & a Law of the same now in full Force.

The New Nation

◆ ❖ ◆

W e have the world to begin againe," an ecstatic Mordecai Sheftall wrote to his son, Sheftall Sheftall, on April 13, 1783. The patriotic Savannah Jew had just learned that the long American struggle for independence was over; he understood that a new era had begun. For America's two thousand or so Jews, the most striking feature of this new era was its emphasis on liberty— liberty from England, liberty from religious establishments, liberty of conscience, liberty for the pursuit of happiness. They watched as church establishments closely linked to England were swept away in the Revolution, and new constitutions, promulgated in almost every state after 1776, promised citizens a greater measure of religious freedom.

Protestant Dissenters—Baptists, Methodists, Presbyterians, and smaller sects—lay behind many of these new freedoms. Their interest in Jews was minimal; it was to achieve equality for themselves, to protect *their* faiths from state encroachment, that they insisted that church and state should be separate and church contributions purely voluntary. The powerful logic of their arguments, couched in the rhetoric of freedom, did much to persuade Americans that liberty of conscience and diversity of belief were part and parcel of the same civil liberties for which so many had just laid down their lives.

There was, however, a disjunction between the radical goals that Dissenters espoused and the social realities that they were prepared to accept. Though they spread the idea of religious liberty, and so helped all minority religions, their battle usually ended with the victory of Protestant pluralism over church establishment. In most cases, laws privileging Protestants over non-Protestants failed to move them.

The extension of religious liberty to Jews and other non-Protestants came about through the work of a second group of

Revolutionary-era thinkers: those inspired by the ideas of Enlightenment rationalism. Classic Enlightenment texts—among them the works of Locke, Rousseau, Grotius, Montesquieu, Harrington, and Voltaire—found many readers in America. Leading patriots like Franklin, Jefferson, Adams, and Paine openly avowed deistic or Unitarian principles. For these men, a utilitarian belief in the value of "all sound religion" was enough. Whether government should encourage religion-in-general as a force for social good, or rely on reason alone to guarantee society's moral order, remained a matter of dispute. Either way, they insisted that Protestantism, for all of its benefits, was *not* a prerequisite for good citizenship.

This Enlightenment view of religious liberty eventually gained the upper hand in America, though Protestant pluralists continued to struggle—with various degrees of success—for many years. In 1777, New York became the first state to extend liberty of conscience "to all mankind," regardless of religion. An anti-Catholic test oath was required only of those born abroad. Virginia's justly famous "Act for Religious Freedom (1785)," originally drafted by Thomas Jefferson in 1779, was both more comprehensive and more influential. It carefully distinguished civil rights from religious opinions, and decreed that "all men shall be free to profess and by argument to maintain their opinions in matters of religion, and that the same shall in no wise diminish, enlarge or affect their civil capacities." Once the United States Constitution, in Article Six and Amendment One, wrote the principles of no religious test, no establishment of religion, and free exercise of religion into federal law, the claims of Revolutionary-era American Jews to equal rights were finally conceded. At least at the national level, an epochal change in Jews' legal status had come about.

Jews themselves played no significant role in this achievement. They did speak up, on a few occasions, for Jewish equality with other faiths, pointing out that they had fought bravely for freedom in the Revolution, "and bled for liberty which they can not Enjoy." They also were spoken about, from time to time, by those who wondered aloud concerning the consequences of permitting Jews (along with Mohammedans, Deists, and Atheists) to hold public office. Most of the debate over religion in American life, however, paid no attention to Jews whatsoever, and the major American documents bearing on religious liberty do not mention them even once. As a result, Jews gained their religious rights on the federal level as individuals along with everybody else—not, as had so often been the case in Europe (and in the American colonies), as a special privilege that set Jews apart as a group.

Yet these federal rights were not binding on the states; they could legislate as they pleased. As a result, some legislatures—notably those in New England, New Jersey, Maryland, and North Carolina—enacted into law only the principles of Protestant pluralism. Jews who refused to avow their faith in the Protestant religion were denied the right to hold state office. The implications of this were absurd: theoretically, a Jew could be President of the United States, but ineligible to hold even the lowliest political position in the state of Maryland. Realizing this, a majority of states granted Jews full rights by 1830 (though New Hampshire held out until 1877). Even this, however, did not result in full Jewish equality. Many Americans continued to view Jews with the greatest of suspicion and worried that a state without Christianity in its laws could not long survive.

1. Widening Religious Liberty in the States

In May 1776, as English governors took flight and war seemed inevitable, the Second Continental Congress recommended that each colony "adopt such government as shall, in the opinion of the representatives of the people, best conduce to the happiness and safety of their constituents in particular, and America in general." This inaugurated a process which by the end of the Revolution resulted in the writing of new constitutions in eleven of the thirteen states; only Connecticut and Rhode Island preserved their old royal charters with minor modifications. Central to each of the new constitutions was a declaration of rights—a response to perceived English tyranny—designed to limit the powers of government and guarantee the rights of individuals. Religious liberty, variously defined, was in each case among the rights guaranteed.

A comparison of these guarantees with those contained in the earlier colonial charters suggests a period of intellectual confusion and ferment as new ideas concerning religious equality for non-Protestants jockeyed with entrenched fears over the specter of non-Protestant rule. The first of the new constitutions to be promulgated, the influential Virginia Declaration of Rights (1776), for example, declared that "all men are equally entitled to the free exercise of religion," a phrase introduced by the young James Madison to replace the "fullest toleration in the exercise of religion," a more restrictive term. But the Declaration said nothing about the rights of non-Protestants to vote and serve in public office, and it included "Christian forbearance" as one of the moral duties that Virginians should "practise . . . towards each other."

New Jersey's constitution (1776) introduced a "no establishment" clause, not previously seen, which the document carefully distinguished from the right to worship according to the dictates of conscience, listed in a separate article. Nevertheless, the constitution, apparently at the insistence of local Presbyterians, continued to enshrine Protestant pluralism in the area of civil rights, rendering Jews second-class citizens.

It was only in religiously pluralistic New York, the state with the largest Jewish community in North America, that the new constitution granted, without any restrictions on office-holding, "free exercise and enjoyment of religious profession and worship, without discrimination or preference." John Jay fought hard at the convention to restrict the rights of Catholics and did manage to inject some anti-Catholicism into the document. No similar slights against Jews, however, even came up for debate. The reasons, according to John Webb Pratt, the historian of church-state relations in New York, is that a consensus had developed behind the proposition "that the state could promote religion by affording the congenial environment within which all sects might develop their full potential for good in the community, short of interfering directly in the affairs of any of them." In no other state where Jews resided at that time did they, as a matter of law, enjoy such complete and unconditional religious equality.

◆   ◆   ◆

Virginia Declaration of Rights, 1776

16. That Religion, or the duty which we owe to our Creator, and the manner of discharging it, can be directed only by reason and conviction, not by force or violence; and, therefore, all men are equally entitled to the free exercise of religion, according to the dictates of conscience; and that it is the mutual duty of all to practise Christian forbearance, love, and charity, towards each other.

◆

New Jersey Constitution, 1776

XVIII. That no person shall ever, within this Colony, be deprived of the inestimable privilege of worshipping Almighty God in a manner agreeable to the dictates of his own conscience; nor, under any pretence whatever, be compelled to attend any place of worship, contrary to his own faith and judgment; nor shall any person, within this Colony, ever be obliged to pay tithes, taxes, or any other rates, for the purpose of building or repairing any other church or churches, place or places of worship, or for the maintenance of any minister or ministry, contrary to what he believes to be right, or has deliberately or voluntarily engaged himself to perform.

XIX. That there shall be no establishment of any one religious sect in this Province, in preference to another; and that no Protestant inhabitant of this Colony shall be denied the enjoyment of any civil right, merely on account of his religious principles; but that all persons, professing a belief in the faith of any Protestant sect, who shall demean themselves peaceably under the government, as hereby established, shall be capable of being elected into any office of profit or trust, or being a member of either branch of the Legislature, and shall fully and freely enjoy every privilege and immunity, enjoyed by others their fellow subjects.

◆

New York Constitution, 1777

XXXVIII. And whereas we are required, by the benevolent principles of rational liberty, not only to expel civil tyranny, but also to guard against that spiritual oppression and intolerance wherewith the bigotry and ambition of weak and wicked priests and princes have scourged mankind, this convention doth further, in the name and by the authority of the good people of this State, ordain, determine, and declare, that the free exercise and enjoyment of religious profession and worship, without discrimination or preference, shall forever hereafter be allowed, within this State, to all mankind: Provided, That the liberty of conscience, hereby granted, shall not be so construed as to excuse acts of licentiousness, or justify practices inconsistent with the peace or safety of this State.

XXXIX. And whereas the ministers of the gospel are, by their profession, dedicated to the service of God and the care of souls, and ought not to be diverted from the great duties of their function; therefore, no minister of the gospel, or priest of any denomination whatsoever, shall, at any time hereafter, under any pretence or description whatever, be eligible to, or capable of holding, any civil or military office or place within this State.

2. The Battle over Religious Freedom in Virginia

Throughout the colonial period, The Church of England was the established church of Virginia, and dissenters were persecuted. This changed in 1776 when, as we have seen, the state's new constitution guaranteed Virginians "free exercise of religion." What remained unclear was, first of all, how broadly the term "free exercise" would be understood, and second, how in the absence of church taxes religion would henceforward be supported. Thomas Jefferson, in the following bill presented to the Virginia Assembly in 1779, proposed to answer both questions at once by defining religion in the broadest possible terms ("all men shall be free to profess, and by argument to maintain, their opinions in matters of religion, and that the same shall in no wise diminish, enlarge or affect their civil capacities") and by forcing churches to rely for their support on voluntary contributions. This unleashed a storm of controversy, including the following response which made the case for a Christian state, one in which "Jews, Mahomedans, Atheists or Deists" would be second-class citizens, excluded from public office, restricted from publishing their views, and forced to pay for the support of Christian worship. In the end, both Jefferson's bill and a bill establishing the "Christian Religion" went down to defeat.

In 1784, Patrick Henry proposed a "general assessment" for "Teachers of the Christian Religion," a plan which would have allowed taxpayers to designate their payments to the Christian denomination of their choice, but made no provisions for non-Christians. The bill might have passed but for the vigorous *Memorial and Remonstrance* (1785) against it penned by James Madison, who attacked the bill as an establishment of religion and compared it to the Inquisition—"it differs from it only in degree. The one is the first step, the other the last, in the career of intolerance."

With the failure of the general assessment, Thomas Jefferson's bill was resurrected and with slight modifications became law in 1786. This not only gave full legal equality to Virginia's Jews (one of whom, two years later, was elected to municipal office), it also set the stage for the Constitution's provisions on religious freedom for which Jefferson and Madison were again heavily responsible. Years later, American Jews would return to the Virginia debate on religious freedom to buttress their case against advocates of a "Christian America" and in favor of radical church-state separation.

❖   ❖   ❖

Thomas Jefferson's bill for religious freedom in Virginia, 1779

Well aware that the opinions and belief of men depend not on their own will, but follow involuntarily the evidence proposed to their own minds; that Almighty God hath created the mind free, and manifested his supreme will that free it shall remain by making it altogether insusceptible of restraint; that all attempts to influence it by temporal punishments, or burthens, or by civil incapacitations, tend only to beget habits of hypocrisy and meanness, and are a departure from the plan of the holy author of our religion, who being lord both of body and mind, yet chose not to propagate it by coercions on either, as was in his Almighty power to do, but to extend it by its influence on reason alone; that the impious presumption of legislators and rulers, civil as well as ecclesiastical, who, being themselves but fallible and uninspired men, have assumed dominion over the faith of others, setting up their own opinions and modes of thinking as the only true and infallible, and as such endeavoring to impose them on others, hath established and maintained false religions over the greatest part of the world and through all time; that to compel a man to furnish contributions of money for the propagation of opinions which he disbelieves and abhors, is sinful and tyrannical; that even the forcing him to support this or that teacher of his own religious persuasion, is depriving him of the comfortable liberty of giving his contributions to the particular pastor whose morals he would make his pattern, and whose powers he feels most persuasive to righteousness; and is withdrawing from the ministry those temporary rewards, which proceeding from an approbation of their personal conduct, are an additional incitement to earnest and unremitting labours for the instruction of mankind; that our civil rights have no dependance on our religious opinions, any more than our opinions in physics or geometry; that therefore the proscribing any citizen as unworthy the public confidence by laying upon him an incapacity of being called to offices of trust and emolument, unless he profess or renounce this or that religious opinion, is depriving him injuriously of those privileges and advantages to which, in common with his fellow citizens, he has a natural right; that it tends also to corrupt the principles of that very religion it is meant to encourage, by bribing, with a monopoly of worldly honours and emoluments, those who will externally profess and conform to it; that though indeed these are criminal who do not withstand such temptation, yet neither are those innocent who lay the bait in their way; that the opinions of men are not the object of civil government, nor under its jurisdiction; that to suffer the civil magistrate to intrude his powers into the field of opinion and to restrain the profession or propagation of principles on supposition of their ill tendency is a dangerous falacy, which at once destroys all religious liberty, because he being of course judge of that tendency will make his opinions the rule of judgment, and approve or condemn the sentiments of others only as they shall square with or differ from his own; that it is time enough for the rightful purposes of civil government for its officers to interfere when principles break out into overt acts against peace and good order; and finally, that truth is great and will prevail if left to herself; that she is the proper and sufficient antagonist to error, and has nothing to fear from the conflict unless by human interposition disarmed of her natural weapons, free argument and debate; errors ceasing to be dangerous when it is permitted freely to contradict them.

We the General Assembly of Virginia do enact that no man shall be compelled to frequent or support any religious worship, place, or ministry whatsoever, nor shall be enforced, restrained, molested, or burthened in his body or goods, nor shall otherwise suffer, on account of his religious opinions or belief; but that all men shall be free to profess, and by argument to maintain, their opinions in matters of religion, and that the same shall in no wise diminish, enlarge, or affect their civil capacities.

And though we well know that this Assembly, elected by the people for the ordinary purposes of legislation only, have no power to restrain the acts of succeeding Assemblies, constituted with powers equal to our own, and that therefore to declare this act irrevocable would be of no effect in law; yet we are free to declare, and do declare, that the rights hereby asserted are of the natural rights of mankind, and that if any act shall be hereafter passed to repeal the present or to narrow its operation, such act will be an infringement of natural right.

◆

"To the Publick," a Christian's response to Jefferson

. . . "To compel a man to pay for propagating opinions he disbelieves and abhors is sinful and tyrannical."

This is drawn up with the covert appearance of attacking the old establishment of a particular church or mode of Christian worship in preference to others, and in that view is raising a ghost to frighten us with. It is a well-known fact, that even the members of that church in the legislature cheerfully relinquished this partial distinction in their favour, and I do not wish to recall it, as I ever thought it unjust; I desire therefore once for all that in anything I have said or may say on this occasion, I may not be misunderstood or misrepresented as favouring any distinctions amongst the various denominations of Christians, which I renounce as narrow, illiberal and unmanly, and only wish to establish Christianity at large, upon a supposition that not only a majority, but the bulk of this community are Christians; and if there be a few who are Jews, Mahomedans, Atheists, or Deists amongst us, though I would not wish to torture or persecute them on account of their opinions, yet to exclude such from our publick offices, is prudent and just; to restrain them from publishing their singular opinions to the disturbance of society, is equally sound policy and a necessary caution to promote the general good; nor is it sinful or tyrannical to compel them to pay towards the support of religious worship, though they do not join in it, since if it be true that this regulation makes men more quiet, better members of society, which I think experience proves, these few will receive a benefit in the quiet enjoyment of their lives and fortunes equivalent to their contribution; or if they think otherwise, may retire from society. . . .

A SOCIAL CHRISTIAN

3. Jews Appeal for Religious Equality

Among the welter of voices that spoke out during the Revolutionary era on the issue of religious liberty, Jews were conspicuous by their silence. Long and bitter experience had taught them that it was safer, as members of a small and much abused minority, to keep a low profile, particularly on issues likely to arouse religious passions. This silence, however, should not be confused with indifference. Jews certainly felt aggrieved at the disadvantages under which they had labored during the colonial era, and as the documents below reveal, once the Revolution was won they began to petition for redress.

Philadelphia, with a Jewish population swelled by refugees from New York, was for a brief period during the war the largest and most important Jewish community in the United States. This made it all the more galling that the state's Declaration of Rights (1776) continued to mandate a religious test acknowledging "the Old and New Testament to be given by

Divine inspiration"—this despite the document's own promise that no one who acknowledged "the being of a God" would be "deprived or abridged of any civil right as a citizen, on account of his religious sentiments." In a bid for equality, and after a general meeting on this subject at Philadelphia's synagogue, Mikveh Israel, the Jewish community's leaders sent the following well-publicized petition to the Council of Censors, a body empowered to inquire into infringements of state law. Note the similarity in form between this petition and the petition of 1655 to the Dutch West India Company (chapter 1). In both cases, petitioners appealed for rights on behalf of Jews as a group, based their case on the usefulness and patriotism of the Jewish community, and hinted at perilous economic consequences should Jews be denied. Though in this case, the petition was quickly tabled, probably because the Council lacked standing to bring about the desired change, the document elicited much favorable comment in the local press.

Almost four years later, one of Mikveh Israel's leaders, the German-Jewish immigrant merchant Jonas Phillips, sent a petition on the same subject to the Constitutional Convention meeting in Philadelphia to draft a new federal Constitution. The convention, of course, was not empowered to amend state laws, and its own discussion on the question of religious tests had already taken place. Phillips' petition is nevertheless significant as the only document of its kind presented to the Constitutional Convention. For all of its lack of polish, it conveys the hopes of the American Jewish community with respect to religious liberty: "The Israelites," Phillips explains, "will think themself happy to live under a government where all Religious societies are on an Equal footing." This goal was finally attained by Pennsylvania Jews (after yet another petition by Jonas Phillips) under the new state constitution of 1790, which qualified for office all who acknowledged "the being of a God, and a future state of rewards and punishments."

❧ ❧ ❧

Petition for equality by the Philadelphia Synagogue to Council of Censors of Pennsylvania, 1783

To the honourable the COUNCIL of CENSORS, assembled agreeable to the Constitution of the State of Pennsylvania. The Memorial of Rabbi Ger. Seixas of the Synagogue of the Jews at Philadelphia, Simon Nathan their Parnass or President, Asher Myers, Bernard Gratz and Haym Salomon the Mahamad, or Associates of their council in behalf of themselves and their brethren Jews, residing in Pennsylvania,

Most respectfully showeth,

That by the tenth section of the Frame of Government of this Commonwealth, it is ordered that each member of the general assembly of representatives of the freemen of Pennsylvania, before he takes his seat, shall make and subscribe a declaration, which ends in these words, "I do acknowledge the Scriptures of the old and new Testament to be given by divine inspiration," to which is added an assurance, that "no further or other religious test shall ever hereafter be required of any civil officer or magistrate in this state."

Your memorialists beg leave to observe, that this clause seems to limit the civil rights of your citizens to one very special article of the creed; whereas by the second paragraph of the declaration of the rights of the inhabitants, it is asserted without any other limitation than the professing the existence of God, in plain words, "that no man who acknowledges the being of a God can be justly deprived or abridged of any civil rights as a citizen on account of his religious sentiments." But certainly this religious test deprives the Jews of the most eminent rights of freemen, solemnly ascertained to all men who are not professed Atheists.

May it please your Honors,

Although the Jews in Pennsylvania are but few in number, yet liberty of the people in one country, and the declaration of the government thereof, that these liberties are the rights of the people, may prove a powerful attractive to men, who live under restraints in another country. Holland and England have made valuable acquisitions of men, who for their religious sentiments, were distressed in their own countries.—And if Jews in Europe or elsewhere, should incline to transport themselves to America, and would, for reason of some certain advantage of the soil, climate, or the trade of Pennsylvania, rather become inhabitants thereof, than of any other State; yet the disability of Jews to take seat among the representatives of the people, as worded by the said religious test, might determine their free choice to go to New York, or to any other of the United States of America, where there is no such like restraint laid upon the nation and religion of the Jews, as in Pennsylvania.—Your memorialists cannot say that the Jews are particularly fond of being representatives of the people in assembly or civil officers and magistrates in the State; but with great submission they apprehend that a clause in the constitution, which disables them to be elected by their fellow citizens to represent them in assembly, is a stigma upon their nation and religion, and it is inconsonant with the second paragraph of the said bill of rights; otherwise Jews are as fond of liberty as their religious societies can be, and it must create in them a displeasure, when they perceive that for their professed dissent to doctrine, which is inconsistent with their religious sentiments, they should be excluded from the most important and honourable part of the rights of a free citizen.

Your memorialists beg further leave to represent, that in the religious books of the Jews, which are or may be in every man's hands, there are no such doctrines or principles established as are inconsistent with the safety and happiness of the people of Pennsylvania, and that the conduct and behaviour of the Jews in this and the neighbouring States, has always tallied with the great design of the Revolution; that the Jews of Charlestown, New York, Newport and other posts, occupied by the British troops, have distinguishedly suffered for their attachment to the Revolution principles; and their brethren at St. Eustatius, for the same cause, experienced the most severe resentments of the British commanders. The Jews of Pennsylvania in proportion to the number of their members, can count with any religious society whatsoever, the Whigs among either of them; they have served some of them in the Continental army; some went out in the militia to fight the common enemy; all of them have cheerfully contributed to the support of the militia, and of the government of this State; they have no inconsiderable property in lands and tenements, but particularly in the way of trade, some more, some less, for which they pay taxes; they have, upon every plan formed for public utility, been forward to contribute as much as their circumstances would admit of; and as a nation or a religious society, they stand unimpeached of any matter whatsoever, against the safety and happiness of the people.

And your memorialists humbly pray, that if your honours, from any consideration than the subject of this address, should think proper to call a convention for revising the constitution, you would be pleased to recommend this to the notice of that convention.

◆

Letter from Jonas Phillips to the Federal Constitutional Convention, 1787

To His Excellency the president and the Honourable Members of the Convention assembled:

Sires
    With leave and submission I address myself To those in Whom there is wisdom and understanding and knowledge, they are the honourable personages appointed and Made overseers of a part of the terrestrial globe of the Earth, Namely the 13 united states of america in Convention Assembled, the Lord preserve them amen—

I the subscriber being one of the people called Jews of the City of Philadelphia, a people scattered & dispersed among all nations do behold with
Concern that among the laws in the Constitution of Pennsylvania, there is a
Clause Sect 10 to viz—I do believe in one God the Creatur and governor of the
universe and Rewarder of the good & the punisher of the wicked—and I do acknowledge the Scriptures of the old & New testament to be given by divine
inspiration—to swear & believe that the new testament was given by divine inspiration is absolutely against the Religious principle of a Jew, and is against his
Conscience to take any such oath—By the above law a Jew is deprived of holding any publick office or place of Government which is a Contridictory [sic] to
the bill of Right Sec 2 viz

That all men have a natural & unalienable Right to worship almighty God
according to the dictates of their own Conscience and understanding & that no
man ought or of Right can be Compelled to attend any Religious Worship or
Creed or support any place of worship or Maintain any minister contrary to or
against his own free will and Consent, nor can any man who acknowledges the
being of a God be Justly deprived or abridged of any Civil Right as a Citizen on
account of his Religious sentiments or peculiar mode of Religious Worship,
and that no authority can or ought to be vested in or assumed by any power
whatever that shall in any case interfere or in any manner Controul the Right
of Conscience in the free Exercise of Religious Worship.—

It is well known among all the Citizens of the 13 united states that the Jews
have been true and faithful whigs, & during the late Contest with England they
have been foremost in aiding and assisting the states with their lifes & fortunes, they have supported the cause, have bravely fought and bled for liberty
which they can not Enjoy.—

Therefore if the honourable Convention shall in their Wisdom think fit
and alter the said oath & leave out the words to viz—and I do acknowledge
the scripture of the new testament to be given by divine inspiration, then the
Israelites will think themself happy to live under a government where all Religious societies are on an Equal footing—I solicit this favour for myself my
children & posterity, & for the benefit of all the Israelites through the 13 united
states of America.

My prayers is unto the Lord. May the people of this states Rise up as a great
& young lion, May they prevail against their Enemies, may the degrees of
honour of his Excellency the president of the Convention George Washington,
be Exhalted & Raise up. May Everyone speak of his glorious Exploits.

May God prolong his days among us in this land of Liberty—May he lead
the armies against his Enemys as he has done heruntofore. May God Extend
peace unto the united states—May they get up to the highest Prosperitys—
May God Extend peace to them & their seed after them so long as the sun &
moon Endureth—and May the almighty God of our father Abraham Isaac &
Jacob indue this Noble Assembly with wisdom Judgment & unanimity in their

Counsells & may they have the satisfaction to see that their present toil & labour for the wellfair of the united states may be approved of Through all the world & particular by the united states of america, is the ardent prayer of Sires

Your most devoted obed. Servant
JONAS PHILLIPS

Philadelphia 24th Ellul 5547 or Sepr 7th 1787.

4. The Federal Constitution and the Jews

On August 27, 1787, the Constitutional Convention meeting in Philadelphia passed what became Article VI, paragraph 3 of the United States Constitution, outlawing religious tests for any "office or public trust under the United States." This was the only mention of religion in the original Constitution (save for the words "Sunday excepted" in Article I, section 7 which obliquely recognized the sanctity of the Christian Sabbath), and departed from the practice of most states, where religious test oaths remained the norm.

Critics of the Constitution understood that the ban on religious tests could result in the election of non-Christians to public office, a proposition so strange as to be terrifying. "No man is fit to be a ruler of protestants, without he can honestly profess to be of the protestant religion," one New Hampshire opponent of ratification remonstrated. Others worried that offering non-Christians complete legal equality might lead them to immigrate in large numbers to America's shores. Both of these issues came up for discussion during the debate in North Carolina over the Constitution's adoption, which is excerpted below. Note two assumptions made by public officials in the debate: first, that all non-Christians—Jews, Muslims ("Mahometans") and pagans—are alike, and second that if such people did immigrate to America their children would in all probability turn Christian.

Jews joined in celebrating the adoption of the Constitution in 1788. In Philadelphia, the "rabbi of the Jews," probably Hazzan Jacob R. Cohen of Congregation Mikveh Israel, walked "arm in arm" with "the clergy of the different Christian denominations" in a grand procession. As the Philadelphia physician and patriot Benjamin Rush pointed out, "There could not have been a more happy emblem contrived of that section of the new constitution, which opens all its powers and offices alike, not only to every sect of christians, but to worthy men of *every* religion." Yet, when the festivities concluded Jews ate conspicuously apart at a special table set aside with kosher food. The symbolism evoked here carried far deeper meaning than anyone could have realized. For while in the eyes of the Constitution all religions were considered equal, each continued to enjoy the right to remain distinctive and unique.

The Constitution as originally adopted lacked a bill of rights. This was intentional; James Madison, for one, considered such guarantees mere "parchment barriers," too weak to withstand majority pressure. "The rights of conscience in particular," he feared, ". . . would be narrowed." In the end, to placate critics and ensure ratification, he compromised. The Bill of Rights, based on amendments that he submitted to the first session of Congress, was ratified in 1791, and the first freedom that it guaranteed was freedom of religion.

◆   ◆   ◆

Constitution of the United States of America

ARTICLE VI
The Senators and Representatives before mentioned, and the members of the several State legislatures, and all executive and judicial officers, both of the United States and of the several States, shall be bound by oath or affirmation to support this Constitution; but no religious test shall ever be required as a qualification to any office or public trust under the United States.

AMENDMENT I
Congress shall make no law respecting an establishment of religion, or prohibiting the free exercise thereof; or abridging the freedom of speech, or of the press; or the right of the people peaceably to assemble, and to petition the government for a redress of grievances.

◆

Debate of the North Carolina Convention, 1788

GOV. JOHNSTON expressed great astonishment that the people were alarmed on the subject of religion. This, he said, must have arisen from the great pains which had been taken to prejudice men's minds against the Constitution. He begged leave to add the following few observations to what had been so ably said by the gentleman last up.

I read the Constitution over and over, but could not see one cause of apprehension or jealousy on this subject. When I heard there were apprehensions that the pope of Rome could be the President of the United States, I was greatly astonished. It might as well be said that the king of England or France, or the Grand Turk, could be chosen to that office. It would have been as good an argument. It appears to me that it would have been dangerous, if Congress could intermeddle with the subject of religion. True religion is derived from a much higher source than human laws. When any attempt is made, by any government, to restrain men's consciences, no good consequence can possibly follow. It is apprehended that Jews, Mahometans, pagans, &c., may be elected to high offices under the government of the United States. Those who are Mahometans, or any others who are not professors of the Christian religion, can never be elected to the office of President, or other high office, but in one of two cases. First, if the people of America lay aside the Christian religion altogether, it may happen. Should this unfortunately take place, the people will choose such men as think as they do themselves. Another case is, if any persons of such descriptions should, notwithstanding their religion, acquire the confidence and esteem of the people of America by their good conduct and practice of virtue, they may be chosen. I leave it to gentlemen's candor to judge what probability there is of the people's choosing men of different sentiments from themselves.

But great apprehensions have been raised as to the influence of the Eastern States. When you attend to circumstances, this will have no weight. I know but two or three states where there is the least chance of establishing any particular religion. The people of Massachusetts and Connecticut are mostly Presbyterians. In every other state, the people are divided into a great number of sects. In Rhode Island, the tenets of the Baptists, I believe, prevail. In New York, they are divided very much: the most numerous are the Episcopalians and the Baptists. In New Jersey, they are as much divided as we are. In Pennsylvania, if any sect prevails more than others, it is that of the Quakers. In Maryland, the Episcopalians are most numerous, though there are other sects. In Virginia, there are many sects; you all know what their religious sentiments are. So in all the Southern States they differ; as also in New Hampshire. I hope, therefore, that gentlemen will see there is no cause of fear that any one religion shall be exclusively established.

Mr. CALDWELL thought that some danger might arise. He imagined it might be objected to in a political as well as in a religious view. In the first place, he said, there was an invitation for Jews and pagans of every kind to come among us. At some future period, said he, this might endanger the character of the United States. Moreover, even those who do not regard religion, acknowledge that the Christian religion is best calculated, of all religions, to make good members of society, on account of its morality. I think, then, added he, that, in a political view, those gentlemen who formed this Constitution should not have given this invitation to Jews and heathens. All those who have any religion are against the emigration of those people from the eastern hemisphere.

Mr. SPENCER was an advocate for securing every unalienable right, and that of worshipping God according to the dictates of conscience in particular. He therefore thought that no one particular religion should be established. Religious tests, said he, have been the foundation of persecutions in all countries. Persons who are conscientious will not take the oath required by religious tests, and will therefore be excluded from offices, though equally capable of discharging them as any member of the society. It is feared, continued he, that persons of bad principles, deists, atheists, &c., may come into this country; and there is nothing to restrain them from being eligible to offices. He asked if it was reasonable to suppose that the people would choose men without regarding their characters. Mr. Spencer then continued thus: Gentlemen urge that the want of a test admits the most vicious characters to offices. I desire to know what test could bind them. If they were of such principles, it would not keep them from enjoying those offices. On the other hand, it would exclude from offices conscientious and truly religious people, though equally capable as others. Conscientious persons would not take such an oath, and would be therefore excluded. This would be a great cause of objection to a religious test. But in this case, as there is not a religious test required, it leaves religion on the solid foundation of its own inherent validity, without any connection with temporal authority; and no kind of oppression can take place. I confess it strikes me so. I am sorry to differ from the worthy gentlemen. I cannot object to this part of the Constitution. I wish every other part was as good and proper.

Gov. JOHNSTON approved of the worthy member's candor. He admitted a possibility of Jews, pagans, &c., emigrating to the United States; yet, he said, they could not be in proportion to the emigration of Christians who should come from other countries; that, in all probability, the children even of such people would be Christians; and that this, with the rapid population of the United States, their zeal for religion, and love of liberty, would, he trusted, add to the progress of the Christian religion among us.

5. "To Bigotry No Sanction, To Persecution No Assistance"

When George Washington assumed the presidency in 1789, letters of congratulations and expressions of esteem poured in from many quarters, following a long-established custom associated with the ascension of kings. The President's replies generally focused on what he knew to be the central concerns of the constituents who addressed him. To the Catholic community, for example, he wrote about equal rights and Catholic patriotism during the Revolution.

The American Jewish community, less centralized and far less well organized than many others, sent three different letters of welcome to Washington, all of them embarrassingly late. Of these, the best known and most important was the address of the "Hebrew Congregation in Newport" (today known as the Touro Synagogue) timed to coincide with the President's visit to that Rhode Island city on August 17, 1790. Redolent with biblical and liturgical language, the letter noted past discrimination against Jews, praised the new government for "generously affording to all liberty of conscience and immunities of citizenship," and thanked God "for all of the blessings of civil and religious liberty" that Jews now enjoyed under the Constitution.

In his reply, Washington addressed what he properly took to be the focus of Jews' interest, religious liberty. Improving a phrase contained in the Hebrew congregation's original letter, he famously characterized the United States government as one that "gives to bigotry no sanction, to persecution no assistance." He also went beyond this to characterize religious liberty as an inherent natural right, distinct from the indulgent religious toleration practiced by the British and much of enlightened Europe.

✦   ✦   ✦

Letter from the Hebrew Congregation of Newport to President Washington, 1790

Sir: Permit the children of the stock of Abraham to approach you with the most cordial affection and esteem for your person and merit, and to join with our fellow-citizens in welcoming you to Newport.

With pleasure we reflect on those days of difficulty and danger when the God of Israel, who delivered David from the peril of the sword, shielded your head in the day of battle; and we rejoice to think that the same spirit which rested in the bosom of the greatly beloved Daniel, enabling him to preside over the provinces of the Babylonian Empire, rests and ever will rest upon you, enabling you to discharge the arduous duties of the Chief Magistrate of these States.

Deprived as we hitherto have been of the invaluable rights of free citizens, we now—with a deep sense of gratitude to the Almighty Disposer of all events—behold a government erected by the majesty of the people—a government which to bigotry gives no sanction, to persecution no assistance, but generously affording to all liberty of conscience and immunities of citizenship, deeming every one of whatever nation, tongue, or language, equal parts of the great governmental machine.

This so ample and extensive Federal Union, whose base is philanthropy, mutual confidence and public virtue, we cannot but acknowledge to be the work of the great God, who rules in the armies of the heavens and among the inhabitants of the earth, doing whatever seemeth to Him good.

For all the blessings of civil and religious liberty which we enjoy under an equal and benign administration, we desire to send up our thanks to the Ancient of days, the great Preserver of men, beseeching Him that the angels who conducted our forefathers through the wilderness into the promised land may graciously conduct you through all the difficulties and dangers of this mortal life; and when, like Joshua, full of days and full of honors, you are gathered to your fathers, may you be admitted into the heavenly paradise to partake of the water of life and the tree of immortality.

Done and signed by order of the Hebrew Congregation in Newport, Rhode Island.

MOSES SEIXAS, *Warden*
Newport, August 17, 1790

◈

President Washington's reply

Gentlemen: While I received with much satisfaction your address replete with expressions of esteem, I rejoice in the opportunity of assuring you that I shall always retain grateful remembrance of the cordial welcome I experienced on my visit to Newport from all classes of citizens.

The reflection on the days of difficulty and danger which are past is rendered the more sweet from a consciousness that they are succeeded by days of uncommon prosperity and security.

If we have wisdom to make the best use of the advantages with which we are now favored, we cannot fail, under the just administration of a good government, to become a great and happy people.

The citizens of the United States of America have a right to applaud themselves for having given to mankind examples of an enlarged and liberal policy—a policy worthy of imitation. All possess alike liberty of conscience and immunities of citizenship.

It is now no more that toleration is spoken of as if it were the indulgence of one class of people that another enjoyed the exercise of their inherent natural rights, for, happily, the Government of the United States, which gives to bigotry no sanction, to persecution no assistance, requires only that they who live under its protection should demean themselves as good citizens in giving it on all occasions their effectual support.

It would be inconsistent with the frankness of my character not to avow that I am pleased with your favorable opinion of my administration and fervent wishes for my felicity.

May the children of the stock of Abraham who dwell in this land continue to merit and enjoy the good will of the other inhabitants; while every one shall sit in safety under his own vine and fig tree and there shall be none to make him afraid.

May the father of all mercies scatter light, and not darkness, upon our paths, and make us all in our several vocations useful here, and in His own due time and way everlastingly happy.

G. WASHINGTON

THREE

In Search of Equal Footing

❖

L egal equality, guaranteed to Jews as Americans by the Constitution and then reaffirmed by George Washington in his letter to the Hebrew Congregation in Newport, did not immediately translate into what Jonas Phillips had called "equal footing." Restrictions on the political rights of Jews remained in force, particularly at the state and local levels, and in myriad ways Jews continued to face discrimination.

This is not surprising. The legacy of religious establishment, centuries of historical experience, the dictates of English common law, and, of course, the religious makeup of the New Nation all tended to elevate Christianity (and more particularly Protestantism) to a privileged position above other faiths. The very word "religion," to most Americans, implied Christianity; that is why, in common parlance, they automatically grouped non-Christians and complete unbelievers together, as in the phrase "Jews, Turks, and infidels." However much they supported religious liberty in theory, as a practical matter they continued to believe that Christianity was essential to civil order and peace, and that the state should be ruled only by God-fearing Protestants.

This disjunction between the promises contained in the Constitution and the realities played out in day-to-day life underlay all of the religion and state issues that challenged the American Jewish community during the period of the early republic. Whenever Jews protested—whether as individuals or as a group—their goal was to achieve civic equality. More often than not, that meant opening up to Jews an advantage formerly available only to Christians.

To this end, late eighteenth- and early nineteenth-century American Jews put forward an interpretation of the First Amendment that placed "equal footing" at its heart. In twentieth-century terms, they advocated a neutral-to-all-religions America with emphasis on freedom *for* religion. They would have found unthinkable what Thomas Jefferson, in his now famous letter to the Danbury Baptists (1802), spoke of as "a wall of separation between church and State," implying a divorced-from-all-religion America, with emphasis on freedom *from* religion.

Working in concert with sympathetic Christians, Jews in this period enjoyed notable success in their quest for religious freedom. Their protests against religious discrimination met with substantial sympathy, they received funds on the same basis as Protestants did in New York, and their long struggle to achieve full political rights in Maryland ended in victory. At the same time, however, Jews learned that legal equality did not protect them from religious importuning. Indeed, the emergence of organized Christian missions to the Jews, in 1816, served as a reminder that many Americans still expected Jews to convert and Christianity ultimately to triumph.

1. Jacob Henry Demands the Right of Conscience

The state constitution of North Carolina (1776), reflecting uncertainties concerning religious liberty that were typical of its day, both promised citizens "the natural and inalienable right to worship Almighty God according to the dictates of their own conscience," and restricted non-Protestants from holding "any office or place of trust or profit in the Civil Department within this State." Nobody actually protested when Catholics assumed public office, nor in 1808 when an intermarried Jew named Jacob Henry was elected to the state legislature. But in 1809, when Henry sought to reassume his seat, his right to it was challenged on constitutional grounds. In response, Henry (probably assisted by North Carolina's State Supreme Court chief justice, John Louis Taylor, who as a Catholic knew that his own position was open to challenge) composed the following celebrated address defending liberty of conscience and his own religious creed. Ironically, he closed with the "Golden Rule"—in its Christian formulation (Matthew 7:12). The address was the first by an American Jew to win widespread notice, and was subsequently reprinted for schoolchildren in a textbook entitled the *American Orator.*

Jacob Henry was permitted to retain his seat on the doubtful grounds that the words "Civil Department" in the state's constitution excluded the legislature. In 1835, an amendment awarded Catholics full rights commensurate with Protestants, but after a stormy debate an exclusion against non-Christians was retained. Jews only won complete equality in North Carolina in 1868.

◆   ◆   ◆

Jacob Henry's address to the North Carolina legislature, 1809

I certainly, Mr. Speaker, know not the design of the Declaration of Rights made by the people of this State in the year 1776, if it was not to consecrate certain great and fundamental rights and principles which even the Constitution cannot impair; for the 44th section of the latter instrument declares that the Declaration of Rights ought never to be violated, on any pretence whatever; if there is any apparent difference between the two instruments, they ought, if possible, to be reconciled; but if there is a final repugnance between them, the Declaration of Rights must be considered paramount; for I believe it is to the Constitution, as the Constitution is to law; it controls and directs it absolutely and conclusively. If, then, a belief in the Protestant religion is required by the Constitution, to qualify a man for a seat in this house, and such qualification is dispensed with by the Declaration of Rights, the provision of the Constitution must be altogether inoperative; as the language of the Bill of Rights is, "that all men have a natural and inalienable right to worship ALMIGHTY GOD according to the dictates of their own consciences." It is undoubtedly a natural right, and when it is declared to be an inalienable one by the people in their sovereign and original capacity, any attempt to alienate either by the Constitution or by law, must be vain and fruitless.

It is difficult to conceive how such a provision crept into the Constitution, unless it is from the difficulty the human mind feels in suddenly emancipating itself from fetters by which it has long been enchained: and how adverse it is to the feelings and manners of the people of the present day every gentleman may satisfy himself by glancing at the religious belief of the persons who fill the various offices in this State: there are Presbyterians, Lutherans, Calvinists, Mennonists, Baptists, Trinitarians, and Unitarians. But, as far as my observation extends, there are fewer Protestants, in the strict sense of the word, used by the Constitution, than of any other persuasion; for I suppose that they meant by it, the Protestant religion as established by the law in England. For other persuasions we see houses of worship in almost every part of the State, but very few of the Protestant; so few, that indeed I fear that the people of this State would for some time remain unrepresented in this House, if that clause of the Constitution is supposed to be in force. So far from believing in the Thirty-nine Articles, I will venture to assert that a majority of the people never have read them.

If a man should hold religious principles incompatible with the freedom and safety of the State, I do not hesitate to pronounce that he should be excluded from the public councils of the same; and I trust if I know myself, no one would be more ready to aid and assist than myself. But I should really be at a loss to specify any known religious principles which are thus dangerous. It is surely a question between a man and his Maker, and requires more than human attributes to pronounce which of the numerous sects prevailing in the world is most acceptable to the Deity. If a man fulfills the duties of that religion, which his education or his conscience has pointed to him as the true one, no person, I hold, in this our land of liberty, has a right to arraign him at the bar of any inquisition: and the day, I trust, has long passed, when principles merely speculative were propagated by force; when the sincere and pious were made victims, and the light-minded bribed into hypocrites.

The purest homage man could render to the Almighty was the sacrifice of his passions and the performance of his duties. That the ruler of the universe would receive with equal benignity the various offerings of man's adoration, if they proceeded from the heart. Governments only concern the actions and conduct of man, and not his speculative notions. Who among us feels himself so exalted above his fellows as to have a right to dictate to them any mode of belief? Will you bind the conscience in chains, and fasten conviction upon the mind in spite of the conclusions of reason and of those ties and habitudes which are blended with every pulsation of the heart? Are you prepared to plunge at once from the sublime heights of moral legislation into the dark and gloomy caverns of superstitious ignorance? Will you drive from your shores and from the shelter of your constitution, all who do not lay their oblations on the same altar, observe the same ritual, and subscribe to the same dogmas? If so, which, among the various sects into which we are divided, shall be the favored one?

I should insult the understanding of this House to suppose it possible that they could ever assent to such absurdities; for all know that persecution in all its shapes and modifications, is contrary to the genius of our government and the spirit of our laws, and that it can never produce any other effect than to render men hypocrites or martyrs.

When Charles V., Emperor of Germany, tired of the cares of government, resigned his crown to his son, he retired to a monastery, where he amused the evening of his life in regulating the movements of watches, endeavoring to make a number keep the same time; but, not being able to make any two go exactly alike, it led him to reflect upon the folly and crimes he had committed, in attempting the impossibility of making men think alike!

Nothing is more easily demonstrated than that the conduct alone is the subject of human laws, and that man ought to suffer civil disqualification for what he does, and not for what he thinks. The mind can receive laws only from Him, of whose Divine essence it is a portion; He alone can punish disobedience; for who else can know its movements, or estimate their merits? The religion I professes, inculcates every duty which men owes to his fellow men; it enjoins upon its votaries the practice of every virtue, and the detestation of every vice; it teaches them to hope for the favor of heaven exactly in proportion as their lives have been directed by just, honorable, and beneficent maxims. This, then, gentlemen, is my creed, it was impressed upon my infant mind; it has been the director of my youth, the monitor of my manhood, and will, I trust, be the consolation of my old age. At any rate, Mr. Speaker, I am sure that you cannot see anything in this Religion, to deprive me of my seat in this house. So far as relates to my life and conduct, the examination of these I submit with cheerfulness to your candid and liberal construction. What may be the religion of him who made this objection against me, or whether he has any religion or not I am unable to say. I have never considered it my duty to pry into the belief of other members of this house. If their actions are upright and conduct just, the rest is for their own consideration, not for mine. I do not seek to make converts to my faith, whatever it may be esteemed in the eyes of my officious friend, nor do I exclude any one from my esteem or friendship, because he and I differ in that respect. The same charity, therefore, it is not unreasonable to expect, will be extended to myself, because in all things that relate to the State and to the duties of civil life, I am bound by the same obligations with my fellow-citizens, nor does any man subscribe more sincerely than myself to the maxim, "whatever ye would that men should do unto you do ye so even unto them, for such is the law and the prophets."

2. Shearith Israel Seeks State Funds for Religious Education of the Poor

Early nineteenth-century Americans assumed that religion and education were closely intertwined. Congress gave legal expression to this assumption in The Northwest Ordinance (1787): "Religion, morality and knowledge being necessary to good government and the happiness of mankind," its second article declared, "schools and the means of education shall forever be encouraged." In New York City, where some four hundred Jews resided, almost all schools were religious in character. Common pay (private) schools assumed the religious identity of their headmaster; charity or "free schools" were supported by the city's churches and could draw upon the state's School Fund. In 1803, Congregation Shearith Israel established a charity school under its auspices named Polonies Talmud Torah. After a successful petition to the State Legislature in 1811, the school was placed on an equal footing with Protestant and Catholic charity schools in the city and received state aid.

The petition that follows, dated January 10, 1813, reflects a developing conflict between church-sponsored charity schools in New York and the nondenominational New York Free School (forerunner of the Public School Society), established in 1805 to educate the city's growing number of religiously unaffiliated poor according to the strict monitorial system pioneered by Joseph Lancaster. Fearing a loss of state funds to the Free School, Shearith Israel spoke out forcefully against separating religion from education and in support of the status quo—a position diametrically opposite to the views expressed by American Jews a few decades later. Siding now with Presbyterians, Roman Catholics, Baptists, and Methodists, the congregation praised religious education as "the greatest foundation of social happiness" and argued on the basis of "the liberal spirit of our constitution" that religiously sponsored charity schools should continue to receive state assistance—which they did until 1825.

◆   ◆   ◆

Petition of Congregation Shearith [Sheerith] Israel on state aid to religious schools, 1813

*To the Honorable
The Legislature of the State of New York,
In the Senate and Assembly Convened.*

SEAL THE MEMORIAL
of Trustees of the Congregation of Sheerith Israel Convened

Respectfully Sheweth,

That a Memorial was presented to the honorable, the Legislature, during their last session, signed by the following religious societies, in their corporate capacity, to wit: Wall-street, Brick, Rutger's and Spring-street, Presbyterian; Roman Catholic; First Baptist and Methodist churches, in recommendation of a Report and Draft of a bill of the Commissioners appointed to organize a System of Education, and the distribution of the School Fund: That the said Commissioners, in their said Report and Bill, have advised the proportion of that Fund, belonging to the city and county of New-York, to be distributed to and among the Charity Schools, within the city and county aforesaid, who were disposed to avail themselves of the same, according to the number of scholars taught in each school, as will appear by said Memorial, to which your Memorialists beg leave to refer, and request that the same may be read by your Honorable Body.

Your Memorialists beg leave further to represent to your Honorable Body, that so far from entertaining any disposition of detracting from the merit of the New-York Free School, they are willing to give it all the praise it has any claim to; they deem it an institution highly laudable in its object in providing for the education of orphans and those unhappy children, whose parents are so lost to every sense of duty as to attach themselves to no religious society; and in this view, your Memorialists are of opinion, that said school is justly entitled to a share of the interest of the School Fund, in common with other Charity Schools in this city; but beyond which, your Memorialists can see no claim it can have to the exclusive patronage of the state bounty.

Your Memorialists beg leave further to repeat in the language of the former Memorial, presented to your Honorable Body, that there are in this city and county a great number of Charity Schools, established by different religious societies, in which poor children are educated under the superintendance and direction of the trustees of each respectively, in such manner and way as is most congenial to the feelings and sentiments of those societies, by which they are governed; which schools are supported principally by the voluntary contributions from individuals, who compose their respective congregations: That the primary object of these societies is to combine religious with literary improvement: That the Legislature are the guardians of the poor children of this state, and as such, will impartially distribute the state Fund: That the policy of rescuing from ignorance, vice and obscurity so many thousands of the rising generation is too liberal and wise to extend its bounty to any speculative system of education, to the exclusion of those poor schools, which are raised and supported on the religious principles of each respective society.

Your Memorialists beg leave further to state, that however they may approve of the New-York Free School in other respects, they conceive it exceptionable on the score of religious instruction. They are informed, that this institution comprizes not less than five hundred scholars, consisting principally of orphans or children whose parents are attached to no religious society; it is evident that a great portion of those children are likely to grow up unacquainted with the principles of any religion: It is in vain to say they may attend the religious worship of their parents, unless they are instructed in their religious principles by some person whose duty it is to perform that office: from irreligious parents they are likely to receive no religious instruction.

Your Memorialists beg leave further to suggest to your Honorable Body, that there are few, if any parents in our community, who have not been educated to some kind of religious worship at some period of their lives, and scarcely any religious society, who have not made provision for the education of its respective poor children, whose religious and literary instruction is governed by trustees chosen from amongst their respective congregations.

Your Memorialists beg leave to remark to your Honorable Body, that the human family are full of attachments of various kinds, of kindred, local habits and situation, and none perhaps more strong than religion, ordained, no doubt, for the wise purposes of promoting a laudable emulation for the advancement of religion, piety and learning.

Your Memorialists beg leave further to represent to your Honorable Body, that they conceive religion the greatest foundation of social happiness—the best pledge of republican institutions—and the greatest security of property, of liberty, and of life—like the dews of heaven, calculated to foster and nourish the germ of genius in the morning of life—what availeth the learning of a Hale, a Newton, or a Locke, without their sense of justice, piety and religion?—what avail courts of justice without just impressions of the solemn obligation of an oath? Of the relative duties which man owes to himself, his family, his country and his God.

Your Memorialists beg leave lastly to state, that they conceive the appropriation of the School Fund to the New-York Free School solely, not only impolitic but unjust, and at variance with the liberal genius and spirit of our constitution—impolitic, because tending in its effects to encourage parents in habits of indifference to their duties of religion, and at the same time inconsistent with that obligation which every government owes to her citizens, of holding out to them every inducement to cultivate that most important of all objects, and without which, education tends only to form the juvenile mind for art, fraud and deception—unjust because calculated to turn to a particular channel, a bounty intended for the benefit of the poor children of the state at large. It is at variance with the liberal spirit of our constitution, which recognizes no distinction in religious worship.

Your Memorialists beg leave to submit to the consideration of your Honorable Body the prayer of their Memorial, and to take and pursue such steps in the premises as in your wisdom you may deem meet.

Your Memorialists have hereunto affixed the Seal of their Corporation, the Tenth day of January 1813. By order of the Board.

M. Gomez
Clerk.

3. Mordecai Noah Protests His Recall from Tunis

The Jewish political journalist and playwright Mordecai Noah was appointed in 1813, at the age of twenty-eight, to serve as American consul to Tunis. He had lobbied for the job as a Jew and won appointment, in part, because it was hoped that he might establish beneficial ties with North Africa's powerful Jewish community. He was also charged with a secret mission to free captured American seamen who had been enslaved in Algeria. Unfortunately, the mission ended badly, and Noah's superiors blamed him and questioned his expenses. They also believed diplomats who intimated that the appointment of a Jew to Tunis had been a mistake. So the decision was made to recall Noah. In order to preserve confidentiality, President Madison decided "to rest the reason pretty much on the ascertained prejudice of the Turks against his Religion, and it having become public that he was a Jew."

The letter recalling Noah on account of his religion soon became public. Noah himself upon his return, and in the following excerpt from his volume of travels (1819), protested angrily that "the religion of a citizen is not a legitimate object of official notice." He cited in his defense both the Constitution and America's 1796 treaty with Tripoli, which (at least in its English language version) described the government of the United States as "not in any sense founded on the Christian religion." With more passion than any American Jew had evoked before, he argued on the basis of his own experience that the government should pay no official attention to religion whatsoever.

❖   ❖   ❖

Consul Mordecai Noah's dismissal based on religion, 1815

. . . Commodore Decatur invited me into the cabin, where, after being seated, he went to his escrutoire, and from among a package of letters he handed me one, saying that it was a despatch from the Secretary of State, and requested me to use no ceremony, but to read it. It had the seal of the United States, which I broke, and, to my great surprise, read as follows:—

"Department of State, April 25, 1815.
"Sir,
"At the time of your appointment, as Consul at Tunis, it was not known that the RELIGION which you profess would form any obstacle to the exercise of your Consular functions. Recent information, however, on which entire reliance may be placed, proves that it would produce a very unfavourable effect. IN CONSEQUENCE OF WHICH, the President has deemed it expedient to revoke your commission. On the receipt of this letter, therefore, you will consider yourself no longer in the public service. There are some circumstances, too, connected with your accounts, which require a more particular explanation, which, with that already given, are not approved by the President.*
I am, very respectfully, Sir,
Your obedient servant,
(Signed) JAMES MONROE.*
"Mordecai M. Noah, esquire, &c. &c.

The receipt of this letter shocked me inexpressibly; at this moment, at such a time, and in such a place, to receive a letter, which at once stripped me of office, of rights, of honour, and credit, was sufficient to astonish and dismay a person of stronger nerves:—What was to be done?
. . . I once more read the letter of Mr. Monroe. I paused to reflect on its contents. I was at a loss to account for its strange and unprecedented tenor; my religion an object of hostility? I thought I was a citizen of the United States, protected by the constitution in my religious as well as in my civil rights. My religion was known to the government at the time of my appointment, and it constituted one of the prominent causes why I was sent to Barbary; if then, any "unfavourable" events had been created by my religion, they should have been first ascertained, and not acting upon a supposition, upon imaginary consequences, have thus violated one of the most sacred and delicate rights of a citizen. Admitting, then, that my religion had produced an unfavourable effect, no *official* notice should have been taken of it; I could have been recalled without placing on file a letter, thus hostile to the spirit and character of our institutions. But my religion was not known in Barbary; from the moment of my landing, I had been in the full possession of my Consular functions, respected and feared by the government, and enjoying the esteem and good will of every resident.—What injury could my religion create? I lived like other Consuls, the flag of the United States was displayed on Sundays and Christian holidays; the Catholic Priest, who came into my house to sprinkle holy water and pray, was received with deference, and freely allowed to perform his pious purpose; the bare-footed Franciscan, who came to beg, received alms in the name of Jesus Christ; the Greek Bishop, who sent to me a decorated branch of palm on Palm Sunday, received, in return, a customary donation; the poor Christian slaves, when they wanted a favour, came to me; the Jews alone asked

nothing from me. Why then am I to be persecuted for my religion? Although no religious principles are known to the constitution, no peculiar worship connected with the government, yet I did not forget that I was representing a Christian nation. What was the opinion of Joel Barlow, when writing a treaty for one of the Barbary States? Let the following article, *confirmed by the Senate of the United States*, answer:

> *"Article 11th*—As the government of the United States of America *is not,* IN ANY SENSE, *founded on the Christian religion*—as it has, in itself, no character of enmity against the laws, religion, or tranquillity of Mussulmen; and as the said States never have entered into any war, or act of hostility against any Muhometan nation, it is declared by the parties, that no pretext *arising from religious opinions,* shall *ever* produce an interruption of the harmony existing between the two countries."

If President Madison was unacquainted with this article in the treaty, which in effect is equally binding in all the States of Barbary, he should have remembered that the religion of a citizen is not a legitimate object of official notice from the government; and even admitting that my religion was an obstacle, and there is no doubt that it was not, are we prepared to yield up the admirable and just institutions of our country at the shrine of foreign bigotry and superstition? Are we prepared to disfranchise one of our own citizens, to gratify the intolerant views of the Bey of Tunis? Has it come to this—that the noble character of the most illustrious republic on earth, celebrated for its justice, and the sacred character of its institutions, is to be sacrificed at the shrine of a Barbary pirate? Have we then fallen so low? What would have been the consequence, had the Bey known and objected to my religion? He would have learnt from me, in language too plain to be misunderstood, that whoever the United States commissions as their representative, he must receive and respect, if his conduct be proper; on that subject I could not have permitted a word to be said. If such a principle is attempted to be established, it will lay the foundation for the most unhappy and most dangerous disputes; foreign nations will dictate to us the religion which our officers at their courts should profess. With all the reflection, and the most painful anxiety, I could not account for this most extraordinary and novel procedure. Some base intrigue, probably one who was ambitious of holding this wretched office, had been at some pains to represent to the government, that my religion would produce injurious effects, and the President, instead of closing the door on such interdicted subjects, had listened and concurred; and after having braved the perils of the ocean, residing in a barbarous country, without family or relatives, supporting the rights of the nation, and hazarding my life from poison or the stiletto, I find my own government, the only protector I can have, sacrificing my credit, violating my rights, and insulting my feelings, and the religious feelings of a whole nation. O!

shame, shame!! The course which men of refined or delicate feelings should have pursued, had there been grounds for such a suspicion, was an obvious one. The President should have instructed the Secretary of State to have recalled me, and to have said, that the causes should be made known to me on my return; such a letter as I received should never have been written, and, above all, should never have been put on file.

4. "An Israelite" Condemns Christian Missions as Unconstitutional

The wave of religious enthusiasm that swept over the United States following the War of 1812 resulted in the establishment of two missionary organizations that sought to convert American Jews to Christianity. When the larger of these, the American Society for Evangelizing the Jews, applied for a state charter in New York, questions arose concerning the constitutionality of missionizing Americans of other faiths. Did evangelization conflict with the "free exercise and enjoyment of religious profession and worship, without discrimination or preference" guaranteed by the state constitution? Would chartering a missionary society violate the spirit of the no establishment clause of the Federal Constitution? To avoid controversy the organization amended its application, and under the name "The American Society for Meliorating the Condition of the Jews" it was soon chartered. But an anonymous "An Israelite" (believed by scholars to have been a non-Jewish freethinker named George Houston), in the following critique of the missionary society in a pamphlet entitled *Israel Vindicated* (1820), refused to allow these questions to rest, arguing for a more expansive interpretation of religious liberty with substantive protections for minority faiths.

◆   ◆   ◆

On the state incorporation of a missionary society, 1820

NO apology is deemed necessary for laying the following letters before the public. In a country, where every man's right to publish his sentiments is held as sacred as his right to think, it cannot be thought surprising that a part of the community, who have long been treated as the outcasts of society, should feel anxious to vindicate themselves from what they consider misrepresentation. It were to be wished that, in conducting a defence of this nature, all allusion to common received opinions could have been avoided; that religious discussions should have been laid aside, and the rights of the parties settled upon the broad principle of equality. This, however, must always remain impossible, where the party attacking, grounds his charges upon theological distinctions, and claims a superiority in this respect over his opponent.

The *"American Society for Ameliorating the Condition of the Jews,"* have assumed this superiority, and, upon that assumption, they have erected a barrier, which, if not broken down, must for ever expose the Jews in this country, to obloquy and contempt, for their adherence to that form of worship which, only, they consider divine. Previous to applying for a charter of incorporation, this society professed merely to have in view the *conversion* of the Jews to the Christian faith. Foreseeing, however, that they would be defeated in their object, if they requested the legislature to sanction an institution formed for *religious* purposes, they found it necessary to *disguise* their real intentions, by adopting a different name from that which originally belonged to the society. They substituted the word *ameliorating* for *evangelizing,* by which suspicion was lulled, and, contrary to the true spirit and meaning of the *constitution,* a law was enacted, giving countenance to one religion at the expence of another; thus establishing an ascendancy over a portion of the community directly subversive of the genuine principles of liberty. The tendency of this measure is obviously to place the Jew below the level of the Christian. It presupposes the former to be in a degraded and uncultivated state, and the latter completely civilized. It recognises the impolitic principle, evidently discountenanced by the constitution, that Christianity ought to be the predominant religion; that those who do not profess it must necessarily be immoral persons, undeserving of the rights of citizens, and whose condition is incapable of amendment, or amelioration, under the profession of any other faith. However derogatory this proceeding may be of the character of those composing the Ameliorating Society, the fact is, nevertheless, put beyond all dispute, by the tenor of the constitution and bye-laws which they have adopted, since they obtained their charter of incorporation.

No one will deny that the Jews have as just a claim to protection as the Christians. But if laws are passed, authorizing the latter to treat the former as a degraded race; if a union of men, honourable from their high standing, and whose very formation as a society, gives countenance to the prevailing calumnies; if such a combination continues to disseminate its pernicious principles, it is impossible that this persecuted people can ever obtain their rights. While pointed at by the finger of scorn; while treated by their fellow-citizens as beings of an inferior cast, they can never employ their talents to advantage for the public good.

. . . In the United States of America, a numerous race is springing up to manhood. The parents of these children are fully alive to the importance of teaching them habits of industry. But to induce them to act accordant with their feelings, every thing must be put out of the way calculated to weaken their confidence. All religious distinctions tending to interrupt social intercourse; all tests precluding the free exercise of the rights of citizenship; all laws countenancing a predominant religion; and all associations, which have other objects in view than the union of the whole community upon the principles of perfect equality: all these must be obliterated and extinguished, before the Jew can be restored to his proper place in society, and to his long lost privileges.

5. The Maryland Jew Bill

Long after religious test oaths had fallen in most states, Maryland's state constitution continued to require anyone assuming "an office of trust or profit" (including lawyers and jurors) to execute a "declaration of belief in the Christian religion." As early as 1797, Solomon Etting, the first prominent Jewish settler in Baltimore, had sought to have this provision changed, but he was thwarted; through the years several other so-called "Jew bills" were either tabled or defeated. In 1818, a non-Jewish legislator named Thomas Kennedy took up the battle on behalf of the Jewish community and introduced a new bill to extend to Jews "the same civil privileges that are enjoyed by other religious sects." The following letter from the Baltimore Jewish businessman Jacob I. Cohen to Maryland representative Ebenezer S. Thomas pleads for support of this measure. It argues for Jewish equality on the basis of "moral rectitude," the federal Constitution, and Jewish patriotism.

The issue of Jewish equality soon became enmeshed in partisan politics. Rural legislators, fearing the growing power of Baltimore (where most of Maryland's Jews lived), voted the bill down in a debate laced with anti-Jewish rhetoric. Supporters of the "Jew Bill," however, refused to give up. In 1825, a bill permitting Jews to substitute a declaration of belief "in a future state of rewards and punishments" finally passed by one vote. It became law on January 5, 1826, and later that same year two Jews won election to the Baltimore City Council.

◆   ◆   ◆

Plea to a Maryland legislator for civil equality, 1818

[December 10, 1818]

E. S. Thomas, Esq.,
Annapolis, Md.

Dear Sir:

Noticing the proceedings of the present legislature of Md., I observe a committee has been appointed in the house of Delegates to bring in a Bill "to extend to persons professing the Jewish Religion the same civil privileges that are enjoyed by other religious sects" and that yourself with Mr. Kennedy by whom the motion was made and Mr. Breckenridge compose that committee.

Having the pleasure of a personal acquaintance with you I am induced from the importance of the subject to address you.

You cannot be aware Sir from not having felt the pressure of religious intolerance, of the emotions excited in the breast of an Israelite whenever the theme of liberty of conscience is canvassed—the subject of religion being the nearest and most vital to the soul of every sectarian it awakens every spark of feeling in support of those unalienable rights which the very nature of man forbids a transfer. On the question of the extension of religious freedom to any sect or denomination, the Jew feels with solicitude for a Brother sufferer and with the anxiety of him for whom the subject is intended particularly to operate, exalts in his success or sinks deeper than before with the pangs which oppression had thrown over him, and in a tenfold degree bends him below his former station.

Judge then Sir how alive to the lightest sound in a prospect of relief from the shackles of temporal jurisdiction towards the enjoyment of rights in common with his fellowmen is the soul of a man heretofore deprived of those privileges, all the dormant faculties of his mind are then elicited and he experiences sensations only felt by those similarly situated and which in extent cannot be comprehended by those who always possessed those privileges and being thus in possession have never had cause to feel the want of.

The motion of Mr. Kennedy at the same time that it reminds us of the indignity of our situation in the States also brings to mind the many blessings our profession enjoys in this country of liberty—that by the Constitution of the United States an Israelite is placed on the same footing with any other citizen of the Union and can be elevated to the highest station in the gift of the government or in the people such toleration is duly appreciated. On the other hand we are not insensible of the protection in our persons and property even under the laws of Maryland still as those obnoxious parts of its Constitution were produced only in times of darkness and prejudice why are they continued as blots on the present enlightened period and on the honor of the State in direct opposition also to the features and principles in the Constitution of the United States.

I can scarcely admit a doubt that on a moment's consideration and reflection a change will be made as the Prayer of Justice and reason.

The grievance complained of and for which *redress* is asked, is that part of the Constitution of Maryland, which requiring a declaration of belief in the Christian Religion prevents a Jew accepting any office his fellowmen might elect him to or think him deserving the enjoyment of—he is thus incapacitated because he cannot *abjure* the principles instilled in him of worshipping the Almighty according to the dictates of his own conscience and take an oath of belief in other tenets as if such declaration of Belief made him a better man or one more capable of exercising the duties of the office which the want of that declaration would deprive him of because he maintains his unalienable rights with a steadfast and upright hand—because he cannot consent to act hypocritically he is deemed unworthy to be trusted and to be as it were disfranchised—thus incapacitating on the very grounds that ought to entitle him to confidence in the discharge of any duty he might be called upon to perform *viz:* a complete independence and unbiased judgment formed on the broad foundation of moral *rectitude.*

To you I'm sure I need not point out the effects resulting from an equal enjoyment of civil rights instead of being borne down by a state of despondency and consequent inaction, those talents idle which otherwise would prompt every effort to a spirit of ambition exhibiting the appreciation of his standing as a Freeman and observing the contrast with that when fettered by temporal authority.

In times of peril and war the Jews have borne the privations incident to such times and their best exertions have been given to their utmost, in defense of the common cause—See the Israelite in the ranks of danger, exposing his life in the defense of the Country of his adoption or of his nativity and then ask the views of the man in such exposure—the cause alone—he bears the brunt of the battle and the toils of the day with the knowledge of having discharged his duty; he retires with the pleasing consolation of mental correctness and the silent approbation of his own conscience—here he rests—having attained the summit of his expectations—Sensible of his worth, his Commander would offer him promotion the honorable and only boon a Soldier aspires to—he cannot—vain are his wishes—the State under whose banners he has fought and bled debars him its acceptance—here Sir, is an evidence of the injustice of the act of the Constitution, and the effect perhaps of that inaction which I have noticed above.

Still stranger tho are the cases requiring the decision of a Jury, look there at the situation of a man professing the Jewish Religion—I wish not to be understood that he could not obtain justice, such is not my meaning—but he is to be judged by men whom perhaps prejudice might influence in their verdict and the very course of justice be *impeded* by mere caprice incident to strong individual feeling.

By the present system a Jew is deprived of a seat in that body where by a liberal construction of matters and circumstances and a free interchange of sentiment on the broad basis of both Jewish and Christian doctrine to "do unto others as you would have others do unto you" might those prejudices be combatted and justice satisfied in its strictest sense. I cannot name the unworthy equality a Jew is placed on trial by Jury. On this great question of right, the guarantee of Freedom and political liberty I will leave you to judge as a legislator and an American Freeman.

Your attention I need not solicit on this occasion, being satisfied of the liberality of your views and the pleasure it would afford you in the opportunity of *redressing* the grievances of your Constituents—A bill relating to an equality of rights intended for the present purposes was reported in the Senate of Maryland during the Session of 1816 and was not acted upon—I do not know why—I confidently trust however that the present legislature will take up the subject with the consideration it merits.

Whatever may be the fate of the proposed bill permit me to request, if not improper that the Ayes and Nays be taken and placed on record on the general question as well as on any previous one, which might involve such general question or be indicative of its final result.

Before I conclude I would remark that previous to my commencing this letter a friend in this city applied to me for such papers as I had in my possession in any way relating to the object proposed by Mr. Kennedy's motion—these I gave him, I would have been glad to have forwarded to you with this but as I learn they will be laid before the committee, it will answer the same purpose as you will then have an opportunity of examining them.

I am,
Dear Sir,
Yours with great Respect,
(signed) J. I. COHEN.

FOUR

Christian America or Religious America?

◆　❖　◆

A merica in the second decade of the nineteenth century was a nation intoxicated with its new vision of democracy, fired with patriotic fervor, yearning to expand to the limits of its frontier, and increasingly zealous in its religious beliefs. A wondrous revival had swept the country, returning thousands to the religious fold, and spawning an empire of benevolent societies intent on doing "good work" in order to hasten the millennium and the coming of God's Kingdom upon earth. Those who earlier feared that freedom of religion would doom America and drive it into deism or atheism learned in this period how wrong they had been. In the wake of what is now known as the Second Great Awakening, the idea that America was a "Christian Country" experienced a dramatic resurgence. Citing the "real object" of the Constitution as well as established principles of common law, many sought to establish Protestantism as the nation's official faith.

The American Jewish community, its numbers swelled by immigrants from England, Holland, Germany, and Poland, determinedly opposed this movement to "baptize the Constitution." References to Americans as a "Christian people," Thanksgiving Day proclamations that excluded Jews by referring to Christianity, discriminatory laws and practices, anti-Jewish slurs and stereotypes, conversionist sallies, efforts to write Christianity into the Constitution—all these and more met with resolute Jewish resistance. Jews called instead for equality of *all* religions, their own included. They did not link their rights to those of nonbelievers, as later generations would. In several cases, in fact, they campaigned for (and won) rights that atheists were specifically denied. The America they advocated was very much a "Religious America," a land where pluralism triumphed over Protestantism and people of all faiths stood on an equal footing.

1. The Case for Christian America

The argument that America was a Christian nation relied both on new interpretations of the Constitution and on traditions carried over from English common law. Supreme Court Justice Joseph Story (1779–1845), a Jeffersonian and one of the most influential American jurists, took the lead in arguing that Christianity underlay the American Republic and should be encouraged by the state. His reading of the First Amendment justified such a conclusion on the basis of history, "sound policy," and "revealed truth," as he explained in his highly influential *Commentaries on the Constitution* (1833) from which the following selections are extracted. More than two decades earlier, Chancellor James Kent, chief justice of New York's highest court, had ruled that religious freedom and church-state separation did not stand in the way of a common law indictment for malicious blasphemy. "We are a Christian people," he wrote in *People v. Ruggles* (1811), "and the morality of the country is deeply engrafted upon Christianity."

The great lawyer and statesman Daniel Webster echoed Kent in an eloquent argument before the Supreme Court in the case of *Vidal v. Girard's Executors* (1844), from which the following paragraph is excerpted. Webster ultimately lost the case, but Justice Story, writing for the Court, did agree that Christianity was part of the common law and was not, as a result, to be maliciously and openly blasphemed.

◆   ◆   ◆

Supreme Court Justice Story on the Christian foundation of America, 1833

1867. Now, there will probably be found few persons in this, or any other Christian country, who would deliberately contend, that it was unreasonable, or unjust to foster and encourage the Christian religion generally, as a matter of sound policy, as well as of revealed truth. In fact, every American colony, from its foundation down to the revolution, with the exception of Rhode Island, (if, indeed, that state be an exception,) did openly, by the whole course of its laws and institutions, support and sustain, in some form, the Christian religion; and almost invariably gave a peculiar sanction to some of its fundamental doctrines. And this has continued to be the case in some of the states down to the present period, without the slightest suspicion, that it was against the principles of public law, or republican liberty. Indeed, in a republic, there would seem to be a peculiar propriety in viewing the Christian religion, as the great basis, on which it must rest for its support and permanence, if it be, what it has ever been deemed by its truest friends to be, the religion of liberty.

1868. Probably at the time of the adoption of the constitution, and of the amendment to it, now under consideration, the general, if not the universal, sentiment in America was, that Christianity ought to receive encouragement from the state, so far as was not incompatible with the private rights of conscience, and the freedom of religious worship. An attempt to level all religions, and to make it a matter of state policy to hold all in utter indifference, would have created universal disapprobation, if not universal indignation.

1869. It yet remains a problem to be solved in human affairs, whether any free government can be permanent, where the public worship of God, and the support of religion, constitute no part of the policy or duty of the state in any assignable shape. The future experience of Christendom, and chiefly of the American states, must settle this problem, as yet new in the history of the world, abundant, as it has been, in experiments in the theory of government.

1871. The real object of the amendment was, not to countenance, much less to advance Mahometanism, or Judaism, or infidelity, by prostrating Christianity; but to exclude all rivalry among Christian sects, and to prevent any national ecclesiastical establishment, which should give to an hierarchy the exclusive patronage of the national government. It thus cut off the means of religious persecution, (the vice and pest of former ages,) and of the subversion of the rights of conscience in matters of religion, which had been trampled upon almost from the days of the Apostles to the present age.

◆

Daniel Webster on Christianity as part of common law, 1844

... In Pennsylvania as elsewhere, the general principles and public policy are sometimes established by constitutional provisions, sometimes by legislative enactments, sometimes by judicial decisions, and sometimes by general consent. But however they may be established, there is nothing that we look for with more certainty than this general principle, that Christianity is part of the law of the land. This was the case among the Puritans of New England, the Episcopalians of the Southern States, the Pennsylvania Quakers, the Baptists, the mass of the followers of Whitefield and Wesley, and the Presbyterians; all brought and all adopted this great truth, and all have sustained it. And where there is any religious sentiment amongst men at all, this sentiment incorporates itself with the law. *Every thing declares it.* The massive cathedral of the Catholic; the Episcopalian church, with its lofty spire pointing heavenward; the plain temple of the Quaker; the log church of the hardy pioneer of the wilderness; the mementoes and memorials around and about us; the consecrated graveyards, their tombstones and epitaphs, their silent vaults, their mouldering contents; all attest it. *The dead prove it as well as the living.* The generation that are gone before speak to it, and pronounce it from the tomb. We feel it. All, all, proclaim that Christianity, general, tolerant Christianity, Christianity independent of sects and parties, that Christianity to which the sword and the fagot are unknown, general, tolerant Christianity, is the law of the land.

2. The Case for Religious Equality

America's Jewish leaders, many of them immigrants who had come to the United States inspired by its promise of religious liberty, spoke out vigorously against the doctrine of Christian America. Casting themselves as defenders of American tradition, they insisted that the doctrines of Christian America ran counter to the plain meaning of the Constitution. Whereas in Europe the state was avowedly Christian and Jews merely tolerated, in the United States, they proclaimed, all alike enjoyed a full measure of religious freedom.

Isaac Leeser (1806–1868), the foremost Jewish religious leader of his day and editor of the *Occident,* the first American Jewish newspaper, was one of the principal figures in the Jewish campaign against Christian America. In the following excerpt from his article entitled "The United States Not A Christian State" (1850), he stresses that whatever America is in practice, it is not Christian as a matter of law.

Nathaniel Levin (1816–1899), a city employee and local Jewish notable in Charleston, offers a broader interpretation of religious liberty in the second excerpt below, part of a response to a toast delivered at a local Jewish charity benefit. Emphasizing that religion is vital to society, his concern on the eve of the Civil War (1859) is to preserve "liberty of conscience"— which, he fears, too close a relationship between church and state must inevitably violate.

✦   ✦   ✦

Isaac Leeser, Christianity is not the state religion, 1850

We have often maintained, both in private conversation and in our writings, that no one can claim for the United States the name of a Christian state, in the legal sense of the words; which does not say that the whole people of the country might not, for all that, be Christians, or sectarians of an especial branch of Christianity. All the words mean to convey, is, that Christianity does, as such, not enter into the polity of the government; and that the constitution, the fundamental law, has no necessary connexion with either the dogmas or precepts of Christianity. The proposition, we always thought, was so evident, that we could not help wondering, and our astonishment is not lessened at this day, that people should even dare to call this a Christian country, and speak of the population as a Christian people; when to a surety they cannot point to a single constitutional clause of the Union, and of nearly all the states, except, perhaps, Massachusetts, New Hampshire, and North Carolina, which demands the existence of Christianity as a prerequisite of the existence of the government. In this, the various authors of the respective fundamental codes, as we may freely call the several union and state constitutions, have shown their wisdom; they found men of the most opposite opinions joined together in this country, and they would not, and could not take upon themselves to decide which should be the *orthodox* or state religion. The laws of the country know nothing of any religious profession, and leave every man to pursue whatever religion he pleases. Nevertheless it is not an atheistical country, and there can be no doubt that more is done for the maintenance of religious establishments here than in any other state; in fact, we should say that more is spent in church-building than there is any occasion for. At all events, it is foolish to pretend to assert that there is a state religion; either that it is Judaism, Christianity, or anything else. All men have an equal right to be here; one does not tolerate the other, nor has he to thank him, *legally,* for leaving him undisturbed, however *practically* the minority are at the mercy of the majority. Might makes right here as well as elsewhere; and the fanatics for all opinions know this perfectly well, and they therefore endeavour to make their views those of the majority, that they may carry them through and force them on the community by the brute power of numbers.

◆

Nathaniel Levin on religious liberty, 1859

When religious establishments extend to the moulding and formation of governments, when religious systems create moral habits that interfere with social happiness, and prostrate political rights, and, when all these influences are brought to bear, so as to consolidate a union of church and state pressing down human rights by a powerful hierarchy: we boldly declare that such a system is anti-social and anti-civilizing, opposed to the rights of conscience, and interferes with the freedom of religious worship.

What affair of life, sir, moral, political, or civil, is not mixed up with religion? What duty of life is there which is not founded on religion? Can you point to a civil institution which is not intimately connected with religion? Begin with matrimony and its duties, birth, death, obedience of children to parents. Are they not all bound up with religion? The duties of office and station: how are they enforced? By religion; by an oath on the Bible, or a solemn affirmation *with God as a witness*, a form even more solemn than that of an oath. Education commences in religion, because it commences on the mother's knee, and religion is the instinct of woman, as it becomes in time the conviction of man. What makes the good citizen? *Not sectarianism*—but religion controlling his moral conduct. What makes the patriot? Religion extended into politics. Separate man from religion in any of the duties of life, and you degrade him to the level of the brute.

Prayer to God—free religious worship is one thing. To take hold of the ignorance and passions of mankind, in order to make them the slaves of an oppressive system of temporal power, is another. Whenever religion is turned to political purposes, it is no longer a right, but a perversion—it is no longer a privilege, but an usurpation.

Religious liberty, as we understand the term, means no more than the right to worship God after the dictates of our own hearts. In other words, it means liberty of conscience, which implies freedom of thought, exercise of judgment—the investigation of reason—the independence of a rational and responsible mind. No human authority can divest us of this right—it is one incident to existence—an original inherent and inalienable right. It is liberty of conscience, sir, that gives dignity to manhood, sacred fire to the soul, immortal breathings to the mind, and lifts us up in near affinity to God. It is this prerogative that gives full and complete enjoyment to all our senses; all our faculties; all our nature; free thoughts; pure feelings; a soaring fancy; an unclouded mind; ideas that revel in the beauty of nature's beams; perceptions clear, vivid, heart-cheering, that unveil an angel of mercy in every ray of light, and acknowledge a blessing in every bounty of God.

3. New York Debates the Appointment of State Chaplains

The custom of opening legislative sessions with a prayer has deep roots in American history. The Continental Congress of 1774 opened with a prayer, and in 1789 the appointment of a chaplain for this purpose won approval from both the Senate and the House. Objections from those (like James Madison) who considered the Congressional chaplaincy an unconstitutional establishment of religion never swayed either Congress or the courts.

Significant objections to legislative chaplains did emerge in New York State in 1829 when a revised statute regularized their hiring and payment. In response to angry petitions, the State Assembly appointed a "Select Committee on the Several Memorials Against Appointing Chaplains to the Legislature," which reported in 1832 that the statute was unconstitutional; the prayers, the chaplains, and the payments were all "without legal authority." The report, excerpted below, then went further, specifically rebutting the opposition claim "that christianity . . . is the law of the land."

The Select Committee's report unleashed a storm of criticism, some of it specifically directed against Assemblyman Mordecai Myers, the report's coauthor, who was an intermarried Jew. The Albany journalist-politician Solomon Southwick, for example, suggested in the second selection below that as a Jew in a Christian state Myers ought to have conducted himself more deferentially. In the end, the legislature did agree to end payments to chaplains, but six years later the vote was rescinded.

✦　　✦　　✦

New York committee opposes legislative chaplains, 1832

Your committee will now proceed to show that the Legislature possess no legitimate authority to associate religious prayers with legislative proceedings, nor to appoint legislative chaplains, nor to appropriate the public money to pay for any religious service: and because,

1st. No such authority has been delegated to them; and,

2d. Because the exercise of such powers is not only repugnant to the constitution, but expressly interdicted by it.

It will not be denied, and hence not necessary to prove that the Legislature is vested with civil powers *only;* and have not been clothed with spiritual jurisdiction. Nor will it be requisite to inquire into the utility of religious prayers, or the obligation to pray, as a religious duty. "Religion is a concern between a man's conscience and his God, with which no human tribunal has a right to meddle." If prayer be deemed an act of religious devotion, the Legislature have no authority officially to perform it, nor to require others to do so, or to attend its performance. The people have not delegated power to the Legislature to perform religious worship of any kind; and if prayers are acts of ecclesiastical character and of religious duty, legislative prayers are acts of supererogation; and legislative acts which transcend the powers delegated by the people to the Legislature, are an official exercise of "power beyond the law," and as unauthorized as they would be if expressly interdicted by those provisions of the constitution which are intended to prevent an alliance of political and ecclesiastical powers, and to preserve the unrestrained exercise and enjoyment of religious opinion.

But the absence of legal authority is not the only objection to which the practice under consideration is obnoxious. It often interferes with the legitimate business of the Legislature, and thus operates unpropitiously to the public interest. Some members of the Legislature, like many of their constituents, conscientiously disapprove of prayers altogether; others are averse to *legislative* prayers; others again do not hold to prayers in *public places;* and amidst the congregated assembly of persons of various religious sects and adverse religious opinions, and who are elected without reference to their religious creeds, there are but few who can at any one time join heartily in the *service.* And the effect produced in the minds of such as are induced by courtesy, or are constrained by a species of legal coercion to attend legislative *prayer meetings,* is anything but piety or "a praying spirit."

Mankind are generally averse to associate in religious devotion with any but those whose feelings and faith accord with their own; and although regard to the opinions of others may often induce some occasionally to listen with respectful attention to a sincere supplicant; yet being, as many of the members of the Legislature frequently are, annoyed by the repeated annunciation of sentiments out of harmony with their own; and finding at length their courtesy greatly overtaxed, their feeling constantly disobliged, and their convictions as often counteracted by attending prayers in which they have no *faith,* and with those with whom they cannot, consistently with their own *creeds,* have any religious communion or fellowship, they usually absent themselves from the legislative chambers until after the ecclesiastical business of the house shall have been concluded. Hence it is, that during prayer time there is seldom more than a lean quorum in attendance, and often less. It was doubtless owing to the extended operation of the same cause, that on one occasion during the present session the *Speaker* adjourned the House of Assembly for want of a quorum to transact legislative business, although a great majority of the members were in and about the Capitol, and appeared in the legislative chamber in a very few minutes after the adjournment.

Having shown that *getting up* legislative religious prayers are inconsistent with the authority delegated to the Legislature, unauthorized by the constitution, and hence an exercise of "powers beyond the law" it would seem superfluous to prove that the Legislature have no legitimate power to appoint legislative chaplains.

It is self-evident and incontrovertible principle, that no person nor body of men have a right to empower others to do *that* which no one, nor any number, have a right to do themselves. The Legislature having no right to convert the legislative chambers into "religious session rooms," nor to transform the legislative assemblies of the political delegates of the people into religious "prayer meetings;" nor any right to attempt, by official vote, to constrain the minority, against their religious opinions, to submit to such an incongruous intermixture of political and religious concerns: *consequently*, they have no right to appoint others to do so; and hence, *conclusively*, have no right to appoint ministers of religion, nor priests of any denomination, to say prayers, or to perform any other kind of religious service for the Legislature.

. . . it is not true that christianity as such is the law of the land. The constitution is the *supreme* law of the land; by virtue of which, the *mosque*, the *synagogue*, the *christian church*, and all other churches and religions are placed on equal grounds. It makes no discrimination between them, nor allows any preference to be given by law to any or either of them. It prohibits none—protects all, but permits no religious creed to be enforced as the law of the land. Hence the law of the land is, that no religious creed, as such, can be recognized as the law of the State; that "all mankind," and therefore every individual "within this State," have an equal and unalienable right to "*believe* according to the dictates of their understanding," and no person, nor "human tribunal," has a right to use the name of *God* or *religion* to make men afraid to avow their honest and conscientious opinions, or in any way to coerce them to act the *hypocrite*, with a view to escape the wrath, or to propitiate the *evil spirit* of religious intolerance and persecution, which is denounced in the christian books and interdicted by the constitution of this State: both of which place clergymen precisely in that situation, which was recognized and approved by their great and acknowledged master. Neither he nor his apostles entered the halls of legislation, except when forced there by his persecutors; nor did he or his disciples ever claim or aspire to participate in the business of civil government, nor assume to be "judges or dividers in Israel." On the contrary, they shunned the political world as a source of contamination, tending to abstract the mind from the study and pursuit of eternal truth, and to pollute it with views and interests incompatible with their clerical vocation. They therefore neither sought nor received political aid, nor the pecuniary emoluments attached to services unknown to them, but which, in the revolution of time and events, have been sought and obtained by their successors.

The result of all the foregoing facts and arguments is, that your committee have arrived to the most satisfactory conclusion, that the association of ecclesiastical duties with political legislative proceedings, is unauthorized by any power delegated by the people—is incompatible with the character of a free government, predicated on the principle of equal rights—uncongenial with the spirit and provisions of the constitution of this State, and that the practice ought therefore to be abolished. That to appoint priests to the office of legislative chaplains, is to appoint them to ecclesiastical or civil office. The former is unauthorized, and the latter expressly interdicted by the constitution, and ought not in future to be repeated. That to take the people's money to pay for religious prayers or any religious service, transcends the legitimate power of the Legislature no less than would a statute law, if enacted expressly to levy a tax upon the people for such purposes.

Your committee therefore are of opinion that so much of the statute laws of this State as prescribe and allow chaplains to be paid out of the public funds, for the performance of religious services or duties are unconstitutional and ought to be expunged from the statute books of this State. For which purpose the chairman of your committee some time since brought in a bill.

And your committee further report, that in several of the memorials referred to their consideration, there are other laws which are represented to infringe the civil and religious liberties of your constituents; the alleged unconstitutionality of which is sustained by such facts and arguments as leave no doubt on the minds of the committee that the exceptions of the memorialists to the several subjects of complaint, are well taken. But your committee not having time to draw up a detailed report on all the matters contained in the said memorials; and not being willing that the memorialists should be misled to believe that their petitions have been neglected, their complaints disregarded or treated with any disrespect, and thus their grievances remain unredressed, your committee, have deemed it proper to recommend the adoption of the following resolutions.

DAVID MOULTON, *Ch.*
M. MYERS.

Resolved, That all legislation on religion, other than pursuant to the constitution, to secure to "all mankind within this State without discrimination or preference" the free and unmolested, enjoyment of the rights of opinion and free discussion, is unjust, unauthorized and unconstitutional.

Resolved, That all existing laws by which any person within this State is co-erced against his conscientious opinions to conform to the religious creeds or doctrines of others, are unjust, unconstitutional, nugatory, and ought to be re-pealed.

Resolved, That to obstruct the public streets or highways with iron chains or other impediments to the free use thereof on Sunday or any other day, is an ex-ercise of power without right, and ought to be interdicted under proper and effectual penalties.

♦

Solomon Southwick's response to the committee report, 1834

After the exhibitions we have given of the pious and devotional practices of the Patriarchs and Prophets of Israel; and after the frightful narrative we have subjoined of the persecutions sustained by the Jews in the Old World, the ques-tion comes home to us with peculiar force:—Did Mr. MYERS, as a Jew, act a modest, consistent, grateful, or a magnanimous part in opposing the choice of Chaplains? It is a serious question for him to answer to his country, his con-science and his God. Standing alone, modesty demanded at least a tacit ac-quiescence in the old and venerated custom. Standing as a Jew, if a faithful one, consistency required his decided support of the measure. But standing as a *Jew,* clothed with the confidence of a *Christian* community; elevated by that *Christian* confidence to the high station of a law-giver—a Jewish *law-giver* in a *Christian* land—a fact never before heard of in any other *Christian* land— was it grateful or magnanimous in him to aim a blow at the Ministers of Chris-tianity? And that, too, under a pretext so flimsy as the one set up by those, who, I venture to say, were then bent, and still are bent, not only on expelling Chap-lains from the Legislature, but expelling *Christianity* itself from the country and the world! I repeat it, it is more in sorrow than in anger, that I make these re-marks. I have ever been the personal friend of Mr. Myers. I would not retaliate upon him, or his race, the blow he has aimed at the Ministers of Christ, and at a Christian custom, sanctioned not only by all the Saints and Sages of Christen-dom, but by all the Patriarchs, Prophets, Priests and Law givers, of the ancient Israel, to whom Mr. Myers and his brethren look up, or ought to look up, as the *"Fathers of the Faithful,"* the "burning and shining lights" of their religion!

I would, however, seriously press upon his attention, and that of his breth-ren, the high privileges which they enjoy in this country, and the proper feelings which they are bound to cherish towards a Christian people, who have so liberally conferred upon them such high and extraordinary privileges; privi-leges which they have hitherto been denied by all the governments of the old world, and which, in this country alone, they have been permitted to enjoy. In this view of the subject, and under such circumstances, I will take the liberty of suggesting such a speech, as Mr. Myers ought to have made, instead of the one which he did make. He ought, I think, to have thus addressed the Chair:—

"MR. CHAIRMAN,—

"I am, it is true, an Israelite by birth, education and principle—and as such am opposed to the Christian Religion. But where am I, and under what circumstances am I placed? I am in a Christian country; and not only so, but in a Christian country, which, rising superior to all bigotry, intolerance, prejudice, or proscription, has elevated my race as high in the scale of society as it has the most favorite members of its own faith. As the consequence of this liberal spirit, this elevation of the long degraded and enslaved Israelite, it has clothed me with its confidence, has made me one of the chosen guardians of its liberties and its laws! And not me alone has it distinguished, but others of my Religion have enjoyed its confidence, and partaken largely of its patronage. Neither civil nor military honors have been denied us; but have, on the contrary, been lavished upon us. Many are the names I could mention, whose brows have been decorated with the honors of this Republic. I have myself borne those honors in the field as well as the cabinet. I see at this moment an Israelite acquiring wealth, fame and distinction as an Editor, on the one hand, and an officer of the government on the other: and the road to wealth, fame and official honors, is thrown broadly open to the whole race. . . .

"Here, Mr. Chairman, this liberty is realised to the Israelites. Here we pray unmolested. Here we sit safely under the shadow of our own vines, and the trees of our own planting, or those planted by others, and by the hand of Nature's God in the Forests that surround us; *and there is no one to make us afraid!* We can freely tune our harps to the songs of our ancient Zion; for we are not in a strange land, nor the captives and the slaves of a Foreign Tyrant: And these blessings have been won for us by the blood of *Christian* martyrs, poured out profusely on many a battlefield, *in the cause of Universal Liberty, and for the Imprescriptible, the Sacred Rights of Man!* The blood of *Warren,* and the toils and the risks of *Washington,* who were *Christian* heroes, to say nothing of thousands of others of the same faith, have raised the Jews, as well as the *Christians,* to the exalted state of Freemen: In short, in no country on the face of the earth, is my race so highly favored, so respectfully and liberally treated, as they are in this land of the brave and the free!

"And shall I, Mr. Chairman, under such circumstances, act the part of the viper in the fable, and sting the bosom of my preserver, my benefactor? Shall I, like that viper, return evil for good, and betray the trust reposed in me, by raising my voice against an ancient, a salutary and venerated custom, not only dear to my benefactors, but sanctioned by the soundest dictates of wisdom and of virtue, of piety and religion? Shall I stifle in my bosom every spark of piety; and every feeling of honor and gratitude, by voting against a measure which my own Religion sanctions, as well as the Religion of my constituents, of those who have generously overlooked my adverse faith, and clothed me with their confidence? And shall I do this, under the flimsy pretext, that it is unconstitutional to offer up Prayers to the God of Heaven and Earth! Why, sir, the Constitution or the Law, that would extinguish in our bosoms the gratitude we owe to our Creator, that forbids us to offer up to him the grateful incense of prayer and of praise, is of itself a nullity; nor can any oath to support so unhallowed and blasphemous an Instrument, be binding upon the honor, the conscience, or the loyalty of any but a savage or a heathen! I will not, then, sir, steep my soul in the lethean dregs of forgetfulness of the God of my Fathers! No, Sir, I will not, I cannot, I dare not act so foul, so treacherous, and so wicked a part. The Law and the Prophets forbid it; for they teach me *to do as I would be done by!* They teach me that Prayer to God is a Sacred duty, which neither men nor nations are at liberty to violate! They teach me that gratitude is a virtue, and that to return good for evil, and not evil for good, is amiable in the sight of men, and well pleasing in the sight of God. It shall never be said of me, therefore, that *Christians* honored me—me, an *Israelite*—with their confidence—and that I betrayed them! It shall never be said of me, that I refused to pray myself, or prevented others from praying, to the God of Abraham, Isaac and Jacob! The sons of *Christians* may disgrace themselves by deserting the faith of their Fathers: but I will not join them in forsaking the God of Israel! Let them do as they please, sir; but, as for me, I will follow the examples of Abraham at Horeb, and Isaac at Beersheba; of Jacob at Bethel, and Moses in the wilderness.

"I therefore move, Sir, that we open our daily sessions by prayer to the ever living God, the Creator, Preserver, and Benefactor of the Universe, that he will graciously smile upon our honest deliberations for the good of this people; and crown them with success!"

I now cheerfully leave the candid reader of every sect, or party, which deserves the name of Jew, Christian, or Republican, to decide, whether if Mr. Myers had pursued the course I have laid down, he would not have acted more prudently, virtuously, and wisely, than he has done: And as to himself, I leave him to his own reflections, to his conscience and his God; and these I hope may bring him back to the ground he has lost, and entitle him to the renewed confidence and esteem of the wise and virtuous of all parties.

4. Thanksgiving Day Proclamations and Jewish Dissents

From America's earliest days, political leaders invited citizens to assemble in their houses of worship to offer thanks to God and to seek God's blessings. Thomas Jefferson opposed this practice, as outside the purview of government, but the custom prevailed. In time, Thanksgiving Day came to be seen as a regular part of the nation's "civil religion."

Precisely because Thanksgiving Day proclamations gave expression to the religious character of the United States, Jews were extraordinarily sensitive to sectarian proclamations directed toward Christians alone. Repeatedly, in the nineteenth century, they protested when they were excluded; in a few cases they boycotted such Thanksgivings entirely. What makes the following 1844 case in South Carolina so unusual is the angry exchange of letters that the Jewish protest provoked. Where politicians elsewhere usually apologized and made amends, Governor James H. Hammond insisted that the United States *was* a "Christian land," and accused his Jewish critics ("inheriting the same scorn for Jesus Christ which instigated their ancesters to crucify him") of seeking to inflict their minority views upon the majority—language that drew an unusually sharp and public Jewish rejoinder. Not since Peter Stuyvesant had Jews clashed with a governor in such an impassioned and stormy exchange over religious liberty and the relationship of religion to the state.

◆　◆　◆

Exchange of letters on South Carolina Gov. Hammond's Thanksgiving proclamation of 1844, with a public protest

At a numerous meeting of Israelites, held at the Masonic Hall, on the 16th of November, Michael Lazarus, Esq., was called to the Chair, and S. Valentine, Esq., requested to act as Secretary.

The Chairman explained the object of the meeting to be in consequence of the Governor's Proclamation of 9th September, the tenor of which excluded the Israelites of this city and State from his invitation to public prayer and thanksgiving. His excellency had been courteously addressed through a public and private source, calling his attention to the fact. *After the lapse of some time, he having declined to notice their complaint,* the following letter was transmitted to his excellency.

To his Excellency James H. Hammond, Governor of the State of South Carolina.

Sir,

The undersigned, Israelites of Charleston, deem it due to themselves as American freemen, sternly and solemnly to protest against the language and spirit of the Proclamation published by your excellency in the Charleston Mercury of the 13th ult. Their voice of firm remonstrance, would have long ere this been heard, but that you had been addressed on the subject by others of our citizens, and we desired to afford you ample time to respond. This you have failed to do; want of time cannot therefore be plead as an excuse, and the silence which courtesy prompted, must now be broken.

That no conflict of opinion may arise as to the precise language of your Proclamation, we here insert it, as it originally appeared, over your official hand and seal.

Executive Department,
Columbia, Sept. 9, 1844.
"By his Excellency James H. Hammond, Governor and
Commander-in-Chief in and over the State of South Carolina.

"Whereas, it becomes all Christian nations to acknowledge at stated periods, their dependence on Almighty God, to express their gratitude for His past mercies, and humbly and devoutly to implore His blessing for the future:

"Now, therefore, I, James H. Hammond, Governor of the State of South Carolina, do, in conformity with the established usage of this State, appoint the first Thursday in October next, to be observed as a day of Thanksgiving, Humiliation and Prayer, and invite and exhort our citizens of all denominations to assemble at their respective places of worship, to offer up their devotions to God their Creator, and his Son Jesus Christ, the Redeemer of the world.

"Given under my hand, and the seal of the State, in Columbia, this ninth day of September, in the year of our Lord one thousand eight hundred and forty-four, and in the sixty-ninth year of American Independence.

By the Governor,
JAMES H. HAMMOND

"ROBT. Q. PINCKNEY,
Secretary of State."

You have thus obviously excluded the Israelites of South Carolina from a participation in the religious observances of the occasion. To do this you have adopted a phraseology as *unusual* as it is offensive. No casuistry however subtle,—no constructions however ingenious, can bring the mind to any other conclusion. It is true, you "exhort our citizens of all denominations to assemble at their respective places of worship," and had you stopped there, you would have been clearly *within* the legitimate sphere of your official duty. But, sir, you go further; and state the particular creed upon which your excellency would have *"all these denominations"* to unite!—*all* are invited "to offer up their devotions to God, the Creator, AND his Son Jesus Christ, the Redeemer of the world." Now, it is scarcely necessary to remind one so profoundly skilled in logic, as well as ethics, as yourself, that to invite one to do that, which you know his conscience forbids, if not a mockery of his feelings, is certainly not far removed from an insult to his understanding; and yet you must, or should have known, that to a respectable portion of your constituents your invitation presented no other features.

Sir, the Israelites of Charleston, while they hold in all proper respect all other denominations of their fellow-citizens, profess themselves a God-serving and prayerful people. They cherish with unfaltering devotion their ancient and holy religion. They contemplate with veneration its sublime truths; and they rely with calm confidence upon its glorious and inspiring promises. They too, in common with all others of the human family, have bowed their heads in humble submission beneath the chastening rod of their Creator, and in their turn, have also had cause, gratefully to acknowledge bounteous blessings bestowed by His beneficent hand. Judge then, sir, what must have been their emotions when they found themselves *excluded* by your Proclamation, from the general thanksgiving and prayer of the occasion!

So utterly repugnant to their feelings—so violative of their accustomed privileges—so widely variant from the ordinary language of such papers—so exclusive in its tone and spirit—did the Israelites of Charleston regard your Proclamation, that, although there are in the city two congregations of them, neither opened their doors for worship on the day you had appointed. Nor could they, with a proper reverence for the hallowed faith of their fathers, have acted otherwise.

Sir, it is not our purpose to enter with you into the discussion of doctrinal points; neither *your* orthodoxy, nor *ours* is now in question. We regard you in this issue *only* as the Governor of South Carolina, and we propose to test the position you have assumed, by that constitution, which you have sworn to support. From that alone do you derive your present authority. Thank God, sir, that noble instrument, together with the Constitution of the United States, presents a glorious panoply of defence against the encroachments of power, whether its designs be bold or insidious. Under its universal and protecting spirit, we do not sue for *toleration,* but we *demand our rights.* Let us refer to first principles. From the reference both the *Governor* and the *governed* may derive salutary instruction. What says then the *first section* of the *eighth article* of the Constitution of South Carolina? The words are these (1st Stat. at L. 191):

"The free exercise and enjoyment of religious profession and worship, *without discrimination or preference,* shall for ever hereafter be allowed within this state to all mankind."

Now, sir, we charge you with such obvious *discrimination and preference,* in the tenor of your proclamation, as amounted to an utter exclusion of a portion of the people of South Carolina. It would seem (and we say it without irreverence) as if the finger of Providence had penned that section of the constitution, in prophetic anticipation of the case in point. From your perversion of it, what monstrous evils might arise? if your excellency could be justified in so framing your proclamations as to shut out the religious privileges of the Israelites, where are we to find the line of limitation? Instead of representing the *whole people* of the state in their various tenets and creeds, the governor would make *his own opinion* the standard of orthodoxy, be it what it may. Episcopacy and Presbytery would in turn exclude each other, as the views of the functionary who may happen to fill the chair might lead. *Individual* prejudice or prepossession would usurp the place of the constitution. An orthodox *Protestant* governor might exclude all who do not come up to his peculiar standard of faith; and the *Catholic,* the *Unitarian,* the Israelite, and numerous other sects, may find their privileges *discriminated* away, and their most cherished opinions crushed or slighted by a gubernatorial preference.

But, sir, while the constitution of our honoured State is cherished by our people, as it now is, the errors or misdeeds of those in authority cannot pass unnoticed, or unrebuked. It is a palladium that throws its broad and protecting influence over all who abide beneath it. It guarantees TO ALL, in its own expressive phrase, "without *discrimination or preference,*" the free and full enjoyment of every right, civil and religious; and we cherish its principles next to the Holy Testimonies of our God! It is a noble covenant of Liberty, won and consecrated by the blood of Heroes. The temple is pure and the shrine is sacred. If desecrated by the minister the fault shall not be ours. It is with hearts warmed by such memories, and minds kindling with such associations, that we now record this our solemn and emphatic protest against your proclamation, as unsanctioned by the letter or spirit of the Constitution, as offensive and unusual in language, as exclusive, arbitrary, and sectarian in its character.

In conclusion, sir, we would remind you that your term of office is about to expire. A few fleeting days, and the robe that you wear will grace the shoulders of your successor. We trust that for your own reputation you will, ere that period arrives, remove the impressions which the act in question has made upon the minds of a large portion of your constituents. We are, very respectfully,

Your obedient servants.

[The above letter was signed by upwards of one hundred Israelites, and transmitted to his Excellency.]

The following reply was received from his Excellency.

"Executive Department,
Silver Bluff, Nov. 4, 1844.

"Gentlemen—I received today your memorial and protest against my Proclamation appointing the third day of October for Thanksgiving, which, in consequence of my allusion to 'Jesus Christ the Redeemer' you denounce 'as unsanctioned by the letter or spirit of the Constitution—as offensive and unusual in language, as exclusive, arbitrary and sectarian in its character.' I have received heretofore several private communications on the subject, and a public letter addressed me through the columns of the Southern Patriot; I made no reply to any of these, because I did not feel myself bound to notice them, and wished to avoid, if possible, a controversy of this nature. Your memorial and protest, however, signed as I perceive it is by over one hundred of the most respectable Israelites of Charleston, rebuking in no measured terms, and demanding, as I understand it, an apology, requires an answer. The simple truth is, that at the time of writing my Proclamation it did not occur to me, that there might be Israelites, Deists, Atheists, or any other class of persons in the State who denied the divinity of Jesus Christ. I could not therefore have intended to wound the feelings of such individuals or associations of them. But I am aware that forgetfulness can never justify a breach of public duty, I do not therefore urge it in the least. And as you force me to speak, it is due to candour to say, that had I been fully on my guard, I do not think I should have changed the language of my Proclamation! and that I have no apology to make for it now. Unhappily for myself I am not a professor of religion; nor am I specially attached by education or habit to any particular denomination, nor do I feel myself to be a fit and proper defender of the Christian faith. But I must say that up to this time, I have always thought it a settled matter that I lived in a Christian land! And that I was the temporary chief magistrate of a Christian people. That in such a country and among such a people I should be, publicly, called to an account, reprimanded and required to make amends for acknowledging Jesus Christ as the Redeemer of the world, I would not have believed possible, if it had not come to pass. I have not examined nor am I now able to refer to the Proclamations of my predecessors, to ascertain whether they have limited their fellow-citizens to address their devotions to the Father or the Son or to the Father only, nor could I verify the motives which might have influenced them to do the one or the other. But I am of opinion that a Proclamation for Thanksgiving which omits to unite the name of the Redeemer with that of the Creator is not a Christian Proclamation, and might justly give offence to the Christian People, whom it invited to worship. If in complaisance to the Israelites and Deists, his name must be excluded, the Atheists might as justly require that of the Creator to be omitted also; and the Mahometan or Mormon that others should be inserted. I feel myself upon the broad ground that this is a Christian community; and that as their chief magistrate it was my duty and my right in conformity with usage, to invite them to return thanks for the blessings they enjoy, to that Power from whence, and that Being through whose intercession they believe that they derive them. And whatever may be the language of Proclamation and of Constitution, I know that the civilization of the age is derived from Christianity, that the institutions of this country are instinct with the same spirit, and that it pervades the laws of the State as it does the manners and I trust the hearts of our people. Why do we observe the Sabbath instituted in honour of Christ? Why do our laws forbid labour on that day or the execution of civil process? it is because we are, and acknowledge ourselves, and wish to be considered, a Christian people. You appeal to the Constitution as guaranteeing 'the free exercise and enjoyment of religious profession and worship without discrimination or preference to all mankind.' If the laws recognising the Christian Sabbath do not violate the Constitution, how can my Proclamation, which was compulsory on no one, do it? If both are unconstitutional, why have not the Israelites commenced by attacking these long-standing laws, and purifying our legislation? Do they deem it easier to intimidate one man, and extract from him a confession and an apology under the apprehension of their fierce and unrelenting hostility, than to reform the State? In whatever situation I have been placed, it has always been my aim to adhere strictly to the Constitution and uphold the Laws. I did not think, and do not now think, that I violated the Constitution of this State by my Proclamation. That forbids the legislature to pass any law restricting the most perfect toleration. I addressed to the Christian community, at their request, a Proclamation inviting them to worship in accordance with their faith; I had neither the power nor desire to compel any one to offer his devotions contrary to his faith, or to offer them at all. Those who did not choose to accept my invitation, were at full liberty to decline it, and if the Israelites refused to open their Synagogues, I had no complaint to make—no penalty to exact. Had they stopped at that, such a manifestation of their disapproval of my Proclamation would have been the more severely felt by me, because of its dignity and its consonance with true religious feelings as I apprehend them. But if, inheriting the same scorn for Jesus Christ which instigated their ancestors to crucify him, they would have felt themselves degraded and disgraced in obeying my exhortation to worship their 'Creator,' because I had also recommended the adoration of his 'Son the Redeemer,' still I would not have hesitated to appoint for them, had it been requested, a special day of Thanksgiving according to their own creed. This, however, was not, I imagine, what the Israelites desired. They wished to be included in the same invitation to public devotion with the Christians! And to make that invitation acceptable to them, I must strike out the corner-stone of the Christian creed, and reduce the whole to entire conformity with that of the Israelites; I must exhort a Christian People to worship after the manner of the Jews. The Constitution forbids me to 'discriminate' in favour of the Christians; and I am denounced because I have not 'discriminated' in favour of the Israelites. This is the sum and substance of your charge. The terms of my Proclamation were broad enough to include all believers. You wished me to narrow it down to the exclusion of ninety-nine hundredths of my fellow-citizens. Neither the Constitution, nor my public duty, would allow me to do this, and they also forbid me to offer any apology for not having done it.

"Many topics in your memorial and its vehement tone I pass over without comment, because I do not wish to go farther in this unpleasant discussion, than briefly to state the prominent grounds on which I justify my conduct. And I cannot but hope that when you come to look dispassionately at the matter, you will perceive that the warmth of your feelings has led you astray, that you have taken offence without sufficient cause, and that in fulminating your wrath at me, you have exhibited a temper which in the end may be more painful to yourselves than it can be to me. Not that I do not regret sincerely that I have so unexpectedly incurred your enmity, but because I suffer little when I am satisfied that I have done no wrong.

> "*I have the honour to be*
> "*Very respectfully, your obedient servant,*
> "J. H. HAMMOND."

All of which the chairman submitted to the consideration of the meeting.

Whereupon, it was, on motion,

Resolved, That the whole subject be referred to a committee, who, after due deliberation, submitted the following

REPORT.

It is evident to your committee, that, on the appearance of the governor's proclamation, the editor of the *Southern Patriot* brought the subject before the executive by stating through the columns of that journal, that the exclusion of the Israelites had given just cause of offence to many citizens of that persuasion. Some time after this, a gentleman, over his own signature, addressed a letter to his excellency, couched in the most respectful language. Had the governor been pleased to instruct his secretary to acknowledge either of these, simply declaring their exclusion an oversight, the matter would have been dropped at that point. But the courtesy usually extended in such cases was withheld on this occasion. His excellency did not, in his own language, "feel bound to answer," and accordingly he took no notice of either. This strange, and as we consider, discourteous course, prompted a large number of Israelites to address him, and his reply to them forms the subject of your committee's present report.

Your committee regret that the positions taken by the Israelites in their letter to his excellency, have been so erroneously construed and misstated in his reply. This of course they regard as unintentional on his part; but as an illustration of the remark, his excellency states in the very first paragraph, that his proclamation is denounced as unusual and offensive, in consequence of his allusion to "Jesus Christ the Redeemer." It will be perceived, by reference to the letter of the Israelites, that such construction cannot be maintained. The only correct interpretation of their language is, that in so framing his proclamation *they* were *entirely excluded* from "a participation in the religious observances of the occasion." That alone was their cause of complaint. Had his excellency, if he had even pleased *specially* to invite our Christian fellow-citizens, only gone a little farther, and extended it, as is customary, *to all other denominations,* no dissatisfaction, in the opinion of your committee, could possibly have existed among the Israelites. And was this an unreasonable expectation on their part? Or would it have been an extraordinary act on the part of his excellency? Assuredly not. He would have been but pursuing the course usual on such occasions—they but enjoying in common with other citizens an established privilege. His excellency states that he had not before him, when he wrote his proclamation, those "of his predecessors," to ascertain their mode of invitation. This your committee regret; for they believe he would have found that *usage* is against him. Of one thing they are assured; that it has been the pride of our governors to show their respect for the constitution, by the address with which they have on all occasions of this kind infused into its spirit what satisfies the most sensitive mind.

It is proper here to remark, that nothing is more common even in monarchical countries, having a state constitution, than for rulers to call on every denomination to offer up prayers at their respective places of worship. This practice prevails even in barbarous countries. If the Nile is tardy in rising, the pacha of a dominant mosque calls on persons of every sect to unite, but does not defeat the object by the mandate, and cry of Allah and Mahomet. Thus, if the governor was absolute, your committee cannot believe that a custom so general would be outraged against the followers of a particular faith. These comparisons, though rather mortifying to those constrained to make them, are nevertheless necessary. His excellency with a written constitution for his guide, has been pleased to act in direct contrast with this course. Your committee are too much in earnest on this subject to notice the sarcasm, temper, or taste of this letter from the "department of state." They decline to comment on these topics—nor is it their right to have been informed of his excellency's creed, any more than if he had been pleased to speak to us of his moral sentiments or private affairs. As citizens of the state, they are aware of the respect due the executive office, and shall not vary from the point of their rights. The feeling on their part is any thing but that of pride, that such a document should be filed among the annals of our state. With the miscellaneous remarks, theological, philosophical, they have as little to do; such views may suit ecclesiastical statesmen, and might form plausible reasons on their part, if efforts are ever made, to subvert the present constitution, and have one uniting church and state; but in the present form of the charter, it bears a far more liberal interpretation than his excellency has given it.

Neither can your committee, for the like reasons, and they are constrained to add in self-respect, properly notice the classification, in which you are included, of "Jews," "Atheists," "Mormons," &c. &c. except to expose the argument. The constitution has nothing to do with the relative numbers of the citizens—with popular or unpopular modes of faith. If either of these classes of citizens formed nine-tenths of the population, and the other tenth were Christians, with the present constitution, his excellency, under his view, must exclude the minority of Christians, and interpret Mormonism, or any other ism, as the religion of the state.

Your committee notice also in his excellency's letter, language which they deem calculated to excite the worst of feelings in our country. They cannot believe that it was penned with such intention, but it has been to them a source of much pain. They would notice particularly his allusion to the crucifixion of Christ, and deprecate it sincerely as tending to excite the prejudices of eighteen hundred years against a small portion of his constituents. They appeal, however, to their fellow-citizens of all denominations to support them in the declaration, that nothing is more common than for Israelites here and elsewhere to subscribe to the erection of churches consecrated to the numerous sectaries of Christianity; and they trust to be found at their post, in defence of the humblest of them, should fanaticism, or outrage of any kind, (which Providence avert,) ever assail them.

But on the main point, your committee in seriousness, as citizens of this state, and of the United States, would be unworthy of the rights secured to them, in common with all others, if they did not protest against the principles set forth in the governor's letter, which if admitted, would form a base sufficient to measure away their rights, and the rights of others, for what affects you now, might at another time be fatal to the rights of other minorities. Such invasions silently creeping in, some future proclamation may make farther discriminations, expressing what the executive means by Christianity, and who are Christians. The worst species of wrong is the partial one that aims at the few; that abandons principles and strives to please numbers. Few or many, popular or otherwise, the Israelites hope to be found always upholding those principles, wherein as American citizens, they of right are at issue with the interpretation of the spirit of the laws as expressed by the governor. They maintain that the state government, like that of the United States, is a government of *equal rights* in religious privileges, as in all other things, and not as his excellency infers, a *government of tolerance*, enabling rulers to give or to withhold. It would be an outrage on the constitution, and on the character of the patriots who made it free and equal, and on our countrymen around us, if any contrivance should make it otherwise. The rights therein secured form the general sentiment of the people of this country, and when attempted to be tampered with, find confirmation from the Congress of the United States, in such manifestation, as in the celebrated report of the Hon. R. M. Johnson, on the petition to arrest the Sunday Mails. To that noble exposition your committee would commend his excellency's attention.

There are numerous observations in the governor's letter, which, however much they may have wounded your feelings as Israelites, we prefer with a view to the suppression of excitement to pass without notice here. Even that impeachment of the purity of your motives conveyed in his question "whether you found it easier to intimidate one man than to reform the state," your committee, while in justice they are compelled to disclaim and repel the insinuation, will also permit to pass without farther comment. They desire to assuage, not to exasperate—and they cannot but believe that much that is harsh and wounding in his excellency's letter, would not have been penned, but for the fact which he himself declares, "that he is not a professor of religion, and is not specially attached by habit or education to any particular denomination."

In conclusion, your committee cannot leave the whole matter with a safer guardian than the public opinion of the country.

After several animated addresses, the report was *unanimously* adopted.

On motion,

Resolved, That these proceedings be published in the public journals of this city, and of Columbia, S.C.

MICHAEL LAZARUS, *Chairman.*

S. VALENTINE, *Secretary.*

5. Reassurances from President Tyler

To uphold their vision of "equal footing," Jews depended on America's presidents. Just as they had traditionally looked to the king for their security, now they expected the president, through his policies, to exemplify what the appropriate relationship of religion and government should be. Reliance on the judicial branch of government, particularly the Supreme Court, came only much later in the twentieth century.

Jewish vigilance in this regard is well illustrated by the following two letters of reassurance sent to Jews by President John Tyler. The first (1841), addressed to the Richmond, Virginia, Jewish leader, Jacob Ezekiel, clarified a reference to "Christian people" in Tyler's call for a national day of prayer to mark the death of President William Henry Harrison. Ezekiel had requested an "explanation . . . as may meet the views of those who do not profess Christianity though believers in the Supreme Being of the world." Tyler appropriately complied. The second letter (1843), addressed to a (self-appointed) Baltimore defender of Jewish rights named Joseph Simpson, responded to a complaint against General-in-Chief of the Army Winfield Scott for allegedly presiding over a missionary conference. Tyler's reply vindicated Scott, offering an interpretation of church-state separation that promised any Jew in public life the equivalent right to "preside in . . . synagogue" and "turn his eye to Judea."

◆   ◆   ◆

Letter from President Tyler on a national day of prayer

Washington, April 19, 1841.
SIR: I beg you to be perfectly assured, that in using the language in my recommendation to the people of the United States to observe the 14th of May as a day for religious exercises, in consequence of the bereavement which the country has sustained in the death of the late President, I designed in nothing to exclude any portion of my fellow citizens from a cordial union in the solemnities of that occasion. In speaking in the first paragraph of the duties of Christian people, I meant in no way to imply that similar duties should not be performed by all mankind. The last paragraph is an invitation to all and excludes the idea of any especial invocation. For the people of whom you are one, I can feel none other than profound respect.

The wisdom which flowed from the lips of your prophets has in time past, and will continue for all time to come, to be a refreshing fountain of moral instruction to mankind—while Holy records bear witness of Divine favors and protection of the God of Abraham and of Isaac and of Jacob, God of the Christian and Israelite, to his chosen people—may I then hope, sir, that this explanation will remove all difficulties, and that your voice and the voices of all your brethren will ascend to our Common Father in supplication and prayer on the day I have suggested.

I tender you assurances of great respect,

JOHN TYLER.

MR. JACOB EZEKIEL.

◆

Letter from President Tyler on separation of church and state

Washington, July 10, 1843.
Dear Sir:
The Notice which you mention in your letter of the 3d instant has only been called to my attention by your reference to it. I presume that it is nothing more

than a contemplated assemblage of certain officers of the army and navy *in their character of citizens and Christians,* having for its object the inculcation upon others, of their religious tenets, for, as they believe, the benefit and advantage of Mankind. A similar call on the part of any other religious sect would be alike tolerated under our institutions. The Government has nothing to do with the publication, nor has it issued from any one of the departments. Whether General Scott is to preside over the meeting, I am not in any way other than through your letter informed. If he attends, it will not and cannot be in his character of General in Chief of the army. He will necessarily for the time being lay aside his sword and epaulets, and appear it is true as a distinguished citizen, but in no other light than as a citizen. Was he a Hebrew and of the same tribe with yourself, his right to preside in your synagogue, if permitted or required by your laws would in no manner affect him in his military character; nor would it make him obnoxious to the censure of the Government for so doing. The United States have adventured upon a great and noble experiment, which is believed to have been hazarded in the absence of all previous precedent—that of total separation of Church and State. No religious establishment *by law* exists among us. The conscience is left free from all restraint and each is permitted to worship his Maker after his own judgment. The offices of the Government are open alike to all. No tithes are levied to support an established hierarchy, nor is the fallible judgment of man set up as the sure and infallible creed of faith. The Mohammedan, if he were to come among us would have the privilege guaranteed to him by the constitution to worship according to the Koran; and the East Indian might erect a shrine to Brahma if it so pleased him. Such is the spirit of toleration inculcated by our political institutions. The fruits are visible in the universal contentment which everywhere prevails. Christians are broken up into various sects but we have no persecution, no stake or rack—no compulsion or force, no furious or bigoted zeal; but each and all move on in their selected sphere, and worship the Great Creator according to their own forms and ceremonies. The Hebrew persecuted and down trodden in other regions takes up his abode among us with none to make him afraid. He may boast as well he can, of his descent from the Patriarchs of Old—of his wise men in council, and strong men in Battle. He may even more turn his eye to Judea resting with confidence on the promise that is made him of his restoration to that Holy Land, and he may worship the God of his fathers after the manner that that worship was conducted by Aaron and his successors in the priesthood, and the Aegis of the Government is over him to defend and protect him. Such is the great experiment which we have tried, and such are the happy fruits which have resulted from it; our system of free government would be imperfect without it.

The body may be oppressed and manacled and yet survive; but if the mind of man be fettered, its energies and faculties perish, and what remains is of the earth, earthly. Mind should be free as the light or as the air.

While I remain connected with the Government be assured, Sir, that so far as the Executive action is concerned, the guarantees of the Constitution in this great particular will know no diminution.

For your kind expression of good will towards me personally, I beg you to accept my thanks along with my best wishes for your health and happiness.

JOHN TYLER

In Defense of Jewish Rights

◆ ❖ ◆

By the Civil War, America's Jewish population had swelled to 150,000 spread across the face of the country. Approximately one American out of every two hundred was Jewish and at least one synagogue stood in every major American city. Rabbis provided leadership to this growing community, national Jewish newspapers fostered communication among its members, the Independent Order of B'nai B'rith (founded 1843) cemented Jewish fraternal ties, and the Board of Delegates of American Israelites (established in 1859) worked to protect the rights of Jews at home and abroad.

This increase in the size, organizational complexity, and visibility of the American Jewish community carried important implications for its involvement in issues of religion and state. For one thing, debates that originally seemed purely speculative concerning the position of Jews (and other non-Christians) in the United States now took on fresh meaning. Suddenly, Jews were no longer just a symbol, a "mythical Jew" akin to "Turks and infidels"; for more and more Americans they had become a living reality, they "lived next door" and had to be treated accordingly.

Second, Jews had an increasing ability, as their numbers and level of community organization grew, to determine their own political fate. They could speak out, lobby, petition, and above all utilize their electoral clout in support of issues that concerned them. Where earlier, Jews, small in number and unable even to vote in some states, were powerless to act on their own behalf, the situation now was different. Perceived challenges to Jewish rights could be forcefully met.

In meeting these challenges, mid-nineteenth-century Jews established patterns that shaped the subsequent course of Jewish involvement in religion and state issues. In each case, the Jewish community was pressed into action by its leaders and newspapers, and demanded equality on the basis of First Amendment guarantees. In each case, spokesmen for the community spoke out boldly, lobbied openly, and took advantage of political opportunities. And in each case, the Jewish community achieved its immediate ends and sensitized American leaders to the growing presence of Jews in their midst. Nevertheless, the goal of "equal footing" proved elusive.

1. The Swiss Treaty

On November 25, 1850, the United States and the Swiss Confederation concluded a commercial and friendship treaty which included the following clause: "On account of the tenor of the Federal Constitution of Switzerland [which restricted the guarantee of religious freedom to Christians], Christians alone are entitled to the enjoyment of the privileges guaranteed by the present Article in the Swiss Cantons." American Jews, who by the terms of this article could be denied entry permits and commercial privileges that Christians traveling to Switzerland were assured, loudly objected and as a result the treaty was returned for amendment. Ratified in 1855, the new treaty made no mention of Christians, but limited "reciprocal equality" to the provisions of local law. This became an issue when it was learned that an American Jewish businessman named A. H. Gootman was denied the right of domicile in Neuchâtel on account of his faith.

In protesting the Swiss treaty to the president, American Jews broke new constitutional ground with the argument that "this government disclaiming all religious distinction as to the political rights of its citizens at home can not consistently recognize such distinctions abroad." Sweeping aside uncomfortable comparisons to "state's rights" and limitations on "the negro" in the South, as well as arguments based on America's national interests, they insisted that the First Amendment was more important and demanded redress. Over the next seventeen years, their hopes were realized and the offending Swiss laws were changed.

◆   ◆   ◆

Protest by American Jews against the Swiss treaty of 1850

This Memorial, Of the undersigned, Delegates of the Israelites from various States of the Union, to his Excellency the President of the United States, *Respectfully represents:*

That a Convention was concluded on the 25th of November, 1850, and proclaimed on the 9th of November, 1855, between the United States of America and the Swiss Confederation, "for friendship, reciprocal establishments, commerce, and for the surrender of fugitive criminals."

The first clause of the first Article of said Convention, reads as follows:

"The citizens of the United States of America and the citizens of Switzerland shall be admitted and treated upon a footing of reciprocal equality in the two countries, *where such admission and treatment shall not conflict with the constitutional* [or legal] *provisions as well Federal as State and Cantonal of the contracting parties.*"

It so happens that certain Cantons of the Swiss Confederation among which [are] Basle and others have laws prohibiting Israelites from sojourning temporarily, domiciliating or establishing themselves permanently. These laws being Cantonal Laws of the Swiss Confederation have been construed to come within the Saving Clause of the above quoted Article of Convention, and in their operation, affect those citizens of the United States who belong to the Israelitish persuasion.

Your memorialists have been elected at general meetings of Israelites of different States, as delegates to lay their grievances before your Excellency, and to pray for that remedy, to which they deem themselves entitled as citizens of the United States. They humbly submit the following suggestions:

The Constitution of the United States—emphatically declares that "no religious test shall ever be required as a qualification to any office or public trust under the United States." and again in Article I, of the amendments to the constitution, "Congress shall make no law respecting an establishment of religion or prohibiting the free exercise thereof."

Ever since the adoption of the Constitution, this government has with a broad and liberal construction of the constitution acted upon those enlightened principles, which have secured the blessings of liberty upon all citizens of the United States without religious distinction. This government disclaiming all religious distinction as to the political rights of its citizens at home can not consistently recognize such distinction abroad. If conventions between different governments are made for any purpose they are made in furtherance of public justice, and more particularly for the purpose of extending the rights of citizens which they enjoy at home, into such other countries. The treaty in question has clearly failed in that object; for when we attempt to enjoy the extension of those rights, we are met by a dark-aged proscriptive law, declaring us unworthy of participating in the rights of our fellow citizens, on account of our professing the Israelitish religion. As citizens of the United States, we can not but consider such a construction antagonistic to the progressive, liberal policy of our government, and unworthy of the philanthropic fame which that policy has achieved; and as Israelites, we must feel mortified, should our government sanction Switzerland's slander upon religion.

Treaties, being laws of the land, must, as to their justness and validity, be tested by the application of principles governing her conduct; and will this treaty stand such a test?

It has been argued, that the commercial advantages this country derives from that treaty, would justify a slight sacrifice of principle; and while your memorialists are satisfied that such are not your Excellency's sentiments, they nevertheless respond, that if such were the policy of our government, Europe's despots would soon ask us mockingly: what is the price of all your liberties? Pecuniary considerations should certainly, least of all, induce a departure from principle.

Your memorialists further represent, that the clause referred to above, conferring reciprocal equality upon the citizens of the two countries, is directly contradicted, if that attempted construction be carried out; because, while it confers equal rights upon all citizens of the respective countries, it contradicts itself, by restrictions under Cantonal laws. But, more than this, there is a strange clashing of the rights of the two governments, as to the effect of their respective constructions of that clause. If it is against the *Cantonal* laws of Switzerland that those citizens of the United States, who are Israelites, come within the benefits of that treaty, then it is at least as clearly against the constitutional laws of the United States, that those citizens be excluded, and yet both Cantonal and constitutional laws of the contracting governments are guarded against a conflict with the articles of convention. The whole subjects [sic] seems thus reduced to the question: Which of the two governments shall yield, and waive its equal right of construction? This pliant clause, then, must refer to such laws only, as do not effect the general purposes of the treaty, and if a choice as to the construction is to be made, that side must be chosen, which has humanity, reason, consistency and the voice of an enlightened, progressive age for its support, and a great and magnanimous republic to proclaim it. While your memorialists take pleasure in expressing in behalf of themselves and of their constituents their implicit confidence in your Excellency's wisdom as to the remedy, and in the firmness to enforce it, they nevertheless humbly suggest, that a construction in accordance with these views, communicated to the Swiss confederation, would be followed by those salutary results, for whose obtention your memorialists are so solicitous. Such action would send a thrill of gratitude through the thousands of Israelitish citizens of the United States—it would be hailed as a timely act of national justice by the people generally, and will engraft itself upon the hearts of your memorialists, never to be effaced.

We beg leave to subscribe ourselves,
Very respectfully,
Your Excellency's most obed't serv'ts.

M. I. COHEN, *Maryland*
REV. DR. H. HOCHHEIMER, *do.*
PH. HERZBERG, *do.*
LEWIS F. LEOPOLD, *Ohio.*

REV. DR. ISAAC M. WISE, *Ohio.*
MARTIN BIJUR, *Kentucky.*
M. M. GERSTLEY, *Illinois.*

Done in Convention, at Baltimore, this 29th day of October, 1857.

2. The Chaplaincy Bill

In connection with the mustering of troops for the Civil War, Congress provided for the appointment of chaplains to the armed forces. Previously, only Protestants had served as military chaplains, but Congress now widened the qualifications to embrace any "regularly ordained minister of some Christian denomination." A proposal to substitute the phrase "religious society" for "Christian denomination," in deference to the "large body of men in this country . . . of the Hebrew faith," was voted down.

The heavily Jewish 65th Regiment of the 5th Pennsylvania Cavalry had a Jewish layman serving as its chaplain, but he was challenged and forced to resign. In his place, as a test case, the regiment nominated Rev. Arnold Fischel of Congregation Shearith Israel of New York. His disallowance set the stage for a Jewish lobbying effort of unprecedented intensity. Spearheaded by Jewish newspapers and the Board of Delegates of American Israelites, the campaign included a nationwide petition drive, a strong bid for non-Jewish support, and a personal plea from Fischel to President Lincoln and members of Congress. Jewish representatives prudently ignored radical claims that the military chaplaincy as a whole violated the Constitution. They warned instead that infringements on

Jewish equality would inevitably spiral down to affect the religious freedom of all. Within a year, this carefully orchestrated effort paid off. On July 17, 1862 a bill reinterpreting the phrase "Christian denomination" to mean "religious denomination" was signed into law.

◆   ◆   ◆

Statement submitted to the United States Senate Committee on Military Affairs by Arnold Fischel, 1861

To the Chairman of the Military Committee.

Sir, Jewish ministers being by law excluded from the office of Chaplain in the Army, the Board of Delegates of American Israelites have, at their own expense, appointed me to attend to the spiritual welfare of the Jewish soldiers in the Camps and Hospitals of the Army of the Potomac, and have, at the same time, deputed me to submit to the proper authorities the injustice inflicted by that law on the Jewish community, who cannot help viewing the same as a violation of the principle of religious equality, guaranteed to all American citizens by the Constitution. With this view, I beg most respectfully to submit to your consideration, the propriety of having erased from the said act of Congress, the words "*of a Christian denomination,*" leaving the religion of the Chaplain to be determined by election, in such a manner as shall fairly represent the sentiments of the volunteers in this respect. Such an amendment would not only be most in accordance with the Constitution, which requires no religious tests as qualification for offices held in the service of the U.S., but it is the only one that can protect the Jewish Community from unjust legislation, the only one that can ensure to them the full benefits of that Constitution, for the maintenance of which they are now freely and lavishly pouring out their blood and treasure. The Israelites have always looked with special affection on this Government, because it was the first to guarantee to them equal political rights with citizens of other religious denominations, and they are, therefore, the more anxious to keep this precious boon inviolate, fearing that this, the first step towards their exclusion from office, may be used as a precedent for further restrictions on future occasions, and finally lead to such oppressive laws as will deprive them of the full privileges enjoyed by other citizens. This subject is of no less interest to the nation in general, than to the Israelites, since history conclusively shows that the union of Church and State owed its origin less to direct legislation than to the gradual encroachment on the principle of religious liberty, which at first affected only a small minority, but eventually extended its baneful influence on all religious denominations that had not the power of controlling the Government of the country, leading to interminable interference with religious matters, to endless struggles for civil power on the part of the oppressed, and finally to fierce strife between the privileged and excluded churches.

Exclusive legislation, which, in this instance, affects the Jews only, may be used as a precedent for the oppression of other religious societies; and we, therefore, consider it to be as much the interest of the nation as of the Israelites, to have no religion specified in the Act of Congress providing for the appointment of Chaplains. Should it be desired by the Military Committee that I present myself before them, to explain more fully the sentiments of the Israelites on this subject, it will afford me great pleasure to comply with their wishes, in the hope that a just request, hitherto not in vain addressed to your august legislative body, may also, in this instance be readily acceded to, especially as it involves the constitutional rights of a large, influential and loyal class of citizens.

3. General U. S. Grant's General Order No.11

General U. S. Grant's 1862 order demanding the expulsion of all Jews from his war zone within twenty-four hours ranks as one of the worst violations of civil and religious rights in American history. The order was an irate, hasty, and highly prejudiced response to wartime smuggling and speculating—crimes engaged in by Jews and non-Jews alike. It wrought untold suffering, especially upon the Jews of Paducah, Kentucky.

Cesar Kaskel, one of those expelled from Paducah, played an important role in having the order reversed within three weeks. He fired off telegrams, communicated with Jewish leaders in Cincinnati, sent a stirring account of the expulsion to the press, collected letters of support, and rushed down to Washington where, in the company of Cincinnati Congressman John A. Gurley, he was admitted to see President Lincoln. Astonished at what he heard, the President immediately instructed General-in-Chief of the Army Henry W. Halleck to countermand the order, and it was revoked.

Although a dismaying reminder of enduring anti-Jewish stereotypes and the insecurities of diaspora Jewish life, the

Grant affair amply vindicated Jews' faith in the President and the Constitution, and demonstrated the power of the Jewish community to successfully win redress—even in wartime. It became an issue again in 1868, during Grant's presidential campaign, when opponents recalled it in an effort to win Jewish votes.

♦   ♦   ♦

Proceedings of the Board of Delegates of American Israelites with respect to General Grant's General Order No. 11 of 1862

At a special meeting of the Executive Committee of the Board of Delegates of American Israelites, held at the city of New York, on Thursday evening, January 8th, 1863. Henry I. Hart, Esq., President, in the Chair:

The President laid before the Committee a copy of General Order No. 11, issued by General U.S. Grant, commanding Department of the Tennessee, December 17th, 1862, and also communications received by him from Washington, with reference to the revocation of the same. Whereupon the following Preamble and Resolutions were proposed, seconded, and unanimously adopted:

WHEREAS. The attention of this Committee has been called by the Chairman to the following "General Order No. 11:"

> *Headquarters Thirteenth Army Corps,*
> *Department of the Tennessee,*
> *Oxford, Mississippi, December 17th, 1862.*

General Order No. 11.]

The Jews, as a class, violating every regulation of trade established by the Treasury Department, also department orders, are hereby expelled from this department within twenty-four hours from the receipt of this order by post commanders.

They will see that all this class of people are furnished with passes and required to leave; and any one returning after such notification, will be arrested and held in confinement until an opportunity occurs of sending them out as prisoners, unless furnished with permits from these headquarters.

No passes will be given these people to visit headquarters for the purpose of making personal application for trade permits.

By order of Major General Grant.

JOHN A. RAWLINS, *A. A. G.*

Be it therefore

Resolved, That we have heard with surprise and indignation the intelligence that, in the present century and in this land of freedom and equality, an officer of the United States should have promulgated an order worthy of despotic Europe in the dark ages of the world's history.

Resolved, That in behalf of the Israelites of the United States, we enter our firm and determined protest against this illegal, unjust and tyrannical mandate, depriving American citizens of the Jewish faith, of their precious rights, driving them, because of their religious profession, from their business and homes by the military authority, and in pursuance of an inequitable proscription.

Resolved, That the Israelites of the United States, expect no more, and will be content with no less than equal privileges with their fellow citizens in the enjoyment of "life, liberty and the pursuit of happiness," as guaranteed by the Constitution of this republic.

Resolved, That it is peculiarly painful to the Israelites of the United States, who have freely tendered their blood and treasure in defence of the Union they love, to observe this uncalled for and inequitable discrimination against them. Claiming to be second to no class of citizens in support of the constitutional government, they regard with sadness and indignation this contumely upon the Jewish name, this insult to them as a community, on the ostensible ground that individuals supposed to be "Jews" have violated regulations of trade, established by the Treasury Department "and department orders."

Resolved, That it is in the highest degree obnoxious to them, as it must be to all fair minded American citizens, for the general body to be made accountable for acts of particular persons *supposed* to belong to their denomination, but, as has been frequently demonstrated, in many cases really professing other creeds. That, if an individual be guilty of an infraction of discipline or offence against military law or Treasury regulations, punishment should be visited upon him alone, and the religious community to which he is presumed to be attached, should not be subject to insult, obloquy or disregard of its rights as a penalty for individual offences.

Resolved, That the thanks of this Committee and of the Israelites of the United States be, and they are hereby, tendered to Maj. Gen. H. W. Halleck, General-in-Chief U.S.A., for the promptitude with which he revoked General Grant's unjust and outrageous order as soon as it was brought to his attention.

Resolved, That a copy of these resolution, duly attested, be transmitted to the President of the United States, the Secretary of War, Maj. Gen. Halleck and Maj. Gen. Grant, and that the same be communicated to the press for publication.

4. The Proposed Christian Amendment to the Constitution

The Civil War stirred religious passions throughout the Union and the Confederacy. Many found signs of God in the great national struggle; some blamed the war on the absence of God and Christianity from the United States Constitution. In 1864, national and local associations linked to the Presbyterian church memorialized Congress to amend the Constitution. They proposed adding to the first sentence in the preamble the mention of "Almighty God," "the Lord Jesus Christ," and the goal of establishing "a Christian government."

The movement for a "Christian Amendment" struck fear in the hearts of American Jews. At stake, from their point of view, was not only their own hard-won equality but American liberty as a whole. They considered vigilance on this issue to be nothing less than a patriotic duty. The document that follows is one of the first Jewish responses to the Christian amendment proposal, drafted for the Board of Delegates by Isaac Leeser and submitted to Congress in 1865. Highlighting the virtues and contributions of the Jewish people, it links the Jewish objective with the "work of the revolutionary heroes," and calls for "the equality of all the citizens of the land . . . no matter what their religious persuasion." In the end, the Christian Amendment failed, as did all similar proposals into the twentieth century. The only legacy of this Civil War movement is an act of Congress dated just five weeks after the Board of Delegates memorial authorizing coins to carry the motto "In God We Trust."

◆   ◆   ◆

Jewish memorial to Congress on a Christian amendment, 1865

THE PROJECTED CONSTITUTIONAL AMENDMENT.
MEMORIAL.

To the Honorable the Senate and House of Representatives of the United States of America in Congress assembled:

The Executive Committee of Board of Delegates of the American Israelites respectfully show, that your memorialists are a permanent Executive Committee from a conference representing about forty congregations of Israelites in various parts of the United States, and have been appointed to watch over all occurrences which may interest the Israelites in their social, religious and political concerns. As such, your memorialists approach your honorable bodies at this juncture, to protest energetically against the amendments to the preamble of the Constitution of the United States as prayed for in the memorial of the Presbytery of Cincinnati, dated September 20th, 1864, and signed by A. J. Reynolds and twenty-one others, and against any changes in the various articles of the Constitution, to make them agree with the amendments as suggested by a conference of ministers and laymen of various denominations held at Philadelphia, on the 29th and 30th of November, 1864, and which, no doubt have been or will be presented to Congress at this or the next session.

Your memorialists take this early opportunity to offer their protest, fearing that an entire silence on their part might embolden the persons who seek to deprive them of their *inalienable* rights which they have hitherto enjoyed under the Constitution, as it was made by the fathers of the Republic, to say, that the universal voice of the country demands the amendment to the Constitution, so as to introduce Christianity as the recognized religion of the land, and thus to prejudice the minds of your honorable bodies in favor of the changes, under the impression that no one would be injured by their adoption.

Your memorialists, too, represent many whose fathers and predecessors came to America, to enjoy civil and religious liberty. Many of their fathers and friends fought in the war of the revolution, and aided to achieve the independence of the country in the contest the colonies waged against Great Britain. Others of those who profess our religion came to this land, called hither to participate in the religious freedom which they were told in their native countries was the common inheritance of all the inhabitants of the Union, let their birthplace be what it may. Many had suffered exclusion from certain rights of man because of their religion, which they cherish as their dearest birthright, as it has been the harbinger of civilization, and has conferred the greatest blessings on the world in the sacred books which compose the Bible, and which they have preserved amidst all the trials and banishments which have afflicted them. Your memorialists appeal to their history in this country and challenge comparison with the best of other persuasions as to their morality, frugality, honesty and industry. They contend that, notwithstanding many discouraging circumstances, many a bitter prejudice to which their name and descent have subjected them, they have contributed their full share, according to their numbers, to the prosperity and development of the country. They had trusted that here, where liberty was guaranteed to all by the charter which the people through their highly endowed delegates devised in 1787, they would be left in peace to pursue the course which Providence in His wisdom had marked out for them in history and revelation. But they observe with the deepest regret that they are threatened with a total withdrawal of their precious rights as citizens equal with any others, by introducing a Christian element in the Constitution. They recognize the full right of every man to worship God as his conscience impels him; they claim no right to denounce the Christian, Mahometan or heathen, for not worshipping the God of Abraham, Isaac and Jacob, or not obeying the laws of Moses as they do. They protest, therefore, against any acts of their fellow-citizens calculated to deprive them of their fullest right to pursue their own conscientious convictions.

The Convention which framed the Constitution was composed of men who surely had full faith in the Creator. Their history proves them not to have been without trust in God. Their not reciting their own creed or any creed in the preamble to the Constitution was owing solely, as your memorialists conceive, to their desire to establish a perfect equality for all modes of belief, leaving it to every one to choose for himself what persuasion he might desire to follow. Your memorialists honestly believe that this omission of a creed has not been hurtful to Christianity, any more than to Judaism. For while the people represented by your petitioners are still a very small minority, the Christian sects number hundreds of thousands, and the spire of the village church is seen near the public school in every vale, and near almost every mountain-top. Schools and colleges are every where erected, and the press, urged by the energetic power of steam, distributes Bibles, books, tracts and cards of Christian teaching, not alone over the entire country, but even in savage lands where the enthusiastic missionary endeavors to diffuse the religion which he professes. Your memorialists cannot believe that the land is cursed by God, because He has not been recognized in the Constitution, or else they would respectfully ask why have eighty years of prosperity blessed it on land and sea, in its basket and kneading trough, in the field and city, on going out and coming in? It is in vain to say, that the absence of a *national* creed renders this an atheistical nation; for the deeds of the people prove the contrary; but were it even otherwise, it would be akin to blasphemy to assert that the offended Deity should be appeased by mere words, which a dialectician can twist to suit his own purposes, and not accept of works which are the true evidences of sincere conviction.

If your memorialists could have the opportunity to appear in person before the proper committees of your honorable bodies, they have no doubt, but that they could offer you many reasons for withholding your assent to the petition from the Cincinnati Presbytery and other similar religious bodies; but they forbear at present, for fear of wearying you, from doing more than presenting their brief protest with a few reasons for it, in the firm hope that you may leave the work of the revolutionary heroes of America unchanged as regards the equality of all the citizens of the land under the organic law, no matter what their religious persuasion may be, by not introducing any clause or clauses which could give to any one more prerogatives than others possess, or only permit some to reside here by the sufferance or toleration of others.

And your Memorialists will ever pray.

New York, January 30th, 1865.

ISAAC LEESER, *First Vice Pres't.*

HENRY JOSEPHI, *Chairman, Executive Com.*

[L. S.]

MYER S. ISAACS, *Secretary.*

SIX

Sunday Laws

♦　◆◆　♦

Sunday laws have their roots in the biblical commandment to "Remember the Sabbath day and keep it holy (Exodus 20:8)." Jews, along with some Protestants, observe the Sabbath day on Saturday, as the Bible enjoins. Most Christians, however, consider Sunday to be the Sabbath day, a change sanctioned in the year 321 by Constantine, the first Christian emperor of Rome, partly from a desire to distinguish Christianity from Judaism in the eyes of the world.

In the seventeenth century, the Puritans, as part of their religious teachings, greatly strengthened observance of the Sunday Sabbath, prohibiting both work and recreation on that day. They brought these principles with them to the New World, with the result that strict Sunday laws—later popularly known as "blue laws"—were enacted in all of the colonies. Religious motivations underlay these regulations, but they also came to be defended on the basis of social justice: they guaranteed all workers a day of rest and the freedom to attend church.

Jews, as well as Seventh Day Baptists, suffered harshly under these laws. Where most Americans worked six days a week, they could work only five. On Saturday they rested to uphold the demands of the Lord and on Sunday they rested to uphold the demands of the state. Many who observed the Sabbath on Saturday ultimately faced a stark choice: they had either to violate the tenets of their faith or to starve. Once church and state were separated and religious liberty guaranteed, those who felt oppressed in this way sought legal redress.

Jews disagreed among themselves concerning what to do. Some sought to outlaw blue laws completely as "an establishment of religion." Others, sympathetic to the fears of working people, accepted the principle of Sunday closing but sought an exemption for those

139

(like themselves) who observed the Sabbath on Saturday. Still others felt that Jews should acquiesce to the will of the majority on this issue, and not expect the state to accommodate their needs.

The battle over Sunday laws proved immensely contentious. Proponents invoked tradition, faith, morality, majority rule, free exercise of religion, police powers, and the state's interest in protecting the rights of workers in defense of Sunday laws. Opponents, many of them also believing Christians, responded with charges of theocracy, religious establishment, loss of personal liberties, persecution of religious minorities, and the imposition on all Americans of Puritan standards to which only some adhered.

In the late 1820s and 1830s the issue of Sunday federal mail deliveries became the focus of national debate. "Sabbatarians," as supporters of Sunday laws called themselves, failed in their attempt to have Congress cut off the transportation and delivery of mail on the Christian Sabbath. Courts, however, proved almost unanimously sympathetic to Sunday laws which state legislatures enacted. Judges in both the nineteenth and the twentieth centuries argued that such laws applied to all citizens equally, demonstrated a secular purpose, and fell well within established state powers.

With the advent of the five-day work week, in the twentieth century, Sunday laws became less significant for most Jews. Subsequently, under pressure from large-scale merchants, such laws in most states were either cut back or repealed. So long as they stood, however, blue laws affected Jews more injuriously than did any other church-state issue. They served as a weekly reminder that, religious liberty notwithstanding, members of a religious minority still paid a stiff price to uphold the tenets of their faith.

1. Petition for a Limited Exemption

Pennsylvania, like many states, forbade "any worldly employment or business whatsoever on the Lord's day." At least one Jew, Abraham Wolff, was convicted in 1816 for breaking this law, while others are known to have been fined for refusing to appear in court on the Jewish Sabbath, which the state did not recognize. In 1838, when Pennsylvania amended its constitution, several Jews drew up the following memorial aimed at amending the state's Sunday law. Conceding that "outdoor occupations . . . might be offensive to the community at large," they sought a limited exemption to permit Saturday Sabbath observers to pursue "their indoor occupations on the First day of the week in a quiet and orderly manner" (or to attend to their fields "if occasion should require the same"). In the end, the strongly-worded memorial was printed but not sent. The Philadelphia Jewish religious leader Isaac Leeser, who preserves this text in a footnote to his *Claims of the Jews to an Equality of Rights* (1841), suggests that only "a few Israelites" supported the initiative—presumably including himself but not the lay leaders of the community with whom he regularly feuded. The document nevertheless remains significant. It represents an early failed attempt to chart a middle ground between the conflicting demands of majority rule and minority rights.

◆   ◆   ◆

Unsent petition to amend Pennsylvania Sunday law, 1838

TO THE HONOURABLE THE MEMBERS OF THE CONVENTION
FOR AMENDING THE CONSTITUTION OF THE
COMMONWEALTH OF PENNSYLVANIA.

The Memorial of the Subscribers, members of the Jewish persuasion, residing within the Commonwealth of Pennsylvania,

Respectfully Showeth:—
That they conscientiously believe the observance of the Seventh day of the week, as a day of rest, to be a divine institution, and a permanent enactment; and as such they feel themselves bound to abstain from all pursuits of labour and gain on that day. Nevertheless, as the law of the state now stands, they are in a measure compelled to rest on the First day of the week also, since they are liable to a prosecution for following their occupations within doors if a complaint is lodged against them. They do not wish to interfere with any man's conscientious scruples; at the same time, however, they are earnestly desirous of following the dictates of their consciences and the religion they profess, without molestation from others who differ from them. They are well aware that the majority of the inhabitants of this commonwealth are Christians, who look upon the First day as holy: still there is no particular religion acknowledged and recognised by the Constitution and Laws of this commonwealth; and your Memorialists do not, therefore, see any reason why they should be

coerced to observe the Sabbath of the majority. They must concede that the majority have a right to rule; but they question the right and propriety of such majority, in a republican country, to impose *religious* obligations upon the minority which that minority do not acknowledge, and cannot acquiesce in without an abridgment of their natural rights and immunities as citizens and equals of a community enjoying an equality of rights, and entitled to the same protection of the laws. Whilst your Memorialists, therefore, are willing to yield any outdoor occupations which might be offensive to the community at large on the First day of the week, and such indoor labours as would tend to disturb them in their public or domestic devotions, they respectfully ask of your assembled wisdom, to insert a clause in the revised Constitution for ever to prohibit any future Legislature from imposing any fine, or other penalties, upon Jews or other observers of the Seventh day, for following their indoor occupations on the First day of the week in a quiet and orderly manner, or for attending to their field labours if occasion should require the same.

And your Memorialists will ever pray.

Philadelphia, January 29, 1838

2. The Case against Sunday Laws

Virginia, notwithstanding its famed Bill for Establishing Religious Freedom, passed a law in 1792 punishing "disturbers of religious worship and Sabbath breakers." The law seems to have been honored largely in the breach, and the fine for violations was small, just $1.67. In 1845, amidst Sabbatarian agitation in many parts of the country, the City Council of Richmond (in the absence of its Jewish president, Gustavus A. Myers) passed a local ordinance "for the more effectual suppression of Sabbath breaking," which raised the fine for violations to between five and ten dollars. As was later admitted, the real motivation of the bill was the fact that on Sunday "the slaves and free negroes, which constitute a larger portion of our laboring class, are out of employment, and therefore much more liable to commit crime." Jews strenuously protested this ordinance, as a violation of their religious equality, and on October 13, 1845, they filed the following petition boldly opposing all Sunday laws as contrary to "the rights of those who entertain different views with regard to the necessity of keeping another day, or of those who deem it immaterial to keep any day of rest at all." Seventeen months later, the ordinance was repealed. When Virginia's state code was revised in 1849, a specific exemption from Sunday laws was enacted for "any person who conscientiously believes that the seventh day of the week ought to be observed as a Sabbath, and actually refrains from all secular business and labour on that day. . . ."

◆   ◆   ◆

Petition protesting Richmond's Sunday ordinance, 1845

To the worshipful, the members of the Common Hall of the City of Richmond:

The petition of the subscribers, Israelites, residing within the limits of the City, humbly sheweth:

That your petitioners are members of a religious community, the object of whose constant endeavour it has always been to demean themselves as order-loving and law-obeying citizens, and they aver, that they may favourably compare with any other portion of the community, in respect to honesty, fair-dealing, and moral deportment. They ascribe this general evidence of good citizenship to the religion which it is their happiness to profess, which has descended to them from a long line of virtuous ancestors, and which in this free State of Virginia, which knows no distinction among its children, secured to them without molestation or hindrance from any religious or political quarter, by those blessed instruments of freedom of body and of conscience, the Constitution of the United States, and the Constitution and the Bill of Rights of our venerable Commonwealth. The Israelites in Virginia have been long known for their sterling character, few indeed have been subjected to arrest and trial for any crime, and the prisons and penitentiaries, they confidently assert, will exhibit but a small portion of their inmates as belonging to their co-religionists. Your petitioners may with pride refer to the names of some of their predecessors who have descended to an honoured grave, some of them in extreme old age, rarely reached except by the pursuit of the strictest temperance and virtue; and they claim that such men as Moses Myers, of Norfolk, Israel and Jacob I. Cohen, Samuel Myers, Jacob Mordecai, Solomon Jacobs, Joseph Marx, Zalma Rehine, Baruch and Manuel Judah, and many others, have left their examples in many respects as merchants and citizens, to be safely followed by others. In times, too, when the country was in danger from invasion by a foreign foe, the Israelites of Richmond snatched up arms at the first alarm, and at the memorable attack on the frigate Chesapeake, they were found foremost amidst those who hastened forward to be ready at the call of their country. They felt themselves blessed that their limbs were free and their hands unshackled to serve the country which looked upon them as children, dear alike with all other persuasions; and they were rejoiced, that feeble as might be their aid, small though their numbers were, they could strike at least one blow against the enemy who threatened the peace of their fireside; for the country, too, was theirs—they were part of the legislative power, alike in the eye of the law, not distinguished by any disqualification because of their belief or religious conduct.

Your petitioners have for their part always entertained the highest affection for the soil of the State, which is theirs, either by birth or adoption, and they mean that should—which God in his mercy forefend—the enemy threaten again our beloved country, to be the foremost among its defenders, and to lavish treasure, blood, and counsel, to insure its safety.

With these feelings animated, your petitioners have perceived, with unfeigned regret, that your honourable body, by its ordinance entitled, "An Ordinance for the more effectual suppression of Sabbath-breaking," passed August 11th, 1845, has endeavoured to abridge their constitutional rights to labour, unobtrusively and within doors, on the first day of the week, called Sunday. The Israelites have no conscientious scruples, which could in any wise make labour on that day appear to them as sinful.—They, however, feel bound, by the dictates of their religion, to observe sacred as a day of worship and abstinence from labour the seventh day of the week, commonly called Saturday; and hence they think that a compulsory rest on the first likewise, would materially injure them in the pursuit of happiness, which is the natural and inalienable right of every man. They are ready to submit to any municipal law which looks towards the preservation of the peace, and upholding of the rights of any, even the humblest individual: hence they would not, against the law of this State, though they might question its authority, compel or induce their domestics of another persuasion, to do the usual amount of day's labour on the Sunday, should they deem resting from labour a religious obligation. They do not wish to enter into an inquiry as to the necessity of any Sabbath or day of rest, on moral grounds: they are satisfied that the institution, as revealed in the Bible, is of paramount importance to man, to reinvigorate him for renewed toil by a day of calm, of rest, and of reflection;—but they contend that they are justly entitled to choose for themselves what day they wish to rest, whilst they do not interfere with any other person. The Bible speaks to your petitioners in emphatic terms of a day of rest on the seventh day of every week, and they deem themselves compelled by their understanding of the Scriptures, to hallow this day as a Sabbath, and no other. They themselves ask for no legislative enactment to require others to rest on their Sabbath, and they contend that no class of citizens has a right, on constitutional grounds, to require them to rest on the first or any other day. It is not evidently an observance without which society could not exist: hence they deem that society at large has no concern with the observation of a Sabbath, as is the case with compulsory honesty, the abstinence from homicide and incest, which infractions, if tolerated, would subvert the structure of civil government, by undermining the basis on which society rests for its security. Your petitioners are perfectly well aware that there is a strong tide setting in favour of keeping more strictly than formerly the first day of the week as a Sabbath, and they know that the term "Lord's Day," formerly in vogue, has latterly given way in most cases to the Jewish term Sabbath, which signifies rest—by which perversion of terms the heads of the dominant churches have endeavoured to make it appear that their adopted day of rest and worship is indeed the biblically ordained day of rest.—Now, your petitioners mean to assert, that even if this assertion were true, and that Sunday-keeping is a portion of the decalogue enactment, it would still be one of those religious observances over which, of right, the civil power in this happy republic has no control any more than over Jewish circumcision, infant baptism of the Episcopal and Presbyterian Churches, the immersion of adults of the Baptists, or the confession and extreme unction of the Roman Catholic body. The policy of the State of Virginia was never intended to favour any religious dogmas; these were left to individuals to choose at their pleasure; and only by implication as against good morals, can any system of worship, even the absurdities of Paganism, be prevented through the legitimate enactments of Legislatures or City Councils.

If, now, it is in the power of your worshipful body to step aside out of the usual course of conservators of the public peace to enact a compulsory keeping of the Sunday, by declaring it to be Sabbath: your petitioners see no limits why next you might not deem infant or adult baptism, the confession or extreme unction, the partaking of the sacrament, or the frequenting of churches, or of all of these acts combined, as legitimate subjects of your vigilance, and to enforce them or any one of them, by an imposition of fines and imprisonment. Your petitioners are well aware that no such attempt against the liberty of conscience is dreamt of; but they especially, since they are in the minority, they will admit immensely so, if compared with the Christian population, feel themselves impelled to raise their voice respectfully but solemnly against this first breach of their right by your legislating for a class, not the whole of the community, which you represent. Your petitioners would respectfully call your attention to one fact, that there are many Christians even in Virginia, who conscientiously reject the Sunday, and keep the Jewish Sabbath, as a day of rest. If, therefore, many Christians observe the first day of the week, there are others who attach no sacredness to it: how then can your worshipful body attempt to fix with certainty, the proper day of the Sabbath, upon the mere clamour of those who profess to be the sole expounders of religion? Your petitioners, indeed, do not see how any one can defend, upon the broad ground of equality, under the law, the wholesale condemnation of one portion of the citizens, for differing upon the propriety of resting on any given day. Suppose the Israelites and Seventh-Day Baptists would be the majority in any community in this state, would not the hue and cry of persecution be raised against them, through the whole length and breadth of the land, for compelling Catholics, Episcopalians, and Methodists, to close their places of business and retire from the field and workshops at sundown of the sixth day of the week? Your petitioners admit that such an act would be an outrage upon the rights of those classes, and with their present mode of thinking, much as they honour the day ordained to them as sacred by their blessed religion, they would raise their voice against those of our fellow-Israelites, who should attempt so to outrage the rights of their Christian neighbours.

Your petitioners see with sorrow the manifestation of the sectarian spirit, which deems it paramount to bring every one to its own mode of thinking. The American United States are the bulwark of liberty, whither the oppressed of all parties have for many years been enabled to come, to be secure against the wiles and tyranny of political and religious oppression. They see, however, with deep regret, that a new spirit is abroad: that the rulers of Churches, and their adherents, are not satisfied with the equal portion of liberty which is theirs in common with all other citizens, but must invoke the aid of civil power to enable them to propagate their doctrines and practices. They feel that this is but the beginning of a revolution backwards, to abridge the rights of individuals, which have been opened as wide as the gates of mercy, by the sages of the Revolution. They believe that your legislation is in contravention of the Constitution and Bill of Rights of this State, by assigning to Sunday-keeping Christians more legal protection than is accorded to Jews and the Seventh-Day Baptists; they therefore feel almost confident, that if an appeal were properly brought before the highest judicial authority of the State, your ordinance would be annulled. But they love peace, and wish to pursue it in the genuine spirit of their religion; they love their fellow-citizens, and are proud of the good sense of the republic; they believe that freemen, when correctly informed, are always willing to act rightly, and repair any wrong which they may have accidentally committed. Your petitioners are therefore anxious to avoid an appeal to the legal tribunal, and they come before your worshipful body as humble petitioners, who crave of your wisdom and sense of justice, not to abridge them in the enjoyment of their religious liberty. They claim to be Israelites from conviction; they claim to remain so unmolested, from the security guaranteed unto them by the fundamental laws of the State, and they appeal to each and all of you, from your own knowledge you have of them, whether they do not deserve, from their uniform good conduct, to be left in undisturbed enjoyment of all the liberties and privileges of freemen, which they have hitherto enjoyed in common with their fellow-citizens.

Your petitioners wish also to state, that it is not for the sake of any profit Sunday labour might bring them, that they ask for the revocation of the to them obnoxious ordinance; for if this were all, they would cheerfully submit. But it is because it acts as a bounty to other persuasions, as an acknowledgment on the part of the city of a particular system or systems of religion, that they complain; and they sincerely think that any unprejudiced person will come to the same conclusion—that the keeping of the Sunday is no subject for municipal regulation, but ought to be referred to the exclusive action of the various ministers of the gospel, who may, if they can do so by persuasion, induce every inhabitant of the land to rest on this day. It is indeed an anomaly in a free and equal country, for the ministers just mentioned to invoke the aid of the civil power to enable them to get their day of rest universally respected; and your petitioners hope that your honourable body will clearly distinguish that in granting such a request, you take away, by so much as it is granted, the rights of those who entertain different views with regard to the necessity of keeping another day, or of those who deem it immaterial to keep any day of rest at all. Virginia has always been foremost in the upholding of liberal principles. The resolutions of '98 are justly the boast of our beloved Commonwealth. Your petitioners earnestly call upon your worshipful body to aid them in making a stand against the spirit of sectarian domination, which is now threatening, by slow degrees, to foist itself upon our country, and to restore them to the rights they would constitutionally enjoy, were it not for the late ordinance and the old State law, which is a dead letter upon the statute book.

And your petitioners, will, as in duty bound, ever pray.

3. The Judicial Defense of Sunday Laws

Solomon A. Benjamin, an English Jew who owned a clothing shop in Charleston, South Carolina, was fined $40 for selling a pair of gloves to a Black man on a Sunday. Rather than petitioning to change the law, as Jews in other municipalities did, he challenged the law in court, claiming that his right to "the free exercise and enjoyment of religious profession and worship, without discrimination or preference," guaranteed by Article 8 of the state constitution, was violated. The City Court in 1846 ruled in his favor. Under South Carolina law, it declared, the Jewish Sabbath and the Christian Sunday should be "precisely equal." On appeal to the Court of Errors, however, the decision was reversed. Judge John Belton O'Neall, for the unanimous court, upheld what became the standard legal defense of Sunday laws: that they were local (police) regulations binding upon Jews and Christians alike. He ridiculed the argument that such laws made it impossible for Jews to observe the biblical commandment "Six days shalt thou labour" and, in a prologue that Jews found particularly offensive, declared that "Christianity . . . is and always has been a part of the common law." "An Hebrew," writing in the *Occident,* condemned the whole tone of O'Neall's decision as intolerant. But an editorial in the *Sunday Times and Noah's Weekly Messenger,* edited by the well-known Jewish lay leader Mordecai Noah, offered a different view, entirely agreeing with the court's decision and suggesting that Benjamin should not have raised the issue in the first place.

◆   ◆   ◆

Judge O'Neall's decision upholding Charleston's Sunday law, 1848

. . . The case before us presents the very simple question, Is a law punishing the sale of goods on the Lord's day, Sunday, a violation of the 1st section of the 8th article of our Constitution, hereinbefore cited and set out? To satisfactorily answer this question, it will be perhaps well to ascertain what was the sense in which the framers of the Constitution used the words, "*The free exercise and enjoyment of religious profession and worship, without discrimination or preference.*" Reading over the words, one would say, the venerable men who framed that article meant to say, that a man might be of any order of religious worshippers, or of none at all; that he might worship God or not, as he pleased; that his worship might be in any form, at any time or place, or none at all; and that for these differences in faith or practice, no difference in civil condition should ever be made by law! It was an abolition of all disabilities—the Christian, Israelite, Mahometan, Pagan, and Infidel, all stand alike in the Government and people of South Carolina. To ascertain, however, more precisely the sense, we may appeal to various other sources. To the 1st article of the amendments of the Constitution of the United States we may very well refer to ascertain the then acknowledged sense: "Congress shall make no law respecting an establishment of religion, or prohibiting the free exercise thereof." This was the general law for all the Union, as standing under the legislation of Congress! There could be no union of Church and State, no religion established by law! Nor could there be any law prohibiting any man from worshipping God as he pleased! These plainly pointed to the evils from which we had escaped, in our separation from England! The Church of England, as an established State religion, had been felt as a great grievance, in at least one of the States of the Union. Against it had been poured the mighty torrent of Henry's resistless eloquence, when "he pleaded against the Parsons' cause." All had felt the pains and penalties imposed by English enactments on all who sought to worship as conscience, not law, dictated. These evils were for ever removed by the amendments above referred to. In the same sense our Constitution was adopted. This may be further illustrated by reading the draught of the Virginia Bill of Rights in 1776. The 16th article of the first draught, by Gov. Mason, will be found in Niles' collection, called the Principles and Acts of the Revolution, 124. It declares that "religion, or the duty which we owe to our Creator, and the manner of discharging it, can be directed only by reason and conviction, not by force or violence; and that, therefore, all men should enjoy the fullest toleration in the exercise of religion according to the dictates of conscience, unpunished and unrestrained by the magistrate: *unless under colour of religion, any man disturbed the peace, the happiness, or the safety of society. And that it is the mutual duty of all to practise Christian forbearance, love and charity towards each other.*" The provision is very much like that in our own Constitution; and its closing declaration of duty shows how much these constitutional principles of toleration rested on Christianity. The general definition of toleration embraced in it, is but an amplification of the words of our Constitution, which were very probably condensed from it! Again, Wm. Livingston, Governor of New Jersey, in 1778, (see Niles' Acts and Principles of the Revolution, 306,) gives a definition of religion: "By religion, I mean," he says, *"an habitual reverence for, and devotedness to the Deity, with such external homage, public or private, as the worshipper believes most acceptable to Him."* "According to this," he says, "it is impossible for human laws to regulate religion without destroying it." It was to secure this privilege of worship, as he has beautifully described it, and this alone, that our constitutional provision was adopted. The sense in which the fathers of liberty used the words, "the free exercise and enjoyment of religious profession and worship without discrimination or preference," has, I think, been sufficiently shown. What abridgment of religious profession and worship is to be found in a law forbidding a shop to be kept open, or goods to be sold on Sunday? I confess, I can see none. If there were any, I presume it will be readily admitted it hardly would have escaped the experienced eye of Dr. Cooper. Yet in his notes to 2d Stat. 707, speaking of this very article of the Constitution, he says; "This does not interfere with the right of the Legislature to incorporate religious societies for civil purposes. *Nor with the right of appointing a Sabbath, or day of rest from labour, as a municipal institution conducive to civil expedience!*" The legislation, objected to on this occasion, is no more than what he allows to be proper and legitimate. It is simply an ordinance for the better observance of the Lord's Day as a day of rest; it simply requires a cessation of public employment in the way of trade or business.

But it is said this violated the free exercise and enjoyment of the religious profession and worship of the Israelite. Why? It does not require him to desecrate his own Sabbath! It does not say, you must worship God on the Christian Sabbath! On the contrary it leaves him free on all these matters! His evening sacrifice and morning worship, constituting the seventh day, he publicly and freely offers up, and there is none to make him afraid. His Sundays are spent as he pleases, so far as religion is concerned. No one dare say to him, in the circle of his own fireside, what doest thou? No one, as he walks the street, would dare say to him, turn in hither and worship as we do!

It is, however, fancied, that in some way this law is in derogation of the Hebrew's religion: inasmuch, as by his faith and this statute, he is compelled to keep two Sabbaths. There is the mistake! *He has his own free and undiminished!* Sunday is, to us, our day of rest! We say to him, simply, *respect us* by ceasing on this day from the pursuit of that trade and business in which you, by the security and protection given to you by our laws, make great gain! This is a mere police, or municipal regulation! If the Israelite were allowed to make the objection, that he could not be constitutionally restrained from pursuing a public business on Sunday, the Infidels would say, as Duke said, all days are alike to me, and therefore, I will at all times pursue my business. Such an assumption is so preposterous, that no one would tolerate it! Yet, in the case of the Town Council vs. C. O. Duke and Alexander Marks, the Infidel and the Israelite placed themselves on the same platform, the 1 § of 8 article of the Constitution. *It is true, the alliance was altogether unnatural.* Still, both together invoked the decision of that good man and good judge, the late J. Martin, on the very question now before us, and he, with his accustomed clearness and power, decided that the Constitution did not prevent the passage of an ordinance to prevent shopkeepers from keeping their shops open on the Sabbath day; and from that decision the parties dared not further pursue their complaint by appeal. It was feared that, like its noble gifted author, it was no more; but I rejoice to find it has been preserved; and I hope, with this opinion, and as one of its main pillars of support, it will be given to the world!

If it were true that the commandment to keep the Sabbath day holy, also required the Israelite to work six days, as closely and faithfully as he is to observe the seventh day, as a day of rest, then indeed there might be a ground to say, that the ordinance which requires him to desist, during Sunday, from a public business, the sale of goods, was unconstitutional. . . . Leviticus xxiii. and 3. contains, as I consider, the commentary of the inspired Lawgiver on, and the explanation of this command. "Six days shall work be done; but the seventh day is the Sabbath of rest, and holy convocation: ye shall do no work therein: it is the Sabbath of the Lord in all your dwellings." The meaning of the commandment is so plain, that I almost fear to add any explanation of my own. In six days the Israelite is to do the work he may have to do: on the seventh he must not work: it is his day of rest! No one ever supposed it could go further. I fancy few among Israel worked every day in the six. If such had been the commandment, it would have been hard again. But it was intended to set apart a day of rest, and not to give a command to labour. The Saviour said, "the Sabbath was made for man and not man for the Sabbath."

So it remains, and so it is intended ever to remain, one day out of seven, as a day of rest: and as such it is essential to every one who labours, be it man or beast, and hence its institution and observance. There is therefore no violation of the Hebrew's religion, in requiring him to cease from labour on another day than his Sabbath, *if he be left free to observe the latter according to his religion.* It is the seventh day, which is to him a holy day, made so by his religion, and to be observed at his peril. All other days are to him indifferent. Hence he can find no abridgment of his religion in being compelled to abstain from public trade, employment, or business, on one of them. If the Legislature, or the city of Charleston were to declare that all shops within the State or City should be closed, and that no one should sell or offer to sell any goods, wares, or merchandise, on the 4th of July or 8th of January in each year, would any one believe such a law was unconstitutional. It could not be pretended religion had anything to do with that! What has religion to do with a similar regulation for Sunday. It is in a political and social point of view a mere day of rest. Its observance, as such, is a mere question of expediency. But, says the argument, on the other side, we would not object to it, if it did not give a Christian a preference over an Israelite. Where is such a provision? There is none such in the law. It is general, operating upon all. The Constitution, in the respect under consideration, considers all the people of South Carolina on whom the Government is to operate as citizens merely. It does not divide them into Christians and Hebrews, or any other classification. If the law be according to *that,* there is no objection. It is true, the Israelite must cease from business on Sunday; so do all others. His religion makes him also observe Saturday! That is not the effect of our law. It is the result of his religion; and to enjoy its cherished benefits, living in a community who have appointed a different day of rest, he must give to its law obedience, so far as it demands cessation from public employment.

The motion to reverse the decision below is granted.

♦

"An Hebrew" condemns the judge's ruling, 1848

. . . I object to the whole tone of the decision, and the *spirit* in which it was written. The Judge, throughout, treats the Jews as though they were not his equals—his fellow-citizens.—He seems to regard them as inferiors, to whom Christian charity has granted the boon of toleration. He says, in so many words, "We say to him (the Jew), simply, *respect us* by ceasing on this day from the pursuit of that trade and business, in which you, by the security given to you, by our laws, make great gain." I protest against these terms, "*you,*" "*us,*" "*our laws.*" Such language is unworthy of an American Judge, and in direct opposition to the *spirit* of our institutions. The Jew receives religious toleration in this country, not as a *boon*, but as a *right*. He stands upon the same platform as his Christian fellow-citizens, and breathes with him, the pure air of American freedom, untainted by bigotry, tyranny, or intolerance. . . .

AN HEBREW.

◆

Sunday Times and Noah's Weekly Messenger editorial sides with the court, 1848

. . . We entirely agree with the court in this opinion. The question has nothing to do with liberty of conscience at all: it is a mere local or police regulation, which should be carried into effect by all religious denominations living in the city and protected by its government. The free exercise and enjoyment of religious opinions and worship secured by the constitution, is not molested by any ordinance requiring shops to be closed on Sunday: hence Sunday is recognized as a day set apart and devoted to rest and religious observance [*sic*]. Freedom of religion means a mere abolition of all religious disabilities. You are free to worship God in any manner you please; and this liberty of conscience cannot be violated. An ordinance for the better observance of Sunday is a mere prohibition of public employment in the way of labor, trade, and business. We cannot in this perceive how liberty of conscience is to be invaded. It does not say to the Hebrew, 'You shall not keep holy the seventh day;' but merely declares that you shall not disturb the Christian by business or labor on his Sabbath. We can see nothing wrong in this. If the Israelites possessed a government of their own, they would assuredly prohibit labor on the Sabbath day. It would be their duty to do so, enjoined by their own law. Why prohibit the Christians from enforcing the same regulations? The question ought not to have been raised. Respect to the laws of the land we live in, is the first duty of good citizens of all denominations.

4. The Limits of Sabbath Legislation

The late nineteenth century witnessed a substantial increase in Sunday law legislation. By 1910, every state except one (California) had enacted some form of Sunday legislation. In 1888, a bill "To Secure to the People the Enjoyment of the First Day of the Week . . . as a Day of Rest, and to Promote its

Observance as a Day of Religious Worship" was introduced in Congress. While it failed, four years later Congress did approve a bill closing Chicago's World's Columbian Exposition on Sunday.

Jews were by no means of one mind as to how to respond to these developments. In 1892, for example, the Central Conference of American Rabbis debated whether to protest the closing of the Columbian Exposition as a violation of "sacred liberties" or to suffer in silence, understanding that Christians sought, much as Jews did, to strengthen the observance of the Sabbath and to ensure all workers one day per week of rest. Rabbi Bernhard Felsenthal of Chicago, addressing the Exposition's "World's Parliament of Religions" in 1893, searched for a middle ground that would at once associate Jews with "friends of the Sabbath," while ensuring that Sunday laws would not be imposed unfairly. In the excerpt that follows, he proposes an alliance on behalf of two legislative guarantees: first, that every congregation shall have full protection from being disturbed in worship; and second, that every American shall have "one day of perfect rest in each week."

◆   ◆   ◆

Rabbi Felsenthal on Sabbath legislation, 1893

... We live, God be praised, in the freest land of the world, in the United States of America, in a land where Church and State are entirely separated, and where every one can follow the dictates of his own conscience and the precepts of his own religion, as long as he does not thereby infringe upon the rights and privileges of his neighbor. Let now the Jew, who desires to keep his Sabbath in his own way, have the undisturbed right to keep it when and how he wishes. And let no unholy and sacrilegious hands attempt to attack the sanctuary of American freedom. May the dark day never come on which it shall be decreed by any legislative or executive power in America that one certain day for keeping the Sabbath and one certain manner of keeping it be *forced* upon unwilling minorities. The Sabbath is a grand and sacred institution—we all agree in that. But its celebration must be left to the individual; it belongs to the category of his eternal and inalienable rights. American liberty, I venture to say, is a still grander and a still holier institution, and the maintenance of it is intrusted to each and every American citizen. We praise the weekly Sabbath, we are sure that from it immense blessings will spring forth—blessings for the mental and for the moral life of individuals, of families, and of society at large.

But what the laws and statutes, enacted or to be enacted by the legislative authorities of our American States, can do for the Sabbath, is this, and only this: They can protect and ought to protect every congregation assembled on their Sabbath for divine worship in a church, or a chapel, or a synagogue, or a mosque, or any other place, against being disturbed in their worship; and they can guarantee and ought to guarantee to each person in our land, and be he the poorest laborer, one day of perfect rest in each week of seven consecutive days. All further Sabbath legislation by the State powers is unnecessary and would be un-American. But let us, let all the friends of the great and sacred Sabbath-institution trust in the power of public opinion. Relying upon this great power and upon the divine blessings of our Heavenly Father, we, all of us and all the friends of the holy Sabbath-institution, can look hopefully toward the future and can rest assured that the land in all times to come will have a Sabbath, a real, genuine Sabbath.

5. Drafting an Exemption

Legislatures in several states agreed to exempt those who kept the Sabbath on the seventh day of the week from major provisions of their Sunday laws. For example, in New York, the state with the largest Jewish population, Saturday Sabbath observers, under an 1885 law, were permitted to engage in "work or labor" on Sunday provided that they did not "interrupt or disturb other persons in observing the first day of the week as holy time." "Secular business," however, was still prohibited in New York on the "Lord's Day." Shops and factories had to remain shuttered.

In an attempt to broaden this exemption, the distinguished lawyer and Jewish communal leader Louis Marshall drafted a bill to allow those who kept an alternate Sabbath to conduct *all* types of business on Sunday. This, he argued in the selection excerpted below, would uphold the spirit of the Sunday laws while mitigating the hardship that they inflicted on "approximately 1,000,000 people." The failure of earlier efforts to defeat blue laws or to have them declared unconstitutional led to this pragmatic legislative approach to the problem. It marked a return to the former strategy of seeking exemptions on the basis of hardship rather than as a matter of right. In New York, this strategy failed: Marshall's bill repeatedly went down to defeat. Similar language, however, was adopted in other states, notably Connecticut.

♦   ♦   ♦

Louis Marshall's bill to permit "secular business" on Sunday

March 10, 1908

To the Committee on Codes of the Senate and Assembly
of the State of New York

I have carefully considered Assembly Bill No. 843, introduced by Mr. Strauss, which is entitled "An Act to amend the Penal Code, in relation to permitting labor and secular business on the first day of the week by certain persons."

The principle which is sought to be established by this bill is an important one, and, in my judgment, should be embodied in the Penal Code, provided, however, that the phraseology should be changed so that the new matter shall read as follows:

"No person who observes the seventh day of the week as the Sabbath, and actually refrains from secular business and labor on that day, or from sundown on Friday to sundown on Saturday, shall be liable to prosecution for carrying on secular business or performing labor on Sunday, provided public worship is not thereby disturbed."

This proposed legislation is intended to extend the policy of Section 264 of the Penal Code, by permitting those who observe the seventh day as the Sabbath, not only to engage in work and labor, as Section 264 now permits, but also to engage in secular business. As the law now stands, a person is permitted to perform work and labor, but his employer who requires that labor in the course of a legitimate business, is not permitted to make use of it lest he should subject himself to a penalty for carrying on a secular business.

There are now in the State of New York, approximately 1,000,000 people who regard the seventh day and not the first day of the week as their Sabbath. They are industrious and law-abiding citizens, and for that reason are placed in a most embarrassing situation by the existing law. To them the first day of the week has no religious sanction, and yet they are compelled to refrain from engaging in their lawful occupations, because the statute of this State declares that they shall not engage in any business on that day, even though their conscientious regard for the behests of their religious faith prohibits them from carrying on business on the seventh day, which is their Sabbath.

As a result, this large proportion of our population is practically compelled to refrain from productive labor on two days of the week, and are thus placed at a disadvantage as against their competitors in business, who observe one day only. This results in an economic waste, which, in the aggregate, amounts to a serious loss to the State, in that a considerable percentage of its inhabitants are arbitrarily prevented from exercising their business faculties and engaging in productive employment on one day of the week, thus reducing their earning capacity by one-sixth. This results in serious hardship to a class of the community which can ill afford so serious a sacrifice. The large majority of these people are dependent upon their daily exertions for their livelihood, and, are, therefore, constrained to either violate their conscience, by engaging in business on a day which they believe to have been divinely set apart as the Sabbath, or to violate the laws of the land, which, as good citizens, they do not wish to do, or to sustain grave financial injury, which is contrary to the best interests of the State.

This condition of affairs has the further tendency, of inducing those who are driven by necessity to violate the present statute, to seek police protection, a condition which is intolerable.

Under the proposed amendment, those who observe the seventh day as the Sabbath, will be permitted to engage in their usual avocations on the first day of the week, provided that public worship is not thereby disturbed. Hence no harm can come to any part of the community, by permitting those who observe the seventh day to labor on the first day of the week; and the policy of the law which underlies our Sunday legislation, will likewise be rendered efficacious, without resultant detriment to any part of the community.

6. The Call for Two Weekly Rest Days— The Five-Day Week

Rabbi Bernard Drachman of New York, an American-born Orthodox rabbi, became a leader in the twentieth-century effort to reinvigorate and promote strict Jewish Sabbath observance. Like many other traditional Jews, he believed that maintenance of the Sabbath was critical to the continuity of Judaism itself. Feeling some kinship toward those who sought to revitalize Sabbath observance among Christians, Drachman also recognized that the economic hardships wrought by strict Sunday laws constituted the greatest single obstacle in his path. His solution was the five-day work week. Speaking in 1915, to the Fourteenth International Lord's Day Congress held in Oakland, California, Drachman, in an address excerpted below, proposed to the assembled Christian leaders a plan "to have two days of rest in the week, one to be purely secular in character and devoted to physical recuperation, the other to be purely religious and devotional." He made similar overtures to labor organizations, bringing them Jewish support for their efforts to cut back the work week to allow increased time for leisure.

♦　　♦　　♦

Rabbi Drachman's address to Lord's Day Congress, 1915

Unfortunately, the Sabbath problem in the modern world is attended with obstacles which render its proper solution a matter of the utmost difficulty.

First, there is the difference of opinion as to the day upon which the Sabbath is to be observed. The Jewish tradition, going back to dim antiquity, to the period of the world's history in which the Sabbath originated and expressed in explicit Biblical precept, tells us that the term Sabbath applies to the twenty-four hours from sun-down on Friday to sun-down on Saturday.

Accordingly the Jews and those Christian sects who agree with the Jews on this point, observe that weekly period as the Sabbath. The bulk of Christendom, of course, for theological reasons satisfactory to it, holds a different view and observes the first day of the week or Sunday as Sabbath. It is idle to expect either of the opposing parties to give up their views on this point. Each party looks upon its stand on the Sabbath question as fundamental to its faith and adheres tenaciously thereto, without thought of surrender.

The observance, therefore, by all of one day as Sabbath is out of the question. Any attempt to enforce such universal observance by legislation would mean a serious wrong to a large part of the community and would be resented as religious persecution and tyranny.

There is another very serious difficulty in the fact that the need of a large portion of the community for a day of recreation and recuperation interferes very greatly with the observance of the one weekly day of rest as a time of worship and religious quietude. The young men and young women who have been tied down for six weary days to hard and exacting toil, who have been confined to the shop and the factory with no opportunity for the bright outdoor life which their young blood demands, are in no mood for church-going on Sunday or Saturday. They want to be out in the open, indulging in the active physical exercise for which, after six days of cramped confinement, their young bodies crave. They want to dance and romp, to play baseball, to row and to ride. They resent the attendance at worship as another form of irksome confinement and if compelled against their will to abstain from the physical activity which they crave and to attend services which they are in no mood to appreciate they are only too apt to turn against religion altogether.

This craving for exercise and recuperation is quite natural and justifiable, yet it is impossible for religious authorities to consent to its unrestricted gratification on the Sabbath. To do so would be to deprive the holy day of its devotional character and would reduce it to a day of merely secular recuperation. There seems to be but one way to overcome the difficulty. That would be to have two days of rest in the week, one to be purely secular in character and devoted to physical recuperation, the other to be purely religious and devotional.

I suggest that the Sunday and Saturday be selected as the days, as they already possess in great measure the required characteristics. The Christian would observe the Sunday as holy time and the Saturday as a secular holiday; the Jew would naturally reverse the process and observe the Saturday as Sabbath and the Sunday for secular recreation. Business and industry would, in this event, be discontinued on both days, except as regards the period from sundown on Saturday until midnight which is not regarded as Sabbath by either religion and which could be usefully employed in providing the necessaries of household and personal use on Sunday.

This, it appears to the writer, would be an ideal solution of the Sabbath problem. It would give ample opportunity for satisfying the needs of both the soul and the body, of doing justice alike to the claims of religion and the sanitary requirements of physical recreation. It would also make an end of the constant strife between observant Christians and Jews as regards the effect of Sunday laws on the latter.

What the Sabbath-keeping Jew resents in the Sunday laws is not the rest-day idea—that is a doctrine of his own faith—but the fact that the selection of the Sunday for general observance puts him in a position of inequality over against the Christian, compels him to restrict himself to five days' business, while his non-Jewish competitor enjoys the full privilege of six. The institution of two days of rest would put all citizens on a plane of equality and remove this long-standing grievance. The idea does not seem impracticable.

The Saturday is already observed to a great extent as a half-holiday in both mercantile and industrial establishments and is found entirely feasible, indeed, very satisfactory and beneficial.

It would not seem to be a matter of great difficulty to add the few morning hours to the holiday and to spread the observance to those sections of the community which have not yet taken it up.

What is needed is a vigorous campaign of education to show the community the eminent desirability of the double weekly holiday from every point of view, sanitary, social and religious. The writer for one is convinced that if the custom of observing two weekly rest-days is ever definitely accepted by the community it will speedily demonstrate its usefulness and desirability and will remain a permanent and cherished institution of our people.

7. The Supreme Court Rules

United States Supreme Court rulings that redefined the meaning of church-state separation spawned a whole series of new legal challenges to Sunday laws in the 1950s. Four different cases wound their way up to the Court, and on May 29, 1961, all four were decided on the same day. Two of the cases, *McGowan v. Maryland* and *Two Guys from Harrison-Allentown, Inc. v. McGinley,* challenged state laws banning the sale of various forms of merchandise on Sunday as the "establishment of religion." The other two, *Braunfield v. Brown* and *Gallagher v. Crown Kosher Super Market,* argued that Orthodox Jews were precluded by the laws from freely exercising their religion, since closing down on both Saturday and Sunday posed them great economic hardship. In each case, these challenges were turned down and the state regulations upheld.

The only Jewish member of the Supreme Court at that time, Justice Felix Frankfurter, penned an important concurring opinion, excerpted below, in which he cited historical precedents, the will of the majority, and "community interests" to explain the Court's reasoning in these cases. Popular opinion, however, had the final word. Many states, in the ensuing years, developed long lists of exemptions to Sunday laws and several repealed them altogether.

◆   ◆   ◆

Supreme Court Justice Frankfurter's opinion upholding state Sunday laws, 1961

Legislation currently in force in forty-nine of the fifty States illegalizes on Sunday some form of conduct lawful if performed on weekdays. In several States only one or a few activities are banned—the sale of alcoholic beverages, hunting, barbering, pawnbroking, trading in automobiles—but thirty-four jurisdictions broadly ban Sunday labor, or the employment of labor, or selling or keeping open for sale, or some two or more of these comprehensive categories of affairs. In many of these States, and in others having no state-wide prohibition of industrial or commercial activity, municipal Sunday ordinances are ubiquitous. Most of these regulations are the product of many reenactments and amendments. Although some are still built upon the armatures of earlier statutes, they are all, like the laws of Maryland, Massachusetts and Pennsylvania which are before us in these cases, recently reconsidered legislation. As expressions of state policy, they must be deemed as contemporary as their latest-enacted exceptions in favor of moving pictures or severer bans of Sunday motor vehicle trading. In all, they reflect a widely felt present-day need, for whose satisfaction old laws are shaped and new laws enacted.

To be sure, the Massachusetts statute now before the Court, and statutes in Pennsylvania and Maryland, still call Sunday the "Lord's day" or the "Sabbath." So do the Sunday laws in many other States. But the continuation of seventeenth century language does not of itself prove the continuation of the purposes for which the colonial governments enacted these laws, or that these are the purposes for which their successors of the twentieth have retained them and modified them. We know, for example, that Committees of the New York Legislature, considering that State's Sabbath Laws on two occasions more than a century apart, twice recommended no repeal of those laws, both times on the ground that the laws did not involve "any partisan religious issue, but rather economic and health regulation of the activities of the people on a universal day of rest," and that a Massachusetts legislative committee rested on the same views. Sunday legislation has been supported not only by such clerical organizations as the Lord's Day Alliance, but also by labor and trade groups. The interlocking sections of the Massachusetts Labor Code construct their six-day-week provisions upon the basic premise of Sunday rest. Other States have similar laws. When in Pennsylvania motion pictures were excepted from the Lord's day statute, a day-of-rest-in-seven clause for motion picture personnel was written into the exempting statute to fill the gap. Puerto Rico's closing law, which limits the weekday hours of commercial establishments as well as proscribing their Sunday operation, does not express a religious purpose. Rhode Island and South Carolina now enforce portions of their Sunday employment bans through their respective Departments of Labor. It cannot be fairly denied that the institution of Sunday as a time whose occupations and atmosphere differ from those of other days of the week has now been a portion of the American cultural scene since well before the Constitution; that for many millions of people life has a hebdomadal rhythm in which this day, with all its particular associations, is the recurrent note of repose. Cultural history establishes not a few practices and prohibitions religious in origin which are retained as secular institutions and ways long after their religious sanctions and justifications are gone. In light of these considerations, can it reasonably be said that no substantial non-ecclesiastical purpose relevant to a well-ordered social life exists for Sunday restrictions?

It is urged, however, that if a day of rest were the legislative purpose, statutes to secure it would take some other form than the prohibition of activity on Sunday. Such statutes, it is argued, would provide for one day's labor stoppage in seven, leaving the choice of the day to the individual; or, alternatively, would fix a common day of rest on some other day—Monday or Tuesday. But, in all fairness, certainly, it would be impossible to call unreasonable a legislative finding that these suggested alternatives were unsatisfactory. A provision for one day's closing per week, at the option of every particular enterpriser, might be disruptive of families whose members are employed by different enterprises. Enforcement might be more difficult, both because violation would be less easily discovered and because such a law would not be seconded, as is Sunday legislation, by the community's moral temper. More important, one-day-a-week laws do not accomplish all that is accomplished by Sunday laws. They provide only a periodic physical rest, not that atmosphere of entire community repose which Sunday has traditionally brought and which, a legislature might reasonably believe, is necessary to the welfare of those who for many generations have been accustomed to its recuperative effects.

The same considerations might also be deemed to justify the choice of Sunday as the single common day when labor ceases. For to many who do not regard it sacramentally, Sunday is nevertheless a day of special, long-established associations, whose particular temper makes it a haven that no other day could provide. The will of a majority of the community, reflected in the legislative process during scores of years, presumably prefers to take its leisure on Sunday. The spirit of any people expresses in goodly measure the heritage which links it to its past. Disruption of this heritage by a regulation which, like the unnatural labors of Claudius' shipwrights, does not divide the Sunday from the week, might prove a measure ill-designed to secure the desirable community repose for which Sunday legislation is designed. At all events, Maryland, Massachusetts and Pennsylvania, like thirty-one other States with similar regulations, could reasonably so find. Certainly, from failure to make a substitution for Sunday in securing a socially desirable day of surcease from subjection to labor and routine a purpose cannot be derived to establish or promote religion.

The question before the Court in these cases is not a new one. During a hundred and fifty years Sunday laws have been attacked in state and federal courts as disregarding constitutionally demanded Church-State separation, or infringing protected religious freedoms, or on the ground that they subserved no end within the legitimate compass of legislative power. One California court in 1858 held California's Sunday statute unconstitutional. That decision was overruled three years later. Every other appellate court that has considered the question has found the statutes supportable as civil regulations and not repugnant to religious freedom. These decisions are assailed as latter-day justifications upon specious civil grounds of legislation whose religious purposes were either overlooked or concealed by the judges who passed upon it. Of course, it is for this Court ultimately to determine whether federal constitutional guarantees are observed or undercut. But this does not mean that we are to be indifferent to the unanimous opinion of generations of judges who, in the conscientious discharge of obligations as solemn as our own, have sustained the Sunday laws as not inspired by religious purpose. The Court did not ignore that opinion in *Friedman v. New York; McGee v. North Carolina; Kidd v. Ohio;* and *Ullner v. Ohio,* dismissing for want of a substantial federal question appeals from state decisions sustaining Sunday laws which were obnoxious to the same objections urged in the present cases. I cannot ignore that consensus of view now. The statutes of Maryland, Massachusetts and Pennsylvania which we here examine are not constitutionally forbidden fusions of church and state.

Appellees in the *Gallagher* case and appellants in the *Braunfeld* case contend that, as applied to them, Orthodox Jewish retailers and their Orthodox Jewish customers, the Massachusetts Lord's day statute and the Pennsylvania Sunday retail sales act violate the Due Process Clause of the Fourteenth Amendment because, in effect, the statutes deter the exercise and observance of their religion. The argument runs that by compelling the Sunday closing of retail stores and thus making unavailable for business and shopping uses one-seventh part of the week, these statutes force them either to give up the Sabbath observance—an essential part of their faith—or to forego advantages enjoyed by the non-Sabbatarian majority of the community. They point out, moreover, that because of the prevailing five-day working week of a large proportion of the population, Sunday is a day peculiarly profitable to retail sellers and peculiarly convenient to retail shoppers. The records in these cases support them in this. . . .

In urging that an exception in favor of those who observe some other day as sacred would not defeat the ends of Sunday legislation, and therefore that failure to provide such an exception is an unnecessary—hence, an unconstitutional—burden on Sabbatarians, the *Gallagher* appellees and *Braunfeld* appellants point to such exceptions in twenty-one of the thirty-four jurisdictions which have statutes banning labor or employment or the selling of goods on Sunday. Actually, in less than half of these twenty-one States does the exemption extend to sales activity as well as to labor. There are tenable reasons why a legislature might choose not to make such an exception. To whatever extent persons who come within the exception are present in a community, their activity would disturb the atmosphere of general repose and reintroduce into Sunday the business tempos of the week. Administration would be more difficult, with violations less evident and, in effect, two or more days to police instead of one. If it is assumed that the retail demand for consumer items is approximately equivalent on Saturday and on Sunday, the Sabbatarian, in proportion as he is less numerous, and hence the competition less severe, might incur through the exception a competitive advantage over the non-Sabbatarian, who would then be in a position, presumably, to complain of discrimination against *his* religion. Employers who wished to avail themselves of the exception would have to employ only their co-religionists, and there might be introduced into private employment practices an element of religious differentiation which a legislature could regard as undesirable.

Finally, a relevant consideration which might cause a State's lawmakers to reject exception for observers of another day than Sunday is that administration of such a provision may require judicial inquiry into religious belief. A legislature could conclude that if all that is made requisite to qualify for the exemption is an abstinence from labor on some other day, there would be nothing to prevent an enterpriser from closing on his slowest business day, to take advantage of the whole of the profitable week-end trade, thereby converting the Sunday labor ban, in effect, into a day-of-rest-in-seven statute, with choice of the day left to the individual. All of the state exempting statutes seem to reflect this consideration. Ten of them require that a person claiming exception "conscientiously" believe in the sanctity of another day or "conscientiously" observe another day as the Sabbath. Five demand that he keep another day as "holy time." Three allow the exemption only to members of a "religious" society observing another day, and a fourth provides for proof of membership in such a society by the certificate of a preacher or of any three adherents. In Illinois the claimant must observe some day as a "Sabbath," and in New Jersey he must prove that he devotes that day to religious exercises. Connecticut, one of the jurisdictions demanding conscientious belief, requires in addition that he who seeks the benefit of the exception file a notice of such belief with the prosecuting attorney.

Indicative of the practical administrative difficulties which may arise in attempts to effect, consistently with the purposes of Sunday closing legislation, an exception for persons conscientiously observing another day as Sabbath, are the provisions of §53 of the British Shops Act, 1950, continuing in substance §7 of the Shops (Sunday Trading Restriction) Act, 1936. These were the product of experience with earlier forms of exemptions which had proved unsatisfactory, and the new 1936 provisions were enacted only after the consideration and rejection of a number of proposed alternatives. They allow shops which are registered under the section and which remain closed on Saturday to open for trade until 2 p.m. on Sunday. Applications for registration must contain a declaration that the shop occupier "conscientiously objects on religious grounds to carrying on trade or business on the Jewish Sabbath," and any person who, to procure registration, "knowingly or recklessly makes an untrue statement or untrue representation," is subject to fine and imprisonment. Whenever upon representations made to them the local authorities find reason to believe that a registered occupier is not a person of the Jewish religion or "that a conscientious objection on religious grounds . . . is not genuinely held," the authorities may furnish particulars of the case to a tribunal established after consultation with the London Committee of Deputies of the British Jews, which tribunal, if in their opinion the occupier is not a person of the Jewish religion or does not genuinely hold a conscientious objection to trade on the Jewish Sabbath, shall so report to the local authorities; and upon this report the occupier's registration is to be revoked. Surely, in light of the delicate enforcement problems to which these provisions bear witness, the legislative choice of a blanket Sunday ban applicable to observers of all faiths cannot be held unreasonable. A legislature might in reason find that the alternative of exempting Sabbatarians would impede the effective operation of the Sunday statutes, produce harmful collateral effects, and entail, itself, a not inconsiderable intrusion into matters of religious faith. However preferable, personally, one might deem such an exception, I cannot find that the Constitution compels it.

It cannot, therefore, be said that Massachusetts and Pennsylvania have imposed gratuitous restrictions upon the Sunday activities of persons observing the Orthodox Jewish Sabbath in achieving the legitimate secular ends at which their Sunday statutes may aim. The remaining question is whether the importance to the public of those ends is sufficient to outweigh the restraint upon the religious exercise of Orthodox Jewish practicants which the restriction entails. The nature of the legislative purpose is the preservation of a traditional institution which assures to the community a time during which the mind and body are released from the demands and distractions of an increasingly mechanized and competition-driven society. The right to this release has been claimed by workers and by small enterprises, especially by retail merchandisers, over centuries, and finds contemporary expression in legislation in three-quarters of the States. The nature of the injury which must be balanced against it is the economic disadvantage to the enterpriser, and the inconvenience to the consumer, which Sunday regulations impose upon those who choose to adhere to the Sabbatarian tenets of their faith.

These statutes do not make criminal, do not place under the onus of civil or criminal disability, any act which is itself prescribed by the duties of the Jewish or other religions. They do create an undeniable financial burden upon the observers of one of the fundamental tenets of certain religious creeds, a burden which does not fall equally upon other forms of observance. This was true of the tax which this Court held an unconstitutional infringement of the free exercise of religion in *Follett v. Town of McCormick.* But unlike the tax in *Follett,* the burden which the Sunday statutes impose is an incident of the only feasible means to achievement of their particular goal. And again unlike *Follett,* the measure of the burden is not determined by fixed legislative decree, beyond the power of the individual to alter. Upon persons who earn their livelihood by activities not prohibited on Sunday, and upon those whose jobs require only a five-day week, the burden is not considerable. Like the customers of Crown Kosher Super Market in the *Gallagher* case, they are inconvenienced in their shopping. This is hardly to be assessed as an injury of preponderant constitutional weight. The burden on retail sellers competing with Sunday-observing and non-observing retailers is considerably greater. But, without minimizing the fact of this disadvantage, the legislature may have concluded that its severity might be offset by the industry and commercial initiative of the individual merchant. More is demanded of him, admittedly, whether in the form of additional labor or of material sacrifices, than is demanded of those who do not choose to keep his Sabbath. More would be demanded of him, of course, in a State in which there were no Sunday laws and in which his competitors chose—like "Two Guys From Harrison-Allentown"—to do business seven days a week. In view of the importance of the community interests which must be weighed in the balance, is the disadvantage wrought by the non-exempting Sunday statutes an impermissible imposition upon the Sabbatarian's religious freedom? Every court which has considered the question during a century and a half has concluded that it is not. This Court so concluded in *Friedman v. New York*. On the basis of the criteria for determining constitutionality, as opposed to what one might desire as a matter of legislative policy, a contrary conclusion cannot be reached.

SEVEN

The Shift to Separationism

◆　❖　◆

T he evolving Jewish position on church-state questions in nine-
teenth- and early twentieth-century America was shaped, in
large part, by the widely held view that America was, and
should remain, a Christian nation. The idea that America was a
"Christian country" had its roots in the colonial period and, as we
pointed out in chapter 4, enjoyed increasing popularity in the after-
math of the Second Great Awakening. In the post–Civil War era,
Protestant efforts to Christianize America experienced another dramatic resurgence, as evangelical Protestant groups lobbied for constitutional amendments officially recognizing Christianity, and
for other religious legislation to translate the idea of a Christian
commonwealth into a reality, and as the rulings of state and federal
courts gave further legitimacy to Protestant claims that Christianity
was part of the common law of the land. During the last decades of
the nineteenth century, moreover, liberal Protestants joined Evangelicals in their calls for a "Christian America" and for the enactment of religious legislation designed to make American government and society more thoroughly Christian.

The last third of the nineteenth century, as Jonathan D. Sarna
notes in his introduction to this volume, "witnessed a momentous change in American Jewish attitudes toward issues of religion
and state." In response to the dramatic revival of efforts to create a
Christian America during the last third of the nineteenth century,
American Jews began to express public support for secular government, and began increasingly to invoke the principle of strict
church-state separation in their ongoing quest for religious equality.
Within the American Jewish community, during this era, leading
Reform rabbis such as Isaac Mayer Wise, Max Lilienthal, and Bernhard Felsenthal became especially ardent separationists, advocating
the secularization of the state and of American public life generally,

and opposing Christian religious legislation in any and all forms. Under the direction of these and other influential Reform leaders, whose shared vision of a secular rather than Christian America found expression in numerous sermons, articles, and rabbinic organizational pronouncements, the doctrine of complete church-state separation would become a central tenet of Reform Jewish thought, as it became the prevailing ideology of the vast majority of American Jews on issues of religion and state.

1. Max Lilienthal Protests

During the post–Civil War decades, Protestant leaders renewed their calls for a "Christian America" and championed "Christian amendments" designed to incorporate references to "Almighty God" and the "Christian" basis of public life into the text of the Constitution. Under the presidency of William Strong, who was appointed to the U.S. Supreme Court in 1870, the National Reform Association (NRA), which had been organized by evangelical leaders to secure a constitutional amendment that would declare "the nation's allegiance to Jesus Christ and its acceptance of the moral laws of the Christian religion . . . on an undeniable legal basis" as part of the "fundamental law of the land," enjoyed increasing influence and prestige, and a burgeoning national membership. Understandably alarmed by such developments, Jewish leaders, such as Max Lilienthal, a prominent Reform rabbi in Cincinnati, denounced the Christian amendment movement, and embraced the doctrine of strict separationism as the best and most legitimate defense against what they perceived to be a Christian-dominated state. In a December 1870 sermon on "God, Religion and Our American Constitution," from which the following paragraphs are excerpted, Lilienthal responds to a resolution, adopted by a Protestant Ministers' conference meeting in Cincinnati, to petition Congress to insert the name of God in the Constitution and to declare America a Christian nation. Time and again, during the early 1870s, Lilienthal voiced eloquent support for the "separation of church and state, entire and complete," a doctrine that he urged all American Jews to endorse. How passionately he felt about this subject is evident from his February 17, 1871 letter to the *Jewish Times,* under the title "Church and State," an excerpt from which is also included below. Lilienthal wrote this letter to protest the formation of a Philadelphia chapter of the NRA and the larger "Christian Amendment" movement of which it was a part.

◆　　◆　　◆

Rabbi Lilienthal denounces the "Christian amendment" movement, 1870

"What do the reverend gentlemen mean and intend by inserting the name of God into our constitution? Was the Almighty Ruler of All Nations less God and Father because His holy name was not mentioned in that holy instrument? Was he less worshipped, less revered and adored by the American people, because the fathers of 1776 wisely refrained from meddling with religious matters?

"Yes, what do they mean and intend by trying to declare by a new amendment to the constitution this nation to be a Christian nation? . . .

"What kind of a Christian nation shall this people be, according to the desire of these reverend gentlemen, a Catholic or a Protestant one? Which one? These gentlemen do not come out in their true colors; they of course mean a Protestant Christian nation. They have as yet too much genuine regard for the American spirit of religious liberty that they shall come forward and declare, we mean a Protestant Christian nation. But do not they by this assertion throw down the gauntlet to the Catholic Church, which ever increases in power, and challenge her to a deadly combat? Or do they presume to avert by such a declaration the dangers they fear from the ever-increasing influence of the Catholic clergy? Do they pretend to put a check on the formidable growth of that Church by adding such an amendment to the constitution?

"They will accomplish thereby neither the one nor the other. They will only add fuel to the threatening fire and put the denominational antagonists into a well-defined array; they will thereby only drill and prepare them for a contest which by such agitations will rather be accelerated than avoided.

"No, my friends, an old, true adage says: 'Let well enough alone'. Our country is in no need of a better name than free America, and our people of no better name than that of an American nation. There is glory enough in the name 'I am an American'. There is security enough against all threatening dangers in our constitution. It will protect and shield us against all temporal or spiritual intrigues and machinations. Let us not wilfully jeopardize its might and power, its wise and well-meant guarantees; let us cling to it at any price as it reads and stands; let us hold firmly to the entire separation of church and state and our beloved country will not only prosper and succeed as heretofore, but will always lead the van of human liberty and civilization. . . ."

✦

Rabbi Lilienthal on the folly of christianizing the nation, 1871

"This new party tries to christianize our nation. The clergy who are at the bottom of the whole movement are no longer satisfied with the proud name of 'America and American Nation'; no, we have to be called hereafter 'Christian Americans' and our country 'Christian America'!

"Nice times these, and a glorious movement this new organization! The trouble is that one can not reason either with bigotry or fanaticism; and that when we Jews protest against this nonsense the rejoinder is made: 'No wonder that the Jews, these old Egyptian petrified infidels, dislike this movement; they do not believe in our Lord Jesus Christ'. That we protest as Americans, or as a race that more than all others has experienced the bitter consequences of a union between church and state and like to warn other people not to revive this dangerous experiment—this fact you can not demonstrate to these modern inquisitors. For they are neuromaniacs in this regard and with such men both reason and history are played out.

"But what a shame to America—no, no, I mean to say to such degenerate Americans who are bent upon degrading and disgracing their God-blessed country in the eyes of all the world! How old, monarchical Europe must laugh in her sleeves at these proceedings in the model republic! While inquisitorial Spain, priest-ridden Italy, ultramontane Austria, and Hengstenberg-Stahl-Prussia proclaim not only the equality of all citizens before the law, but the entire separation of church and state; while one after another adopts the broad principle of the immortal Count di Cavour, *'Chiesa libera in libero stato'*—'A free church in a free state', Americans are not ashamed of reviving the old exploded union and of recklessly throwing away the brightest gem in the American diadem, the priceless jewel of religious liberty.

"At the head of the movement in the state of Ohio is the Evangelical Association of this city. About three or four years ago, several ministers traveled on one of the Ohio railroads. Seriously discussing the state of religious affairs in this country, they resolved upon an 'aggressive policy'. Fearing the continuous growth of the Catholic Church, scared by her powerful organization and concerted action, and reviewing the numberless sects of their Protestant Church, they wished to counteract the growing influence of Rome, and to thwart the schemes and plots of the Jesuits.

"No course would have been more natural, in order to effect this aim, than to cling to the spirit of our constitution, to assert and to maintain at any price the separation of church and state and to oppose 'Roman Infallibility' by the repeated declaration of religious liberty. All pretensions of the Roman clergy to a division of the school fund, to donations from the public treasury for the support of sectarian institutions, would have been silenced by the words, 'The state has nothing to do with the church; the state ignores her altogether'.

"But instead of pursuing this wise and truly American policy they now hit upon the supreme folly of christianizing the country and the constitution. . . ."

2. For a Secular America

In opposing the prevailing Protestant vision of a "Christian America," late nineteenth-century leaders of Reform Judaism became ardent supporters of the doctrine of strict separation. They enthusiastically propounded a vision of a secular state. This was to their mind the most effective response to the argument that America was a Christian Commonwealth, and that Christianity was the law of the land. Legal equality for non-Christians in America, they contended, depended upon (and derived naturally from) a secular government that separated church and state completely. If the state had no religion, it could not impose Christian religious values or instruction on its Jewish citizens. As Jews, they were not disturbed by critics who charged that separationism smacked of irreligion or atheism. Rabbi Bernhard Felsenthal, a prominent Reform rabbi in Chicago, in the following selection written in 1875 to prove that "ours is not a Christian civilization," argued that religion did not belong in government or the workplace. If the separation of church and state is indeed "atheistical," he exclaimed, then "may our constitutions and state constitutions remain 'atheistical', just as our manufactories, our banks, and our commerce are."

♦   ♦   ♦

Rabbi Felsenthal, the non-Christian morality of the modern state, 1875

Neither in fact nor in law has this assertion ("this is a Christian country, and ours is a Christian civilization") the least foundation. On the contrary, this is not a Christian country, and ours is not a Christian civilization. If the expressions "Christian country" and "Christian civilization" shall not be considered meaningless, hollow phrases, but if a sense is to be connected therewith, then these expressions have no other meaning than the following, viz.: the distinguishing features of Christianity characterize all our public and private life, and the superstructure of our polity is based upon the foundation of this peculiar Christianity.

What are the distinguishing features of Christianity said to give character to our country and our civilization? I suppose that our protesting fellow citizens will not claim that Christian dogmatism is thus all-prevailing. For this would be such a flagrant contradiction of the existing state of things that even the dimmest eye would perceive it as such. But they will probably insist that Christian ethics are at the bottom of all modern civilization, and that their spirit permeates all the public life of our country and all our American institutions. Let us examine this assertion for a moment. The distinguishing features of Christian ethics, whereby the same differ from other ethical systems, are love, meekness, submission even to wrong (Matt. 5:38–41; Luke 6:20; I Cor. 6:7). As sublime and idealistic as this principle of "love" and of submission to wrong appears upon first sight, it is nevertheless a fact that in our sublunary world and in real life it is not carried out, and cannot be carried out, and ought not to be carried out. Not submission to wrong, not meek suffering of injustice, but standing up manfully for one's rights, and battling for the same, if necessary, with all energy and all courage, resisting and resenting wrong with all might and means, that is it and not Christian "love" that characterizes our modern civilization.

The modern world regards it even as a moral duty for every man thus to battle for his rights; for, in standing up for his own rights the individual assists in better securing for human society right and justice *in abstracto*. Instead of the Christian doctrine, "Suffer injustice," the modern un-Christian or perhaps anti-Christian civilization teaches "Do not suffer injustice; resent it; and if any one smite you upon your right cheek, do not turn to him your left cheek, but strike back, have him properly punished, and help thereby to maintain the virtues of justice and manhood in the world." Such are the un-Christian ideas permeating the politics of all Christendom, and the codes of all modern states; and in no state of the Union, nor anywhere else, is there a lawbook which is characterized by Christian "love," and which therefore could be designated Christian.

3. Against Religious Legislation

As early as 1876, the newly organized Union of American Hebrew Congregations, in adopting the resolution included below, affirmed its commitment to the doctrine of church-state separation and to the ideal of secular government, by expressing its public support for the "Congress of Liberals" in its "noble and energetic" efforts "to secularize the State completely." In response to a growing number of proposed "Christian amendments" to the Constitution submitted to Congress during the early 1890s, and a Congressional proposal for a national Sunday law, Reform Rabbis devoted numerous sermons to the dangers of religious legislation, which they urged their congressional representatives to actively oppose. In 1892, the issue of the Sunday closing of the World's Fair to take place in Chicago the following year, which was generating heated legislative debate on the floor of Congress, came before the Central Conference of American Rabbis, the newly-created rabbinic arm of the Reform movement. The historic resolution adopted by the CCAR, which is also included below, did not address the World's Fair closing issue itself. However, it registered the Reform Rabbinate's emphatic "protest against all religious legislation as subversive of religious liberty," and support of the separationist doctrine upon which they believed Jewish religous equality in America was predicated.

◆   ◆   ◆

Resolution of the Union of American Hebrew Congregations commending the "Congress of Liberals," 1876

Whereas, It is one of the greatest aims and objects of this Union of American Hebrew Congregations now in session in Washington City, to encourage and to sympathize with any movement, with any organization or association which promotes religious liberty, and endeavors to uphold the great principle of equality as expressed in the constitution of this great Republic; therefore be it

Resolved, That this Convention tenders its sincerest expressions of sympathy and gratification to the "Congress of Liberals" for their noble and energetic efforts in their convention just held in Philadelphia, to secularize the State completely and to protest against all such laws of State or States, which are calculated to endanger the bulwarks of perfect freedom and Justice.

Be It Resolved, That the President of the Union of American Hebrew Congregations appoint a Committee to draft suitable resolutions and the same be transmitted to the Secretary of the "Congress of Liberals."

◆

CCAR resolution protesting religious legislation, 1892

The resolution as amended was then adopted. It reads thus:

Whereas, There is a growing tendency toward the introduction of religious legislation in many States of the Union, and even at the National Capital.

Whereas, Such legislation is antagonistic to the principles of our country's Constitution, thereby endangering the stability of all American institutions; therefore, be it

Resolved, That it is the sense of this Conference that we, as a body of American ministers, while thoroughly recognizing the value of religious sentiment, do emphatically protest against all religious legislation as subversive of religious liberty.

4. Justice Brewer and the Jews

The prevailing nineteenth-century Protestant view that America was a Christian nation gained further legitimacy in 1892 when the U.S. Supreme Court, in *Church of the Holy Trinity v. United States,* for the first time explicitly embraced the Christian state idea. Equating religion with Christianity, and citing judicial decisions affirming the historic interconnection between Christianity and the common law, the Court unanimously ruled that "we find everywhere a clear recognition of the same truth: . . . this is a Christian nation." The Justice who wrote the decision, David Brewer, son of a Protestant missionary, defended and developed his views in three lectures delivered at Haverford College in 1905, and published as *The United States—A Christian Nation,* that same year. Arguing that Christianity was the "best of all religions" and "a mighty factor in the life of the Republic," and seeking to explain why America had always been and would remain a Christian nation, Brewer relegated Judaism to the level of a tolerated creed. The publication of Justice Brewer's book generated vocal and widespread condemnation throughout the American Jewish community. A comprehensive Jewish response was published in 1908 by Philadelphia attorney, Isaac Hassler. Calling the Justice's views "erroneous and mischievous," as well as un-

American, Hassler's pamphlet, *A Reply to Justice Brewer's Lectures*, from which the following selections are taken, provided a detailed critique of Brewer's main points. Claiming that the legal recognition of Christianity was a relic "of a barbarous age," and rejecting Brewer's view that Judaism was merely a "tolerated creed," Hassler insisted that equality is the principle, "upon the platform of which there is neither tolerance nor tolerated."

◆   ◆   ◆

Isaac Hassler replies to Supreme Court Justice Brewer's lectures on the Christian state, 1908

. . . It is a discouragement when our leaders, our men of culture, our broad-minded men of affairs exhibit a narrowness of view which we should only expect in the ignorant or the prejudiced. It is particularly surprising when a man of high judicial office gives utterance to a view which is narrow or sectarian, and which is opposed to the spirit of that very instrument under which he holds his judicial tenure.

The three lectures, the first entitled "The United States a Christian Nation," the second "Our Duty as Citizens," and the third, "The Promise and Possibilities of the Future," delivered a short time ago to the students of Haverford College by Justice David J. Brewer, of the Supreme Court of the United States, challenge, the first in its very title, and all three in their content, the attention of the student of civics and constitutional law, no less than of the plain citizen to whom the fundamental principles of civic equality and the entire separation of church and State mean something. The lectures attracted wide notice in the newspapers at the time and must have been a great comfort to those who still insist on mixing up religion and government as they were a source of regret to those who believe that these two things must not be mixed at all and who were sorry to see so able a man and Judge as Mr. Justice Brewer express views in their judgment erroneous and mischievous. Whatever the view taken, the lectures are worthy of a review.

*   *   *

The lectures attempt to derive our civic life, its obligations and duties, not so much from our relation to the State as citizens in a purely political sense, but from Christian virtues and doctrine, giving to these a legal and a civic status not properly found in our fundamental State papers. That you may rapidly get a view of the scope of the three lectures, it may be mentioned that the first, "The United States a Christian Nation," argues that this is a Christian nation, first, according to history and law; second, by the fact of the multitude of Christian educational agencies; third, by the preponderance of Christians in the population.

The second lecture, "Our Duty as Citizens," derives those duties from the fact of our Christianity; as citizens we are bound to further its influence, "because of its essential importance to the country."

The third lecture postulates that Christianity is the key of the "Promise and Possibilities of the Future of this Nation."

* * *

The argument, then, amounts to no more than this; most of the colonists were Christians; many of the colonies had distinct religious predilections or establishments, and their founders mixed the economic side of their projects with pious hopes of a religious monopoly, their own; to argue anything from this today is to turn back the pages of history and use the unwise political principles of a past and gone age in a totally different, emancipated present.

The same argument applies to recitals from the constitutions of the new States adopted after the Revolution, nearly all of which contained distinct Christian preferences and positive requirements; some providing for the public support of the Christian religion by appropriations from the public funds, or by the laying of a tax; others requiring a "profession of the Christian faiths" as an indispensable condition to holding office; some required Protestant Christian qualifications, being aimed obviously at Catholics. Some of these provisions lasted for many years; some still hold in the constitutions of the States. Does anybody argue for them today? And will anyone fairly argue their justice or draw any conclusion other than that they are the relics of a barbarous age, sectarian and un-American? The very course of elimination which, little by little, they have suffered, shows that the enlightened sense of the American people opposes these ancient and worn-out principles, and the recent action of France shows that the enlightened sense of the world moves in the same direction in which the United States has, or has always been supposed to have, moved. Those that remain, as in some of the constitutions of the New England States, remain just as bad habits will cling—they are hard to get rid of. But you cannot found a good argument on a bad habit.

* * *

This Republic is called a Christian nation then by a perversion of historical and legal truth by the force of the majority, and the fact that it is called a Christian nation imposes no duty whatever upon any citizen, except the duty to combat the idea. The duties of citizens are derived from the fact that they are citizens, partners in the national enterprise. Ask the Deist, or the Jew, or the Agnostic whether the fact that this Republic is called by somebody a Christian nation imposes any duty upon him, and he, of course, will say, naturally, "no." All can be good citizens, whether they are Christians, Jews, Agnostics, Infidels, Unitarians, Buddhists, Deists or any other kind of religionist or non-religionist. Will it be asserted that Americans who are not Christians are not good citizens, ipso facto? Ask such a man whether he feels any lack of power to discharge his duties as a good citizen, such as to vote honestly and intelligently, to pay his taxes, to take an interest in the affairs of his community, his State, his country, to serve his country in the field, if necessary, in time of war, and he will say "no." His own religious system, whatever that may be, is quite sufficient for his private purposes; his sense of civic obligation may be fostered by the morality taught him in his church or he may not go to a church at all; yet he is no less a good citizen. The Christianity of some of our greatest men has been of a shadowy character. Thomas Jefferson was a Deist. Who will deny his entire patriotism and his whole-souled Americanism? But this matter carries its own refutation.

There is no doubt, as Justice Brewer says, that Christianity is entitled to the tribute of respect. So are all religions which are sincerely held, and it merely demeans a religion to force upon it the artificial support of the law. But when Mr. Justice Brewer carries the respect which he has in mind to the extreme of making this statement:

"From the standpoint of citizenship the treatment of Christianity may be regarded as in some respects similar to that which is accorded and is due to the national flag."

we must enter our respectful dissent. All religions must be respected. None is to be placed on such a plane as to be accorded the general sentiment with which the flag, typical of the sovereignty of the whole people, is held, because Christianity is simply the private belief of those who profess it.

But the logic of Justice Brewer's premises requires him to ask that citizens who do not share in Christian beliefs ought "ever to bear in mind the noble part Christianity has taken in the history of the Republic," and he says: "Strike from the history of this country all that the Christian Church has done in the interest and to further the cause of peace and there is not as much life left as was found in the barren fig tree." He mentions that it has stood for education and benevolence—as if it stood for these more than any other good religion; and if it did, that gives it no greater official status. And he concludes: "When one who loves his country realizes this fact, does there not appear before him a clear vision of his duty to further its influence?" No one denies that Christianity has been a civilizing factor. No fair-minded person will deny that other religions and systems of philosophy also have been civilizing factors; and it is to be supposed that each believes his own to be the best of the factors making for civilization. As a Jew will not call upon a non-Jew as a national duty to promote Judaism, because he thinks it is a civilizing factor of the highest value, so Christianity cannot call upon the Jew, or any other non-Christian, to promote

Christianity as a civic duty. These duties are essentially private and personal, and a citizen is not in any sense required to further the influence of a religion in which he does not believe. Will the Protestant persecuted in the countries of Greek Christian persuasion be moved to further the influence of the Greek Christian Church because it is the predominant religion of the country and because its adherents assert that the very life of the country depends upon it?

* * *

This survey indicates the contents of Justice Brewer's lectures. There are other errors of the usual kind in the lectures in assuming virtues and ideals to be Christian which were virtues and ideals long before Christianity appeared in the world; as e.g. the ideal of universal peace, which the Justice gives credit for to Christianity, though he cites texts from the Jewish Bible which disprove his statement; so he speaks of the "Christian" doctrine of the fatherhood of God and the brotherhood of man as one which this Republic stands for. This is only Christian by appropriation. But then this is like the common error of calling everything good "Christian," and need not be dwelt on.

As a whole, the point of view or attitude of mind of the lectures discloses the persistence of religious ideas, a thought with which this paper began. Upon no other theory can an argument such as was made by the learned lawyer be excused or explained. A principle promulgated hundreds of years ago in the mother country, with its established church, a principle petrified in judicial precedent, is carried down by the ultra conservatism of the law and the unconscious bias of Christian judicial minds into the jurisprudence of a country which has no established church and which revolted from the restricted liberties of the mother and proclaimed a new policy. The historical documents which we were guilty of when we were an infant people in our swaddling clothes, closely tied to the maternal apron-string, we are told still mark us as a Christian nation, though we thought we had cut that string and stood out firmly on our own legs, with our eyes set in a new direction. We are told that this is not so; that while we have no established church we have a favored religion. I cannot help thinking that they who thus think in sincerity and earnestness that they add to the strength and glory of this nation by such assertions, really lower it again to the levels from which we thought we had permanently arisen.

The Jew is a distinctively, perhaps the distinctively, non-Christian element in the American population. There are many others who do not yield any active allegiance to the Christian faith, but since they are not easily grouped, they are not as easily distinguishable. All these non-Christian citizens, with their Christian fellow-citizens, all citizens as such, have the privilege of combating an erroneous idea, a bit of flotsam brought down by the currents of the past. I say "privilege" because citizens who take this attitude take the real American attitude and are merely asserting the principle of fair play and equality.

There are a great number of well-meaning people in the United States who are so conscious of the rectitude of their purposes and the entire value of their ideas that they benevolently insist on making all come up to and adopt their standards and doctrines. Against this philanthropy it is sometimes necessary to set the unreasoning Constitution of the United States. The statesmanlike utterance in the Smoot case of the Senator of Pennsylvania may be commended for perusal in this connection. And I cannot do better than quote a sentence or two from that statement, as a recent reminder that the American Government has no concern whatever with religion: "In this country of ours religious belief is not an offense or a defense. A man may believe what he chooses without fear of molestation from the law or privation of his civil rights." "Nor am I disposed to challenge the wisdom of the fathers of this government who provided that in such matters every man should be protected in his individual belief."

Let the platform be: Government and law in America shall not favor any religion nor intermeddle with religion in any way whatever. This will lead to the best unity, mutual respect and entire equality and maintain the real strength and best glory of this Republic.

EIGHT

Religion in the Public Schools

+ ◆ +

A s noted earlier, the issue that stood at the heart of the church-state debates in late-nineteenth- and twentieth-century America and affected American Jews significantly concerned the emotional question of religion in the public schools.

The development of the free public school system in antebellum America coincided with the immigration of tens of thousands of German Jews, who embraced the public school ideal, and whose children flocked to these schools in ever increasing numbers. By the 1860s and 1870s, American Jews had become ardent supporters of public school education, enthusiastically embracing the opportunities and promise offered by a free, tax-supported school system open to all children, rich or poor, of all religious faiths. The vast majority of Jewish children were enrolled in public schools, receiving their religious instruction in Sabbath, Sunday, or supplementary afternoon congregational schools established and maintained by the Jewish community. For nineteenth- and early-twentieth-century American Jews, many of whom were new immigrants to these shores, the public schools had become important vehicles of Americanization and integration into American society, where students were taught the democratic values and civic virtues necessary for good citizenship. Public education not only inculcated reading, writing and arithmetic, but fostered religious and moral virtues.

Believing that religion and religious instruction should remain a private matter, the province of the church or synagogue, Jewish leaders such as Isidor Busch, Isaac Mayer Wise, and Max Lilienthal advocated the ideal of nonsectarian, religiously-neutral public school education. "It is our settled opinion here," Wise wrote as early as 1870, "that the education of the young is the business of the State, and that religious instruction . . . is the duty of religious bodies. Neither ought to interfere with the other." Over the years, as Lloyd Gartner has suggested, Wise's "settled opinion" became Jewish communal "ideology."

This Jewish commitment to nonsectarian public school education was not universally shared. Public schools in most parts of the United States, from their very inception during the three decades prior to the Civil War, had been culturally Protestant, requiring compulsory Bible reading and classroom prayers as well as other devotional exercises. "The schools," one historian writes, "were permeated with a missionary Protestantism that their proprietors associated with general morality." Jews who attended America's public schools then and later, vividly recalled the "Christian ambience" of the classroom: the school day often began with morning religious exercises, including readings from the Protestant King James version of the Bible, the recitation of the Lord's Prayer, and the singing of hymns. Christian holidays such as Christmas and Easter were regularly celebrated. Massachusetts, and then several other states, enacted laws mandating Bible reading and school prayer. Public schools should not be "godless," Massachusetts legislators proclaimed. While they agreed that "sectarianism" was constitutionally prohibited, religion—by which they usually meant Protestantism—was not. Politicians, Protestant clergymen, and professional educators alike, spurred by their desire to assimilate and control the largely Catholic immigrants, fought for control of the public school curriculum and called for a new emphasis on "moral education," which was understood to be predicated upon Protestant religious teachings and values.

During the last two decades of the nineteenth century, evangelical Protestant groups and their leaders, in response to Catholic and Jewish efforts to remove religion from the classroom, began a concerted campaign to restore the practice of reading from the King James Bible and the reciting of daily prayers as part of school exercises, where these had been halted, and to strengthen the religious component of public school education throughout the country. Jews overwhelmingly opposed these efforts, believing based on past experience that such teachings (which often included the reading of anti-Jewish passages from the New Testament) would be blatantly offensive to Jewish sensibilities. Religion, Jews argued, should be practiced at home or at church—not in the classroom.

Beginning in 1906, the Central Conference of American Rabbis (CCAR), the Reform rabbinical organization, led the largely successful Jewish fight against the spread of Bible reading and other religious exercises in the schools. Determined to protect Jewish school children and to fight for their religious liberty, it established a standing Committee on Church and State to combat "sectarianism in the public schools" and to marshall the necessary evidence to prove that "morning religious exercises" in most public schools involved "Protestant religious worship," and as such, were both offensive to religious minorities and un-American. "Church and School," it argued, "must be divorced." The committee published a well-researched pamphlet entitled *Why the Bible Should Not Be Read in the Public Schools,* which was distributed in every state where the issue was being debated, and organized effective protests calling for church and state to be separated.

The CCAR position on the issue of religion in the schools would remain the prevailing one within the American Jewish community for decades to come. It came to be shared by the Synagogue Council of America (representing all branches of American Judaism) and by the National Jewish Community Relations Advisory Council (NJCRAC), representing a wide spectrum of Jewish Community Relations agencies, including the American Jewish Congress and the American Jewish Committee. In 1948, these two umbrella organizations formed a Joint Committee on Religion and the Public School (later the Joint Advisory Committee on Religion and State), which formulated public statements and drafted legal briefs in opposition to prayer, Bible reading, religious holiday observances in the public schools, and the teaching of religion under the guise of "moral and spiritual values." Their policy statements and positions represent what many consider to be the Jewish communal consensus on these issues.

Yet, as some of the documents included in this section indicate, Jewish views on these issues have never been quite so monolithic. As much as they opposed sectarianism in the public schools, many Jews felt that there should be some accommodation for classroom Bible reading and prayer in the schools. A number of Jewish leaders staunchly favored "released time" proposals for religious instruction outside the public school premises, believing such proposals to be both constitutional and "highly commendable." During the 1960s, a vocal minority of rabbis and other Jewish leaders would publicly support school prayer as well.

1. "Temples of Liberty Unpolluted":
The Development of Jewish Attitudes toward
the Public Schools

The middle decades of the nineteenth century witnessed a significant transformation in the educational practices of American Jews. In the 1840s, wealthier Jews often sent their children to elite Jewish private schools or other private academies, and poorer Jews, particularly immigrants, might attend synagogue-run schools that taught both Jewish and general subjects. One generation later, by the 1870s, these schools had all closed, and the vast majority of American Jews attended public schools, pursuing their Jewish studies in supplementary programs that met after school or on weekends. Rather than opting for a parochial school system of their own, as Catholics did, Jews decisively cast their lot with public education. They did so, however, with the clear understanding that, as the Cincinnati Jewish leader Julius Freiberg put it in 1874, the public schools would stand firm as "temples of liberty . . . not polluted by sectarianism."

The debate between proponents of Jewish schools and proponents of public schools erupted in 1855 into the pages of the American Jewish monthly, the *Occident*. Isidor Busch (later Bush) of St. Louis, who had immigrated just six years before from Vienna where he had been involved in both Jewish publishing and radical politics, urged Jewish parents to send their children to the public schools, which he described as a "grand institution." Attacking Jewish day schools as "separationist," he advocated the establishment of "good Sabbath, Sunday and evening schools for religious and Hebrew instruction only." The *Occident's* editor, the Jewish traditionalist Isaac Leeser, strongly disagreed. To him the American public school was less a "temple of liberty" than a fundamentally Christian enterprise where Jews, as a tolerated minority, were intimidated into concealing their faith. In a note appended to Busch's article he reiterated his longstanding belief that Jewish children should attend Jewish schools.

◆ ◆ ◆

Isidor Busch in praise of public schools, 1855

The income of the St. Louis public schools during the year 1854, amounted to $87,088.55, and is increasing every year. The value of its real estate in St. Louis far exceeds one million of dollars! Religious, or rather Christian instruction has been kept out of its system by its wise founders, and I have some reason to believe that this has been done partly, with regard to our confession. One of the directors of the present school-board is an Israelite (Mr. Adolph Levi). He, and every good republican, whatever his individual religious views may be, will watch, that no sectarian influence shall ever be permitted to control it. And *why* should we refuse to participate in the blessings of this grand institution, towards whose support we contribute our mite, and to the benefits of which we are fully entitled?

Thus we have arrived at the second question; and I do not hesitate to declare that, after mature reflection and due consideration of all its bearings, I am utterly opposed to all sectional or sectarian schools, nor would I change my opinion if our means were as ample as they are deficient.

* * *

It is my firm conviction, that a Jewish school, embracing all branches of instruction, could not exist for one year in St. Louis, and would at the same time be prejudicial, in many respects, to our children; that it would be resorted to but by a very small number, and would thus leave by far the greater number of our sons and daughters without all religious instruction. And I believe, on the other hand, that by devoting our zeal, means and energy to an exclusively religious school, in the way we have proposed, sending our children at the same time to our public schools for the acquirement of other branches of learning, the result would exceed our most sanguine expectations:—that thus our children will become good pious Israelites, and worthy American citizens, our pleasure in life, our support and pride in the eve of our days.

Say you will try it, and let us join hand in hand.

◆

Isaac Leeser's reply

Mr. Bush overrates the advantage of a public school education, and underrates the difficulties of evening religious schools. The mode of instructing children in the Hebrew, &c., in the extra hours, has been tried and has signally failed; if the success in St. Louis will be more in accordance with the wishes of its advocates, let time show. We are content to let experience justify or condemn the efforts we have made, and caused others to make, in establishing separate Jewish schools.

2. The Nineteenth-Century Case for Nonsectarian Public Schools

Having cast their lot with the public schools, American Jews in various cities labored to purge the schools of practices that they considered sectarian, notably Bible readings and the recitation of Christian prayers. Sometimes they worked hand in hand with Catholics, who resented the reading of the Protestant King James translation of the Bible in the schools, preferring the Douay version that they considered authoritative. Many Jews found both of these English versions unacceptable, since they reflected Christian interpretations of the text in their translations and headnotes, and also included the New Testament that Jews do not recognize.

The issue of the Bible in the public schools became particularly divisive in nineteenth-century Cincinnati, a city with large numbers of Protestant, Catholic, and Jewish schoolchildren. After many years of wrangling, and in an effort to make the public schools all-inclusive, the Board of Education in 1869 ended Bible readings and resolved that "Religious instruction and reading of religious books, including the Holy Bible, are prohibited in the Common Schools of Cincinnati." Rabbi Isaac Mayer Wise of Cincinnati, in an editorial published in his newspaper, the *American Israelite,* and excerpted below, endorsed this decision, arguing that "We want secular schools and nothing else." He and many of his fellow Reform Jews opposed both Protestants who sought to inject their faith into the public schools and Catholics who sought state funds for schools of their own. The Superior Court of Cincinnati in the celebrated case of *John D. Minor, et al. v. Board of Education of Cincinnati, et al.* threw out the Board's order, in a majority decision that extolled the Bible's "sacred character." The Supreme Court of Ohio, however, reversed this decision, calling for a "hands off" policy on matters pertaining to religion as well as "protection to the minority."

A few years later in San Francisco, a community similarly divided among children of different faiths, the public schools again served as a battleground between those alarmed at "God-less" schools and others sworn to protect them from becoming "sectarian." Rev. John Hemphill, pastor of the city's Calvary Presbyterian Church, published two sermons demanding the recitation of the Lord's Prayer in the public schools. In reply, Joseph R. Brandon, a Jewish lawyer who has been described "as the leading defender of the civil rights of California Jewry in the nineteenth century," published a pamphlet, excerpted here, in which he lauded "unsectarian education," describing it as "the hope and salvation of the Jew." Akin to Rabbi Wise, he claimed the middle ground for Jews, calling for vigilant pro-tection of the public schools from "sectarianism, whether in the garb of Catholic priest, or Protestant minister."

◆　　◆　　◆

Rabbi Wise for secular public schools, 1869

The war cry for and against the Bible in the public schools of Cincinnati is loud, emphatic, and even passionate. . . . We have said nothing on the topic, because our readers know that we are opposed to Bible readings in the schools. We want secular schools, and nothing else. Nor has the State a shadow of a right to support any other. As Jews, we do not want any body to teach our young ones the religion of our fathers. We do it all ourselves. Our schools for this special purpose suffice to do it all right. We do not like to see our young ones indoctrinated by headings contrary to truth, and translations often refuted by men like Gesenius, Ewald, Hitzig, Umbrelt and other honest critics and acknowledged linguists. We do not wish our young folks to hear their teachers say things in school which the scholars know to be contrary to truth, and in many instances know better than the teacher. It places the master in an awkward light before his pupils. It does no damage to our cause, because one hour weekly in our Sabbath schools upsets all the sectarian precepts imposed in a week upon a scholar; it damages the reputa-tion of the teacher with his scholars. We can not be in favor of the Bible in the public schools, although we have no material objections to urge against it from our religious stand-point.

From a general stand-point, however, we are opposed to Bible readings in the public schools. The American people consists of a conglomeration of nationalities and sects united by the Constitution and laws of the United States, the common interests, and the love of liberty and independence. The gist of the whole is, we agree to disagree on every point except the public government, which we agree to support, maintain and obey. This is in perfect consonance with our ideas of personal freedom, civil and religious liberty. It is admitted that a free government relies for its very existence on an enlightened people. Therefore we must have schools. Hence we have public schools to the purpose of educating enlightened citizens. Again, it must be the object of a good government to aid in the development of the resources and wealth of the country. Intelligence is the main wealth of a people. Little Rhode Island is wealthier than the large and fertile Basarabia. The intelligence of a people is cultivated first and foremost in the schools. Therefore, again, we have public schools. The morals of a people are always in strict proportion to its intelligence and freedom. Therefore all the bombastic and grandiloquent phrases like "the basis of all civilization," "the groundwork of public morals," "the fundamental principle of Christian government," and all the like actually mean nothing in this connection. The public schools are institutions for the education of free, intelligent and enlightened citizens. That is all. To this end we need good secular schools and nothing else.

The State has no religion; because we, the people who are the State, agreed to disagree on this essential point. Having no religion it can not impose any religious instruction on the citizen, adult or child. The Bible is the book of religion, all admit this; by what right is it imposed on the public schools? We disagree on this book which some call the Bible and others call a mutilated translation thereof. Who has a right to force upon the community that particular Bible in the public schools or anywhere else? Citizens have the unquestionable right to maintain that they agreed to disagree on religion, and to hold you to the contract in the management of the public schools.

*   *   *

If churches, chapels, preachers, ministers, deacons, Sabbath schools, tracts, teachers, parsons and pious women, street preachers, prayer meetings, revivals, camp meetings, missionaries, colporteurs, &c., can not guard Christianity against the advances of infidelity, the Bible readings in the public schools, thus much is certain, can not do it. If that reading promulgates Christianity, then it is undoubtedly contrary to the Constitution and laws of Ohio, which prohibit the State to support any particular form of religion.

The arguments in favor of the Bible in the public schools are all vulnerable, however pompously they may be announced. If we are to be one people, we must remove the disuniting elements from our State institutions [and strive to?] afford the benefit of education to all, in order to unite all in the bonds of cultivated intelligence. The growth of freedom depends on the progress of enlightenment, and *vice versa*. Enlightenment springs from the sciences. Therefore let us have good secular schools, and let the churches care for the progress of religion.

◆

Joseph Brandon on protecting public education from sectarianism, 1875

Mr. Hemphill, in his cry about Godless schools, evidently represents that class of men who must see the name of God stamped upon everything; who are uneasy because it does not appear in the Constitution of the United States, and are continually agitating to get it there, as the first step to sectarianizing the Government. What doctrine is this? Cannot things speak of God to the soul of man without the letters of His name being graven upon them? Do flowers speak to us of Him?—yet we find not His name on them. Do we see the lightning assume the form of the letters of His name, or hear the thunder pronounce the sound?—yet, *they* speak to us of Him. Does the wind shriek His name to us in the tempest, or whisper it in the zephyr?—yet they speak to us of Him. Do the heavens declare His glory, and the earth His handiwork?—"There is no speech, there is no language, yet their voice is heard." And if the name of God does not appear in the Constitution of the United States, surely to him who has God in his heart His hand is seen therein, and he may exclaim with the magicians of Egypt, "The finger of God is here." . . .

The hope of all thinking men as the means to this end is education—education of the highest order—the cultivation of science, the exercise of reason, *unlimited* in its objects; but to this end it must be UNSECTARIAN. None must be shut out from that light which is to dissipate the clouds of bigotry and prejudice, and hasten the appearance of the cloudless sky of which we have spoken, and whence the heavenly dew distils.

Education—unsectarian education is the hope and salvation of the Jew, as of all who have passed through religious persecution; for it is from the deep, dark clouds of ignorance, which bespeak its absence among men, that the direst shafts of bigotry and persecution which have fallen upon our people and others have proceeded. Well, indeed, and earnestly may we labor for its diffusion, and seek not to drive children from, but to persuade and invite them to the common schools by removing all obstacles in the way.

Let our education be of the widest kind. Let reason and religion, too long divorced, too long at enmity, be reconciled. Let all of us, with free thought and free, unsectarian education, seek to lift ourselves and our fellows above the clouds of ignorance, sectarianism and prejudice, until these clouds can be dissipated. . . .

No, reader; because sectarian prayer has not been permitted in the schools, the friend of true education and true religion need not wail with

Mr. Hemphill—that a battle has been lost—that Rome has conquered. He may rather rejoice that free thought, free education, free religion has gained a victory over the churchmen of all denominations: that the great principle has at last been enunciated, that the State, which should be the common parent and protector of all its children—majority or minority—few or many—will not lend its aid to dispense the particolored light of any particular sect, but only that colorless, illuminating principle which is common to all; and let us fervently hope, and at the same time be vigilant, that sectarianism, whether in the garb of Catholic priest, or Protestant minister, rob us not of the victory.

America's flag—the star-spangled banner—should symbolize the roof of that grand, common, unsectarian, religious temple of all mankind—THE CLOUDLESS SKY!

3. Should the Bible Be Read in the Public Schools?

Proponents of Bible reading were not swayed by calls to make the public schools "nonsectarian." Concerned by studies showing that large numbers of schoolchildren, particularly the children of immigrants, received no religious education at all, they argued that children, at the very least, needed to hear the Bible in school. As a result, many efforts were made in the first decades of the twentieth century to mandate Bible reading in the schools by law and to restore such readings where they had earlier been abandoned.

Alarmed at these efforts, the Central Conference of American Rabbis, through its newly created Committee on Church and State, issued a widely distributed pamphlet entitled "Why the Bible Should Not Be Read in the Public Schools." In this pamphlet, which is excerpted below, the Reform rabbinic organization predicated its opposition to Bible reading on American and universalistic values, rather than on specific Jewish communal concerns. Instead of calling for "unsectarian schools," as nineteenth-century Jews did, they stressed the value of church-state separation. Both "progress" and America's "manifest destiny," they claimed, depended on keeping religion and state apart.

Louis Marshall, longtime president of the American Jewish Committee and one of the most respected lay leaders of the Reform movement, disagreed. As he makes clear in the following letter to his cousin, Benjamin Stolz, he felt that he had himself benefited from "hearing the Bible read daily from the King James version," and believed that Jewish public school students of his day would benefit no less. Fully aware of the abuses that sometimes resulted from Bible readings, Marshall differed from most of his Jewish colleagues in believing that compromise on this issue was possible. His goal was to obviate "sound objections" while still conferring on the country's youth "the advantage of familiarizing itself with the noblest ethical teachings the world has yet known, couched in the purest of English."

❖　　❖　　❖

CCAR, "Why the Bible Should Not Be Read in the Public Schools," 1906

"Promote as an object of primary importance," said Washington in his Farewell Address, "institutions for the general diffusion of knowledge. In proportion as the structure of a government gives force to public opinion, it is essential that public opinion should be enlightened." In his "Notes on the State of Virginia," published in 1787, Jefferson wrote: "Every government degenerates when trusted to the rulers of the people alone. The people themselves therefore are its only safe depositories. And to render even them safe, their minds must be improved to a certain degree." "The existence of a republic," said the United States Commissioner of Education in 1874, "unless all its citizens are educated, is an admitted impossibility." In accord with these views, the public school has become a recognized and prominent institution in American life. We are almost all agreed that the welfare of the country demands the education of its citizenship, and that this end can best, can indeed only, be attained thro[ugh] the system of free schools. But we are not so agreed upon the things these schools should teach. There are those who argue that the school curriculum amounts to nothing which makes no provision for religious instruction. Could they have their way, they would have religion taught in all the public schools. Unable to bring this about, they insist that the schools should introduce Bible readings, prayers, and sectarian hymns. The individual who dare to criticize this plan, is usually attacked as an atheist or infidel, seeking to undermine the pillars of the republic, to make this a godless country, and so bring it to ruin. As a matter of fact the critic may be thoroughly religious by nature, enthusiastically observant of the details of the denomination to which he belongs, loyal in every way to the land in which he lives, and interested in its welfare. Yet he objects to religious exercises in public institutions. How can he justify his objection?

"Religion," said James Madison, "is not in the purview of human government. Religion is essentially distinct from government, and exempt from its cognizance. A connection between them is injurious to both." This conviction is fundamental to our Federal Constitution. When it says "Congress shall make no law respecting an establishment of religion," it means to affirm that there shall never be in this country a connection between Church and State. Now the public school is a state institution, established unquestionably for secular purposes, while Bible reading, recitation of prayer and the singing of sectarian hymns, are purely religious exercises. To put these exercises into the public schools is to unite Church and State, and so to rebel against the spirit of the Constitution.

There was a time when Church and State were everywhere one. For a century and a half, the leaven has been at work, bringing about a separation between the two. In that time the cause has made great progress. Today the signs of the times point unmistakably to its ultimate victory. Here and there the connection still exists, but the day is not distant when it will altogether disappear. To insist upon the retention of religious exercises in our public school, or to try to introduce them at this late day, is to attempt to turn back the hands of time, to resurrect a dead past, to struggle vainly against manifest destiny.

It is interesting to observe that the rapid progress life has made in every way during the past one hundred years has been synchronous with the growing separation of Church and State. It is not an accidental coincidence. For the finest and largest development has taken place in those lands where a State Church is unknown. Where it still exists, tho it grant every privilege to those not its communicants, the development tho commendable, has been, in practically every instance, not as great. The countries which have developed least, and which today seem so far behind the times, and so out of place, are those where the connection between Church and State is still so intimate that dissenters are considered aliens, and are subject to political discrimination. If we are interested in the growth of our country we shall do everything in our power to keep Church and State apart.

Our public schools belong to the State. They are expressions not of denominational but State interest. They were established not by the members of a particular sect to educate their own children, but by the people as a whole, so that all the children of the land might receive the instruction that would fit them for citizenship. These schools are attended by children whose parents have every shade of religious belief. They are supported by taxes paid by every member of the community, whatever the character of his creed, even tho he disavow any creed, and without regard to the question as to whether or no, he has children of school age to take advantage of the educational opportunities thus provided. In one word they are public and not private schools, and therefore must be conducted in such a way that all those interested may have equal privileges, and receive exactly the same recognition. Private schools are owned and controlled by private individuals, and therefore the public has absolutely no right to question or dictate their internal administration. The curriculum may be liberal or narrow, denominational or undenominational, the rules may be exacting or lenient. Children who attend these schools must obey, and parents who send them, must be content to have them obey. There may be religious exercises, there may be even religious instruction. But there is no room for complaint, because the institutions are private, and the owners have a right to conduct them as they please, providing only they do not deceive their patrons as to the manner of such conduct. The case is altogether different where the public schools are concerned. These schools are built by the people, supported by them, and attended by their children. In one word they are the public's schools, wherefore care must be taken that their curriculum should consider impartially the rights of all those responsible for their maintenance. Religious exercises in our public schools may please the majority, but they wrong the minority. In plain language they discriminate.

*　*　*

Anyone can read the Bible, but a special equipment is required to teach it. Few of our public school teachers possess this equipment. When we engage them we examine them along purely secular lines. We exact no religious test of them. A course which is eminently proper and sensible. But tho we are not concerned with their religious beliefs, or with what they know of religion in general, we permit, in some instances compel them, to read and speak and sing about religion to our children. A poor religious teacher can only stunt the religious development of the child.

Suppose, as is sometimes the case, the teacher is a Catholic or a Jew. The Bible version generally used in our schools is a Protestant translation. Is this teacher to be compelled to use this version? When in his reading, he comes to interpretations with which he does not agree, shall he introduce changes into the text to make it correspond with his belief? Is he apt to risk the displeasure of the authorities by reading passages which confirm his own position, or will he sacrifice his self-respect, by reading selections, which meet the approval of his superiors, but the burden of which belies his own conviction? Has a public school system a right thus to embarrass its teachers, to subject them in this indirect way to what is virtually a religious test, and so restrict the freedom of their conscience?

And since there is no religious qualification for teaching in our public schools, suppose an atheist is given charge of a class. Like the other teachers he has the privilege of reading any Bible chapters he pleases, and insinuating into them the interpretations that suit his fancy. Now the influence the Bible exerts on men and women, depends in a measure on the manner in which it is presented to them during their childhood. Read to them reverently, and they may view it with reverence. Read to them cynically, and they may learn to scoff at it.

Under existing circumstances, what is to prevent a teacher to whom the Bible is but an ordinary book, from reading it in such a way as to make the children of his class share his views?

Reading the Bible in the public schools usually leads to the introduction of other religious exercises altogether sectarian in character. Sometimes it is supplemented by exegesis. The teacher becomes a commentator and interpreter. Gradually the teacher becomes preacher. In one school in New York a principal preached on the religious message of all the holidays. In another school in Brooklyn, a teacher delivered a regular course of sermons, on the tenets of the faith he professed. Out in Nebraska a teacher devoted the period intended for the reading of the Bible, to instructing the children in preparation for baptism, while in another instance, later brought into court, a teacher frankly confessed, that since she was allowed to read the Bible to the children as she pleased, she felt herself privileged to teach them the fundamental doctrines of her church. Most of the schools which permit Bible reading, supplement the reading with sectarian prayers and hymns. Some of them permit special celebration by the children of all the religious holidays of the year. Some decorate the rooms with sectarian pictures. In a certain school ministers were invited to open the sessions with prayer. In one instance the guest took advantage of the opportunity to preach an evangelistic sermon that would have done credit to a revival meeting. The point is that as soon as we allow the Bible to be read in our public schools, that moment we open their doors to a host of other religious features, that in the end will affect their efficiency.

* * *

Religion is a concern of the individual alone, a matter between a man and his God. The state and therefore a public institution belonging peculiarly to the state, and so to all the people, has absolutely no right to interfere with it. But the moment religious exercises are admitted into the public school, the State if it does not suggest, sanctions such interference.

There is no uniform statute regulating the reading of the Bible in the public schools. In fact, there is no explicit law in any of the State constitutions or State statutes except one dealing directly with this question. Hence the question must finally be submitted to the Court of Appeals in the State where it is raised, and left to the Supreme Court for decision. The decision is, in nearly all cases, based on the interpretation of a clause in the State constitution or statutes, which, while not stating specifically about the use of the Bible in the public schools, contains some provision relating to sectarian instruction.

* * *

. . . Theoretically the people of the United States of America proclaim their belief in the absolute separation of Church and State. Yet it is extremely false to imagine that the civil power and religion are wholly disassociated.

The remedy for all these flagrant actualities that belie our theoretical proclamation of the divorce of Church and State can be gotten only in one way. We, the people of the United States, must make such laws as shall be explicit and sufficiently catholic to cover all cases where the church trespasses on the territory which we have theoretically but not practically proscribed her.

The voters in each commonwealth of the Union should be vigilant and see to it that the Legislature enacts such specific measures as to prohibit the reading of the Bible in the common schools for religious purposes, and it may just as well be declared once for all that wherever the Bible is used in the public schools it is solely for religious purposes.

Appeals to school Boards, and memorials to school authorities, have in many cases proven futile. The State must step in and checkmate the insinuating sectarianism that threatens to change the fundamental principles of our government. The prophecy "that we shall have a national issue on this matter of school reform, and that it will be as vehement as any national issue has ever been," may be open to considerable doubt, but it is almost a certainty that the problem of public school education will be made a State issue in State elections. It is well to begin to pave the way for that time and to be prepared for the battle when it will be at hand. The ballot and it alone will finally settle the persistent question of "The Bible in the Public Schools."

Church and School must be divorced. Neither petitions, nor quarrels, nor any other indirect means, will keep them apart. The State will write the bill of divorcement. The citizens will dictate it. The people that are mortally afraid that this complete separation will engender danger should be reminded of the words of Whittier:

"Nor heeds the sceptic's puny hands,
    While near her school the church spire stands;
Nor fears the blinded bigot's rule,
    While near her church spire stands her school."

◆

Louis Marshall for compromise on Bible reading, 1922

November 21, 1922

To Benjamin Stolz

I am in receipt of yours of the 20th instant with regard to the action taken by the Board of Education of Syracuse directing the reading of the Bible in the public schools, concerning which you desire my opinion.

The subject is one which has aroused much contrariety of opinion in various parts of the country. In some quarters there has been much indignation manifested at the thought that the Bible should be read in the public schools. I can very well recognize the strength of the argument of those who are opposed to the compulsory reading of the Bible. While the King James version is a magnificent piece of literature and the most perfect example of good English that one can find, the translators were by no means free from theological bias, and in consequence, from the standpoint of Catholics and Jews, it contains many objectionable features. As you know, the Catholics have their own translation, the Douay version, and the Jews have found it necessary to make their own translation in order to conform with the original text and to eliminate the many Christological passages and references which are not contained in that text.

If all pupils attending the public schools were discriminating and had the benefit of religious training in Sunday Schools or at their homes, the reading of the Bible from the King James version would do no harm. The difficulty, however, is that a large majority of pupils have had no such training as would enable them to understand and recognize the differences between the various versions, and are apt to be confused, to say the least. When I attended the public school the morning sessions were not only opened by reading from the Bible, but also with prayer. The Catholic children were permitted to retire at the time of such reading, but it always was the subject of comment and was most unpleasant and disagreeable for them. It tended to mark a classification between the pupils, which I then felt and still feel was unjustifiable. A large number of the teachers who read the Bible were considerate in the selection of the readings. They chose the Psalms and Proverbs and other books which were of such a nature as to give offense to nobody. On the other hand there were teachers who confined their readings entirely to the New Testament. Some were extremely offensive. There were those who made it a point to read about the crucifixion of Christ on Good Friday. There were others that laid emphasis on sections of the Bible which was reflected in the actions of the Christian pupils toward the Jewish pupils. There is no question that some of the teachers possessed the missionary spirit and were exceedingly narrow. On the other hand I may say from my own experience that, although I read the Bible at home and especially a German translation, I profited greatly from hearing the Bible read daily from the King James version. My first acquaintance with the New Testament was derived from these readings. The familiarity which I then acquired has been greatly impressed upon my memory and has been a valuable addition to my vocabulary. It certainly did not harm me as a Jew, nor as a man.

There are, of course, others who, hearing the Bible read without proper guidance, might be mentally disturbed. Personally I believe that it would not do our Jewish children a bit of harm to become familiar with the Bible even though it be read in the public schools. It will probably be the only way in which many of them would ever gain the slightest familiarity with the Book of Books. Save in exceptional instances they do not read it in their homes and they read very little of it in their Sabbath Schools, and, what is worse, only a very small percentage of the Jewish children attend any Sabbath School.

If all teachers could be depended upon to make the proper readings there would be no possible objection to familiarizing the pupils with the noble teachings of the Bible and the majestic English of the King James version. The trouble, however, is that many teachers lack judgment, are bigoted, and their familiarity with the Bible is so limited that very little benefit can be derived from their reading of it. If a list of readings could be agreed upon by the representatives of the Protestant, Catholic and Jewish parts of the community, not only would there be no resultant harm, but much good would come from such reading. Of course we must preserve religious liberty in its spirit and essence. We cannot permit our schools to be used by bigots or fanatics for denominational propaganda. We must not permit readings which would offend the parents of Catholic or Jewish children. Some method should be found by which all interested persons can agree upon a programme which will obviate the sound objections that exist to the reading of certain portions of the Bible and at the same time confer upon the youth of this country the advantage of familiarizing itself with the noblest ethical teachings the world has yet known, couched in the purest of English.

I do not think that the subject should be considered in any public meetings, which are apt to become acrimonious and to produce unnecessary excitement and bitterness of feeling. It is rather a subject which should be taken up by the leaders of thought of the various religious bodies throughout the country, and I have no doubt that if this is done the problem, which is now a serious one, may be simplified. . . .

4. Nonsectarian Education in the Public Schools

For all that they opposed prayer, Bible reading, and all forms of sectarianism in the public schools, many Jewish leaders in the late nineteenth and early twentieth century sympathized with Christian fears that schools devoid of religious values might become secular and "godless." Seeking to reconcile their belief in church-state separation with their commitment to non-religious ethical instruction, prominent Reform rabbis began to espouse a position advanced earlier by both the Ethical Culture movement and some Protestant denominations and pressed for the introduction of courses in religion-based ethics in the public schools. As early as 1881, Bernhard Felsenthal, a

Reform rabbi in Chicago and, as we have seen, a leading Jewish proponent of church-state separation, called for "instruction in unsectarian ethics." In a letter to the *Nation,* the first selection included below, he sketched out a program of "systematic ethical instruction," carefully avoiding any mention of God, covering all grades, and embracing such concepts as "virtue and vice, equanimity and passion, good and evil, true and untrue, egoism and altruism and so forth." Subsequently, in 1911, the Central Conference of American Rabbis' Committee on Church and State began to debate this question. In a paper presented to the CCAR's annual convention, excerpts from which are included in the second selection below, Tobias Schanfarber, a rabbi of Congregation Anshe Maariv in Chicago, raised an objection to secular ethical education in the public schools. Arguing that ethics could not be divorced from religion, and that "the secular character of the public schools should be maintained sacred and inviolable," he concluded that there was no need for separate, formal courses in religion-based ethics in America's schools. Other Reform rabbis, however, believed that the schools had a responsibility to inculcate ethical and moral values. In the third selection below, El Paso's Rabbi Martin Zielonka, appealing to "all who have the welfare of childhood at heart," dissented from Schanfarber's arguments. "In our anxiety to keep religion out of the schools," he warned, "let us not prove our excessive zeal by seeking to keep out moral instruction."

◆   ◆   ◆

Rabbi Felsenthal calls for public school instruction in "unsectarian ethics," 1882

To the Editor of The Nation:

Sɪʀ: A number of citizens of Chicago have recently submitted a petition to the Board of Education of this city, asking that instruction in unsectarian ethics be given in all grades of the public schools here.

The subject is, no doubt, of high importance. Intellectual culture must be supplemented by moral culture. Intellectual culture alone, if not controlled by moral principles, is liable to become a curse instead of a blessing. But have state authorities or communal authorities the right to provide the means for moral culture to go beyond providing for instruction in reading, writing, and arithmetic? We claim that they have, and we add that not only have they the *right*, but it is their *duty* to train the future citizen in good morals. This duty, however, is far too much neglected. Our schools suffer under the great fault that they pay too little attention to the *education* of the children, and lay all their stress upon *instruction*—upon instruction in so-called practical branches of study. "Utility" is the name of the guiding-star which directs the course of the majority of our schools. But vulgar utility ought not to be the chief end and object of the schools. They have not fulfilled their great and holy mission when they produce good arithmeticians, efficient bookkeepers, smart business men. They have not come up to their ideal height if they consider it their main aim and purpose so to bring up our youth that they may successfully run along in the race after riches. Our schools ought to strive after higher ideals. They should be among the most potential factors for elevating the nation to a higher plane of morality. The too materialistic character of our schools should be counterbalanced by introducing into them a number of studies such that, even if they be without any visible and measurable value in practical life, they will yet have the tendency and potency to ennoble the heart, to refine the sentiments, to purify the will, and to give to life a higher turn altogether.

A systematic and regular course in unsectarian ethics would be a great help to this end, while casual, well-meant remarks by the teacher would be of no particular educational value.

It is not difficult to grade properly the rich material of undenominational ethics. In the lower grades already it is possible to give instructive, impressive, and attractive lessons to the children on their duties toward their parents, teachers, schoolmates, toward older people, and so forth. In the next higher grade their hearts might be impressed with the duties of employers toward their employees, and of employees toward their employers, with the mutual relations of members of a family, with the duties of the citizen toward the State and the Government, etc. In another grade the children might be taught, to their mental and moral benefit, that while the ambition to raise one's self and to ameliorate the conditions of his life is praiseworthy, yet it becomes every person, under unalterable circumstances, to be satisfied with and reconciled to his station in life; that man ought to be just and honest in all his actions, true and reliable in all his utterances, faithful and diligent in whatever he is obliged to do, charitable and kind to those who are in need, etc. The character of the children might also receive a proper and lasting direction by showing them the moral beauty of having order in all things, of being temperate in various ways, of withstanding manfully all temptations to do wrong, etc. In the next grade the pupils might be advanced enough to pursue a systematized course of ethics, and now would be the proper time to generalize, and to define such conceptions as virtue and vice, equanimity and passion, good and evil, true and untrue, egoism and altruism, and so forth. For the highest grade of our schools we would recommend instruction in empirical psychology, analyzing of characters of men as they appear in every-day life, in history, and in fiction; and, no doubt, such instruction would be of the greatest advantage, intellectually and morally, to the pupils attending our schools.

In imparting such lessons it would be well for the theoretical instruction to be supported and illustrated by stories and examples, which would make these lessons doubly interesting and attractive to the children. In connection there with, classical sentences and aphorisms, full of true wisdom, and sayings and verses from the poets and other great master minds of all ages and nations would have to be explained to and memorized by the children. Their spiritual horizon would thus become greatly widened, and in their youthful days they would gather in a mental store of excellent wise sayings, which, in their advanced years, would be for them an invaluable, refreshing source of joy and happiness, and, possibly, a quickening power for a noble conduct of life.

Some may now admit systematic ethical instruction to be a most important, nay, a most urgent reform in our national system of education. Yet they may say, Where can the time be found for this new study? Our children are already overburdened. They are overburdened. Take off, then, those horrid, stupefying drills in spelling—in spelling even rarely used Greek and Latin words; diminish the useless stuff of geographical and historical details, of names and dates and numbers which the children have to cram into their minds; aim for mental development, and avoid pernicious one-sided cultivation of the memory; and then sufficient time will be found for ethical instruction. And ethical instruction will prove to be a means of ethical education.

—*Respectfully*, B. F.

◆

Rabbi Schanfarber proposes a CCAR resolution against ethical instruction in public schools, 1911

. . . The whole question of ethical instruction in the schools is still in a vague, indefinite and indefinable shape. We are groping for some common ground, but we fail to find it save as we maintain the secular character of the schools. We can not find it in some common denominator belonging to all religions, because in reality no such common denominator exists. The book prepared by the "Chicago Woman's Educational Union" known as "Readings from the Bible," in which an attempt was made to gather from the old and New Testament selections which would be agreeable to all religions, would make the poorest kind of a text-book for moral instruction. That book, in the hands of the teacher whose inclinations were in that direction, would make a most fruitful source for propaganda for the dominant faith.

We can not find the common ground by setting aside a certain time and allowing the followers of different religions to enter the school and permit them to instruct their own children in the particular tenets of their faith, because this would render nugatory the secular character of our schools.

We can not find the common ground in permitting morality to be taught without the religious sanction, for the vast majority of religionists are opposed to having ethics taught that way. To all of these propositions vital objections can be raised, but it seems to me that the least or no objection can be taken to the incidental instruction in ethics by means of the activities of the school life and in connection with the other subjects already taught, and here ample opportunities are afforded to build up the moral life of the child. And this moral training will be all the more effective because it comes informally and without the conscious effort on the part of the teacher or the child. The preachy method of teaching morality is deprecated by a large number of teachers in their reports of the work done at their schools along these lines.

Both Jews and Christian, agnostic and atheist agree that in its ultimate analysis the purpose of the public school is the formation of character and the creation of good citizenship. I believe that our public school system of instruction always has had this aim in view. Even though ethics are not definitely and directly taught, it would be a libel to label our public schools, as is sometimes done by narrow credists, as godless and atheistic. For they are always surrounded by a moral and even religious atmosphere, even though these subjects have no place in the curriculum. And what the child needs in the school, as well as in the home, is not so much ethical instruction as it is moral atmosphere, contact with morality in action. The State law demands of its teachers that they be morally pure and of good character. Retaining their positions is contingent upon this fact. After all the most important factor in the school life of the child is the personal influence of the teacher. One Horace Mann is worth more than all the didactic, moral instruction and all the text-books on morality. The state laws demand that the pupils must be moral. If they are not they are placed in Parental Schools and Schools for the Delinquent. In several States of the Union to maintain the democratic character of the schools the ban has been placed upon the fraternity secret society. The schools have ample opportunity to create civic pride and to appeal to the patriotic side of the child's life by means of the patriotic holidays which they celebrate, such as Lincoln's and Washington's birthday, Thanksgiving and Decoration Day, Flag and Peace Day. All of this would indicate that in an indirect way the schools are providing for the formation of good character and the creation of good citizenship. We can scarcely begin to estimate what it means for higher civilization by the attendance of a child for seven or eight years upon our public schools. The discipline of the schools is a most potent factor in the training of morals. The punctuality and regularity that are demanded, the orderliness and cleanliness that are made imperative, the lessons of obedience and reverence for the rights and feelings of others as human beings that are exacted, the sanctity of property and the necessity for truthfulness which characterize every schoolroom mean more for the development of the ethical sides of the child than all the moral maxims that it might learn by rote. . . .

To sum up the contentions of this paper I will put the conclusion in the form of a resolution:—

Whereas, it is the sense of this Conference that ethical instruction should not be given without the religious sanction and, whereas, this Conference believes that the secular character of the public schools should be maintained sacred and inviolable, be it therefore resolved that:

This Conference goes on record as opposed to the introduction of ethical instruction in the public schools, save as it is incidental to the school activities and in connection with the other studies already prescribed in the curriculum. . . .

◆

Rabbi Zielonka's dissent, 1911

. . . I feel that we can accomplish more by admitting the necessity for ethical instruction and then impressing the religious sanction for the same in our religious schools, than by continually combatting religious instruction. The latter movement is gaining, rather than losing, ground in most States. All are not so fortunate as to have a Supreme Court with the foresight and courage of the one in Illinois.

Our secular schools are a reaction against the priest-ridden schools of the 18th century and as such, are as one-sided as were the latter. Suppressing ethical instruction because the influence of religious bodies and religious instruction had proven baneful, has developed one side of education at the expense of the other.

*   *   *

State schools are supported for the purpose of creating good citizens. Citizens can only then be good, when they possess good characters. Why then, should not our schools educate directly for good characters? Our churches have not succeeded fully. Revelations in the business world and in municipal government prove that something vital is lacking in the make-up of our citizenship. Our homes, due to the conditions of labor, become, less and less, factors in character building, and we can only turn to our schools if we would replace, to some extent, the former influences for an ethical life. At the same time we must urge the churches to increase their activities in the field of ethics.

*   *   *

We need not worry about the teachers. If the need is at hand teachers to cope with the situation will be prepared in the training schools. And if special teachers be deemed best then, men fully capable and properly trained for this branch of service will come forward, even as we have found them for all other branches of service.

In conclusion, I would say with Prof. Coe, "morals are not religion and religion is not morals, nevertheless full grown religion includes morals." In our anxiety to keep religion out of the schools let us not prove our excessive zeal by seeking to keep out moral instruction. I feel that much can be attained and finer manhood and womanhood be reared, by allowing our public schools to give instruction in ethics. Our religious schools can then be so organized as to take up the work done the week previous in the public school and giving it *our* religious sanction. I, believe that we should not oppose ethical instruction in the public schools, and I, for one, am ready and willing to try it.

5. The Debate over the Gary "Released Time" Plan

Some of the same concerns that motivated the debate over the teaching of ethics in the public schools fueled fears, especially among rabbis, concerning the consequences of growing religious illiteracy amongst young Americans, and Jews in particular. Studies showed that knowledge of the Bible and of the Jewish ethical tradition were noticeably declining within the American Jewish community, and that many Jewish children were receiving no religious education whatsoever. In response, a growing minority of Jewish leaders endorsed "released time" proposals for religious instruction within the framework of the public school system. Under these plans, children were released from school for a period of time during the day, for moral and religious instruction under the auspices of their church or synagogue. They then returned to school to continue their secular studies. Introduced in Gary, Indiana in 1913, this so-called "Gary Plan" generated considerable Jewish communal discussion and debate.

One outspoken and articulate opponent of the Gary Plan, Isadore Montefiore Levy, a member of the New York City Board of Education, explained his opposition to this plan in a letter to the *New York Times* (November 5, 1915), which is reprinted as the first selection below. Rabbi Samuel Schulman of New York City, on the other hand, supported the plan with certain changes. He urged his colleagues within the Central Conference of American Rabbis (CCAR) to endorse it, and to become more accommodationist and proreligious in their policies. His arguments in support of the plan, delivered as part of an address to the CCAR Convention in 1916, are included in the second selection below. As with ethical education, so too with released-time programs, the Jewish community was divided and failed to speak with one voice.

◆   ◆   ◆

Isadore Levy's argument against the Gary Plan, 1915

To the Editor of The New York Times:

So much comment has been aroused by the provision for religious instruction incident to the Gary school system, that this unique feature merits careful attention on the part of all those who have the welfare of our schools at heart. Indeed, the criticism and discussion of this feature have assumed such proportions that they threaten to overshadow the other salient features of the Gary idea.

This religious provision may be briefly described as follows: The daily school program sets aside a certain period during the school day to be devoted to religious training. The children are grouped according to their religious beliefs. They are met outside of the school by their religious instructors, and, under their care, are taken to their respective churches or religious institutions. When through with the period assigned exclusively to religious instruction the children are sent back to school to continue their studies. It is to be noted that this religious instruction is given during the school session, but outside of the school. Each denomination receives instruction in the formal tenets of its religion, by its duly authorized religious teacher.

We are thus confronted with the great problem of whether religious instruction should be presented to school children during school hours, but outside of the school building. It is now being tried in Public School 45, Bronx, and a committee is now devising ways and means of introducing it in all the schools.

The average layman is well contented to go the even tenor of his way and leave the educational experts to wrestle with the educational problems, but this incidental scheme for religious instruction has caused the layman to concentrate his attention upon the Wirt plan and judge the entire plan by his opinion of its religious feature. This is both undesirable and unfortunate, for the reason that an open-minded study of this system is thereby made difficult.

Total separation of school and religion has heretofore been accepted as sound public policy. As a result, our school system has heretofore escaped religious criticism save by the few religious zealots who have attacked our schools as being "godless."

To revolutionize our system by the introduction of the religious feature would be to open the floodgate to a tide of possible bitterness and hatred. School children are peculiarly susceptible to this, and their minds would at once be poisoned. Their religious belief and prejudices would be awakened and intensified. No longer would the children in our classrooms dwell together in peace and harmony.

Called upon to attend the church or religious institution, the child would awaken to the gulf which divides him from his classmates of different religious belief. The cohesion and harmony so essential to the classroom would be destroyed. His religious prejudices, no longer dormant, would cause pain to others.

The school child whose religious belief is in the minority would be made miserable, for he would become the butt and target of his fellow-beings, and none can be so unconsciously cruel as our thoughtless youth. Good fellowship, well-being, and harmony, so characteristic of our common schools today, would be destroyed. Only recently, if a newspaper report be correct, a boy of Public School 45, Bronx, where the experiment is now being tried, came home from school complaining that he had been insulted by his fellow-playmate because of his religious belief. The nihilist, anarchist, and agnostic have threatened to organize their own school. Thus we would lose our opportunity to mold the character of their children and make them firm believers of our institutions.

The teachers of our school system are themselves members of diverse religious denominations. Nor would they, the teachers themselves, escape this infection. That fraternal feeling and social relation so essential to the efficiency of the schools would be a thing of the past. The esprit de corps for which the teachers have long been noted would disappear.

There is really no need for religious instruction in our schools. The shepherds of our flock—our priests, rabbis, and ministers, men deservedly eminent for their faithfulness to their trust—have long imparted instruction to our youth and guided their souls. It is very doubtful whether many of them favor this idea of religious instruction. All denominations have at all times given religious instruction outside of the schools and have kept religion and school apart with excellent results.

The school system has no right to call upon the church for religious instruction. To meet this burden which may be suddenly thrust upon them, the various religious denominations will be compelled to hire quarters near the schools and to engage teachers to give religious instruction. This will cause many churches to undergo greater expenses than they can afford. If these churches would be rendering the city a service by such religious instruction, then such services should be paid for. This would at once create an opening wedge and sooner or later religious corporations would demand that they be reimbursed from the public treasury, the provision of the Constitution notwithstanding.

It is doubtful whether this idea of religious instruction as an essential part of the school curriculum can successfully weather a legal assault. If suit is brought to determine the validity of this feature of religious co-operation the courts would be certain to question its constitutionality. It is with reluctance that the courts have sustained the reading of the Bible in school. . . .

In addition to this, other legal problems suggest themselves. Has the school a right to send children outside of the schools for religious instruction during school hours? What are the rights of the schools against parents, if parents object? What is the legal liability of the schools for injuries resulting to children while going to and from religious instruction? These problems are not academic but of practical importance, the determination of which sooner or later will come before the courts.

The suggested idea of introducing religion in common schools is an indirect menace to democracy. It is vital to the existence of our schools that they be free from all outside religious influence. Our religious denominations would sooner or later make our schools a battlefield upon which would be fought their ancient enmities. We ought not to pave the way for their ultimate control of the school. It would be harmful to religion and harmful to us. Our school has long been regarded as the cradle of democracy. This has been one of its unique and most valuable features. Whatever menaces the school, then, menaces democracy.

ISADORE MONTEFIORE LEVY

✦

Rabbi Schulman in support of the Gary Plan, 1916

It is necessary to become clear in thought as to just what is our attitude towards the religious life of the American people of which we are a part. We must continue to be jealous of our rights as a religious minority. But that does not mean indifference on our part to the welfare of the larger majority of the American people to which we belong. Owing to our being a minority religion and, therefore, jealously watchful of our rights, we may, in matters of Sunday observance and religious instruction of the nation, easily and thoughtlessly drift into a purely secular and indifferent position. This would be both contrary to the genius of Israel and to the American spirit. It is a difficult and delicate problem and it is about time that we supplement our negative attitude with some positive contribution towards a possible solution of it.

Our business as Jews is to have a positive message, urging the growth of religious education in the land. And as Americans, we must not forget that the American people has always been profoundly religious. The principle of the separation of Church and State is not the positive one of the secularization of life on behalf of infidelity, agnosticism or ethical culture, indifference to Theism or any historic religion. The principle of the separation of Church and State is the negative one, which aims at preventing the infringement upon the rights of conscience. The State, according to it, is not to do anything which will force the conscience of any individual. But where possible, the State does show appreciation and respect for religion and courtesy to its representatives. For example, the public sessions of our Legislature are opened with prayer. It is the custom in the country that impressive public meetings are opened with prayer. Chaplains are appointed in our army and navy to meet the various religious needs of soldiers and sailors. Religion is recognized as indispensable for the moral education of men and therefore as making for good citizenship. The State shows courtesy to religion by recognizing a religious marriage as a civil validity. In other words, the real meaning of the principle of the separation of Church and State, as developed in this country, is to create a strong religious life in a free State by making that religious life dependent upon individual initiative and effort.

Our purpose, therefore, as Jews, should be to encourage the religious life of all churches and, at the same time, jealously to be on our guard lest the spirit of sectarianism encroach upon government or the schools to the detriment of our rights as a minority. Our ideal would be for the American people to observe one day of rest in seven and, at the same time, for a conscientious Jew to be allowed to observe his own Sabbath without his being forced to rest on two days, which for the overwhelming majority, is an economic impossibility. And with respect to the ethical and religious education, our purpose as Jews should be not merely the negative one of opposing the introduction of Bible reading in the public schools, because it is a piece of sectarianism, but the efficiently active and positive one of utilizing whatever methods are offered with which we can sympathize, which aim at improving the knowledge of the Bible and the general ethical and religious culture of the American nation.

*   *   *

The best plan which offers the greatest promise and which I permit myself to greet most enthusiastically, is the Gary plan, because it seems to me to meet most effectively all the circumstances of our unique American situation. The Gary plan, as is well known, is a large, general plan for increasing the length of the school day. The school day for the child is to cover not only study, but work and play. All possible aspects of the child life are in some way to be reached by the school, stimulated, watched over and accounted for. Within this large scheme, opportunity is to be offered to such children, whose parents desire them to obtain religious instruction, to take the hours in the day necessary for such instruction. The instruction is not to be given in the school. It is not to be paid for by school authorities. It is not even to be credited in school grading. All that the school is to do in connection with it is to obtain records from the teachers that impart religious instruction of the presence of the children for that purpose. And thus a record is kept of the time in which the child is absent from the school. In other words, the child uses an hour that might be given, say, to amusement, for the purpose of receiving moral and religious instruction. Its absence is accounted for and it cannot be considered a truant.

The great value of this plan consists in a number of things. In the first place, it meets all objections of those who hold that it is not the business of the school, supported by the taxes of all citizens, to impart religious instruction. It does not emphasize religious differences amongst the children within the school building, as would be the case if the school were divided for religious instruction amongst various denominational teachers. The school remains secular. At the same time the school, representing the nation, gives its moral support to religious instruction, in the sense that it considers the time spent on it well spent and necessary for the child's welfare. The imagination of the child will be impressed with the fact that religion is a serious matter, that it is as important for life as any other subject in the school and that three and four days in the week ought to be given to it. At present, the mere relegation of religious instruction to one day in the week tends to make the child regard it as less important than arithmetic or geography or languages. And, indeed, I hold that for effective instruction in religion we should have more time than what is now given to it.

The Gary system would make religious instruction an integral part of the education of the child, would give it a dignity, because of its connection with the educational scheme, which it now lacks, would coordinate it more with the national life and, at the same time, would bring no pressure to bear upon any child in the direction of sectarian instruction; would do nothing insidious and would not force the conscience of any parent who had strong convictions against religious instruction. Not the least advantage of the Gary plan is that it is a splendid challenge to the churches themselves. We Jews ought to welcome this plan. It ought to be a stimulus to our earnestness and energy. We, too, ought, wherever possible, to make arrangements for the religious instruction of our children more than once a week. We, too, ought to provide for the religious education of the masses of Jewish children, by cooperating with this plan.

6. Preserving the Rights of Nonpublic Schools

Notwithstanding the Jewish community's support for non-sectarian public schools, it played a notable role in preserving the right of parents to opt out of the public schools and to educate their children under parochial or private auspices. In 1922, amidst a frenzy of anti-immigrant nativism and anti-Catholicism, the State of Oregon had passed a law requiring all able-bodied and teachable students to attend public schools. Although Jews were scarcely affected—there were no more than twelve Jewish day schools in the entire United States at that time and none in Oregon—Louis Marshall, representing the American Jewish Committee, filed an *amicus curiae* brief before the Supreme Court challenging the constitutionality of Oregon's law and attacking as "an invasion of liberty" any attempt to make public schools "the only medium of education in this country." He asked the Court to affirm the basic right of parents to send their children to parochial schools and thus provide for their "religious instruction, the importance of which cannot be minimized." Ruling in the case of *Pierce v. Society of the Sisters of the Holy Names of Jesus and Mary* (1925), the Court indeed overthrew the Oregon statute. In what has been described as the "Magna Carta" of American parochial schools, it established the right of nonpublic schools to do business and the liberty of parents to direct the upbringing and education of their children.

◆　　◆　　◆

Louis Marshall defends the right to attend private and religious schools, 1925

. . . This legislation is clearly calculated to confer upon the public schools a monopoly of education. That necessarily would tend to the suppression of all religious instruction, the importance of which cannot be minimized. Under our system of government the State is powerless, as it should be, to give religious instruction. That is a right and a duty which rests upon parents, upon the churches and the synagogues. If private, parochial and denominational schools are, however, to be deprived of the right to educate the children, and the parents are forbidden to send their children to such schools, then we shall be in precisely the same situation as that which now exists in Russia. There it is strictly forbidden to give religious instruction of any kind to children until they reach the age of eighteen years.

Fundamentally, therefore, the questions in these cases are: May liberty to teach and to learn be restricted? Shall such liberty be dependent on the will of the majority? Shall such majority be permitted to dictate to parents and to children where and by whom instruction shall be given? If such power can be asserted, then it will lead inevitably to the stifling of thought. If the will of a temporary majority may thus control, then it is conceivable that it may prohibit the teaching of science, of the classics, of modern languages and literature, of art, and of nature study. A majority might reach the conclusion that the teaching of the Darwinian theory, or of the philosophy of Kant or Spinoza, or the ideas of Montesquieu, or of Jeremy Bentham, or of John Stuart Mill, or of Emerson, should be prohibited. In some parts of this country a majority, if it possessed the power, would unquestionably limit instruction in the public schools to the Three R's. New York has recently witnessed an attempt to eliminate from the handbooks of history used in the public schools, any references to England which were not to its discredit, and any reference to America which, although truthful, did not indicate that it had at all times been immune to criticism.

Recognizing in the main the great merit of our public school system, it is nevertheless unthinkable that public schools alone shall, by legislative compulsion rather than by their own merits, be made the only medium of education in this country. Such a policy would necessarily lead to their deterioration. The absence of the right of selection would at once lower the standards of education. If the children of the country are to be educated upon a dead level of uniformity and by a single method, then eventually our nation would consist of mechanical Robots and standardized Babbitts.

* * *

There is nothing in the public school which is culturally superior to the private, parochial and religious schools; nor can it be said that the teachers are possessed of moral or intellectual or other qualities which make them the superiors of the men and women who have in the past taught and who are now teaching in private and parochial schools. Is it intended to say that those who are wedded to the principles of freedom to such an extent that they are ready to lay down their lives for it, are not correctly instructed in the fundamental principles of freedom?

* * *

Those who send their children to private and parochial schools because of their creed are charged with constituting antagonistic groups and as absorbing "narrow views of life." In other words, parents who are anxious for the future welfare and happiness of their children and who seek to dedicate them to moral, ethical and religious principles, are denounced for sending their children to private and parochial schools, because, forsooth, the views of life which they there absorb are characterized as "narrow."

What does that mean but an attempt on the part of the protagonists for this law to sit in judgment upon their fellow-citizens whose ideals differ from theirs? How does such a mental attitude differ from that which prevailed when governments sought to enforce uniformity of religious beliefs and punished nonconformists as criminals? With the most extraordinary ingenuousness they look upon those of other cults as striving "not for the good of the whole but for the supremacy of themselves." What about the cult of those who adopted the resolutions which are described as "the inspiration for the Act," of those who are seeking to force the youth of this country into the public schools and to destroy private and parochial schools, regardless of the wishes of parents and guardians and of the various religious elements in our population?

This is a demonstration of the evils of intolerance and of the dangers inherent in this legislation, which undermines the fundamental concepts of liberty and which has the inevitable tendency of carrying us back to those evil days which preceded the adoption of our American Constitutions.

The noble words uttered by the President on his inauguration a few days ago, redeclare the great truth which is ignored in this legislation:

"The fundamental precept of liberty is toleration. We cannot permit any inquisition either within or without the law or apply any religious test to the holding of office. The mind of America must be forever free."

It is respectfully submitted that the judgments appealed from should be affirmed.

LOUIS MARSHALL,
for the American Jewish Committee,
Amicus Curiae.

7. Prayer in the Public Schools— The Debate over *Engel v. Vitale*

Seeking a compromise means of promoting school prayer without antagonizing members of different faiths, the New York Board of Regents, in 1951, composed a twenty-two word nondenominational prayer, which it recommended for daily use in public schools throughout the state of New York. The prayer was voluntary: students not wishing to participate could leave their classrooms when it was recited. In 1958, after the school board of Hyde Park, Long Island, adopted the Regents' Prayer for use in its classrooms, a suit was brought by a local resident claiming that, despite its nonsectarian form, the Regents' Prayer violated the establishment clause of the First Amendment and was unconstitutional. The suit made its way to the U.S. Supreme Court, and in a landmark 1962 decision

(*Engel v. Vitale*) the court outlawed all such state-composed prayers, even if seemingly nonsectarian, as constituting an impermissable establishment of religion.

Although some Jews had accepted the Regents' Prayer, the vast majority now supported the Court's decision in *Engel v. Vitale*. Indeed, in an expression of near-unanimous Jewish organizational sentiment, the Synagogue Council of America and the National Jewish Community Relations Advisory Council had filed an *amicus* brief advocating the very position that the Court endorsed. In their brief, excerpts of which are included in the first selection below, the Jewish agencies argued that the prayer constituted "an establishment of religion," and that allowing for nonparticipation did not make it constitutional. As if in response to those who equated opposition to prayer in the schools with antireligious hostility, they insisted that "the thousands of rabbis and congregations who have authorized the submission of this brief can hardly be characterized as being 'on the side of those who oppose religion.'"

Yet some Jewish leaders dissented from the widespread community support for *Engel*. Rabbi Menachem Schneerson, the Lubavitcher Rebbe, for example, approved of the Regents' Prayer, and publicly challenged the Court's ruling. In the second selection included below, Rabbi Schneerson criticized *Engel* on the grounds of "Halacha (Jewish law) and common sense." "It is necessary to engrave upon the child's mind the idea that any wrongdoing is an offense against the divine authority and order," Rabbi Schneerson argued, and he called upon all Jews committed to the Torah to work for the decision's reversal.

♦   ♦   ♦

Jewish agencies support the Supreme Court decision outlawing state-composed prayers, 1961

Brief of Synagogue Council of America and National Community Relations Advisory Council as Amici Curiae, *Supreme Court of the United States, October Term, 1961,* Engel v. Vitale.

This Court has granted certiorari to review a decision of the New York Court of Appeals which affirmed lower court decisions upholding the validity of the action of the Respondent School Board in instituting the practice of daily recitation in the public schools of the so-called "Regents' Prayer." The text of this prayer is as follows:

"Almighty God, we acknowledge our dependence upon Thee, and we beg Thy blessings upon us, our parents, our teachers and our Country.". . .

First, the officially promoted acknowledgment of dependence upon God and the invocation of His blessings constitute a preference of theistic religions over non-theistic ones and, secondly, the engaging in public prayer constitutes a preference of those faiths which sanction the practice over those to which it is offensive.

The acknowledgment of dependence upon Almighty God and the prayer to him for His blessings necessarily constitute official assertion by the public school officials of the existence of a personal God who can and will respond to prayer and grant the blessings prayed for. This official assertion of a belief in the existence of God prefers some religions over others, specifically theistic religions over those which are non-theistic.

Nor is the "Regents' Prayer" acceptable to all religions that posit the existence of a personal God. For example, even among theistic religions, there are innumerable varieties and gradations of creed and doctrine concerning: (1) the very possibility of the Deity's present intervention in the course of creation (theologically dominated "special providence") and the conditions under which special providence may be hoped for without irreverence; (2) the propriety of addressing prayers to the Deity that seek to sway or influence the exertions of divine will; and (3) the propriety of assuming that the Deity, in dispensing blessings, can be induced to recognize the political boundaries of a specific country. . . .

Experience has shown that sooner or later so-called non-denominational religious exercises acquire sectarian additions and deviations. Moreover, what is non-denominational to the majority frequently is sectarian to the minority. Many Protestant public school authorities have designated as non-denominational the King James version of the Bible, which is unacceptable to Catholics, and the Lord's Prayer, which is unacceptable to Jews.

Children of different religions pray in different ways. Some kneel and cross themselves, some clasp their hands and bow their heads. Some pray with head covered and some with head uncovered. And to some all public oral prayer is objectionable. . . .

Even if the Regents' Prayer were truly non-sectarian, its collective recitation under public school sponsoring would still be unconstitutional. The First Amendment, the Court held in *Everson, McCollum, McGowan* and *Torcaso,* as well as in *Zorach v. Clauson,* 343 U.S. 306, imposes upon government an obligation of neutrality not merely as between competing sects and faiths, but also as between religion and non-religion. Under the principles set forth in these cases, a government not only may not aid one religion or prefer one religion over another, but also may not "aid all religions.". . .

While the issue of voluntariness vs. compulsion is perhaps relevant in respect to the attack on the practice involved in the present suit under the free exercise aspect of the First Amendment, it is completely irrelevant in respect to the establishment aspect. Here the critical test is not compulsion (although in respect to religious practices or teachings compulsion would violate the establishment ban as well as the free exercise guaranty), but state aid to religion. Hence, even if pupil participation in the prayer were entirely voluntary—which we deny—the First Amendment's ban on establishment would still be violated by the aid accorded religion by the State through its public school system and by State participation in religious affairs. . . .

Children of minority religious groups particularly are faced with a dilemma whenever religion intrudes upon the public school—a dilemma which is always hard and frequently is cruel. They must either subject themselves to being singled out as non-conformists or they must participate in religious practices and teachings at variance with what they learn at home or in their religious schools. It is understandable that not infrequently some of them choose the second alternative as the lesser evil, and that Catholic and Jewish children will participate in Protestant religious practices in violation of their religious convictions and upbringing rather than subject themselves to the pain of not belonging.

We submit that under the guaranty of separation and religious freedom, American children may not be placed in this dilemma by public school authorities. They may not be compelled to choose between being forced or influenced to profess a religious belief or disbelief. It was to avoid the oppression and bitterness which Old World experience had shown to be an inevitable concomitant of governmental intrusion in religion, that the fathers of our country gave constitutional protection to the principle that "religion is wholly exempt from [government's] cognizance.". . .

[The] equation of opposition to religious practices in the public school with opposition to religion is unfortunately widespread. But its being widespread does not make it true.

This brief is submitted on behalf of the coordinating bodies of 70 Jewish organizations, including the national bodies representing congregations and rabbis of Orthodox, Conservative and Reform Judaism. The thousands of rabbis and congregations who have authorized the submission of this brief can hardly be characterized as being "on the side of those who oppose religion." Many Christian groups and publications have similarly expressed opposition to the Regents' Prayer. . . .

The stated purpose of the Board of Regents in formulating the challenged prayer and in urging its collective recitation daily in the public schools is to inculcate in the children an appreciation of the moral and spiritual values shared by most Americans. But it is unreal to expect that an appreciation of moral and spiritual values can be communicated to our children by the rote recitation in the classroom of the prayer recommended by the Regents or of any other formalized prayer. Whatever is good and meaningful in prayer must inevitably be lost by its mechanical repetition in an atmosphere devoid of the religious spirit which only the home, church and synagogue can provide. . . .

Since the adoption of the First Amendment, the United States has escaped much of the bitter religious conflict and sectarian strife which have riven other parts of the world and driven men to violence and bloodshed. That good fortune has been due in no small part to two of the truly great contributions the American people have made to western civilization: the concept of the separation of church and state and the free public school system. The first, by protecting religion against the intrusion of civil authority and by making it impossible for the state to become a battleground for sectarian preference and favor, has preserved both our political freedom and our religious freedom. The second, by providing for the education of our children on terms of complete equality and without cognizance of their differences in religious beliefs or disbeliefs, has been the cornerstone of our American democracy. The intrusion of religion upon the public school system, as we have shown in this brief, both threatens the separation of church and state and challenges the traditional integrity of the public schools. That instruction, if permitted and sanctioned as sought by respondents, will greatly endanger the institutions which have preserved religious and political freedom in the United States and which have prevented religious warfare in this nation.

◆

Letter from the Lubavitcher Rabbi on the need for public school prayer, 1964

Greeting and Blessing:

In reply to your inquiring as to whether or not there has been a change in my views on the question of prayer in the public schools, inasmuch as this issue has again become a topic of the day in connection with congressional efforts to introduce a constitutional amendment to permit certain religious exercises in the public school.

Let me assure you at once that my views have not changed. As I stated then, my views are firmly anchored in the Torah, Torath Chayim. Their validity could therefore not have been affected by the passing of time. On the contrary, if there could have been any change at all, it was to reinforce my conviction of the vital need that the children in the public schools should be allowed to begin their day at school with the recitation of a nondenominational prayer, acknowledging the existence of a Creator and Master of the Universe, and our dependence upon Him. In my opinion, this acknowledgment is absolutely necessary in order to impress upon the minds of our growing-up generation that the world in which they live is not a jungle, where brute force, cunning, and unbridled passion rule supreme, but that it has a Master who is not an abstraction, but a personal God; that this Supreme Being takes a "personal interest" in the affairs of each and every individual, and to Him everyone is accountable for one's daily conduct.

Juvenile delinquency, the tragic symptom of the disillusionment, insecurity, and confusion of the young generation, has not abated; rather the reverse is the case. Obviously, it is hard to believe that the police and law-enforcing agencies will succeed in deterring delinquency and crime, not to mention completely eliminating them at the root, even if there were enough police officers to keep an eye on every recalcitrant child. Besides, this would not be the right way to remedy the situation. The remedy lies in removing the cause, not in merely treating the symptoms.

It is necessary to engrave upon the child's mind the idea that any wrongdoing is an offense against the divine authority and order.

At first glance this seems to be an essential function of a house of prayer and of the spiritual leaders. However, anyone who does not wish to delude himself about the facts of house of prayer attendance, both in regard to the number of worshipers and the frequency of their visits, etc., must admit that shifting the responsibility to the house of prayer will not correct the situation. Nor can we afford to wait until the house of prayer will attain its fitting place in our society, and in the life of our youth in particular, for the young generation will not wait with its growing-up process.

Children have to be "trained" from their earliest youth to be constantly aware of "the Eye that seeth and the Ear that heareth." We cannot leave it to the law-enforcing agencies to be the keepers of the ethics and morals of our young generation. The boy or girl who has embarked upon a course of truancy will not be intimidated by the policeman, teacher, or parent, whom he or she thinks fair game to "outsmart." Furthermore, the crux of the problem lies in the success or failure of bringing up the children to an awareness of a Supreme Authority, who is not only to be feared, but also loved. Under existing conditions in this country, a daily prayer in the public schools is for a vast number of boys and girls the only opportunity of cultivating such an awareness.

8. Christmas in the Public Schools

How Jews, as a religious minority, should respond to the annual celebration of Christmas in America's public schools is an issue that has long divided the American Jewish community. Since the late nineteenth century, some Jews have viewed Christmas as a secular national holiday, not unlike Thanksgiving or the Fourth of July: a universal celebration of peace and goodwill, in which all patriotic Americans, regardless of their religious faith, could and should participate. These Jews argue that Christmas, having become part of America's "civil religion," a "universal holiday," neither Christian nor Jewish, may be celebrated in the public schools with Jews participating. For as a legally mandated national holiday, it holds no Christological significance whatsoever. Most Jews, however, disagree, viewing Christmas as a decidedly sectarian holiday, specifically Christian in its origins and character. They insist, in the words of the American Jewish Congress, that "the observance of the day which marks the birth of the Savior is nothing and can be nothing but a Christian religious holiday." Advocating a strict separation between religion and state on this issue, many Jewish leaders have urged parents to complain to public school principals about Christmas celebrations and to actively protest if their complaints are ignored.

As the issue of Bible reading and prayer in the schools receded, the Christmas issue came more and more to the forefront of religion-in-school debates. Already by the 1940s and 1950s, a Jewish communal consensus had begun to emerge in opposition to Christmas celebrations in the schools, to the public display of nativity scenes and creches at school assemblies, and to the singing of Christmas carols in the classroom. Led by the American Jewish Congress and the Central Conference of American Rabbis (CCAR), Jewish communal organizations also opposed joint Chanukah-Christmas observances. "We must not allow ourselves to be drawn into the embarrassing and contradictory position," argued the CCAR's Committee on Church and State in its annual resolution that is included as our first selection below, "that we are not opposed to sectarianism in public schools when something of Judaism is introduced and that our adherence to the principle of separation of church and state is only invoked when another religion wants to make use of the public schools to further its own special religious purposes." In more recent decades, this growing Jewish communal consensus in opposition to any and all religious holiday observances in public schools has been reflected in the several important policy statements of the Synagogue Council of America and the National Jewish Community Relations Advisory Council's Joint Advisory Committee on Religion and State, particularly its oft-quoted 1962 "Statement of Principles on Religious Holiday Observances in Public Schools" which we have included as our second selection below.

Nevertheless, some Jewish leaders and thinkers still consider Christmas celebrations to be forms of an American civic faith that Jews should not find troubling or offensive. In the third selection included below, "A Rabbi's Christmas," Jakob J. Petuchowski, a prominent Reform rabbi and theologian who for many years (until his death in 1992) was a distinguished professor at Hebrew Union College–Jewish Institute of Religion in Cincinnati, and for whom "the sound of Christmas carols" was "music to my ears," explains why he "dissociates himself completely from the battle waged each winter by various Jewish organizations against the festival of Christmas."

◆   ◆   ◆

CCAR resolution on religious day celebrations in the public schools, 1937

On the question of the introduction of Christian or Jewish holyday celebrations or observances into the public schools, the Committee on Church and State recommended to the conference the following stand, which was approved by the C. C. A. R. at the 1937 Conference held in Columbus, Ohio:

> "Another question of general interest, not new but with a novel slant, is that of the Christological programs during the mid-winter holidays.

> "For years this Committee has contended that religious programs no matter how popular, interesting and attractive, have no place in tax supported public educational institutions. No exceptions were made for Christmas or Easter. They, like other religious festivals, could not possibly be given without very definite denominational background and implications and the public school room was no place for them. The Committee has always realized that its declaration was in all too many localities no more than a voice calling in the wilderness, but it stood by its convictions and still does so.

> "It is, therefore, with keen regret that the Committee notices that in some communities, our people, being unable to eliminate Christmas or Easter programs,

have asked that Hanukkah and Passover programs be also allowed and in at least two states Yuletide and Hanukkah, Passover and Easter form the content of programs in public schools.

"Your Committee strongly disapproves of this and urges the members of the Conference not to encourage the celebration of Hanukkah and Passover in public schools. We must not allow ourselves to be drawn into the embarrassing and contradictory position that we are not opposed to sectarianism in public schools when something of Judaism is introduced and that our adherence to the principle of separation of church and state is only invoked when another religion wants to make use of the public schools to further its own special religious purposes. Your Committee recommends that the Conference go on record as disapproving the giving of Hanukkah and Passover programs in our public schools."

◆

"Statement of Principles on Religious Holiday Observances in Public Schools," 1962

In keeping with the principles underlying the relationship of religion and public education set forth in the joint resolutions of the Synagogue Council of America and the National Community Relations Advisory Council regarding sectarian practices in the public schools, and reaffirming those principles and applying them to the specific question of religious holiday observances in the public school, we state:

1. We are opposed to the observance of religious holidays in the public elementary and high schools because in our view such observance constitutes a violation of the traditional American principle of the separation of church and state.

2. Joint religious observances such as Christmas-Hanukah and Easter-Passover, are in our opinion no less a breach of the principle of separation of church and state and violate the conscience of many religious persons, Jews and Christians alike.

3. Where religious holiday observances are nevertheless held in public schools, Jewish children have a right to refrain from participation. We recommend that the local Jewish communities take such action as may be appropriate to safeguard this right of nonparticipation.

4. We urge that local Jewish communities consult with the Joint Advisory Committee of the Synagogue Council of America and the National Community Relations Advisory Council before taking formal or public action on all these matters.

◆

Jakob J. Petuchowski, "A Rabbi's Christmas," 1991

In order not to raise false hopes in the hearts of those who still have the expectation that one day all Jews will convert to Christianity, it might be best to begin with a few disclaimers. The writer of this article does *not* believe in the Trinity. He does *not* believe that Jesus of Nazareth was either a part of the Godhead or the Messiah expected by the Jews. In other words, the writer of these lines is *not* a Christian.

But the writer of these lines also dissociates himself completely from the annual battle waged each winter by various Jewish organizations against the festival of Christmas, or at least against the public observance of Christmas. For one thing, although he does not himself celebrate Christmas in his own home, he rather likes the sights, the sounds, the smells, and the tastes of Christmas. Nor is he beyond relishing such traditional German Christmas delicacies as *Lebkuchen* and *Stollen*—coming, as he does, from a German-Jewish background where those bakery goods figured prominently in the observance of the Jewish winter festival of Hanukkah. Colorfully decorated Christmas trees and crèches, in the homes of Christian friends and in public places, delight his eyes; the sound of Christmas carols is music to his ears; and he avidly follows the rubrics and the pageantry of the Papal Midnight Mass on his TV screen.

Still, all of that is a matter of mere externals. What really intrigues him is the fact that millions of his non-Jewish fellow human beings are celebrating the birthday of a *Jewish* child. And they are doing so by extolling the values of peace and good will. All the more misplaced, he thinks, are the efforts by some supposedly Jewish organizations to arouse, through their battles against Christmas symbols in public places, the ill will and resentment of Christians— at the very time when the Christian religion, more than at other times of the year, inspires its followers with irenic and philanthropic sentiments.

Suppose that one day half of the world, including the United States, were to take note of the contributions made to human thought by the seventeenth-century thinker of Jewish origin, Baruch Spinoza, by instituting an annual celebration of his birthday—including the public display of Spinoza's lens-grinding workshop. Would the various Jewish organizations now fighting public Christmas displays also fight the public observance of Spinoza's birthday? Hardly. In fact, they might even enthusiastically welcome it—in spite of the fact that Spinoza had severely criticized the faith of his Jewish ancestors, and had been excommunicated by the rabbinical authorities of Amsterdam.

Or what would happen if there were an annual International Sigmund Freud Day, including public displays of replicas of the couch which once stood in Freud's Vienna consulting room? Would Jewish organizations now fighting public Christmas displays fight that display, too? Hardly. In fact, they might even enthusiastically welcome it—in spite of the fact that Freud had proudly proclaimed his own atheism, and had included the religion of his Jewish ancestors among the rest of the world's religions, all of which he described as illusions.

What, then, is so different about celebrating the birthday of that Palestinian Jew through whose influence, as already noted by the great twelfth-century Jewish thinker, Moses Maimonides, the words of Israel's Torah have been spread to the far corners of the earth? Why does the public celebration of the birthday of Jesus of Nazareth, including the public display of replicas of the Bethlehem crèche, arouse such Jewish animosity?

The reasons are varied and complicated. Traditionally, in spite of its role in spreading major Jewish teachings throughout the world, Christianity, to put it mildly, has not been an unmixed blessing for Jews. Not only the words of the Torah were spread throughout the world in Jesus' name; that same name was also invoked when, throughout the centuries, Christians murdered Jews by the thousands, burned them alive, confiscated their goods, restricted the way in which they could earn their livelihoods, and confined them to overcrowded and unsanitary quarters. The Christian ideals of peace and good will did not extend beyond the entrance of the ghetto. This may no longer be the case today. But Jews have long memories. To many of them, the sign of the Cross is still a reminder of pogroms and persecutions. Their attitude toward Christianity and toward Christianity's founder is, therefore, a highly ambivalent one.

That is particularly true of those Jews—and they tend to be the most Orthodox followers of the faith—whose own personal and family background in Eastern Europe still approximated most closely the conditions of Jewish life in the Christian Middle Ages. Those Jews certainly cannot be expected to "enjoy" Christmas.

Yet, and here we come to an apparent paradox, these East European Orthodox Jews are *not* in the forefront of those who protest most vociferously against the public display of Christmas symbols or the public celebration of that festival. In fact, not only are they not in the forefront; most of them have nothing at all to do with the organizations that lead the battle against the public observance of Christmas in the name of *the* "Jewish Community."

That battle is led by a different type of Jew altogether. He or she is most likely to be a secularist of Jewish origin, who has no use for any kind of religion; and that includes the religion into which he or she was born. And in that battle, the secularist of Jewish origin is liable to be joined by a fellow Jew of the Reform Jewish denomination, which—in its increasingly radical departures from traditional Jewish belief and practice—is itself more and more becoming a wing of American secularism. Such Jews seek alliances with all the other secularist forces in the country that want to denude the "public square" of every last trace of religious influence. They keep insisting upon a strict enforcement of the separation of church and state—enforcement to a degree certainly never anticipated by the founders of the republic.

In other words, what we are really dealing with in this annual battle against public Christian observance is not so much a "Jewish" attack on that observance as it is a *secularist* one—with some of the prominent secularists identifying themselves as Jews. They are the same people who fight *non-denominational* prayers in public schools, the use of public school facilities for meetings of high school religious-interest groups, and state support of private schools. They fight with equal vigor the attempts by other Jewish groups to have Jewish religious symbols exhibited alongside the Christian ones, such as the efforts of the Chabad (Lubavitch) group of Orthodox Jews to place a Hanukkah candelabrum on the public square when a Christmas tree is put up there, which would be a fitting demonstration of America's religious pluralism. They are, in other words, not singling out Christianity. They are against the public manifestation of religion *per se*—even (or perhaps particularly) against the public manifestation of the religion of their own ancestors.

The invocation of the First Amendment as authority for the campaign against the public display of any and all religious symbols seems to involve the demand that the state "establish" the religion of Secularism as the official religion of the United States—which would, to say the least, be a rather curious use of the First Amendment. But even if one were to grant, for argument's sake, that the lawyers employed by the American Jewish Congress, the (Reform) Union of American Hebrew Congregations, and similar organizations have established the "true" meaning of the First Amendment, i.e., that the amendment really and truly rules out the public display of a crèche or a Hanukkah candelabrum, one would still be entitled to wonder what those organizations hope to gain by stirring up animosities every winter.

Traditional Jewish teaching includes the principle of *liphnim mishurat hadin* (cf. Babylonian Talmud *Baba Qamma* 100a and elsewhere), which means that, on occasion, it is preferable not to make use of the full extent to which the law, strictly interpreted, entitles one to go. For there is, after all, a "higher law," which is adumbrated in Deuteronomy 12:28, "You shall do what is good and right in the sight of the Lord your God." Several passages in Jesus' Sermon on the Mount seem to incorporate that principle. It is not a case of "abolishing" the law, but rather, if one so desires—and if one does so to one's own, and not the other person's, hurt—of not pressing the full extent of what the law provides. That, admittedly, may not be an everyday occurrence in traditional Jewish life (although the pious will always strive for it), but it is a manifestation of a higher degree of piety. Some of the ancient rabbis even sought to find biblical basis for such transcendence of biblical law.

It would seem to this writer that, even if the strict constructionists of the separation of church and state could demonstrate beyond a shadow of a doubt that the public display of Christmas symbols infringes upon that "separation," Jews might still prefer to abide by the principle of *liphnim mishurat hadin,* of *not* running to the courts in order to get the spontaneous expression of their neighbors' piety interfered with by the law. After all, what are we to think of a "Judaism" that is so weak that it feels threatened by the display of a crèche at City Hall, or by the sound of a Christmas carol at a public school assembly? Why, then, not show some generosity on the Jewish side at a season of the year when Christians celebrate the birth of the Jew in whose name they proclaim peace and good will to humankind?

And it is, to be quite honest, not *only* a matter of superior generosity. Life in the medieval Christian world—in which, by the way, we no longer happen to live—certainly was no bed of roses for the Jews. But Jews fared infinitely *worse* in those modern societies from which the God of Abraham and of Jesus had been banished. If Jews cannot forget the Middle Ages, they owe it to themselves to remember the most recent past, too. One could argue, therefore, that the very self-interest of the Jews is at stake in preventing the United States from becoming a totally godless society.

Jews may not accept the dogmas and the theology associated with the Christmas story. They would, in fact, cease to be Jews if they did. Nor would they be acting in good taste if, without accepting the Christian belief structure, they were to celebrate Christmas in their own homes. (And it does not help much if they try to justify the Christmas tree in their home by saying that it was originally a pagan, rather than a Christian, custom—as though Judaism approved of paganism!) But they can still recognize in the *Christian* observance of Christmas one of the factors that help maintain the religious character of our society—in which Jews, too, with their own beliefs and practices, and with their very lives, have a considerable stake.

That is why this writer will continue to wish his Christian friends a "Merry Christmas" at Yuletide, and rejoice in the fact that those friends join the angelic choir in proclaiming glory to God in the highest, and peace among humankind on earth. He will most certainly not object at all to the public display of his friends' symbols of religious faith. Indeed, he will continue to be moved by awe and wonder that, through the influence of one of his own remote cousins, some of the words of Judaism's Torah have been spread to the far corners of the earth.

9. *Lee v. Weisman* and the Continuing Issue of Public School Prayer

In the 1962 case of *Engel v. Vitale,* the Supreme Court, as we have seen, ruled that a state-sponsored prayer recited by public school students was unconstitutional. Thirty years later, in the case of *Lee v. Weisman,* as we have also noted, the Supreme Court extended the principle of *Engel* to hold that a state may not sponsor prayers at middle and high school graduation ceremonies.

The case arose in Providence, Rhode Island, where middle and high school principals regularly invited members of the city's clergy to offer invocation and benediction prayers as part of their schools' graduation ceremonies. In June 1989, Leslie Gutterman, the rabbi of Temple Beth-El in Providence, delivered a nonsectarian prayer, at the eighth-grade gradu- ation of one of the city's middle schools, "praising God for the legacy of America where diversity is celebrated and the rights of minorities are protected" and for "its court system where all can seek justice." His prayer was challenged by Daniel Weisman and his daughter Deborah, a member of the middle school's graduating class, who sued the Provi- dence School Board, arguing that Rabbi Gutterman's com- mencement benediction violated the Supreme Court's 1962 (*Engel v. Vitale*) ban on public school prayer. In a five-to-four decision, the Supreme Court agreed, stating that gradu- ation ceremony benedictions such as Gutterman's, however nonsectarian, were unconstitutional, and explaining that its ban on graduation prayers and benedictions in this case was a logical extension of three decades of court decisions (since *Engel*) regarding organized prayer in the public schools. Despite this ruling, the U.S. Court of Appeals for the Fifth Circuit (and other lower courts) subsequently decided that student-led graduation prayer was constitutionally permiss- able, a position that the Supreme Court seems to have en- dorsed. This has led some observers to predict that the impact of the *Lee v. Weisman* ruling will be less profound than initially anticipated.

Most Jewish organizations and leaders applauded the Su- preme Court's ruling in *Lee v. Weisman* as a great victory for religious freedom. Even Rabbi Leslie Gutterman, the Reform rabbi who delivered the contested benediction, seemed pleased by the Court's decision. As indicated in the selection below, he was ambivalent about offering the prayer in the first place. "The decision is in the best interest of all civil libertarians," Rabbi Gutterman observed when the Court's ruling was an- nounced. "That the official posture of the government be neutral bodes well for diverse faiths."

◆   ◆   ◆

Rabbi Gutterman on his commencement benediction, 1989

Anyone who remembers me from Mr. Krable's Algebra I class at Whittier Junior High School in Flint, Mich., knows I've done my share of praying in public schools. Inevitably, I'd panic before an exam was distributed. After lifting my eyes heavenward in sincere petition, I remember asking the same question I still ask now that prayer is my profession: "Will this turn out to have been helpful?"

In the almost 20 years I've been a rabbi in Rhode Island, I've given my share of invocations. I offered public prayers when the Civic Center was dedicated, at inaugurations of governors and mayors, at retirements and installations. I've prayed at testimonials, roasts, hospitals' annual dinners and a college commencement. Sometimes the atmosphere has been heady. I've sat next to Elizabeth Taylor, Henry Kissinger, Gen. William Westmoreland and former President Gerald Ford.

At more occasions than I care to remember, I'm seated at one end of a dais, with a colleague of Christian faith seated at the other. There we perch like two bookends, more than aware that the opening prayer one of us will give may be considered a short, possibly pleasant interlude between cocktails and salad. One of the tricks of the trade is to request to give the opening prayer—so we can then go home and enjoy our own salads.

Sometimes I wonder if I am too eager to say yes to a public invocation because of the event's prestige. So, as a balance, I frequently accept invitations to pray at events that I believe will assuredly escape public notice. For example, a few weeks ago I said yes to a request to deliver an invocation and benediction at Nathan Bishop Middle School in Providence, although it was an occasion I approached with ambivalence because it stirred up unsettled feelings I have about public prayer.

As it turned out, those prayers were covered by Channels 6, 10, and 12 and by the Providence Journal-Bulletin.

The graduation at Nathan Bishop highlighted the thornier issues which surround prayer at civic occasions. A prayer can be unwittingly divisive. For example, many Jews wait with bated breath to hear whether a Christian minister will pray in the name of Jesus. This year I was a proud parent at the Classical High School graduation and I admit to inordinate feelings of gratitude after the lovely, sensitive benediction delivered by a priest. It was a benediction any rabbi could have spoken in good conscience.

Most of us try to frame our public prayers in universal, inclusive language, using words that are nonsectarian. On the other hand, if we make a public prayer so general, could it not end up being innocuous and meaningless? And what about the minister who might protest that his prayer is not authentic unless he invokes Jesus, his Lord and Savior? Need we be reduced to praying "to whom it may concern"?

After a temporary restraining order was sought to stop my coming to Nathan Bishop Tuesday, I consulted with a dear friend who is a respected and beloved Dominican priest, a professor at Providence College. He is sensitive to the constitutional issues involved, but sincerely feels it is meaningful to remind people at every public opportunity of the spiritual dimensions of life, even if our words fall on some deaf ears. Maybe he's right.

But I still feel more at home praying in the midst of sympathetic fellow worshippers. When I speak at public events, I can only hope that my presence and my prayers will not alienate anyone.

Chief U.S. District Judge Francis J. Boyle will soon be grappling with some of the competing legal claims. I wish him well. I'll remember him in my prayers.

The National Conference of Christians and Jews provides guidelines to schools for appropriate prayers in a pluralistic society. But even the NCCJ admits that "prayer of any kind may be inappropriate on some civic occasions."

I am still not certain whether a school graduation is such an occasion.

NINE

Religion and the State

The New Consensus

◆ ❖ ◆

B eginning in 1948, with the landmark Supreme Court case *Mc-Collum v. Board of Education,* which outlawed released-time programs such as the Gary Plan (see chapter 8, part 5), American Jewish communal leaders united in resolute opposition to any religious practices and symbols in the public arena. Jewish survival and freedom are most secure, they came to believe, echoing the language of the Supreme Court itself, where the wall separating religion and the state is strongest and least secure where religion and government are intertwined. A month after the *McCollum* decision, the Joint Committee on Religion and the Public School (later the Joint Advisory Committee on Religion and State) formulated an important statement of principles embodying the organized Jewish community's new public position. "The maintenance and furtherance of religion are the responsibility of the synagogue, the church and the home," declared the Joint Advisory Committee, which also went on record in opposition to released and shared time, government support for private religious schools, religious observances in the public schools, and the teaching of religion under the guise of "moral and spiritual values." Emboldened by the Supreme Court, Jews now loudly reaffirmed their adherence to the principle of the strict separation of religion and state.

For several decades, Leo Pfeffer, one of America's foremost scholars of church-state relations, was the preeminent Jewish spokesman for this separationist position. As staff attorney and for many years director of the American Jewish Congress's Commission on Law and Social Action, he did more than anyone else to shape and further the legal doctrine of strict separationism, espoused by the

Joint Advisory Committee on Religion and State, whose public statements and legal briefs he himself helped draft.

Instead of embracing what is generally referred to as the "narrow" interpretation of the establishment clause of the First Amendment, Pfeffer and his colleagues on the legal staffs of the American Jewish Committee, the Anti-Defamation League of B'nai B'rith, and the Joint Advisory Committee, consistently invoked the "broad interpretation" of the clause first espoused by the United States Supreme Court in its 1947 *Everson* decision, wherein the Court first claimed that the establishment clause "was intended to erect a wall of separation between Church and State." The "intent" of the First Amendment, Pfeffer and his colleagues argued, was "not merely to prohibit the establishment of a state church but to preclude any government aid to religious groups or dogmas." Henceforward, they emphasized the establishment clause of the First Amendment, rather than the free exercise clause, as the best guarantor of both religious freedom and religious equality. They assumed that the two clauses were "two sides of the same coin," expressing the unitary principle "that freedom requires separation." The "complete separation of church and state is best for the church and best for the state, and secures freedoms for both," Pfeffer loudly proclaimed. This was the principle upon which the new post–World War II Jewish consensus on issues of religion and state was predicated. To most American Jews, at least for several decades, the new consensus seemed logically consistent, historically convincing, and strategically wise in terms of the Jewish community's manifest interests.

1. Jewish Legal Action through the Courts

With the landmark 1940 Supreme Court decision of *Cantwell v. Connecticut,* in which the Court reversed the state's conviction of three Jehovah's Witnesses, the Supreme Court became increasingly involved with issues of religion and state. *Cantwell,* by incorporating the free exercise clause into the Fourteenth Amendment and applying it to the states, opened the door to federal litigation in this area. As a result, Jewish organizational activity in the church-state arena shifted ever more from the legislatures toward the courts. Beginning in 1945, with the establishment of the American Jewish Congress's

Commission on Law and Social Action (CLSA), litigation, heretofore avoided by the organized Jewish community, became
the standard Jewish communal technique for advancing the
separationist agenda that Jewish leaders had come increasingly
to espouse. While the American Jewish Committee and the
Anti-Defamation League often joined the CLSA in Jewish legal
action through the courts, the CLSA, which was the strictest
on the principle of church-state separation, invariably took
the lead in filing legal briefs and initiating litigation. In the
selection excerpted below, Will Maslow, a founding staff attorney and the first legal director of the CLSA, and subsequently
the executive director of the American Jewish Congress, outlined the legal strategy and tactics of the CLSA that guided its
approach in this area for several decades.

◆   ◆   ◆

Will Maslow on the strategy and tactics of the American Jewish Congress, 1972

. . . Unlike a private citizen, who can insist at any time on legal redress for his
private grievances, AJC must first persuade those upon whose behalf it acts
that its proposed course of action is necessary and desirable and that the gains
from such action outweigh the risks. A church-state case is not an ordinary
pocketbook action of concern only to the litigants. An objection, for example,
to the performance of a Nativity play in the public schools may be considered
by some an attack on religion itself; a protest against the use of government
funds to aid parochial schools may be regarded as an act motivated by anti-
Catholic bigotry. If the plaintiff is identified as a Jew or his cause is publicly
sponsored by a Jewish organization, the local Jewish community council may
fear that other Jews, not involved in the litigation, may become the targets of
ostracism or boycott or that latent anti-Semitism may erupt or that the harmonious relations existing between Christians and Jews in a community may
be disrupted.

AJC has always believed that such fears are exaggerated and reflect the basic
psychological insecurity of a minority group (see Maslow, *Is American Jewry
Secure,* Congress Weekly, March 27, 1950). We are convinced by experience
that whatever hostile reactions occur will quickly subside and that in the long
run a religiously-oriented Christian community will respect a courageous and
principled defense of religious liberty by a Jewish organization. In any event,
AJC believes that the fear of arousing or aggravating anti-Jewish prejudices
should not deter an effort to defend religious liberty where serious violations

are involved and that some degree of temporary resentment is preferable to acquiescence in deliberate constitutional violations.

Nevertheless, because AJC believes strongly that local Jewish community councils fill an indispensable need in reaching a community consensus, it follows scrupulously the policy of not initiating any controversial local course of action without prior discussion with the appropriate representatives of such councils. AJC has almost never undertaken a local project against the deepfelt convictions of a community council.

The process of "clearance" and coordination with national organizations is much looser and AJC exercises a greater freedom of independent action on national issues.

*　*　*

The civil rights and civil liberties aspects of CLSA's work are fully articulated in a seminal article by the late Alexander H. Pekelis, chief consultant to AJC's Commission on Law and Social Action, entitled "Full Equality in a Free Society" (Pekelis, *Law and Social Action,* pp. 218–260, Cornell U. Press, 1950). Basic to that program is the conviction that ours is and must remain a culturally pluralistic society which gains in richness and variety by encouraging religious and ethnic groups to preserve their own cultures and that American democracy and freedom will be strengthened by such diversity. We are committed therefore to the proposition that our government and its officials should treat no religion as predominant and none as subordinate. Indeed, we believe strongly that religious liberty is best preserved when our government remains strictly and severely aloof from all religious affairs. We believe, in language which has been affirmed on four occasions in the last fourteen years by the Supreme Court, that such neutrality is best cultivated by the absolute avoidance of "laws which aid one religion, aid all religions or prefer one religion over another" and that such neutrality is impossible if any "tax, in any amount, large or small" is "levied to support any religious activities or institutions whatever they may be called." Such financial support, we contend, embroils the state in religious controversies, encourages religious and civil divisiveness, penalizes non-believers and compels the taxpayer of one faith to support the religious institutions of another in violation of conscience and religious liberty. We are convinced that our country's history demonstrates that church and synagogue are at their strongest when they must depend exclusively on their spiritual resources for their strength and sustenance and not on the coercive or supporting arm of government. Finally, we agree with Justice Jackson's prophecy in the *Zorach* case that: "The day that this country ceases to be free for irreligion it will cease to be free for religion—except for the sect that can win political power."

To safeguard the precious inheritance bequeathed to us by Madison, Jefferson and the Founding Fathers, AJC seeks to win ever-increasing popular understanding and support of these principles. Our primary task is therefore an educational one. Our efforts are directed first to the Jewish community, then among the legal profession and finally the public generally. . . . Generalized educational efforts are, however, not sufficient to bring about compliance with the principles laid down in the First Amendment. Negotiation with government officials and particularly school officials is necessary. . . . Where education and negotiation fail, the only alternatives are an appeal to public opinion or an appeal to the courts. Unconstitutional policies of a school official or a school board may be reversed if a public campaign of protest can be organized. Whether such a campaign can be mounted depends upon an assessment of the strength of the opposing forces and particularly of the courage and unity of the local Jewish community on this issue.

Litigation in the sensitive areas of religious liberty and separation of church and state is comparatively infrequent. It takes a rare amount of courage for an individual, particularly a member of a minority religious group, to challenge in the courts the religious practices strongly advocated by a majority and sometimes an overwhelming majority in a local community. Where the potential plaintiff is the parent of a school child, he must also weigh the dangers of hostility to his child by its classmates. Nevertheless, there are courageous plaintiffs ready to stand by their principles.

* * *

With limited resources and the necessity to defend religious liberty from almost constant attack at every level of government and in almost every state, AJC has had to adopt a selective strategy. Obviously, one overwhelming legal or legislative victory that will once and for all dispose of the problem is impossible. AJC's strategy is therefore to attack gross breaches of the First Amendment and by the gradual accumulation of a series of favorable rulings buttress the wall that separates church and state.

A system of fluid priorities has therefore been developed. Thus we believe that financial grants by the state to religious institutions are less significant than governmental coercion, whether flagrant or subtle, to compel participation in religious exercises of another faith. The most important battleground for us therefore is the public school system because immature children are involved and because the state compels their attendance. . . .

Of course, any suit or legislative campaign which promises lasting results is preferable to one that attacks a transitory evil. Similarly a proceeding that may result in a new or significant precedent, particularly one capable of extension and development, is more desirable than the reaffirmation of well-established rule.

Considering the forces opposed to our concept of church-state separation and religious liberty, AJC is more frequently compelled to take defensive actions to maintain present positions and is rarely able to seek to heighten the wall of separation. But this strategy must of course remain flexible.

* * *

The strength of the opposing forces dictates another strategical consideration: that violations, however, blatant, should not be attacked if they are likely to be regarded as *de minimis* by judge or legislator. Thus AJC brought no suit challenging the . . . law that added the words "under God" to the statutory pledge of allegiance (36 U.S.C. 172).

* * *

The Jewish community is, of course, not monolithic, even in a formal organizational sense, and there is rarely a single Jewish position on every church-state issue. On some issues, there is a sharp conflict in the stands taken by Jewish groups. The Anti-Defamation League, for example, for many years urged school authorities to promote joint Christmas-Chanukah celebrations while AJC was opposing observance of all religious holidays in the public schools as unwise and unconstitutional. On the issue of Federal aid to education, all of the Jewish groups that have taken a position have opposed aid to parochial schools or church-operated colleges with the exception of an ultra-Orthodox splinter group not represented in the national Union of Orthodox Jewish Congregations.

But even when formal policy positions are identical, Jewish groups frequently differ on questions of emphasis, tactics and the desirability of taking public stands. The American Jewish Committee, for example, almost always opposes litigation challenging strongly-rooted religious practices in the schools as likely to engender more harm than good.

AJC has frequently allied itself with Protestant groups in challenging violations of the separation principle. . . . AJC has also sought to maintain cooperative relations with local Catholic bodies whenever it finds itself in agreement with that church on particular issues. . . . The closest relationship between AJC and a non-sectarian group in these issues is that with the American Civil Liberties Union. Although our general positions on religious liberty are not identical (the ACLU has endorsed a limited form of Federal Assistance, with certain qualifications, to church-connected colleges), AJC and ACLU have jointly brought test cases, jointly filed briefs amicus and worked together in countless ways.

* * *

. . . Jews constitute about 3% of the national population although in New York State they comprise almost 15%. Their influence with most legislatures is weak, particularly when there are countervailing religious pressures. AJC has therefore understandably relied heavily on the courts for the protection of religious liberty. That is not to say that judges are not influenced by currents of popular feelings or prejudice. But judges, unlike legislators, are guided by a tradition of objectivity and independence, a tradition that requires decisions to be based on the record and statutes or constitutions interpreted in a way that will fulfill their original purpose.

AJC hopes that these lawsuits will also serve as means of educating the American people to the inestimable value of America's great contribution to the art of government: the wall of separation between church and state. It will continue its efforts to show that strong fences make good neighbors and that only by separating church and state will each thrive.

2. Leo Pfeffer: Apostle of Strict Separationism

During his forty-year (1945–1985) association with the American Jewish Congress's Commission on Law and Social Action, as staff attorney, director, and special counsel, Leo Pfeffer advised, planned, and argued more church-state cases before the United States Supreme Court than anyone else in American history, while at the same time making an enduring contribution to church-state thought and scholarship. More than any other single individual, he combined the roles of thinker and participant, theoretician and practitioner, in his continuing efforts to shape and further the legal doctrine of strict separationism. Indeed, it has been widely recognized that his major books, such as *Church, State, and Freedom* and *God, Caesar, and the Constitution,* along with his articles and legal briefs, constitute the most "polished expression" of the strict separationist constitutional position. His "broad" interpretation of the establishment clause, and his view that religion and state were meant to be completely independent and "absolutely" separate, left a profound impact on church-state thought and jurisprudence, and shaped Supreme Court decision-making during his lifetime.

Pfeffer's "absolutist" approach to the First Amendment, while enjoying widespread popularity within the Jewish community, did not go unchallenged. Critics, both within the Jewish community and without, accused him of being an "extremist" in the separationist positions that he espoused. A reflective autobiographical essay written by Pfeffer suggests that he himself was somewhat ambivalent about his role. As he reveals in the first selection below, "pragmatic consider-ations" underlay his stance. "Any compromise," he believed, "becomes too often the starting point for further compro-mises." He also attributes his views to his experiences and perceptions growing up as an Orthodox Jew in a Christian so-ciety. In the second selection included below, he recalls his formative years in the public schools of Manhattan's Lower East Side, where he was constantly reminded of his minority status. His subsequent opposition to proposals for released-time instruction in New York City's public schools, he reveals, "was hardly surprising in view of my childhood experience with the released-time proposal."

◆   ◆   ◆

Leo Pfeffer's autobiographical reflections, 1985

In 1911 (I was then two years old), my father, an Orthodox rabbi, left my birth-place, a small ghetto town in Austria-Hungary, to explore the possibilities of obtaining a pulpit in the United States. Within six months he was successful, and the family, consisting of three daughters and two sons (I was the young-est), emigrated to America to settle in the lower east side of New York City.

The apartment in which we lived was necessarily close to the synagogue that my father served as rabbi. It was, however, about a mile from the closest yeshivah, known officially as the Rabbi Jacob Joseph Elementary School. For that reason, I was sent to Public School 15, located but two short streets from our apartment. There are only two things relating to my attendance at the school that I remember. The first was the daily Bible reading in the assembly. The reading was done by the school's principal, Miss Knox—as far as the pupils knew that was her full name. She was gray-haired and probably a Protestant. The reading was limited to the book of Psalms, which I assume was from the King James version. I assume, too, that the limitation was based upon the reality that almost all the pupils in the school were Jewish.

The second experience was also related to my future career. In the middle of my 4A term, the first semester of the fourth year, the public school educational authorities received and were considering a proposal to introduce released-time religious instruction into the schools. This was long before the Supreme Court's decision in *McCollum v. Board of Education,* and I think that the pro-posed program would have been based upon in-school instruction. Whatever the case might be, in the end the proposal was not adopted. My parents, how-ever, did not wait for that. I was immediately withdrawn from Public School 15 and enrolled in the yeshivah.

Upon graduation from elementary school, I was enrolled in a yeshivah for secondary school students, known as the Rabbi Isaac Elchonon Talmudical Academy, which later expanded into the arena of higher education under the name Yeshivah University. My collegiate education was received at the City College of New York, and my law degree was granted by New York University in 1933. I was admitted to the bar in December of that year. In 1937, I married Freda Plotkin, whom I met when we were both members of Young Israel Synagogue of Manhattan. It was because of her, by sheer chance as a coconspirator, that I later entered the field of church-state relations.

In 1944, our first child, Alan, was born. Our other child, Susan, was born three years later. Freda was then employed as a secretary in the Women's Division of the American Jewish Congress, and, after an effort of several months to continue her career while mothering a child, she gave up and resigned from her position. She informed me that the organization was expanding its committee on law and legislation and had openings for lawyers. I applied for a position, was accepted as a staff member of the Commission on Law and Social Action (CLSA), and started work on 1 October 1945. . . .

My first assignment as a staff member of the Commission on Law and Social Action was to prepare a memorandum on the pros and cons of released time for religious instruction. The American Jewish Congress was considering whether to take a position on the subject and, if so, what position to take. Why I was selected for the assignment, I do not know. It may be that I was the only member of the staff who had a religious education. It may be that in my application for employment I noted that I had written some articles that were published in religious-oriented Jewish periodicals. Or it may have been purely a matter of chance. If the last option was the fact, then chance was very good to me, for the memorandum I prepared setting forth both sides of the controversy indicated quite clearly that I opposed the released-time program primarily, though not exclusively, on constitutional grounds. This is hardly surprising in view of my childhood experience with the released-time proposal. In any event, the memorandum resulted in my being assigned responsibility for litigation involving religious freedom and church-state issues.

* * *

Lawyers and scholars cognizant in the field of free exercise of religion and church-state relations are aware that I am frequently characterized as an absolutist or extremist or doctrinaire or unrealistic or uncompromising. Even if I would, I could not challenge the thrust of the characterizations. My briefs, writings, and lectures manifest my commitment to absolutism in respect to all First and Fourteenth Amendment rights.

Like other civil liberties defenders, I recognize that absolute freedom of religion or of speech or of assembly is not possible, but that hardly proves anything. The reality that no person is immortal does not mean that the medical and pharmaceutical professions should be abolished.

Aside from my deep commitment to the religion clauses as a matter of sincerely held principle, pragmatic considerations impel me to defend an absolutist position. "The same authority," James Madison said, "which can force a citizen to contribute three pence only of his property for the support of any one establishment may force him to conform to any other establishment in all cases whatsoever." Absolutists serve an important function in church-state law; any compromise becomes too often the starting point for further compromises. The recent compromise that led to the enactment of a law accepting prayer at the secondary school level will most assuredly not end the crusade for the return of religion to all public schools of whatever level.

During the thirty years since I submitted my first Supreme Court brief in the *McCollum* case until the present writing, the Supreme Court has had three chief justices—Fred M. Vinson, Earl Warren, and Warren E. Burger. In respect to this period, we realistic absolutists could hardly have been happier. The Court did allow released-time religious instruction off public school premises, and somewhat restricted state financing of church-related colleges, but in the main, church-state separationism was triumphant. So, too, was the principle of free exercise, and, in respect to this aspect, the Supreme Court has done more than quite well.

3. Safeguarding Religious Liberty: The "Official" Jewish Position on Church-State Relationships

One indication of the broad Jewish consensus on issues of religion and state was the ability of a wide variety of disparate and diverse Jewish organizations, representing all of the different religious movements in Judaism as well as a host of community relations organizations, to formulate joint statements of policy under the auspices of the Joint Advisory Committee of the Synagogue Council of America and the National Jewish Community Relations Advisory Council (established in 1947). To mark the tenth anniversary of this unique umbrella organization, it published "a concise, comprehensive and systematic presentation," in one document, of its various policy statements for use as a general guide for Jewish organizations, agencies, and communities. Entitled *Safeguarding Religious Liberty* (1957), the pamphlet was widely distributed and frequently reprinted. It reflected the "shared conviction of all the organizations that . . . the wall of separation between state and church created by the Constitution must be scrupulously maintained."

The revised edition of *Safeguarding Religious Liberty*, published in 1971 and reprinted below, presents the official consensus position of the American Jewish community on a range of church-state issues, including basic principles, religion and public education, Sunday laws, religious symbols on public property, and related concerns. For the most part, the text was unchanged from 1957, an indication that the major Jewish organizations continued to hold to their established positions. Yet, the 1971 edition, unlike its predecessor, does include a demurral on the part of two Orthodox Jewish organizations, the Rabbinical Council of America and the Union of Orthodox Jewish Congregations of America, on the issue of governmental aid to religiously-controlled schools. The Joint Advisory Committee's inability to obtain consensus on this issue pointed to cracks in the wall-to-wall coalition that had stood for twenty-five years, and adumbrated further challenges that would, in time, undermine it. By the time another twenty-five years passed, the coalition was dead and both the Joint Advisory Committee and the Synagogue Council had passed out of existence.

✦　　✦　　✦

"Safeguarding Religious Liberty," a general guide, 1971

DECLARATIONS OF PRINCIPLE

These declarations constitute a statement of principles from which the positions of the many Jewish agencies on various specific practices are derived.

Religion has always been and continues to be the central core of Jewish life. We urge all religious groups to unite in an intensified national program, designed to enroll all the children of our country in religious educational institutions of their respective faiths. We urge the religious bodies to avail themselves of all media of mass communication for this program, such as the press, radio, motion pictures, speakers' platforms, and special dramatic projects.

The American democratic system is founded in large part upon ethical and moral concepts derived from the great religions of mankind. The preservation and fostering of these concepts are essential to the fullest realization of the American ideal; and their growth and development as major forces in American life should be the deep concern of every citizen.

Religious liberty is an indispensable aspect of democratic freedom; indeed it is the very foundation of American democracy. As a nation of people attached to many different religious faiths, or to none, we owe our survival and our unity to the universal acceptance of the uniquely American concept that the relationship between man and God is not and may not be subject to government control or regulation.

The growth of democracy in the United States is in large measure a product of that unique principle in our basic law that puts religion outside the jurisdiction of the state. Any impairment of that principle threatens religious liberty and brings other basic freedoms into jeopardy.

The maintenance and furtherance of religion are the responsibilities of the synagogue, the church and the home, and not of the public school system; the utilization in any manner of the time, facilities, personnel, or funds of the public school system for purposes of religious instruction should not be permitted.

The public schools must recognize the realities of religious differences in the community and among their pupils. They should continue as they have done throughout their history to teach pupils that acceptance of and respect for such differences are basic to American democracy and contribute toward harmonious living in a free society. This implies no need, however, on the part of the public schools to teach religious doctrines or to teach about religious doctrines.

STATEMENTS OF POSITION

RELIGION AND PUBLIC EDUCATION

Moral Values and Religious Concepts
The teaching of morality, ethics and good citizenship has, down to the present, been accepted as a primary responsibility and a desirable goal of the public schools. It is our contention that the public school must continue to foster commitment to the moral and ethical values basic to such instruction. Regrettably, in public discussion of this responsibility, these values have frequently been linked with espousal of the beliefs and attitudes of particular religions or of "religion-in-general." We hold that the public school must not seek or assign theological sanctions for the values it seeks to inculcate in the children of our heterogeneous population. Such sectarian instruction is and must remain the responsibility of the home, the synagogue and the church.

"Objective" or "Factual" Teaching About Religions
The public schools must and should teach with all possible objectivity the role that religions have played in the life of mankind in the development of so-

ciety. In so doing, they must at all times be aware that it is the primary respon-sibility of the home, the synagogue and the church to provide religious instruction, and must therefore refrain from any sectarian and partisan pre-sentations in the curriculum. Religions, particularly those of the west, have significantly affected the history, ideas and institutions of our society. Public school teachers will therefore find it necessary, useful and appropriate to in-clude references to the role of these religions in human affairs, not excluding references to the doctrines or tenets of faith groups, when these are intrinsic to the subject matter being studied. Teachers may also find that sacred books of many religions, including the Bible, used as source or reference books, will help to enrich courses in literature, history and the social studies, particularly as they illuminate the ideas and life styles of the communities by which those sacred books are revered.

However, we oppose any such instruction in the public schools that will, in the guise of teaching *about* religions, actually be covert religious instruction, *i.e.*, the teaching of a sectarian religion or of "religion-in-general." We insist that parents have the exclusive right to choose their own religious instructors who function in a setting proper for such instruction.

Teaching of a "Common Core"

We are opposed to any public school program that seeks to inculcate as doc-trine any body of principles, beliefs or concepts that is represented as the "common core" of several or all religious faiths. The effort to extract from the religions current among us such a common denominator or "common core" can lead only to a watering down, a vitiation, of all that is spiritually meaning-ful in every religious faith. We submit, moreover, that attempts at religious inculcation in the public schools, even of articles of faith drawn from all reli-gions and endorsed by representatives of all, violate the traditional American principle of separation of church and state.

Use of School Premises for Religious Purposes

We are opposed to the use of public school premises during school hours for religious education, meetings, or worship. Where public school premises are made available after school hours to civic groups outside the school system, they should be made available on the same basis to religious groups.

Religious Practices and Observances; Joint Religious Observances

Mindful of the dangers inherent in any violation of the traditional Ameri-can principle of separation of church and state, we are opposed to religious practices or observances in the public elementary and high schools, including:

The reading or recitation of prayers
The reading of the Bible (except as included in a course in literature)

The distribution of Bibles or religious tracts
The singing of religious hymns
The granting of school credits for religious studies
The wearing of any type of clerical garb by public school teachers on school premises
The holding of public school classes on the premises of religious institutions
The taking of a religious census of pupils

We are opposed to the observance of religious festivals in the public elementary and high schools because in our view such observance constitutes a violation of the traditional American principle of the separation of church and state.

Joint religious observances, such as Christmas-Chanukah and Easter-Passover, are in our opinion no less a breach of the principle of separation of church and state and violate the conscience of many religious persons, Jews and Christians alike.

Where religious holiday observances are nevertheless held in public schools, Jewish children have a right to refrain from participation. We recommend that local Jewish communities take such action as may be appropriate to safeguard this right of non-participation.

Released Time and Dismissal Time
We believe that Jewish communities are justified in objecting to released time or dismissal time programs.

Inherent in dismissal time are many, though not all, of the faults of released time. Nevertheless, when confronted with the necessity of a choice, we regard dismissal time as less objectionable.

Where a program of released time or dismissal time is in effect, or may be adopted, the Jewish community shall insist upon the following safeguards against possible abuses:

1. No religious instruction shall be given on public school premises.
2. The administrative machinery of the public school system shall not be employed to record or encourage attendance at religious instruction centers of students who avail themselves of released or dismissal time programs.
3. There shall be no proselytizing on school premises.
4. All children participating in such programs shall be dismissed together, and all grouping, separation, or identification by religion or by participation or non-participation in such programs shall be avoided.
5. Children shall not be assembled on public school premises for the purpose of being led to religious instruction centers nor shall any representative of such religious instruction center meet the children on such

premises to facilitate the operation of either program.

Governmental Aid to Religiously Controlled Schools

With the exception of the Rabbinical Council of America and the Union of Orthodox Jewish Congregations of America, we are opposed to governmental aid to schools under the supervision or control of any religious denomination or sect, whether Jewish, Protestant, or Catholic, including outright subsidies, transportation, text-books and other supplies. (The RCA and the UOJCA believe that government reimbursement for the expenses of the secular programs of religious schools is not a violation of the separation principle, and they favor such reimbursement.)

We are not opposed to the use of any school for the provision of lunches, or of medical and dental services to children.

Closing of Public Schools on Jewish High Holy Days

It is our view that whether or not public schools should be closed on Jewish High Holy Days is exclusively an administrative question to be decided by the public school authorities in the light of their own judgment as to the advantages or disadvantages involved. In some communities the public school authorities might find that the large number of absences of Jewish children and teachers make it impossible to engage in any fruitful educational work and therefore justifies keeping the schools closed in the interests of economy and efficiency. In other communities, public school authorities may reach a different conclusion. In either event, the Jewish community can have no special interest in the decision.

Therefore, we recommend:

1. It should be the concern of the Jewish community that no Jewish child or teacher shall be penalized for remaining away from school on a Jewish religious holiday.
2. Jewish organizations or leaders should not request the public school system to close the schools on Jewish religious holidays.
3. Where the public school system, as a matter of school administration, wishes to close the schools on Jewish holidays, and requests an opinion from Jewish organizations or Jewish community leaders, no objection should be interposed by such Jewish representatives, provided the record is made clear that the decision was made purely for administrative reasons and that the Jewish community has not requested such action.

Baccalaureate Programs

When exercises or programs marking graduation from public school and conducted under the auspices or with the participation of the public school authorities (popularly called Baccalaureate Programs) are religious in their nature or contain religious elements, they violate the principle of separation of church and state. We oppose such religious programs.

We deem such school-sponsored exercises or programs a violation, whether they take place on or off public school premises and whether during or after school hours; nor is it material that attendance at such programs may be declared to be voluntary. Since the education provided in the public schools must not be religious, the ceremony conducted by the public school authorities marking the termination of the period of education likewise must not be religious. We do not, of course, oppose non-religious commencement or graduation exercises, but we urge that they be held either in the school or in a place other than a church or synagogue and either during school hours or at some other time not conflicting with the religious requirements of any of the school population, so that there may be no bar to attendance by any of the graduating body.

We respectfully urge that rabbis invited to participate in such baccalaureate or religious graduation exercises or programs or in religious elements thereof should decline to do so, stating to the school authorities their reasons for so declining.

RELIGION AND PUBLIC POLICY

Sunday Observance Laws

The principle of religious liberty is impaired if any person is penalized for adhering to his religious beliefs, or for not adhering to any religious belief, so long as he does not interfere with the rights of others or endanger the public peace or security.

We believe that compulsory Sunday observance laws violate this principle, since they involve the use of state power to compel persons to conform to or to refrain from practices that find their basic sanction in particular religious beliefs and teachings.

Accordingly, we oppose the enactment or expansion of compulsory Sunday observance laws. We urge that at the very least existing Sunday observance laws be amended to exempt from their operation persons whose religious convictions compel them to observe a day other than Sunday as a religious day of rest.

We do not oppose, and indeed regard as salutary, laws requiring gainfully occupied persons to observe one day of rest in each week. We hold, however, that the choice of the day to be so observed should be a matter of individual preference.

Religious Symbols on Public Property

We oppose the erection of religious statues or the placing of religious sym-

*This opposition does not extend to the appropriate designation of places of religious worship on military installations and in other establishments where the movements of per-

bols on publicly-owned property.* Public parks, city halls, governmental office buildings and similar premises are purchased and maintained out of taxes imposed upon all persons, irrespective of their religious beliefs or affiliations. The presence on such premises of religious statues or symbols constitutes in effect a dedication of the premises to one sect or creed, to the exclusion of others. The expenditure of governmental funds or the use of governmental property for religious purposes, moreover, is a serious impairment of the principle of separation of church and state. Experience has shown that the placing of religious statues or symbols on public property divides the community along religious lines and brings about interreligious disharmony and acrimony.

These evils are substantially aggravated when religious statues or symbols are placed on public school premises. In such cases, sensitive and defenseless children, rather than mature adults, are principally affected. Moreover, attendance at school is not voluntary but is by compulsion of law. To compel children to obtain their secular education in an atmosphere charged with a religion violative of their beliefs is to deny them their full religious liberty as well as to breach the relationship of confidence and trust that should mark their school experience.

Question on Religion in U.S. Census

We are opposed to the inclusion in the federal census of any questions regarding religious affiliation or belief for the following reasons:

- The asking of such questions by census takers would be in violation of the constitutional guaranty of freedom of religion. The United States Supreme Court has expressly declared that, under the freedom of religion provision of the Bill of Rights, no person may be compelled to profess a belief or disbelief in any religion. Persons questioned by census takers are subject to conviction and punishment as criminals if they refuse to answer. However, even if the element of compulsion be eliminated, we would regard the asking of questions about religious affiliation or belief as violative of the constitutional guaranty of religious freedom.
- The asking of such questions would violate the constitutional guaranty of the separation of church and state; for it would, in effect, make the federal government an agent of religious groups and employ government instrumentalities for church purposes.
- The asking of such questions would constitute an unwarranted infringement upon the privacy of Americans. In a totalitarian society no interest of the people is deemed outside the jurisdiction and concern of the state. In a democracy, on the other hand, the state has only such powers and such jurisdiction as are freely granted to it by the people; certain aspects of the

---

sonnel are restricted, or to the marking of graves with symbols of the religious faith of the deceased.

people's lives are held inviolable; chief among these is the relation of man to his Maker. In a democracy committed to the separation of church and state the religion of the people is not a proper subject of government inquiry.

• The asking of such questions would create a dangerous precedent, the consequences and implications of which cannot be anticipated. For 180 years our government has refrained from including questions concerning religion in the census. Abandonment of this tradition would inevitably lead to further encroachments upon the liberties of Americans.

TEN

A Question of Priorities

F or several decades, Leo Pfeffer's view that "the complete separation of church and state is best for the church and best for the state, and secures freedoms for both" seemed to most American Jews to be both historically convincing and in their own best interest. But the separationist position espoused by Pfeffer and his colleagues did not go entirely unchallenged even in its heyday. In articles published during the 1950s and 1960s, Will Herberg and a small group of other Jewish thinkers began to call for a reassessment of the prevailing consensus. The authors of the Constitution never intended to erect a "wall of separation," said Herberg. The establishment clause of the First Amendment, he felt, had been profoundly misunderstood: although the Founding Fathers did not want to favor any single religion, they were not against helping all religions, or all religion, equally. "Neither in the minds of the Founding Fathers nor in the thinking of the American people through the nineteenth and twentieth century," he wrote, "did the doctrine of the First Amendment ever imply an ironclad ban forbidding the government to take account of religion or to support its various activities."

During the 1960s and 1970s, other prominent Jewish thinkers, such as Milton Himmelfarb, editor of the *American Jewish Year Book,* Professor Jakob J. Petuchowski of Hebrew Union College–Jewish Institute of Religion in Cincinnati, and Professor Seymour Siegel of the Jewish Theological Seminary in New York, began to develop a strong Jewish argument for the desirability of greater religious involvement in American public life. While supporting state aid to parochial schools and questioning Jewish opposition to public school prayer, they (like Herberg) began to publicly challenge and criticize the prevailing Jewish separationist consensus.

One of the central issues behind this reassessment was whether the government should give aid to parochial schools. During the 1960s and 1970s, Orthodox Jews had abandoned their opposition to such aid in the hope of obtaining funds for their own Jewish day schools. They began to argue, as Catholics had before them, that education in a religious setting benefited not only members of their own faith but also the nation as a whole, and that money used to support secular studies at these schools should not be denied just because the schools also taught religious subjects. A growing number of Jewish religious leaders and intellectuals had begun to recognize the "justice" of the Catholic claim to public support of parochial schools, in the form of textbooks, bus transportation, and school lunches, and even to the point of contributing to the tuition of pupils and the salaries of teachers. "In principle," as Herberg put it, "there is no reason why the religious school should be barred from governmental support because of what is said or implied in the First Amendment." In 1965, Rabbi Moshe Sherer, executive vice president of the Orthodox Agudath Israel of America, testified before Congress in support of federal aid to private and parochial schools, arguing that Jewish day schools faced "extremely difficult financial circumstances." In the late 1960s, a group of young Orthodox Jewish lawyers and social scientists organized the National Jewish Commission on Law and Public Affairs (COLPA), to support aid to parochial schools and to promote the rights and interests of the "observant Jewish community."

Since the 1940s, there has been a dramatic increase in the number of Jewish day schools throughout the United States. Whereas there were only 33 such institutions in the United States in 1940, there were 237 in 1960 and, by 1990, there were 604. During these years the growing Orthodox Jewish consensus that only through day school education can Judaism survive also came to be shared by an increasing number of leaders within the Conservative and Reform movements of American Judaism. While Orthodox-sponsored day schools still predominate, first the Conservative and then the Reform movement organized a growing number of day schools that enroll thousands of Jewish students each year.

Throughout the 1970s and 1980s, the growth of Jewish day schools outside the Orthodox community prompted some Conservative and Reform rabbis and educators to rethink their earlier opposition to state aid as well. In a seminal article published in 1970 (and reprinted below), Rabbi Seymour Siegel found increasing support within both the Conservative and Reform movements for the view "that the strengthening of the Day School movement is essential for the maintenance of religious life," and "vital to Jewish survival." As a result, he argued, "Jewish parents are now more sympathetic to the plight of Catholic parents," who have long been claiming "that without government aid for parochial schools they are carrying a double load of taxation and that the special financial burden of supporting children in church-related institutions constitutes, in effect, a threat to their religious freedom."

1. Will Herberg and the Jewish Critique of Strict Separationism

During the 1950s and 1960s Will Herberg, author of *Judaism and Modern Man* and an eminent Jewish theologian and sociologist of religion, emerged as an outspoken proponent of government support for parochial schools and as the most vocal Jewish critic of judicial efforts to outlaw Bible reading and prayer in the public schools. As early as 1952, in an article published in *Commentary* magazine, which is the first selection included below, he urged Americans of all faiths to rethink their views on issues of church and state in American life. Criticizing his fellow Jews, he called for a reassessment of the prevailing Jewish consensus concerning separation of church and state and the role religion should play in public life. "By and large," he wrote, those who speak for the American Jewish community "seem to share the basic secularist presupposition that religion is a 'private matter.'. . . The American Jew must have sufficient confidence in the capacity of democracy to preserve its pluralistic . . . character without any *absolute* wall of separation between religion and public life. . . ." A decade or so later, frustrated by liberal Jewish support for the 1963 Supreme Court decisions banning the Lord's Prayer and Bible reading in the schools, he pleaded for a restoration of religion to a place of honor in American public life: "Within the meaning of our political tradition and political practice," he wrote in the second selection included below, "the promotion [of religion] has been, and continues to be, a part of the very legitimate 'secular' purpose of the state. Whatever the 'neutrality' of the state in matters of religion may be, it cannot be a neutrality between religion and no-religion."

◆   ◆   ◆

Will Herberg's challenge to strict separationism, 1952

It can hardly be denied that the intervention of most Jewish bodies in the current church and state controversy has generally not tended to allay the sharpening religious cleavage in American life. It has often operated on principles in some ways even more extreme and basically secular than those of the Protestant guardians of the "wall of separation." It has shown little understanding of the realities of the educational and cultural situation as it confronts the religious parents, Christian or Jewish, who take their faith seriously as the substance of life.

Religious leaders, lay educators, and parent groups have in recent years become increasingly disturbed over the religious vacuum in public education, which is felt to have serious moral and spiritual consequences. With due consideration to constitutional limitations, a number of ways have been proposed to strengthen the foundations of the public school by compensating for the religious emptiness that is devitalizing it. President Van Dusen of Union Theological Seminary and former Dean Weigle of Yale have suggested a "common core" program of religious education; others have looked to various schemes of dismissed or released time to provide a partial remedy. All of these suggestions are animated by the desire to preserve the public school for its undoubted merits as a vehicle of cultural unification and to obviate the necessity of establishing separate church schools.

How has the most vocal Jewish opinion reacted to these proposals? Almost entirely in the negative, and often violently: spokesmen representing a broad segment of organized Jewish community life applauded the Supreme Court's invalidation of released time in the McCollum case, joined in the opposition to the New York released-time program and criticized the Supreme Court's validation of it, opposed Bible readings in schools, opposed the New York Board of Regents' suggestion of a daily prayer, and of course opposed every variety of aid, direct or indirect, to religious schools. I am not trying to make a case for any of these plans or programs; they may all be very properly criticized as impracticable and ineffective. Indeed, it may even be contended, with considerable show of reason, that under present-day American conditions, with the bewildering diversity of cult that characterizes our "pluralistic" society, the practical difficulties in the way of any acceptable program of religion in the schools are quite insuperable. Perhaps that is so; nevertheless, all of the plans and suggestions, however impracticable in themselves, do point to a problem that cannot be ignored, especially by those who are so much concerned with repelling attacks on the public schools.

What answer have Jewish spokesmen had for parents and educators? Only this: school and religion must be kept rigorously apart; no religion in the school or in any conceivable association with it; let the schools inculcate in the children "basic moral principles" and "social ideals," the place for "religion" is the home and the church. Leaving aside the psychological unreality of this kind of mechanical division of labor, which flies in the face of any view of personality held by modern educators themselves, how can such a reliance upon secularism to do the work of moral education be supported? It is, in fact, not supported. It is simply taken for granted that "basic moral principles" and "social ideals" are autonomous, and can and should be established, validated, and inculcated without reference to religion. Nor is any consideration given to the actual realities of the American situation. Many argue that the literally godless education the child receives in the typical public school can be supplemented by religious teaching in home and church. But is it not usually the school, where the child spends so much of his waking day, that exerts the primary formative influence on his mind, so that whatever reactive influence there is, is likely to proceed from school to home, rather than the reverse? The school establishes the priority and prestige of ideas, and the child who becomes habituated in the school to thinking about things exclusively in secular and naturalistic terms is more than likely to regard the religious ideas he finds floating around in the average home or church with indifference and contempt. Even if the home could "compete" with the school for the soul of the child, the very idea of such competition is somehow shocking.

I am not suggesting that all parents feel this way or that the school is exclusively guilty in what has been called the "religious illiteracy" of the American child. On the contrary, many parents, including many Jewish parents, see no place for religion in education, or for that matter in life, and are quite happy at the extrusion of religion from the schools. Even those parents who have a religious interest only too easily tend to overlook their own failure and the failure of the church in their readiness to blame everything on the school. This must be admitted, and yet it remains a fact that to large numbers of our citizens the present pattern seems increasingly questionable. For it operates to make the schools into instruments acting toward and sanctioning the rejection of religion, whereas we Americans are, as the Supreme Court put it in its opinion on the recent New York released-time case, "a religious people whose institutions presuppose a Supreme Being." Need we recall that while the propaganda of atheism is protected under the Constitution, non- or anti-religion has never enjoyed and does not now enjoy the same public status as religion? Anyone who doubts this might try proposing that the federal government commission atheist or "humanist" chaplains on a par with Jewish and Christian! The public school system, in effect, reverses this relation, and makes non- or anti-religion the established "religion" in public education. No wonder that dissatisfaction with the public school has been growing.

Operating under a concept of the separation of church and state more rigid and absolute than even that held by doctrinaire Protestants, most Jewish community leaders have paid little heed to these realities of the situation. A few, however, particularly among the Orthodox, have attempted something positive. Feeling it undesirable or impossible to change the character of the public schools, and realizing the feebleness of most after-school religious education, they have undertaken to set up religious day schools. The movement is not yet very extensive. In 1945, there were perhaps 75 such schools throughout the country; today, there may be over 150, almost all operating on the elementary or pre-elementary levels; attendance has increased rather more than proportionately. Some Jewish religious leaders outside the Orthodox camp have endorsed the idea, but lay opinion seems generally opposed. Significant too is the line taken by some of its religious advocates in justifying it. In a recent article defending Jewish day schools, the Orthodox author was very much concerned to point out that after all Jewish day schools were utterly different from analogous Catholic institutions because the latter, the Catholic schools, employed their own religiously oriented textbooks, while the Jewish schools used the regulation public school texts and curricula, merely adding a program of "Jewish knowledge." Note how the "separation of church and state" is now duplicated *within* the Jewish school: all subjects of everyday, worldly concern, presumably not only mathematics, but also history, the social sciences, literature, and the humanities, are taught from the same textbooks and in the same secular spirit as in the public schools; to this is added some "Jewish instruction," which must in the nature of the case be peripheral and irrelevant. So far has the spirit of secularism permeated Jewish thinking, even that which considers itself strongly religious.

It is worthwhile to pause at this point. I think no informed observer will care to deny that of all comparable groups in this country Jewish community leaders, including leaders in the synagogue, appear most secular-minded in their public attitude on matters of church and state. In what other American religious community, for example, could the proposal be advanced by respected *religious* leaders—out-Blansharding Blanshard—that American democracy be made the vehicle of a "common American faith" to be inculcated in the public schools with all the paraphernalia of a religious cult? Yet that is substantially the idea that a number of influential Jewish religious leaders have been advocating for years. By and large, those who speak for the American Jewish community, whether they be rabbis or laymen, religious individuals or men and women avowedly secular-minded, judging by their public expressions, seem to share the basic secularist presupposition that religion is a "private matter"—in the minimizing sense of "merely private"—and therefore peripheral to the vital areas of social life and culture, which latter are held to have non-religious foundations. Jewish religion, if it is affirmed at all, is affirmed as something to be *added to* the common life, not as something that pervades and is inextricably involved in every aspect of it. Separation of church and state is thus at bottom advocated as only one phase of the separation of religion from life.

How has this come about? How could this isolation of religion from life have arisen in a group with whom religion has traditionally been conceived as coterminous with life? Basically, it seems to me, it is due to the conviction, widely held though rarely articulated, that because the Western Jew achieved emancipation with the secularization of society, he can preserve his free and equal status only so long as culture and society remain secular. Let but religion regain a central place in the everyday life of the community, and the Jew, because he is outside the bounds of the dominant religion, will once again be relegated to the margins of society, displaced, disfranchised culturally if not politically, shorn of rights and opportunities. And it is well to note that by "religion" in this context, it is Christianity that is meant, and by Christianity primarily Catholicism. The Catholic Church still remains in Jewish eyes the standard form of Christianity and the prime symbol of Christian persecution. Deep down, it is Catholic domination that is feared. Such are the anxieties that beset many American Jews, and it cannot be denied that they have much justification. Religion has so often with good conscience been turned into an instrument of exclusive privilege that one can well understand the feeling of those who believe that democracy requires the eviction of religion from public life and the thorough secularization of society.

Yet in the long run such a view is short-sighted and self-defeating. Jewish survival is ultimately conceivable only in religious terms; and when its *raison d'être* is whittled down to a few "supplemental" factors, survival itself loses much of its meaning. Furthermore, a thoroughly "de-religionized" society would make Jewish existence impossible. But a "de-religionized" society is itself for long impossible. Ultimately, man finds the autonomy which secularism offers him an intolerable burden, and he tends to throw it off in favor of some new heteronomy of race or nation, of party or state, that the idolatrous substitute faiths of the time hold out to him. In such idolatrous cultures, the Jew is inevitably the chosen victim; the lesson of history and contemporary experience seems clear on this head. The way of the Jew in the world is not and never will be easy; it will certainly not be made any the easier by his throwing in his lot with an increasingly total secularism, which both invites and is helpless to withstand the demonic idolatries of our time. The American Jew must have sufficient confidence in the capacity of democracy to preserve its pluralistic libertarian character without any *absolute* wall of separation between religion and public life. After all, the Jew is no less free in Britain, where church and state are more closely linked.

The fear felt by Jewish leaders of the possible consequences of a restoration of religion to a vital place in public life is what throws them into an alliance with the secularists and helps make their own thinking so thoroughly secular. They feel the problem primarily in terms of the Jew's status as member of a minority group. The minority-group defensiveness, which we noted in contemporary Protestantism, is of course far more intense among Jews; indeed, it may probably be said to be the most influential determinant of the policy and activities of many leading Jewish groups in this country. Public assistance to religious schools, it is felt, would mean overwhelmingly aid to Christian, primarily Catholic schools, with Jewish schools sharing to a relatively insignificant extent. Released or dismissed time, in most communities, would mean the invidious isolation of a handful of Jewish children amidst large numbers of their Protestant and Catholic schoolmates. Reading the Bible would necessarily mean reading the "Christian" Bible, that is, the King James version, even if only Old Testament passages were read. And so on. In every case, the "intrusion" of religion into public life, it is feared, would result in situations in which Jews would find themselves at some disadvantage—greater isolation, higher "visibility," an accentuation of minority status. Uneasy memories of past persecution and oppression are stirred up. The most elementary defensive strategy would seem to dictate keeping religion out of public life at all costs; hence the passionate attachment of American Jews to the secularist-Protestant interpretation of the principle of separation of church and state. It is a question, however, whether defensive strategy is, after all, the highest wisdom of Jewish existence and survival.

* * *

American Jews even more than Protestants, must rid themselves of the narrow and crippling minority-group defensiveness. Just because Jews in this country occupy such a curious "third" position between Protestants and Catholics, their responsibilities are great. We must rethink the problem of church and state, of religion and life, as it affects the Jew and as it affects the entire nation. We must be ready to abandon ancient fears and prejudices if they no longer conform to reality, and we must be ready to strike out boldly in new directions required by the times. There is no need for—indeed there is every need to abandon—the anxious search for injuries and grievances which has characterized so much of the Jewish "defense" psychology. On the question of aid to religious schools, I do not believe we have much to fear from any of the proposals thus far suggested. On the question of teaching religion in the public schools, I have yet to see a plan that seems to me wise or practicable, and perhaps there is none. But these questions will continue to be raised by many citizens seriously concerned with the problem, and we owe it to ourselves and to them to give fair and sober thought and discussion to their point of view, without attempting to throw it out of court in advance. Should not our community leadership more openly reflect the genuine religious interest of Jews and their concern over the religio-ethical education of their children, which has always been strong, however confused by the felt pressures and demands (often misunderstood) of the new American environment—a concern that every observer reports at high and rising tide in the present decade? That the question of public and private schools, and of church and state in education, can be discussed from the Jewish point of view in a sober, constructive, un-prejudiced manner may be seen from Hayim Greenberg's exploratory article last year in the *Yiddisher Kemfer*. We urgently need more of such thinking.

Finally all of us, Catholics, Protestants, Jews, and secularists too, must realize the seriousness of the present tensions and our responsibility to do everything in our power to allay them, certainly not to exacerbate them.

♦

Herberg's support for religion in public life, 1963

The crucial passage in Justice Clark's majority opinion in the *Schempp* and *Murray* (Lord's Prayer and Bible reading) cases, is no doubt the following:

> ... to withstand the strictures of the establishment clause [of the First Amendment] there must be a secular legislative purpose and a primary effect that neither enhances nor inhibits religion.

This passage well reflects the strange incoherence of the majority opinion as a whole. For the second part of the criterion it offers ("neither enhances nor inhibits religion") not only does not follow from the first ("secular legislative purpose"), but stands in obvious logical and historical contradiction to it.

The Federal Government is indeed restricted to "secular" purposes. That is because it is a state, not a church; and, in our Western tradition, the jurisdiction and activities of the state have almost always been understood as limited to the promotion of the common good in the civil order, which (I presume) is what Justice Clark means by "secular purpose." Note well that this restriction of the state to the civil ("secular") order is not a peculiarly American "separationist" notion derived from the First Amendment; it is, as I have said, deeply rooted in our Western tradition, and rests upon the primary distinction between State and Church, which was at least as clear to Augustine and Thomas Aquinas as it is to the justices of the Supreme Court. With this part of Justice Clark's criterion, there can be no quarreling; it deserves all the emphasis it can get.

But the second part of Justice Clark's test of constitutionality does not follow from the first; rather it contradicts it. *For the promotion of religion may well be seen as a major "secular" purpose of the state in its furtherance of the common good of the civil order.* This was the almost universal conviction of Americans at the time of the adoption of the federal Constitution; and it has remained the conviction of the American people, and the practice of federal and state government to this very day, despite the confusion introduced by recent Court decisions.

The Northwest Ordinance of 1787 is widely recognized as a significant reflection of the best mind of the American people at the outset of their career as a nation. Perhaps the most celebrated article of this ordinance is Article 3, which reads as follows:

> Religion, morality, and knowledge being necessary to *good government* and the happiness of mankind, schools and the means of education shall forever be encouraged [my emphasis].

Two years before, in 1785, what was probably the first state university in this country, the University of Georgia, was established. The charter of the university—adopted, let us remember, not in "theocratic" New England but in "Jeffersonian" Georgia—included the following paragraph:

> When the minds of the people in general are viciously disposed and unprincipled, and their conduct disorderly, a free government will be attended with greater confusion, with evils more horrid, than the wild, uncultivated state of nature. It can only be happy when the public principles and opinions are properly directed, and their manners regulated. This is an influence beyond the sketch of laws and punishments, and can be claimed only by religion and education. It should therefore be among the first objects of those who wish well to the *national prosperity*, to encourage and support the principles of religion and morality . . . [my emphasis].

Documentation could be multiplied; but the point, I think, is clear: the promotion of religion, along with the promotion of morality and education, is understood as a legitimate, indeed an imperative purpose of the state *in the promotion of "good government" and "national prosperity."* This was a recognized principle at the time of the emergence of the new nation.

The very first Congress, which ratified the First Amendment, also assigned certain funds to subsidize Christian missionaries among the Indians; and, in one case at least, if my memory serves, the missionary thus subsidized was a Roman Catholic. This action, which must shock and outrage every conscientious "separationist," was hardly taken out of a deep concern for the Christian religion, and emphatically not out of a predilection for the Roman Catholic Church. It was taken because it was obvious to all thinking people that religion (in this case, of course, Christianity) was "necessary to good government"; and the promotion of religion among the Indians—even, where expediency dictated, the Roman Catholic version of religion—was important for the national welfare. It was with this *"secular"* motive that the Congress moved, thus acting upon a well-established principle.

This principle has not changed either in theory or in practice, despite the protests of a few doctrinaires. Why do we exempt religious, along with educational and charitable institutions, from the burden of taxation which might otherwise crush them? Because we recognize that religious institutions along with the others, perform an indispensable *public* ("secular") service. Why do we support an extensive chaplaincy system in the armed forces? Because we recognize that the chaplain in the armed forces performs an indispensable *public* ("secular") service essential to the national welfare. If, as Justice Douglas said some years ago in the majority opinion in the *Zorach* case, "we are a religious people whose institutions presuppose a Supreme Being," it would seem to be stultifying to prohibit the government from *in any way* promoting the activities of religion serving to strengthen our social institutions by strengthening their "presupposition"? And, in fact, the government has not been so inhibited, as we all know.

Theologians may very well have their qualms about a religion that is thus converted into an instrument for strengthening the secular order of society. This aspect of the problem I hope to discuss in a later article. Here, however, my point is something quite different. My point is that, within the meaning of our political tradition and political practice, the promotion has been, and continues to be, a part of the very legitimate "secular" purpose of the state. Whatever the "neutrality" of the state in matters of religion may be, it cannot be a neutrality between religion and no-religion, any more than (to recall the language of the Northwest Ordinance) it could be a neutrality between morality and no-morality, knowledge and no-knowledge. All three, in our American conviction, are necessary to "good government" and "national prosperity"; and all three fall within the legitimate scope of the friendly assistance of the state.

2. The Debate over State Aid to Parochial Schools

The issue of whether the government should provide aid to parochial schools has been a central focus of the debate, both nationally and within the Jewish community, on the relationship between religion and state. In 1965, when Congress debated the Elementary and Secondary Education Act (ESEA), which proposed to extend $2.3 billion dollars to the nation's elementary and secondary schools including private and parochial schools, Jewish communal leaders testified before Congress on both sides of the question. Leo Pfeffer, the American Jewish Congress attorney and legal scholar who did so much to shape the legal doctrine of strict separationism and was a vocal opponent of the ESEA, led the battle against state aid to parochial schools. In the following selection, published in 1966, he explains the reasons for his opposition, in the process criticizing those Orthodox Jewish leaders who claim "that the Jewish day school system needs the money desperately and without it cannot survive." In the second selection, Rabbi Moshe Sherer, the executive vice president of the Orthodox Agudath Israel of America, attacks Jewish separationists for their "rabid opposition." Rabbi Sherer also testified in 1965 before Congress, arguing that Jewish day schools face "extremely difficult financial circumstances" and that denial of tax aid to these schools would constitute "a discrimination which is not in accordance with basic American ideals."

◆   ◆   ◆

Leo Pfeffer on religion, the First Amendment, and the ESEA, 1966

Initially, I suggest what is quite obvious: there is no significant desire within the Jewish community to change the First Amendment insofar as it forbids religious practices and teachings within the public school. . . . Whatever discontent there is within the Jewish community relates to that aspect of the First Amendment which forbids governmental aid to religious schools. We must therefore give serious consideration to the question whether the Amendment is severable, and whether we can weaken or modify one aspect of it without gravely threatening, if not critically weakening, the other. We cannot, I believe, do this. There are not two First Amendments, one keeping religion out of the public schools and the other keeping public funds out of parochial schools. We must, therefore, weigh carefully whether the financial assistance our day schools may receive through a breach in the wall of separation is worth the price we pay for it in relinquishment of constitutional protection for our children in the public schools. It must always be remembered that only a small percentage of Jewish children attend private schools; at least 90 percent attend public schools, and it is not likely that this proportion will change radically in the foreseeable future. . . .

I have encountered . . . the following principal arguments in favor of a change:

(1) The war is over. American Jewry made a valiant fight, but the enactment of the Elementary and Secondary Education Act of 1965 marks the end of the era of strict church-state separation and the beginning of a new era of church-state cooperation, particularly in the field of education. Whatever may have been the validity of the Jewish position, the American people, through their

representatives in Congress, have spoken and it is futile, if not unpatriotic, to resist further.

(2) An absolutist, doctrinaire position is sterile. We must be prepared to make some accommodations, lest we find our efforts completely ineffective.

(3) We have lost all our allies. The Jewish community was practically alone in its opposition to the enactment of the 1965 Act without amendments safeguarding the principle of church-state separation. Both the National Council of Churches and the National Education Association, two of our staunchest allies in the past, supported the bill.

(4) Even if we do not retreat from our position of opposition to direct, financial aid to parochial schools, we can and should endorse legislation whose purpose is to aid the child rather than the school.

(5) Since our last conference, Vatican II has completed its work. A new spirit of interfaith friendship has spread across America. The Catholic Church has changed, or at least clarified, its long-standing teaching of Jewish responsibility for the crucifixion of Jesus. American Jewry should express its appreciation by adopting a less rigid position on an issue on which the Catholic community feels so deeply.

(6) The plight of the Jewish day-school system is desperate. Jewish federations, it is said, refuse to support it adequately, and unless help is obtained from the Federal and state governments, many of our schools will have to close their doors. . . .

Fourteen years ago the Supreme Court handed down its decision in the *Zorach* case upholding New York City's released-time program. What was most distressing was the language of the Court's opinion, written by Justice Douglas, which rejected an absolutist approach to church-state separation. It stated that "The First Amendment . . . does not say that in every and all respects there shall be a separation of church and state"; that "We are a religious people whose institutions presuppose a Supreme Being"; and that "When the state encourages religious instruction or cooperates with religious authorities . . . it follows the best of our traditions."

There was exultation in the camps of Amalek; gloom and despair in the tents of Israel. The impression was widespread throughout the country that absolutism, if not church-state separation itself, was dead. . . .

A Lively Corpse

Church-state separation is far from dead. It has never been more alive and vigorous. Should you think this an extreme, unrealistic, wishful appraisal, I offer the following items of evidence to support it:

(1) *The judicial record.* Since the *Zorach* case, the decisions of the Supreme Court have expressed an absolutist approach to the First Amendment, as reflected in the *Torcaso* (Maryland Notary Public), the *Engel* (Regents Prayer) and *Schempp* (Bible reading) cases. . . .

If church-state separation is dead the news has not yet reached the courts.

(2) *The litigation record.* The June, 1966 issue of the American Jewish Congress litigation docket shows that at least thirty suits are now pending in the courts throughout the nation challenging invasions of the religion clause of the First Amendment. The organizations specifically concerned with church-state separation are more active in the courts today than ever.

(3) *The defense of the First Amendment.* American religious, political, cultural and intellectual leadership unanimously rallied to the defense of the First Amendment in the efforts of Congressman Becker and Senator Dirksen to weaken it. At the outset of Becker's campaign to overrule the Supreme Court's prayer decision, there were few who were rash enough even to hope that it could be defeated. The Becker Amendment perhaps never did die; it just faded away. The Dirksen Amendment has not died; but I am sufficiently rash to predict that it too will fade away.

(4) *The decennial census.* In 1957 the U.S. Census Bureau decided to include in the 1960 census a question on religious affiliation. We felt that this would constitute a violation of the First Amendment and expressed our opposition. Within a relatively short period we were able to mobilize widespread opposition to the proposal, with the result that it was dropped.

(5) *The Peace Corps.* Originally, the Peace Corps planned to use church organizations as part of its overseas program. Again we were the first to protest this as a violation of church-state separation. Other groups and denominations followed suit, with the result that the Director of the Peace Corps announced a decision not to use religious organizations in carrying out the program.

(6) *The 1965 Federal Education Act.* This, and its predecessors—the College Aid Act and the Anti-Poverty or Economic Opportunity Act—are the principal bases for the assertion that church-state separation is now of interest only to historians. But the evidence to support this is far from clear. There is much in the history of these acts indicating a strong commitment on the part of the American people to the principle of church-state separation. . . .

In sum, the First Amendment is dead only if we allow ourselves to be talked into believing it is dead. . . .

Jews and the Ecumenical Spirit
The same ecumenical spirit which explains American Protestantism's willingness to make some accommodation to Catholic demands for governmental funds, is undoubtedly exerting some similar influence within the Jewish community. We seem indeed to have entered an era of good feeling. We especially have reason to be accommodating; the same Vatican Council that issued the schema on the Jews also issued a schema declaring the moral obligation of government to support schools maintained by religious groups. If we accept one decree of the Council, how can we gracefully reject the other?

Speaking for myself, I have a far less enthusiastic appreciation of the Declaration on the Jews than most spokesmen of organized Jewry. But even if we take the most optimistic approach to the Declaration, it is, I submit, irrelevant to our consideration of the question before us. If we believe the demands of the Church are just, we should support them. If we do not believe they are, there is no more reason that we should support them in gratitude than that we should for that reason alter our traditional views on the place of Jesus in the Jewish religion.

* * *

Of all the arguments seeking to justify Jewish demand for an acceptance of governmental funds for schools the one that has the least validity is the assertion that the Jewish day-school system needs the money desperately and without it cannot survive. It is absurd to urge that the Jewish community needs governmental aid to maintain its day-school system. If but ten percent of what is spent weekly on the gaudy Bar Mitzvah, or ten percent of what is spent on erecting and maintaining temple edifices or so-called Jewish hospitals, were set aside for the Jewish day-school system, it would have more money than it would know how to spend and could take care many times over of every Jewish child seeking enrollment.

◆

Rabbi Sherer criticizes Jewish opposition to ESEA, 1965

The new education bill, by bestowing its benefits upon the disadvantaged religious-school children along with their public school counterparts, serves to remove the *cherem* which doctrinaire devotees of Church-State separation have sought to place on religious school students.

It is this *principle of recognition* accorded to the Yeshiva student, over and above any immediate financial advantages, which makes the President's education bill a document of major importance to the Jewish community.

It is now five years since Agudath Israel, alone among Jewish organizations, took up the cudgels for this principle and conducted a continuing campaign in Washington and in other areas for this cause. During this half decade the general climate has radically changed among *all* segments of America's citizens; the atmosphere has become increasingly favorable to the demands of the religious schools. As the American public learned the true facts, it gradually discarded many of the myths spread by the opponents of religious school aid. This change in public opinion has been clearly indicated by the Gallup Poll.

Within the Jewish community too, new winds began to stir as individuals and groups had second thoughts. As the justice of the religious schools' demands gradually pierced through the clatter of confusing and conflicting

declarations, many reappraised their stand. The result: Today many of the opponents of school aid have switched and others who equivocated lost their
shyness and are joining this battle. Slowly the pendulum of the Jewish consensus has swung toward the pro-federal-aid camp.

The President's education bill is the factor which crystallized some of this
new sentiment. Because it limited the scope of its benefits to the student, omit-
ting any direct grants to schools, this bill narrowed down the area of controversy to the point that even the votaries of Church-State separation could
accept it without compromising their convictions. This was best demonstrated
when the staid American Jewish Committee jumped on the bandwagon and
issued a warm public endorsement of the basic provisions of this legislation.

However, two groups among Jews—the American Jewish Congress and
Reform Judaism—are determined not to budge one inch in their stubborn
stand to deny federal-aid, not only to religious schools, but to their students as
well. . . .

[W]hen hearings began on Capitol Hill on the Administration's education
bill, the American Jewish Congress dispatched spokesmen to Washington to
sound the alarm about the impending doom of America's public school system
if the legislation would be enacted. . . .

The spokesman of Reform Judaism also appeared at these hearings to help
fan the flames of fear concerning "mushrooming" religious schools. . . .

Oddly enough, the spokesman of Reform Judaism prefaced his statement
with a declaration that "Our traditional love of learning has impelled us to
create, as our own religious responsibility, a vast network of private educational institutions for the perpetuation of Jewish religious values" and, he
added, "without receiving any federal aid." This spurious contention does not
even merit rebuttal. No intelligent person could compare the financial costs of
the all-day Yeshivot, and their heavy budgets for religious and secular departments, with the relatively tiny costs of the Sunday Schools of Reform Judaism.
Instead of a "traditional Jewish love of learning," the statement of the Reform
Jewish group reeks of their traditional abhorrence of the "separatist" religious
parochial schools—a "mitzvah" of Reform Jewish dogma which most of their
spiritual leaders have been fulfilling with great fervor. . . .

Fortunately, the President's education-aid-bill has received the overwhelming support of American organizations and educational groups of all faiths.
The prestigious 900,000–member National Education Association, long a foe
of any aid to parochial schools, endorsed this bill, as have many other groups
traditionally opposed to direct grants to religious schools. In this general atmosphere of consent, the rabid opposition of the American Jewish Congress
and Reform Judaism sticks out like a sore thumb.

These Jewish groups are not only hitting at an educational effort which is
important for all Americans. Even more, the raucous position taken by the
A.J.C. in *every* area where there could be found the slightest suspicion of state

assistance to religion, has gravely damaged the Jewish image in this country. The Jewish defence agencies, which spend so many millions of dollars annually to create "good public relations," would be able to sharply curtail their budgets if the A.J.C. would cease its activities in delicate areas, which only fan the flames of prejudice.

With the warm bi-partisan support that this legislation enjoys, its enactment seems assured. The Orthodox Jewish community now has two specific tasks ahead:

• The first order of business, since funds from the provisions of this bill will be channelled through the states, is the organization of associations of Jewish all-day schools on a state-wide level. This will assure that the local education authorities negotiate directly with the heads of the Yeshivo movement, and not with any self-appointed non-Orthodox Jewish educational agencies. Sad experience of the past has shown that where Orthodox institutions were not united, the non-Orthodox took advantage of this division to step in and claim rights to represent Yeshivos for whom they have no right to speak. Torah Umesorah could be the logical group to undertake this huge organizational effort, which should unite all segments of the Yeshivo and Bais Yaakov movement in this country on a state-wide basis.

• The Orthodox Jewish community should not be lulled—by this favorable turn of events—into a false sense of security about the ultimate rectification of the injustice from which our Yeshivos now suffer. We are about to win the first round, but we are still very far from the day when Yeshivos will receive federal aid for their secular studies programs, which they rightly deserve. The struggle for justice must be pursued further with wisdom and tenacity. The entire Orthodox Jewish community must become involved in this all-important struggle, whose successful outcome can radically alter the chances for survival of the broad masses of American Jewry.

3. The Rise of COLPA

The National Jewish Commission on Law and Public Affairs (COLPA) was established in 1965 by a group of young Orthodox Jewish laymen, mostly lawyers, to defend the interests of Orthodox Jews in church-state matters, particularly with respect to Sunday laws, employment discrimination, and in support of state aid to parochial schools. Dedicated to providing "legal and legislative services to Orthodox Jewish organizations and individuals, without charge, by submitting briefs to courts and preparing other legal materials," it effectively served as a counterweight to the legal staffs of the American Jewish Congress and other separationist agencies. In the ensuing years, COLPA has appeared as *amicus curiae* in numerous church-state cases before the courts, on issues ranging from the legal rights of Jewish Sabbath observers to tuition tax credits. COLPA has played a particularly important role in sensitizing American courts to the problems that arise when the requirements of Jewish religious law conflict with society's normal practices, and in securing "reasonable accommodation" of these practices under the free exercise clause of the First Amendment.

In the following selection, one of COLPA's founders, Marvin Schick, then a professor of political science and constitutional law at Hunter College of the City University of New York, provides an analytical review of COLPA's early history and litigation in the church-state field.

◆   ◆   ◆

Marvin Schick on the creation of COLPA, 1967

Probably the most meaningful, although almost unreported, development in recent years in American Jewish affairs is the new vigor and confidence manifested by Orthodox Jewry as it goes about its business. Still in many respects the weakest of the three "branches" of the community—particularly with respect to nominal organizational resources—Orthodoxy has risen mightily from a position of near impotence only a generation ago to the point that it now sets the style, if not the pace, for many of the transactions that occur within the world of American Jewry.

*   *   *

In view of this situation, it is no surprise that in public affairs matters the Orthodox are increasingly following new paths and policies. Twenty years ago, at the time of the first burst of Supreme Court activity in the church-state area, there was no peculiarly Orthodox expression of opinion and those groups that took a position on, for instance, government aid to parochial schools, adhered rather ritualistically to the strict separation of church and state which has become one of the hallmarks of American Jewry. To be sure, there were some dissenting views, such as on the issue of release time programs for public school students, but these were faint and feeble and did little to disturb the popular American and Jewish image of a community united on church-state relations. More recently, on a matter directly affecting the interests of religious Jews, the Sunday Closing laws, Orthodox Jewry for the most part, and certainly until late in the game, let the American Jewish Congress and other non-religious groups lead the battle for fair treatment of Sabbath observers.

*   *   *

The idea that Orthodox Jews could effectively deliver a message to politicians was immeasurably strengthened when, after the New York Legislature took no action, a meeting to discuss the Blue Laws was set up between Governor Rocke-feller and Orthodox leaders. In the course of the meeting, following urgent requests that he support amendment of the state law, the Governor remarked that for the first time he understood why the Sunday Closing requirement was onerous to Sabbath observers, something he could not feel when the case was presented by Jews who themselves did not keep the Sabbath.

So, the fact was that Orthodox Jews could benefit by acting on their own behalf. Moreover, the next year, when the law was amended they discovered that it was rather easy to communicate and meet with public officials, includ-ing the big shots. Significantly, it was the recognition of interest and not religion or ideology that dictated the new practice of at least quasi separatism.

At about the same time, there was renewed ferment in the church-state area. The Catholic Church was making substantial headway in its massive effort to obtain support for government assistance to parochial schools. This, coupled with the pressure on Washington for legislation that would provide financial help on the elementary and secondary levels for local school districts, set the stage for a nation-wide debate over inclusion of church-related schools in any aid to education law. Urged on by President Johnson, most interested parties—public education officials, political leaders, teacher organizations, and Catholic and Protestant spokesmen—recognized that it was a practical (and not ideological) matter over which reasonable men might differ and sup-ported at least some forms of federal assistance to parochial schools. Yet, the bulk of the organized and articulate Jewish community, robot-like invoked the holiness and oneness of the First Amendment and proclaimed their opposition to any "breach in the wall separating church and state." This idol worship how-ever did not paralyze the thought processes of Orthodox leaders who were, as a feature of the situation outlined in the opening paragraphs of this report, beginning to have ideas that it might be a good thing for the state to do some-thing which might help the Hebrew Day Schools. First Agudath Israel of America and Torah Umesorah (The National Society of Hebrew Day Schools) and then other Orthodox groups publicly announced their support of certain forms of government help, so that by the time that the Elementary and Sec-ondary Education Act (ESEA) was adopted by Congress in the spring of 1965 the entire organized Orthodox community was in favor of at least child benefit type programs such as busing, textbooks, and remedial services for parochial school children.

Passage of ESEA posed a serious challenge to the Orthodox community, which was not unexpected since, dialectically, success often creates responsibilities that otherwise would not be incurred. Even before Congress finally acted, it was obvious that a legal attack would be launched against the federal program by the diehard opponents to its enactment. . . . Orthodox Jewry did not have any agency for dealing with legal and legislative problems in an orderly and professional manner. It was to fill this need that the National Jewish Commission On Law and Public Affairs (COLPA) was created. . . .

Three persons were responsible for the establishment of COLPA: Rabbi Moshe Sherer of Agudath Israel, Reuben E. Gross, and the writer. The three of us had been among the very first in the Orthodox camp to argue for a new position on governmental aid, and the idea for an Orthodox "legal aid" group apparently came to each of us during the debate over ESEA.

*　*　*

. . . By the spring of 1966 we had become involved in the two areas that now occupy most of our attention. These are governmental aid to parochial schools and the promotion of the rights of Sabbath observers.

4. The Breakdown of Consensus

Echoing Herberg and COLPA, new voices within the American Jewish intellectual community began to speak out on church-state issues in the late 1960s, in opposition to strict separationism and in favor of a more proreligion stance. Thus, writing in *Commentary* in 1966 on the subject of public aid to parochial schools, in the first selection included below, *American Jewish Year Book* editor Milton Himmelfarb argued:

> It is time we [American Jews] actually weighed the utility and cost of education against the utility and cost of separationism. All the evidence . . . points to education, more than anything else, influencing adherence to democracy. . . . All the evidence points to Catholic parochial education having the same influence. . . . Something that nurtures a humane, liberal democracy is rather more important to Jews than twenty-four-karat separationism.

. . . It is not true that freedom is most secure where church and state are separated. . . . Separationism is potentially tyrannical. . . . It is harsh to those who prefer nonpublic schools for conscience' sake; and it stands in the way of a more important good (and a more important safeguard of Jewish security), the best possible education for all.

Writing four years later in the second selection included below, Rabbi Seymour Siegel, a professor at the Jewish Theological Seminary, argued for the abandonment of the Jewish separationist position altogether. In a plea that he (and others) would reiterate many times over the following two decades, Siegel called "for the Jewish community to revise its stand" on church-state questions generally, and especially "to support the public officials who are in favor of state aid to all schools, including parochial schools, day schools, and *yeshivot*." Noting that "it has been considered one of the givens of American Jewish life that the Jewish community, speaking through its agencies, would be on the side of the strict separationists," Siegel pointed to the breakdown of this consensus, to the "signs that this once solid front is not holding." "There is a growing feeling, not limited to the Orthodox," he maintained, "that whatever were the good reasons for this stance in the past, it does not serve Jewish interests today."

◆   ◆   ◆

Milton Himmelfarb on the wall of separation, 1966

The Jews are probably more devoted than anyone else in America to the separation of church and state. At times, hearing some of us talk about separation, or reading the statements of our organizations, one has the impression that we also think ourselves more loyal to the Constitution and more skilled in its interpretation—although of course nobody ever says that in so many words. Thoughts protected against expression, as this one is, can be foolish. We are not more loyal to the Constitution or more skilled in its interpretation, we are only more separationist. And with every passing year our separationism comes closer to being part of the "old order" that Tennyson, in those verses that used to be so popular, wanted to see "yielding place to new;/ . . . Lest one good custom should corrupt the world."

*   *   *

It is time we actually weighed the utility and cost of education against the utility and cost of separationism. All the evidence in America points to education, more than anything else, influencing adherence to democracy and egalitarianism. All the evidence points to Catholic parochial education having the same influence. (And all the evidence points to Catholic antisemitism as probably less than Protestant.) Something that nurtures a humane, liberal democracy is rather more important to Jews than twenty-four-karat separationism.

There is another thing related to the Catholic parochial schools that we ought to weigh in the balance of Jewish interest. Outside the American consensus stand the far Right and the antisemites. (There is antisemitism on the outside Left, too, and among some of the young Jews in it.) It is good to broaden the consensus, to bring inside those who are outside. They change when they come inside.

* * *

Jews have special reason for being grateful to the public school: it helped make the America of opportunities for newcomers, and it trained us to seize the opportunities. It has also helped to make American culture receptive and inclusive, with everything *that* has meant to us. So we are all for the public school. At the same time, we tell each other horror stories about what it has become. If we can, we either send our children to private schools or move to where the public schools are not too public. Meanwhile, out there, some others are less attached than we to the public-school idea and system and are asking rude questions about it, aloud. They are even suggesting that the attachment is a cultural lag, unsuited to the new times.

When this is suggested on behalf of the Catholics, we find it easy to dismiss the suggestion as illiberal. But now it has been suggested on behalf of the Negroes, and we cannot so easily dismiss that. Christopher Jencks, for instance, has argued that the public-school systems of the big cities are so diseased with bureaucracy and inertia that they cannot reasonably be expected to recover and do the job they are supposed to do. In their place, he proposes, the government should give parents the money needed for educating their children; and then the parents, having formed suitable associations, can set up their own schools and hire their own teachers.

Whatever the merits of that particular proposal, Catholics might want to use governmental tuition payments for parochial-school education. What objection could there be then?

To repeat: It is not true that freedom is most secure where church and state are separated; separation and separationism are not the same; even in America, separationism is potentially tyrannical; separationism needlessly repels some from the democratic consensus; it is harsh to those who prefer nonpublic schools for conscience' sake; and it stands in the way of a more important good (and a more important safeguard of Jewish security), the best possible education for all.

*   *   *

Historically, establishment has gone with monarchy: throne and altar, crown and mitre. Separation has gone with a republic: no king, no bishop. And in fact England, Denmark, Norway, and Sweden have established churches and are monarchies. Republicanism was once even more of a fighting creed than separation, but who in Great Britain or Scandinavia is excited by republicanism any longer? It has become an irrelevance, an anachronism. While monarchies have shown that they can be decent and democratic, republics have shown that they need not necessarily be either decent or democratic. In America separationism may soon be just as anachronistic, if only because our establishmentarians are not much more numerous than our monarchists.

Even the metaphors are coming down with mustiness. "Wall of separation" may have sounded good once, but if you say it to a young man now he is as likely as not to think you mean the wall that separates Berlin. Leave it to a poet: "Something there is that doesn't love a wall."

◆

Seymour Siegel advocates state aid for all schools, 1970

. . . It has been considered one of the givens of American Jewish life that the Jewish community, speaking through its agencies, would be on the side of the strict separationists. However, there are signs that this once solid front is not holding. There is a growing feeling, not limited to the Orthodox, that whatever were the good reasons for this stance in the past, it does not serve Jewish interests today. . . .

I am one of the number who believe the time has come for the Jewish community to revise its stand on this question and to support the public officials who are in favor of state aid to all schools, including parochial schools, day schools, and *yeshivot.*

I am not competent, of course, to discuss the constitutional question which will be decided in the courts. However, as has been frequently pointed out, the Jewish community is not rigorously separationist. It does accept the notion of the government paying chaplains in the army and in state-supported institutions; has fought for the continuation of the tax exemption for religious facilities (which, of course, represents an indirect government subsidy) and has received manifold benefits from the state in many ways. It is clear that the so-called wall of separation between church and state is more like a hedge, where if you really want to, or have to, it is not too difficult to get through.

There are good reasons, in my judgment, to support efforts to ease the financial burden of those who are providing their children with alternative education. They are founded on the growing interest in the day school within all the segments of the Jewish community. The Orthodox have thrown most of their educational eggs into the basket of integral education. There is more and more realization in the Conservative movement that the strengthening of the Solomon Schechter Day School movement is essential for the maintenance of religious life. Even the Reform movement, once positively antagonistic, seems to be opening such schools, recognizing that they are vital to Jewish survival. So Jewish parents are now more sympathetic to the plight of Catholic parents. They have been claiming that without government aid for their parochial schools they were carrying a double load of taxation and that the special financial burden of supporting children in church-related institutions constituted, in effect, a threat to their religious freedom.

The latter argument is of some interest. It says: the guarantee of the free exercise of religion is endangered if parents who, as a matter of conscience, wish to educate their children according to the tenets of their faith, are taxed so heavily that the economic burden makes the practice of their religion prohibitive.

*   *   *

. . . In past years, Jewish parents, as a matter of personal distance, tended to be unsympathetic to this argument. Now that they are in the situation they can see the cogency of the argument that the parochial schools perform an important social function and therefore merit some financial support from the state. . . .

A telling argument against aid to church-related schools is that such assistance would wreck the public school system. We Jews owe a great deal to the public school system. It was the chief agency of Americanization of the immigrant and made possible, in large measure, the stunning success of the American Jewish community in the economic, cultural and political spheres. However, it would be folly not to realize that both the ethnic communities in America and the public school have changed. It is clear that most Jews are *born* American and they have to *become* Jews, in contrast to our parents' generation when they were *born* Jews and had to *become* Americans. There is a good deal that plagues our public schools. Much has been written about the malaise affecting them. Homogenizing Americans is not our problem. Constructive pluralism is. If we are to attain it, as many options as possible should be left open for parents and their children in the educational enterprise. . . .

We should not keep our gaze backward. The notion of the separation of Church and State which was championed so vigorously by such thinkers as Spinoza and Mendelsohn reflected their justified fears that a "religious" state would exclude the Jew. But in pluralistic America where there are constitutional guarantees against the establishment of any *one* religion and where the prevailing ethos ordains that Judaism is one of the "three religions of democracy," the strengthening of parochial schools would not endanger the Jewish status as a full citizen. What endangers Judaism is ignorance and an all-pervasive secularism. To fail to recognize this change in the cultural climate and to hold on to positions better suited for other times is folly. Peter Viereck, professor of Yale, has perceptively remarked that anti-Catholicism is the anti-semitism of the liberals. It would be dishonest not to admit that a good deal of the opposition to state aid stems from the undeniable fact that the main beneficiaries would be the Catholics. . . .

Today, I am arguing, such prejudice is intolerable and state aid would be good for the Jewish community and for the general welfare. So it would serve us better if Jewish organizations were to promote government help, insofar as our constitution allows it, rather than fight against it. Realistically, of course, even if the state were to be generous to religious schools this would not completely remove the burden now borne by parents of children in yeshivot and day schools. But even some help is important. This should not, of course, absolve the dispensers of Jewish communal funds from helping our educational efforts to the best of their ability.

I do not question the integrity and the ability of our agencies who have taken such a vigorous stance on the question of Church and State. I do think that they served us well in the past. However, conditions have changed and the Jewish community has changed. Today, it would seem to me more prudent and more true to Judaism to urge our states and local authorities to recognize that education must be supported wherever it is being fostered—both in private and public schools.

ELEVEN

Old Principles and New Rights

The Free Exercise Debate

The First Amendment to the Constitution contains two vital clauses. The first, known as the establishment clause, decrees that "Congress shall make no law respecting an establishment of religion." The second, known as the free exercise clause, also limits Congress from prohibiting the "free exercise" of religion. Cases involving Sunday blue laws, school prayer, and state aid to parochial schools, the issues that historically most concerned the American Jewish community, focused upon the establishment clause. Jews argued that these practices tended to "establish" Christianity as America's state religion, in direct contravention of First Amendment guarantees. The "wall of separation" that Jewish organizations fought to uphold likewise related to the establishment clause. By blocking any manifestation of religion in the public sphere Jews sought to ensure that no religious establishment would ever come into being.

As the Jewish consensus on religion and state broke down, some began to question whether the Jewish community devoted too much attention to the establishment clause at the expense of free exercise claims. These critics, many of them Orthodox Jews involved with COLPA, wondered whether it wasn't more important to focus on such issues as the right to keep the Jewish Sabbath without losing one's job, or the right to wear religious headgear, or the right to obtain kosher food while in jail. Instead of forging alliances with religious liberals and atheists and "clamoring for an impenetrable wall of separation," they called upon American Jews to link hands with religious believers in defense of free exercise liberties.

Surprisingly, the "liberty" that most frequently found its way into court was not one that the creators of COLPA anticipated, or for that matter one that most religious Jews considered of top priority. Yet the issue—the liberty to display a Chanukah menorah (candelabrum) on public property—underscored in a way that no previous issue had the chasm that divided defenders of the old Jewish consensus from their "free exercise" critics.

For years, American Jews had argued on the basis of the establishment clause that religious symbols did not belong on public property; they particularly fought against nativity scenes that some communities displayed during the Christmas season. Now, on the basis of the free exercise clause ("The First Amendment . . . guarantees individuals the right to practice their religion without fear"), the Chabad (Lubavitch) organization, an independent Orthodox Hasidic movement directed by Rabbi Menachem Schneerson, undertook to place a Chanukah menorah "in town squares and shopping malls, alongside highways and byways and waterways." The campaign divided the Jewish community and pit Jews against one another in court. Never before had divisions within the Jewish community on the issue of religion and state been so publicly displayed.

While the menorah issue captured most of the headlines, COLPA and its "free exercise" allies were busy litigating a range of other cases—some of which are detailed in this chapter—designed to help religious Americans (and Orthodox Jews in particular) to observe the tenets of their faith. Where these issues did not appear to raise "establishment clause" concerns—for example, in cases involving prisoners who sought to adhere to Jewish law while in jail—the Jewish community was sometimes able, as before, to effect an uneasy consensus. But as the documents below amply illustrate, consensus, even when it was achieved, masked a critical difference in outlook and communal strategy.

Those who place primary emphasis upon a high wall of separation believe that religious establishment—state-sponsored Christianity—constitutes the greatest danger facing the American Jewish community. They advocate the privatization of religion and the secularization of the state as far more desirable alternatives. By contrast, those who place primary emphasis on "free exercise" believe that religious indifference—which they blame, in no small part, on state policies—constitutes the greatest danger facing the American Jewish community. In advocating the accommodation of religion, public displays of religion, and affirmative state support for religion, they seek to redress past inequities and to stem the assimilationist tide.

1. Do Jews Have the Legal Right to Observe the Sabbath?

In 1964 President Lyndon B. Johnson signed the Civil Rights Act, Title VII of which made it unlawful for an employer to engage in practices tending "to deprive any individual of employment opportunities or otherwise adversely affect his status as an employee, because of such individual's . . . religion." In 1972, Title VII of the 1964 Civil Rights Act was amended to provide: "The term 'religion' includes all aspects of religious observance and practices, as well as belief, unless an employer demonstrates that he is unable to reasonably accommodate to an employee's or prospective employee's religious observance or practice without undue hardship on the conduct of the employer's business." Under these provisions of the Civil Rights Act as amended in 1972, it is the obligation of the employer to continue to employ a worker who refuses on religious grounds to work on Saturday, which he or she observes as the Sabbath. The employer must make any reasonable accommodations to the religious needs of employees and applicants for employment that cause no "undue hardship on the conduct of the employer's business."

In the case of *Estate of Thornton v. Caldor* (1985), this amended Civil Rights act of 1972 was invoked by the U.S. Supreme Court as it determined how far a state can go in protecting an individual Sabbath observer's right to the free exercise of his or her religion. In an eight-to-one ruling, the Supreme Court struck down a Connecticut statute that prohibited employers from forcing their employees to work on their chosen Sabbath. The statute in question had been enacted by the Connecticut General Assembly in 1977, when the state's Sunday-closing laws were repealed, to protect church-going employees from being forced to work on their Sabbath. The Supreme Court ruled, however, that the new law, which stated that "no person who states that a particular day of the week is observed as his Sabbath may be required by his employer to work on such day," was too absolute, and went beyond the Civil Rights Act's standard of "reasonable accommodation" to an employee's religious beliefs and practices. Thus, the Court held, the Connecticut Sabbath law imposed an "undue" burden or hardship on employers, by requiring them to make "absolute" rather than only "reasonable" accommodation to a religious employee's observance of his or her Sabbath.

In its case before the U.S. Supreme Court, Thornton's Estate was represented by attorneys from the National Jewish Commission on Law and Public Affairs and the American Jewish Congress, who maintained that all Sabbath observers, Orthodox Jews and religious Christians alike, had a legal right to observe their Sabbath. In their brief to the Court, portions of which are included below, they argued that the Connecticut Sabbath law should be upheld because it protected a Sabbath observer's legal right to the free exercise of his or her religion. In making the argument on behalf of Thornton's Estate before the Court, Nathan Lewin stated that it should be constitutional for a state to protect all religious people from "the cruel choice between their livelihood and the divine commandment" of honoring the Sabbath.

◆   ◆   ◆

Argument before the Supreme Court on Sabbath observance, 1985

For as long as Western civilization has accepted a seven-day week, it has also recognized one day of the seven as a religious day of rest. The term "Sabbath" has, since the days of the Bible, been defined as the day of the week set aside by divine command for rest and cessation of weekly labor. The issue in this case is whether a State, acting through its legislature, may constitutionally deny a private employer the privilege of forcing an employee to perform labor on the one day in seven which the employee's religious faith recognizes as the Sabbath. The Connecticut Supreme Court held that a law which prohibits such private interference with religious practice is a "law respecting an establishment of religion" within the meaning of the First Amendment. In our view, this Court's decisions—based on the history and purpose of the Bill of Rights—teach that rather than constituting an "establishment of religion," a law which protects Sabbath-observers against adverse employment consequences attributable to their Sabbath observance is a means of preserving and protecting the "free exercise" of religion—an objective which is at least equal in value and stature to the goal of preventing government "establishment" of religion. . . .

This case concerns a law which explicitly protects Sabbath-observers—*i.e.*, those who believe that a particular day of the week is a divinely ordained day of rest—from suffering adverse economic consequences because they carry that belief into practice. The Connecticut Supreme Court concluded that since the law "comes with religious strings attached" (Pet. App. 13a), it is, *ipso facto,* unconstitutional. The court reasoned that a provision of law designed "to allow those persons who wish to worship on a particular day the freedom to do so" (Pet. App. 14a) is unconstitutional because it has a purpose that is other than "secular." We submit that the First Amendment was never intended to prohibit federal, state or local government agencies from safeguarding the rights of people to worship—or to refrain from labor—on the day of the week that they deem sacred.

It has long been established "that the State may not establish a 'religion of secularism' in the sense of affirmatively opposing or showing hostility to religion, thus 'preferring those who believe in no religion over those who do believe.'" *Abington School District* v. *Schempp,* 374 U.S. 203, 225 (1963), *quoting Zorach* v. *Clauson,* 343 U.S. 306, 314 (1952). Our First Amendment differs fundamentally from Article 52 of the Constitution of the Union of Soviet Socialist Republics, which recognizes that "the church . . . is separated from the State," but which grants freedom only for the dissemination of "anti-religious propaganda" and gives no equivalent protection to expression that favors or supports religion. *See* A. P. Blaustein and G. H. Flanz, *Constitutions of Countries of the World,* Constitution of the Union of Soviet Socialist Republics, tit. II, ch. 7, art. 52 (Oct. 7, 1977) at 29. This Court has acknowledged that hostility to religion "would be at war with our national tradition as embodied in the First Amendment's guaranty of the free exercise of religion." *Illinois ex rel. McCollum* v. *Board of Education,* 333 U.S. 203, 211–212 (1948). "We are a religious people whose institutions presuppose a Supreme Being." *Zorach* v. *Clauson,* 343 U.S. 306, 313 (1952).

Justice Jackson's warning against "convert[ing] the constitutional Bill of Rights into a suicide pact" (*Terminiello* v. *Chicago,* 337 U.S. 1, 37 (1949)) has often been quoted. *See American Communications Association* v. *Douds,* 339 U.S. 382, 409 (1950); *Kennedy* v. *Mendoza-Martinez,* 372 U.S. 144, 160 (1963); *Haig* v. *Agee,* 453 U.S. 280, 309–10 (1981); *Aptheker* v. *Secretary of State,* 378 U.S. 500, 509 (1964). A similar warning may be sounded against converting the First Amendment into a death warrant for religion, or, more particularly, into a license entitling private citizens to destroy religion with acts of bigotry.

The Court below concluded that a legislature is constitutionally disabled from providing statutory protection to "those persons who wish to worship on a particular day" (Pet. App. 14a) because the purpose of such a law is religious, not secular. Government would, by the same reasoning, be prohibited from protecting by law those persons who *believe* in the Jewish, Christian, or Moslem faiths, even if they engage in no practice and commit no act that affects their employment. Any law prohibiting discrimination in employment based on religious belief would, by a parity of reasoning, offend the Establishment Clause because its purpose would be "religious" rather than "secular."

The Establishment Clause mandates no such absurd result. It must be read together with the complementary Free Exercise Clause "in light of the single end which they are designed to serve." *Abington School District* v. *Schempp*, 374 U.S. 203, 305 (1963) (Goldberg, J., concurring). That basic purpose (*id.*):

> is to promote and assure the fullest possible scope of religious liberty and tolerance for all and to nurture the conditions which secure the best hope of attainment of that end.

It is "our remarkable and precious religious diversity as a nation . . . which the Establishment Clause seeks to protect." *Lynch* v. *Donnelly*, 104 S. Ct. 1355, 1371 (1984) (Brennan, J., dissenting).

It is firmly accepted that the Establishment Clause forbids the "sponsorship, financial support, and active involvement of the sovereign in religious activity." *Walz* v. *Tax Commission*, 397 U.S. 664, 668 (1970). *Accord, Committee for Public Education and Religious Liberty* v. *Nyquist*, 413 U.S. 756, 772 (1973); *Wisconsin* v. *Yoder*, 406 U.S. 205, 234, n.22 (1972); *Gillette* v. *United States*, 401 U.S. 437, 450 (1971). Equally important, however, the Establishment Clause's mandate of *benevolent* neutrality forbids not only intentional, "active, hostility to the religious . . . ," but also "a brooding and pervasive devotion to the secular and a passive, or even active, hostility to the religious." *Abington School District* v. *Schempp*, 374 U.S. 203, 306 (1963) (Goldbert, J., concurring). "[C]allous indifference" to the needs of religious observers runs counter to the Constitution. *Zorach* v. *Clauson*, 343 U.S. 306, 314 (1952).

Decisions of this Court make clear that nothing in the Establishment Clause prevents government from protecting religious observers against discrimination in private employment, even though such protection appears to grant special treatment to religious, as opposed to secular, needs. "'Neutrality' in matters of religion is not inconsistent with 'benevolence' by way of exemptions from onerous duties." *Gillette* v. *United States*, 401 U.S. 437, 454 (1971). In fact, when seemingly neutral government requirements impose a discriminatory burden on religious observers, the Free Exercise Clause frequently requires singling out religious beliefs and practices for special protection. . . .

2. Do Jewish Prisoners Have the Legal Right to Kosher Food?

The eating of food certified by Jewish religious authorities as being "kosher" is central to the observance of the Jewish

dietary laws, and a matter of religious obligation for observant Jews.

In 1975, Rabbi Meir Kahane, founder of the militant Jewish
Defense League, sued the Allenwood (Pennsylvania) federal
penitentiary, to which he had been remanded for parole violation, to provide him with kosher food during his incarceration
in the prison facility. As his attorney argued in the first selection included below, to deny kosher food to a religiously observant Jewish prison inmate, such as Rabbi Kahane, was to
deny that inmate the free exercise of religion guaranteed by
the First Amendment: "The free exercise clause embraces both
the freedom to believe and the freedom to act according to
those beliefs. . . . The government, in its control of prisons,
is precluded from denying religious observance to inmates. Its
obligation to permit religious observances is an extension of
the position that no one can be burdened or punished by the
state for having the 'wrong' religious beliefs."

Although in May 1975, Brooklyn Federal Judge Jack Wein-
stein directed the Federal Bureau of Prisons to provide kosher
food to Rabbi Kahane, his ruling was a limited one. Kahane
had hoped that his suit would establish a legal precedent entitling every Jewish prison inmate to kosher food as a matter
of constitutional right. "This fight will continue until a court
ruling is handed down establishing *the constitutional right of
every Jew,* who so wishes, to have kosher food regardless of cost
or problems for the prison," Kahane vowed. In fact, the free
exercise arguments that his attorneys made on his behalf did
prove influential. Jews, Muslims and members of other faiths
now regularly appeal to the courts under the First Amendment, seeking the right to observe the tenets of their faith
while incarcerated.

◆　　　◆　　　◆

Attorney for Rabbi Kahane on prisoners' right to kosher food, 1975

A person does not lose his basic humanity and constitutional rights because
he has been convicted or is serving a term in prison. In this respect we differ
fundamentally from some governments which consider its citizens' rights forfeited upon incarceration and engage in abuses of prisoners that amount to
a form of slavery. Our courts have made it clear that, to the extent consonant

with effective administration of correctional institutions, the First Amendment rights of prisoners cannot be ignored:

> "[A] policy of judicial restraint [concerning prison administration] cannot encompass any failure to take cognizance of valid constitutional claims whether arising in a federal or state institution. When a prison regulation or practice offends a fundamental constitutional guarantee, federal courts will discharge their duty to protect constitutional rights."

*   *   *

Rabbi Henry Siegman, Vice-President of the Synagogue Council of America, testified that his organization, which has assisted the Federal Bureau of Prisons for the past fifteen years in providing Jewish chaplains, regularly requested that the Bureau provide kosher food to Jewish prisoners, but had been unsuccessful. He and other witnesses testified, without contradiction, that kosher food could be provided, using modern technology, with no inconvenience to a large institution serving meals to a predominantly non-observant population. They gave detailed descriptions of how this could be accomplished using the regular kitchen equipment of the institution with no appreciable administrative difficulties. . . .

*   *   *

. . . Where the government has total control over people's lives, as in prisons, a niche has necessarily been carved into the establishment clause to require the government to afford opportunities for worship. . . . The government, in its control of prisons, is precluded from denying religious observance to inmates. Its obligation to permit religious observances is an extension of the position that no one can be burdened or punished by the state for having the "wrong" religious beliefs.

3. Does a Jewish Soldier Have the Legal Right to Keep His Head Covered?

In the celebrated 1986 Supreme Court case of *Goldman v. Weinberger*, an Orthodox Jewish Air Force officer named Simcha Goldman challenged the military's uniform dress requirements that prohibited him from wearing a *yarmulke*, a skullcap, while serving on duty. Goldman, an Orthodox Jew and an ordained rabbi serving as a clinical psychologist in an Air Force hospital, normally kept his head covered at all times in accordance with Orthodox Jewish practice. When outdoors, he wore the regulation Air Force cap; when indoors, he wore a small cloth skullcap. In May 1981, Goldman's superior officer notified him that wearing a *yarmulke* indoors while in uniform violated an Air Force dress code regulation, and ordered him to remove it or face a court martial. Goldman, represented by attorneys from COLPA, filed suit, claiming that this regulation infringed upon his First Amendment right to the free exercise of his religion. In their legal brief to the Supreme Court, excerpts of which are included below, Goldman's attorneys based their case on "the very heart of the protection afforded by the Free Exercise Clause of the First Amendment." The Supreme Court, nevertheless, upheld the Air Force: The First Amendment's free exercise protection, it ruled, did not require the military to accommodate Captain Goldman's religious beliefs.

In a sharp dissent, praised by all segments of the organized Jewish community, Justice Brennan lamented the fact that "The Court and the military services have presented patriotic Orthodox Jews with a painful dilemma—the choice between fulfilling a religious obligation and serving their country." Orthodox Jewish servicemen, noted Brennan, would now be required to violate the tenets of their faith "virtually every minute of every working day."

Congress subsequently enacted federal legislation to overturn *Goldman v. Weinberger.* Drafted by Nathan Lewin, the COLPA attorney who argued Simcha Goldman's case before the U.S. Supreme Court, and passed by both houses of Congress as an amendment to the Defense Authorization Law, this new law required the armed services to allow its members to wear a "neat and conservative" skullcap if it would not interfere with their duties. Later, in response to another Supreme Court decision limiting free exercise (*Employment Division, Department of Human Resources of Oregon v. Smith*), this one involving the sacramental use of peyote by Native Americans, Congress passed what became known as the Religious Freedom Restoration Act. Strongly supported by the Jewish community, the act requires the government to demonstrate a "compelling state interest" before religiously mandated activities may be challenged.

◆ ◆ ◆

COLPA's defense of the right to wear a yarmulke, 1985

. . . [W]earing a yarmulke has absolutely no impact on the rights or conduct of others. It is a personal mark of religious identity and an individualized acknowledgment of a Divine Creator. It is, in this regard, no different from symbolic devotion or prayer. Hence it is at the very heart of the protection afforded by the Free Exercise Clause of the First Amendment.

Yarmulkes are generally understood to be a form of religious observance. They are commonly seen and accepted in today's society wherever Orthodox Jews are found. University campuses—particularly on the East Coast—have substantial numbers of young men who wear yarmulkes. On the streets of New York City, Los Angeles, Chicago, or Miami, yarmulkes are commonplace. They are increasingly visible in centers of commerce, including retail businesses, brokerage houses, and stock exchanges. Attorneys wearing yarmulkes can be found in the state and federal courthouses of New York, and attorneys wearing yarmulkes have been permitted to sit in the Bar Section of this Court and attend oral arguments.

Wearing a yarmulke is a form of silent devotion. It is the functional equivalent of prayer, because it manifests one's belief in a Supreme Being. When he first described the First Amendment's dual provision as "building a wall of separation between church and State." Thomas Jefferson also declared that man "owes account to none other for his faith or his worship, [and] that the legislative powers of government reach actions only, and not opinions." 8 Works of Thomas Jefferson 113, quoted in *Braunfeld v. Brown*, 366 U.S. 599, 604 (1961). Wearing a yarmulke is as private and nonintrusive as are belief and prayer. Hence there is rarely any justification for government interference with this observance, and it is entitled to the same protection against legislative encroachment as is afforded to prayer or other forms of worship.

◆

Defense Authorization Law amended to allow religious apparel

SEC. 508. WEARING OF RELIGIOUS APPAREL BY MEMBERS
OF THE ARMED FORCES WHILE IN UNIFORM

(a) In General—Chapter 45 of title 10, United States Code, is amended—
(1) by redesignating section 774 as section 775; and
(2) by inserting after section 773 the following new section 774:

"§ 774. Religious apparel: wearing while in uniform

"(a) GENERAL RULE.—Except as provided under subsection (b), a member of the armed forces may wear an item of religious apparel while wearing the uniform of the member's armed force.

"(b) EXCEPTIONS.—The Secretary concerned may prohibit the wearing of an item of religious apparel—

> "(1) in circumstances with respect to which the Secretary determines that the wearing of the item would interfere with the performance of the member's military duties; or
>
> "(2) if the Secretary determines, under regulations under subsection (c), that the item of apparel is not neat and conservative.

"(c) REGULATIONS.—The Secretary concerned shall prescribe regulations concerning the wearing of religious apparel by members of the armed forces under the Secretary's jurisdiction while the members are wearing the uniform. Such regulations shall be consistent with subsections (a) and (b).

"(d) RELIGIOUS APPAREL DEFINED.—In this section, the term 'religious apparel' means apparel the wearing of which is part of the observance of the religious faith practiced by the member."

(b) CLERICAL AMENDMENT.—The table of sections at the beginning of such chapter is amended by striking out the item relating to section 774 and inserting in lieu thereof the following:

> "774. Religious apparel: wearing while in uniform.
> "775. Applicability of chapter."

(c) REGULATIONS.—The Secretary concerned shall prescribe the regulations required by section 774(c) of title 10, United States Code, as added by subsection (a), not later than the end of the 120-day period beginning on the date of the enactment of this Act.

4. Can a Secular Judge Compel a Religious Divorce?

The alarming rise in the American divorce rate in recent years has exacerbated the problems created by the interplay and clash between secular and religious divorce. Under Jewish religious law, a marriage validly entered into can be terminated only by the death of the husband or wife, or by the issuance of a traditional religious divorce, known as a Get. Since only the husband has the right to give or accept a Get, there have been numerous instances in which the wife has been unable to re-marry after the civil divorce by virtue of the refusal of the husband to do so. In recent years, as several scholars have noted, individuals embroiled in divorce litigation have turned with increasing frequency to the civil courts to compel a recal-citrant husband to give or accept a Get. Since Judaism views marriage as a religious contract, and the Get as the only valid bill of divorcement to dissolve this religious contract, the courts have had to decide whether or not it is constitutionally permissible on First Amendment grounds for the state to be-come involved in the issues of Jewish marriage and divorce.

In recent years, several American civil court decisions have held that the Ketubah, the marriage contract which is always read as an integral part of the Jewish marriage ceremony, is a legally binding agreement enforceable by a secular judge in the civil courts, and that prenuptial commitments stipulated within the Ketubah concerning the procurement of a Get after the granting of a civil divorce, are enforceable by the secu-lar courts as well. In the landmark case of *Avitzur v. Avitzur,* the New York Court of Appeals ruled that a Ketubah commonly used by the Conservative Movement in American Judaism, containing a prenuptial agreement binding husband and wife to submit the issue of the giving of a Get to Rabbinical arbi-tration before a Beth Din (a Jewish legal tribunal having the authority to advise and counsel upon matters of Jewish law re-lating to marriage and divorce, including the granting of a Get), is indeed a valid and legally binding contract, which the civil courts have the power to enforce. When Susan and Boaz Avitzur were married in 1966, they had signed this Conserva-tive Ketubah, containing the stipulation that, in the event of civil divorce, they "hereby agree to recognize the Beth Din of the Rabbinical Assembly and the Jewish Theological Semi-nary" as the Rabbinic tribunal before which to submit the issue of procurement of a Get, and to abide by any decisions of that body. After having obtained a civil divorce in 1978, how-ever, when Susan summoned her husband to appear before the Conservative Beth Din and grant her a religious divorce in accordance with his initial agreement stipulated to in their Ketubah, he refused to do so. The New York Court of Appeals ruling, excerpts from which are included in the first selec-tion below, decided in favor of Susan Avitzur, holding that the prenuptial agreement signed by the Avitzurs to arbitrate their differences before the Conservative Movement's Beth Din was legally binding and enforceable in a secular court of law. Thus Boaz Avitzur was compelled to appear before the Beth Din.

In recent years, in the legislative arena as well as in the courts, new legal remedies have been sought to compel a recalcitrant spouse, who has sued for civil divorce, to give or accept a religious divorce. In 1984, the New York State Legislature passed a bill known as the Get Law, predicated upon the assumption that the Ketubah can be viewed as a contractual agreement between husband and wife, which compels a recalcitrant spouse to give or accept a Get following a civil divorce. This legislative bill, drafted by lawyers from COLPA, which we have included as the second selection below, provides that a final judgment for annulment or divorce will not be rendered unless the party suing for annulment or divorce has "taken all steps solely within his or her power to remove all barriers to the defendant's remarriage following the annulment or divorce." In other words, according to this law, a husband will not be able to obtain a civil divorce without first giving his wife a Get, thus permitting her to remarry.

◆　　◆　　◆

New York Appeals Court rules that a Ketubah is legally binding, 1983

WATCHLER, J.

This appeal presents for our consideration the question of the proper role of the civil courts in deciding a matter touching upon religious concerns. At issue is the enforceability of the terms of a document, known as Ketubah, which was entered into as part of the religious marriage ceremony in this case. The Appellate Division held this to be a religious covenant beyond the jurisdiction of the civil courts. However, we find nothing in law or public policy to prevent judicial recognition and enforcement of the secular terms of such an agreement. There should be a reversal.

Plaintiff and defendant were married on May 22, 1966 in a ceremony conducted in accordance with Jewish tradition. Prior to the marriage ceremony, the parties signed both a Hebrew/Aramaic and an English version of the "Ketubah". According to the English translation, the Ketubah evidences both the bridegroom's intention to cherish and provide for his wife as required by religious law and tradition and the bride's willingness to carry out her obligations to her husband in faithfulness and affection according to Jewish law and tradition. By signing the Ketubah, the parties declared their "desire to *** live in accordance with the Jewish law of marriage throughout [their] lifetime" and further agreed as follows:

> "We, the bride and bridegroom *** hereby agree to recognize the Beth Din of the Rabbinical Assembly and the Jewish Theological Seminary of America or its duly appointed representatives, as having authority to counsel us in the light of Jewish tradition which requires husband and wife to give each other complete love and devotion, and to summon either party at the request of the other, in order to enable the party so requesting to live in accordance with the standards of the Jewish law of marriage throughout his or her lifetime. We authorize the Beth Din to impose such terms of compensation as it may see fit for failure to respond to its summons or to carry out its decision."

Defendant husband was granted a civil divorce upon the ground of cruel and inhuman treatment on May 16, 1978. Notwithstanding this civil divorce, plaintiff wife is not considered divorced and may not remarry pursuant to Jewish law, until such time as a Jewish divorce decree, known as a "Get", is granted. In order that a Get may be obtained plaintiff and defendant must appear before a "Beth Din", a rabbinical tribunal having authority to advise and pass upon matters of traditional Jewish law. Plaintiff sought to summon defendant before the Beth Din pursuant to the provision of the Ketubah recognizing that body as having authority to counsel the couple in the matters concerning their marriage.

Defendant has refused to appear before the Beth Din, thus preventing plaintiff from obtaining a religious divorce. Plaintiff brought this action, alleging that the Ketubah constitutes a marital contract, which defendant has breached by refusing to appear before the Beth Din, and she seeks relief both in the form of a declaration to that effect and an order compelling defendant's specific performance of the Ketubah's requirement that he appear before the Beth Din. Defendant moved to dismiss the complaint upon the grounds that the court lacked subject matter jurisdiction and the complaint failed to state a cause of action, arguing that resolution of the dispute and any grant of relief to plaintiff would involve the civil court in impermissible consideration of a purely religious matter. Plaintiff, in addition to opposing the motion, cross-moved for summary judgment.

Special Term denied defendant's motion to dismiss, noting that plaintiff sought only to compel defendant to submit to the jurisdiction of the Beth Din, an act which plaintiff had alleged defendant bound himself to do. That being the only object of the lawsuit, Special Term was apparently of the view that the relief sought could be granted without impermissible judicial entanglement in any doctrinal issue. The court also denied plaintiff's entanglement in any doctrinal issue. The court also denied plaintiff's motion for summary judgment, concluding that issues concerning the translation, meaning and effect of the Ketubah raised factual questions requiring a plenary trial.

The Appellate Division modified, granting defendant's motion to dismiss. Inasmuch as the Ketubah was entered into as part of a religious ceremony and was executed, by its own terms, in accordance with Jewish law, the court concluded that the document constitutes a liturgical agreement. The Appellate Division held such agreements to be unenforceable where the State, having granted a civil divorce to the parties, has no further interest in their marital status.

Accepting plaintiff's allegations as true, as we must in context of this motion to dismiss, it appears that plaintiff and defendant, in signing the Ketubah, entered into a contract which formed the basis for their marriage. Plaintiff has alleged that, pursuant to the terms of this marital contract, defendant promised that he would, at plaintiff's request, appear before the Beth Din for the purpose of allowing that tribunal to advise and counsel the parties in matters concerning their marriage, including the granting of a Get. It should be noted that plaintiff is not attempting to compel defendant to obtain a Get or to enforce a religious practice arising solely out of principles of religious law. She merely seeks to enforce an agreement made by defendant to appear before and accept the decision of a designated tribunal.

Viewed in this manner, the provisions of the Ketubah relied upon by plaintiff constitute nothing more than an agreement to refer the matter of a religious divorce to a nonjudicial forum. Thus, the contractual obligation plaintiff seeks to enforce is closely analogous to an antenuptial agreement to arbitrate a dispute in accordance with the law and tradition chosen by the parties. There can be little doubt that a duly executed antenuptial agreement, by which the parties agree in advance of the marriage to the resolution of disputes that may arise after its termination, is valid and enforceable (e.g., *Matter of Sunshine*, 40 NY2d 875, affg 51 AD2d 326; *Matter of Davis*, 20 NY2d 70). Similarly, an agreement to refer a matter concerning marriage to arbitration suffers no inherent invalidity (*Hirsh v Hirsch*, 37 NY2d 312; see *Bowmer v Bowmer*, 50 NY2d 288, 293). This agreement—the Ketubah—should ordinarily be entitled to no less dignity than any other civil contract to submit a dispute to a nonjudicial forum, so long as its enforcement violates neither the law nor the public policy of this State (*Hirsch v Hirsch, supra*, at p. 315).

Defendant argues, in this connection, that enforcement of the terms of the Ketubah by a civil court would violate the constitutional prohibition against excessive entanglement between church and State, because the court must necessarily intrude upon matters of religious doctrine and practice. It is urged that the obligations imposed by the Ketubah arise solely from Jewish religious law and can be interpreted only with reference to religious dogma. Granting the religious character of the Ketubah, it does not necessarily follow that any recognition of its obligations is foreclosed to the courts.

It is clear that judicial involvement in matters touching upon religious concerns has been constitutionally limited in analogous situations, and courts should not resolve such controversies in a manner requiring consideration of religious doctrine (*Presbyterian Church v Hull Church*, 393 US 440, 449; *Serbian Eastern Orthodox Diocese v Milivojevich*, 426 US 696, 709; *Jones v Wolf*, 443 US 595, 603; see e.g., *Reardon v Lemoyne*, __ NH__, __[Dec. 23, 1982]. In its most recent pronouncement on this issue, however, the Supreme Court, in holding that a State may adopt any approach to resolving religious disputes which does not entail consideration of doctrinal matters, specifically approved the use of the "neutral principles of law" approach as consistent with constitutional limitations (*Jones v Wolf, supra,* at p. 602). This approach contemplates the application of objective, well-established principles of secular law to the dispute (*id.* at p. 603), thus permitting judicial involvement to the extent that it can be accomplished in purely secular terms.

The present case can be decided solely upon the application of neutral principles of contract law, without reference to any religious principle. Consequently, defendant's objections to enforcement of his promise to appear before the Beth Din, based as they are upon the religious origin of the agreement, pose no constitutional barrier to the relief sought by plaintiff. The fact that the agreement was entered into as part of a religious ceremony does not render it unenforceable. Solemnization of the marital relationship often takes place in accordance with the religious beliefs of the participants, and this State has long recognized this religious aspect by permitting duly authorized pastors, rectors, priests, rabbis and other religious officials to perform the ceremony (Domestic Relations Law, §11, subds 1,7). Similarly, that the obligations undertaken by the parties to the Ketubah are grounded in religious belief and practice does not preclude enforcement of its secular terms. Nor does the fact that all of the Ketubah's provisions may not be judicially recognized prevent the court from enforcing that portion of the agreement by which the parties promised to refer their disputes to a nonjudicial forum (see *Ferro v Bologna*, 31 NY2d 30,36). The courts may properly enforce so much of this agreement as is not in contravention of law or public policy.

In short, the relief sought by plaintiff in this action is simply to compel defendant to perform a secular obligation to which he contractually bound himself. In this regard, no doctrinal issue need be passed upon, no implementation of a religious duty is contemplated, and no interference with religious authority will result. Certainly nothing the Beth Din can do would in any way affect the civil divorce. To the extent that an enforceable promise can be found by the application of neutral principles of contract law, plaintiff will have demonstrated entitlement to the relief sought. Consideration of other substantive issues bearing upon plaintiff's entitlement to a religious divorce, however, is appropriately left to the forum the parties chose for resolving the matter.

Accordingly, the order of the Appellate Division should be reversed, with costs, and defendant's motion to dismiss the complaint denied.

◆

New York law links civil and religious divorce, 1984

47. 1984 N.Y. Session Laws ch. 945. The amended law now reads (deletions from the 1983 version are in brackets, additions are in italics):

1. This section applies only to a marriage solemnized in this state or in any other jurisdiction by a person specified in subdivision one of this section.

2. Any party to a marriage defined in subdivision one of this section who commences a proceeding to annul the marriage or for a divorce must allege, in his or her verified complaint: *(i) that, to the best of his or her knowledge,* that he or she has taken or *that he or she* will take, prior to the entry of final judgment, all steps solely within his or her power to remove any barrier to the defendant's remarriage following the annulment or divorce; *or (ii) that the defendant has waived in writing the requirements of this subdivision.*

3. No final judgment of annulment or divorce shall thereafter be entered unless the plaintiff shall have filed and served a [verified] *sworn* statement [that]: *(i) that, to the best of his or her knowledge,* he or she has, prior to the entry of such final judgment, taken all steps solely within his or her power to remove all barriers to the defendant's remarriage following the annulment or divorce; *or (ii) that the defendant has waived in writing the requirements of this subdivision.*

4. In any action for divorce based on subdivisions five and six of section one hundred seventy of this chapter in which the defendant enters a general appearance and does not contest the requested relief, no final judgment of annulment or divorce shall be entered unless both parties shall have filed and served [verified statements that each has] *sworn statements: (i) that he or she has, to the best of his or her knowledge,* taken all steps solely within his or her power to remove all barriers to the other party's remarriage following the annulment or divorce; *or (ii) that the other party has waived in writing the requirements of this subdivision.*

5. *The writings attesting to any waiver of the requirements of subdivisions two, three or four of this section shall be filed with the court prior to the entry of a final judgment of annulment or divorce.*

6. As used in the [verified] *sworn* statements prescribed by this section "barrier to remarriage" includes, *without limitation,* any religious or conscientious restraint or inhibition, *of which the party required to make the verified (sic) statement is aware, that is* imposed on a party to a marriage, under the principles [of

the denomination of] *held by* the clergyman or minister who has solemnized the marriage, by reason of the other party's commission or withholding of any voluntary act. *Nothing in this section shall be construed to require any party to consult with any clergyman or minister to determine whether there exists any such religious or conscientious restraint or inhibition.* It shall not be deemed a "barrier to remarriage" within the meaning of this section if the restraint or inhibition cannot be removed by the party's voluntary act. Nor shall it be deemed a "barrier to remarriage" if the party must incur expenses in connection with removal of the restraint or inhibition and the other party refuses to provide reasonable reimbursement for such expenses. "All steps solely within his or her power" shall not be construed to include application to a marriage tribunal or other similar organization or agency of a religious denomination which has authority to annul or dissolve a marriage under the rules of such denomination.

[6] 7. No final judgment of annulment or divorce shall be entered, notwithstanding the filing of the plaintiff's [verified] *sworn* statement prescribed by this section, if the clergyman or minister who has solemnized the marriage certifies, in a [verified] *sworn* statement, that he or she has solemnized the marriage and that, to his or her knowledge, the plaintiff has failed to take all steps solely within his or her power to remove all barriers to the defendant's remarriage following the annulment or divorce, provided that the said clergyman or minister is alive and available *and competent* to testify at the time when final judgment would be entered.

[7] 8. Any person who knowingly submits a false [verified] *sworn* statement under this section shall be guilty of making an apparently sworn false statement in the first degree and shall be punished in accordance with section 210.40 of the penal law.

9. Nothing in this section shall be construed to authorize any court to inquire into or determine any ecclesiastical or religious issue. The truth of any statement submitted pursuant to this section shall not be the subject of any judicial inquiry, except as provided in subdivision eight of this section.

5. Do Jews Have the Legal Right to Light a Menorah in the Public Square?

The Chabad (Lubavitch) organization's vigorous campaign, beginning in the 1970s, to construct privately funded Chanukah menorahs on public property in cities throughout the United States precipitated a heated debate within the American Jewish community over whether it was constitutionally permissible and proper to do so. The issue, as popularly understood, involved a basic question: should the public square be devoid of any religious symbols, or should it be open to all religious symbols, including the creche and menorah. Liberal Jewish organizations, such as the American Jewish Congress and the Reform Movement's Central Conference of American Rabbis, have staunchly opposed the placing of menorahs (as well as creches) on public property, as an unacceptable breach of the "wall of separation" between religion and state. Orthodox Jewish groups such as Chabad and COLPA, by contrast, argued that Jews have a legal right to ask for menorahs to be placed on public property, especially alongside the permissible symbols of Christmas. Opponents of public menorah displays saw them as a violation of the establishment clause; proponents saw them as an expression of the very neutrality with regard to all religions that the First Amendment was enacted to guarantee.

In the following 1978 letter to Rabbi Menachem M. Schneerson, the leader of the Chabad (Lubavitch) organization, Rabbi Joseph B. Glaser, then the executive vice president of the Central Conference of American Rabbis, voiced his opposition to the Lubavitch campaign to erect menorahs on government property, calling it "as much a violation of the constitutional principle of separation of church and state as is the erection of Christmas trees and creches depicting the birth of Jesus. It weakens our hand when we protest this intrusion of Christian doctrine into the public life of American citizens. . . ." In his reply, also printed below, Rabbi Schneerson, the Lubavitcher Rebbe, tried to "allay" Glaser's "apprehensions." After presenting an alternative understanding of the First Amendment, he emphasized that the Lubavitch organization placed menorahs on public property to encourage Jewish religious identity and observance ("Torah and Mitzvoth") as well as Jewish religious pride. "Where Chanukah lamps were kindled publicly," he wrote, "the results have been most gratifying in terms of spreading the light of Torah and Mitzvoth, and reaching out to Jews who could not otherwise have been reached. . . ." Their correspondence highlights the fundamental differences in outlook of these two leaders. Not only did they read the Constitution differently, they also embraced very different priorities and goals.

In 1989 the Supreme Court, in the case known as *Allegheny County, City of Pittsburgh and Chabad v. ACLU,* ruled that a

Chabad-sponsored menorah standing next to a Christmas tree in front of Pittsburgh's City Hall did not violate the First Amendment. The issue divided the Jewish community. As the responses included below illustrate, underlying these divisions lay a fundamental disagreement concerning what was best for the American Jewish community. Nathan Lewin, a vice president of COLPA and the attorney for Chabad in the *Allegheny* case, who also litigated several other important church-state cases before the federal courts, argues that public displays of a menorah symbolize to all the fact "that America is a country where Jews are welcome and are first class citizens," and "engender emotions of pride and confidence among Jews who see them." Banishing menorahs from public places, he believes, would mean "derogating religion and denying to Jews the equal access to public forums that are available to secular organizations. . . ."

By contrast, Rabbi Allan Nadler, director of the YIVO Institute for Jewish Research, reflects the erstwhile consensus and still widespread Jewish view that "the kindling of huge menorahs in public places across America opens a dangerous constitutional can of worms. It can very easily backfire on the Jewish community by undermining the principle of freedom from established religion, which has always been such a blessing for American Jewry."

✦   ✦   ✦

Exchange of letters between Rabbi Joseph Glaser and Rabbi Menachem Schneerson on the menorah issue, 1978

Central Conference of American Rabbis
Office of the Executive Vice President

April 25, 1978

Rabbi M. M. Schneerson
770 Eastern Parkway
Brooklyn, N.Y. 11213

Dear Rabbi:

It has come to my attention that Lubavitcher chassidim are erecting hanukkiot and holding religious services in connection therewith on public property in various localities throughout the United States at Hanukkah time.

This is as much a violation of the constitutional principle of separation of church and state as is the erection of Christmas trees and creches depicting the birth of Jesus. It weakens our hand when we protest this intrusion of Christian doctrine into the public life of American citizens, and thus, it is really not worth the value received.

I would very much appreciate an opportunity to meet with you to discuss the matter further, and also to indulge a desire I have had for a long time to know you personally. I feel that we have many common interests, and want to explore them with you.

My warmest good wishes for the remainder of the Pesach season.

Shalom,
RABBI JOSEPH B. GLASER

Central Conference of American Rabbis
Office of the Executive Vice President

May 31, 1978

Rabbi M. M. Schneerson
770 Eastern Parkway
Brooklyn, New York 11213

Dear Rabbi:

Following up on my letter of April 25 suggesting that we discuss religious observances, particularly the kindling of *Hanukkiot,* held on public property, I was pleased to receive a telephone call from your office inviting me to send our views for your consideration and response.

As believing Jews, Lubavitcher Chasidim, Reform Jews, and others share the conviction that the *mitzvah* of kindling *Hanukkiot* should be fulfilled by all Jews. Likewise, that the lights should be placed in the windows, or even outside, of Jewish homes and synagogues "to proclaim the miracle," is a practice we encourage. All that we question is the necessity and desirability of holding this or similar religious ceremonies on public property.

The *mitzvah* is fulfilled when *Hanukkiot* are lit on Jewish property. So there is no halachic necessity for doing so on public property. We believe public-property religious observances are not only unnecessary, but undesirable. Allow me to explain why we feel that way.

As you know, the American Constitution provides for the separation of "church and state." The relative comfort of Jews in the United States has resulted in part from the application of that principle. By constant vigilance we Jews, and other Americans who believe that the full freedom of religion which church-state separation provides is important, have managed to minimize violation of the Constitutional principle. Of particular note in this context, we have had considerable success in recent decades in preventing Christmas displays, creches especially, on public property, and in preventing religious assemblies and prayer-periods in public schools. Thus we and our children are not forced—as Jews in many nations are—to support Christianity through our taxes or to be exposed, and have our children exposed, to government sanctioned proselytizing. The civil courts have repeatedly agreed that we and our children need not be exposed to Christian observances which we find offensive.

Clearly Jewish religious observances and displays on public property are no less a violation of the doctrine of church-state separation than are Christian observances and displays. And when Jews seek to violate the Constitutional principle we weaken our hand in our ongoing efforts to prevent Christian violations.

There is a second reason for our concern about Chabad's practice of holding *Hanukkah* observances on public property. For the reasons outlined above, in several communities Jews have objected to these observances. Heated debates in the Jewish community has spilled over into the general community and has been reported by the media. Surely the sad spectacle of Jews publicly fighting with other Jews is a *chillul hashem*. I must tell you in all candor that we continue to receive complaints about this particular Chabad practice, and thus I have no doubt that the disputations will continue and possibly even end up in court. Since you and we have no difficulty "proclaiming the miracle" via *Hanukkah* observance on private property, continued confrontation serves no positive Jewish purpose, and indeed is counter-productive.

Our request of you, then, is simply that in your role as leader of the Chabad Lubavitch movement you direct a cessation of *Hanukkiot* lightings or other religious observances on public property. I would be happy to meet personally with you or your representatives to discuss the matter further.

Shalom,
RABBI JOSEPH B. GLASER

By the Grace of G-d
3rd of Sivan, 5738
Brooklyn, N.Y.

Dr. Joseph B. Glaser
790 Madison Avenue
New York, N.Y. 10021

Greeting and Blessing:
    This is to confirm receipt of your letter of May 31, and I regret the unavoidable delay in replying to it more promptly. In it you express your reservations

about the kindling of *Hanukkiot* in public places on the ground of (a) the principle of separation of church and state, and (b) it being "counter-productive."

Had I received your letter years ago, when this practice started, I would have had a more difficult task of defending it, for the simple reason that the expected positive results were then a matter of conjecture. But now, after the practice and the results have been observed for a number of years, my task is an easy one, since the general acclaim and beneficial results have far exceeded our expectations. The fact is that countless Jews in all parts of the country have been impressed and inspired by the spirit of Chanukah which had been brought to them, to many for the first time. Indeed, the eternal and always timely message of Chanukah—the victory of the outnumbered forces of light over the overwhelming forces of darkness that attempted to make Jews forget G-d's Torah and Mitzvoth (as we say in the prayer of "V'Al Hanissim")—struck a responsive cord in the hearts of many Jews and strengthened their sense of identity with the Maccabbee of all ages.

This year, too, now that some six months have elapsed since Chanukah and reports have come in from various places where Chanukah Lamps were kindled publicly, the results have been most gratifying in terms of spreading the light of the Torah and Mitzvoth, and reaching out to Jews who *could not otherwise* have been reached, either because some of them are unaffiliated with any synagogue, or, though loosely affiliated, always thought that religious practices belong within the confines of a synagogue and do not relate to the personal everyday life of the individual. It was precisely through kindling the Chanukah Lamp in public places, during "ordinary" weekdays, with dignity and pride, that it was brought home to them that true Judaism is practised daily, and that no Jew should feel abashed about it.

With regard to the "Constitutional" question, I can most assuredly allay your apprehensions on this score. I am fully certain that none of all those who participated in, or witnessed, the kindling of a Chanukah Lamp in a public place (and in all cases permission was *readily* granted by the authorities) felt that his or her loyalty to the Constitution of the USA had been weakened or compromised thereby. Indeed, many expressed surprise that this practice had not been inaugurated many years earlier, seeing that the U.S. Congress opens with a religious invocation by a representative of "one of the major religions" in this country; and, surely, the U.S. Congress, comprising each and every State of the Union, is *the* place where the Constitution of the USA should be most rigidly upheld. There is surely no need to belabor this point.

As for your stating that some Jews did object to the ceremony on Constitutional grounds, to my knowledge these were exceptional and isolated instances. Moreover, I dare say, that (entre nous) the objectors, though ostensibly citing the Constitution, were motivated by other sentiments; a plausible assumption, since they are identified with organizations that thwart every effort to get State aid for Hebrew Day Schools and Yeshivoth to alleviate their burden of the *secular* department and other "non-religious" needs. Be it noted that the money that would have been received in such aid carries the motto, "In G-d We Trust!" It is lamentable that as a result of this attitude thousands of Jewish children have been *deprived* of their right to Jewish education. It is not surprising, therefore, to see such an appalling rate of intermarriage, nor is it surprising, however sad and deplorable, that the vast majority of intermarriages take place among the ranks of young people who have been deprived of Jewish education, for one reason or another.

In view of your expressed concern for the preservation of Judaism in this country and for the protection of our children against proselytizing, etc., I am encouraged to take advantage of this unexpected exchange of correspondence between us to express my ardent hope that you will use your influence to put an end to the *destructive* fight against State aid to parochial schools—at any rate insofar as the secular department is concerned, so as to enable Jewish Day Schools and Yeshivoth [to] open their doors to the maximum number of students, starting with the next school year and thereafter. For, only an adequate Jewish education can preserve our young generation and future generations from alienation, intermarriage and complete loss, G-d forbid.

I hope and pray that *everyone* who has a voice and influence in Jewish community affairs and is concerned for the preservation of Jews and Judaism in this country no less than for the preservation of the American way, will indeed act in the spirit of the basic principle of "this Nation *under G-d*, and government of the people, by the people, and *for* the people," including also the Jewish people, and do *everything* possible for the good of every Jewish child, that he and she remain Jewish, marry a Jew, and live Jewishly; and, of course, a good Jew is also a good American.

With prayerful wishes for an inspiring Yom Tov of Mattan Torah, and the traditional blessing to receive the Torah with joy and inwardness,

Sincerely yours,
M. SCHNEERSON

Central Conference of American Rabbis
Office of the Executive Vice President

August 14, 1978

Rabbi M. M. Schneerson
770 Eastern Parkway
Brooklyn, New York 11213

Dear Rabbi Schneerson:

Thank you for your letter of the 3rd of Sivan which was delivered to me at Oxford University where I am doing some very interesting research in a comparative study of the Anglo-American and Jewish laws of self-incrimination. I graduated law school before entering the rabbinate and have maintained an interest in legal studies.

Knowing how busy you are and that your health has not been good, I deeply appreciate your taking the time to send me such a full reply. However, I can see that we are very much in basic disagreement.

You place a great deal of importance on the fact that the kindling of the Hanukkiot in public places has received general acclaim and that countless Jews in all parts of the country have been impressed. I must point out respectfully that constitutional matters are not decided by *vox populi* except in the extreme case where a constitutional amendment is being considered, and even then there are federalist safeguards. Constitutional law, which is what we are talking about, is a matter of principle and not of passing popularity. It follows that those who participated in, or witnessed, the kindling of a Hanukkah lamp in a public place feeling, as you say, that their loyalty to the Constitution of the United States had not been weakened or compromised thereby, are not the arbiters of such an issue. Neither are the authorities who you report readily granted permission for the kindling. Nor is the United States Congress which indeed, lamentably begins its sessions with a religious invocation. You are quite correct when you say that "surely the U.S. Congress, comprising each and every State of the Union, is *the* place where the Constitution of the U.S.A. should be most rigidly upheld." Unfortunately, all too often, this is not the case. Time after time, the United States Supreme Court, which *is* the place and the only place, where ultimately the U.S. Constitution is upheld, has struck down law after law passed by the Congress, as unconstitutional. This is also true in reference to acts of other governmental bodies, Federal, State and local, legislative and executive or administrative.

By the way, it is only very recently that the words "under God" were added to the Pledge of Allegiance, rather arrogantly, many of us thought, by President Eisenhower, whose understanding of the American process and constitutional principle was probably the least of all the presidents of the United States from George Washington to the present. No one took it very seriously, as it had no particular legal force, and no one really wanted to "come out against God," which is part of the reason that your impression is that Jewish objection to the kindling of the Hanukkiot in public places is "to my knowledge . . . exceptional and isolated instances." We should add to that the fact that Jews do not like to oppose Jews in public and thus the far more substantial opposition than you realize exists has been muted up to now. If you are referring to Lincoln's Gettysburg address, it must be remembered that this was a personal affirmation of Lincoln, to which he was entitled, and for which I am grateful; Eisenhower, on the other hand, both cheapened and abused the phrase, and its underlying concept, when he promulgated it into the Pledge of Allegiance by Presidential decree. It is not correct to say that "the objectors, though ostensibly citing the Constitution, were motivated by other sentiments." I am one of those objectors and I must protest against such an allegation. It is my opinion that the principle of separation of Church and State, firmly imbedded in the United States Constitution, exalts religion by keeping the state out, and that any intermingling of religion and state cheapens, weakens and subordinates to the state religion. The lamentable experience throughout Europe is eminent proof of that, as testified to by Alexis de Tocqueville in his classic work on Democracy in America which I urgently recommend you read. There, de Tocqueville, a French scholar of the 19th Century, glories in the vigorous and healthy state of religion in America and accounts for it by citing the sharp separation of religion and state in this country. He deplores the opposite situation in Europe. Further, if you would justify Hanukkiot kindling under the rubric of "civil religion," this, too, would be inappropriate. The proponents of civil religion clearly draw the line at sectarian prayer and practice of any sort, and what could be more sectarian than our Hanukka, celebrating our national deliverance from Syria, our cultural reassertion, the miracle of the cruse of oil in our very own, highly exclusive Temple?

The matter of government support for religious schools, which you bring into our correspondence, has always been a most painful one for me. I feel very deeply about Jewish education and make every effort to strengthen it. I have supported Jewish day schools, and shall continue to do so, under all auspices, including the most Orthodox. But, for the reasons given above, I have steadfastly opposed any kind of direct, or dangerously indirect, government support. The moment the camel gets its nose under the tent, the inhabitants thereof are in trouble. The wall of separation between religion and state is like a dike; the slightest breach is a dangerous portent of a torrent to follow. Your own reasoning is a classic example thereof. You point to the prayers uttered in the halls of the Congress as justification for the kindling of Hanukkiot in public places, and then move right on to call for government subvention of religious based schools. Ultimately, this must lead to government intervention in matters theological and in the moral areas where religion must have full sway and unimpeded conscience. There can be no "deals" between secular power and religious authority. Inevitably, religious authority will be subordinated and crushed. To mingle religion and state is to pervert American democracy and to endanger American religion.

I want to assure you, dear Rebbe, that I believe in, worship and commune with God as deeply, as fervently, and as intensively as you do, and cherish and work for the perpetuation of Judaism as much and as indefatigably. It is for these reasons, as well as out of respect for the brilliance of the founding fathers of the United States of America, that I urge you to research the matter further and to reconsider your policy.

Finally, I must disagree with your opinion that there is some intrinsic value to individual Jews involved in the public lighting and blessing of the Hanukkiot. I think it might be just the opposite. Ultimately, the survival of Judaism depends on the home, which is where the Hanukkia should be lit. People coming to public places to observe (not really participate in) this ceremony are being involved in a kind of public, almost flamboyant religious exercise instead of in a sacred home ritual. From that standpoint also, I think the matter should be reconsidered.

My very best wishes to you.

> *Shalom,*
> RABBI JOSEPH B. GLASER

◆

Nathan Lewin, "Making a Case for Menorahs on Public Property," 1991

The tide has turned in the battle to permit privately funded Chanukah menorahs to be constructed on public property. The legal issue used to be whether cities could constitutionally permit menorahs to be placed near governmental buildings or in public parks. That was resolved more than two years ago when the Supreme Court, in a landmark case arising in Pittsburgh, held that it was not an establishment of religion to permit a large Chabad-Lubavitch menorah adjacent to the city's Christmas tree in front of Pittsburgh's City Hall.

Today's constitutional issue, being litigated across the country, is whether cities must allow private menorahs to be exhibited in "public forums"—that is, at locations where private speeches and exhibits on various subjects have traditionally been permitted. One illustration is Cincinnati's Fountain Square—an area in the heart of downtown where demonstrations, public gatherings and private displays have always been encouraged.

Cincinnati refused for many years to allow a Lubavitch menorah to be displayed at Fountain Square, even though there had been private banners and rallies at the square from time immemorial. Last year, shortly before Chanukah, the city authorities again turned down the request that an 18-foot high menorah be erected at Lubavitch's expense. Lubavitch initiated a lawsuit against the city and, after a brief hearing in federal court, the city was ordered to permit the menorah display for all eight days of Chanukah.

The federal court of appeals rejected Cincinnati's expedited request to have the trial court order overturned. The court of appeals ruled that religious speech could not constitutionally be discriminated against. If a square or a park is thrown open for private speech on secular subjects, it cannot be closed to religious speech.

Contrary to the protestations of organizations such as the American Jewish Congress, Lubavitch has consistently represented the menorah to be a religious symbol which, when erected in a public square, has the constitutional protection of religious expression. No fewer than ten times in his decision in the Pittsburgh case, Justice Harry Blackmun—who wrote the dispositive opinion that decided the case in favor of the menorah—referred to the menorah as a religious symbol.

Opponents of the menorah displays have falsely asserted that those who want the menorahs erected are defending menorahs as "secular symbols" and thereby deprecating the religious significance of menorahs. In fact, in all cases litigated in federal courts, the menorah has been characterized by its supporters as a religious object that symbolizes the religious holiday of Chanukah.

It is entirely appropriate that, at a period of the year when Americans are submerged in constant reminders of the important Christian religious holiday being celebrated by the overwhelming majority of American citizens, there be some official acknowledgment that some Americans celebrate other religious holidays.

In my brief to the Supreme Court in the Pittsburgh case, I noted that Chanukah was a relatively minor holiday in the Jewish calendar, and that its importance in the case grew out of the fact that it arrives at the end of the secular calendar year. A menorah display in front of a city hall tells the residents of an American city that there are various religious holidays celebrated in December and that America is a country where Jews are welcome and are first-class citizens.

The fact is that menorah displays engender emotions of pride and confidence among Jews who see them. Jewish children feel like outsiders when, in December of every year, they are surrounded by the ever-present symbols of a Christian holiday. If a menorah shines amidst the evergreens, wreaths, reindeer and holly, a Jewish child (or adult) can identify with it and sense the hospitality and generosity which has been a part of this nation's tradition.

Banishing menorahs from public places means derogating religion and denying to Jews the equal access to public forums that are available to secular organizations, gospel groups and evangelical meetings. Cincinnati decided, after its initial defeat in the trial and appellate courts, to abandon its antimenorah position and to amend its municipal regulations to allow the menorah display that had been forbidden for many years.

Other cities are also belatedly recognizing that no sensible public policy is advanced by doctrinaire resistance to the exhibition on public property of a plainly private religious symbol. Only the American Civil Liberties Union, the American Jewish Congress and other secular Jewish organizations are putting up a last-ditch fight.

◆

Allan Nadler, "Lubavitchers setting fire to wall of separation," 1991

The Chanukah menorah is the great Jewish symbol of religious freedom. It commemorates the proud overthrow of a cruel religious autocracy by an ancient oppressed minority. How ironic then that this very symbol has of late become the vehicle for a grossly public and widespread violation of precisely that amendment to the American constitution that was formulated to prevent the "establishment of religion" and thereby protect minorities from the tyranny of religious subjugation.

For the past decade, the chasidic Lubavitch movement has, with remarkable zeal, pursued a vigorous campaign of erecting Chanukah menorahs and engaging in public religious ceremonies in which prominent civic and political personalities participate in the benedictions and rituals surrounding the lighting of the candles.

From city hall in Los Angeles, to the steps of the state house in Des Moines, to Independence Hall in Philadelphia, the Lubavitchers have deliberately targeted the most public of public places in which to display their oversized menorahs.

This public lighting campaign has been proudly documented twice by the Lubavitchers in glossy, hardcover volumes titled "Let There Be Light" and ". . . And There Was Light," respectively pictorial accounts of public lighting ceremonies across America and around the world.

In celebration of a holiday that champions religious freedom as no other does, these menorahs have contributed to the most widespread breach of the "wall of separation" between religion and affairs of state that guarantees Americans of all faiths—not the least Jews—complete religious freedom.

And far from being the unintended consequence of naive religious enthusiasm on the part of the chasidim, the menorah-lighting campaign has had a very deliberate political effect. ". . . And There Was Light," for example, published in 1987, contains a preface that argues that these public religious ceremonies are in perfect harmony with the First Amendment, followed by a full-page photograph of then-President Ronald Reagan accepting a copy of the earlier volume, "Let There Be Light."

Indeed, the public menorahs reflect the political philosophy of a rebbe who, among his other positions, advocates prayer in the public school system and the reintroduction of anti-abortion legislation.

The Lubavitchers' aggressive menorah-lighting campaign has not been without widespread, and potentially dangerous, religio-political consequences. As far back as 1984, the Catholic League, taking note of the precedent set by the erection of a huge menorah in New York's Central Park, successfully petitioned for the re-institution of a public nativity scene in the park—a display that had been proscribed for 60 years.

And in court cases in a number of states the Lubavitchers have joined forces with Christian activists to ensure the presence of Christmas symbols, along with menorahs, on the steps of state houses and in the corridors of city halls. Christians who are this season inspired by the reintroduction of long-banned Christological displays such as creches on public property have the Lubavitcher chasidim to thank.

It has been argued, in defense of the Lubavitch menorahs, that signs of Christmas are ubiquitous in this season and that the menorah is no more offensive than the Christmas lights and decorations that have always been routinely tolerated on public property. It is essential, however, that the exact nature of permissible public holiday displays be very carefully defined. There is a crucial distinction that must be drawn between vague symbolic reminders of a festive season, and ritual objects actually used in religious ceremonies.

*　*　*

The kindling of huge menorahs in public places across America opens a dangerous constitutional can of worms. It can very easily backfire on the Jewish community by undermining the principle of freedom from established religion, which has always been such a blessing for American Jewry.

While public lightings may appear to some as a splendid, ultimate form of pirsumei d'nisa [the publicizing of the miracle of Chanukah], such religious exhibitionism is in no way mandated by Jewish law. Moreover, even if it were so mandated, the mitzvah of publicly broadcasting the miracle of Chanukah, is, as we have seen, entirely subordinate to pragmatic concerns for Jewish security and welfare. And there are few, if any, legal institutions, so basic to that security as the constitutional wall separating church and state.

Suggestions for Further Reading

I. The Colonial Era

Cohen, Naomi W. *Jews in Christian America: The Pursuit of Religious Equality.* New York, 1992.

Curry, Thomas J. *The First Freedoms: Church and State in America to the Passage of the First Amendment.* New York, 1986.

Faber, Eli. *A Time for Planting: The First Jewish Migration, 1654–1820.* The Jewish People in America, vol. 1. Baltimore, 1992.

Goodman, Abram Vossen. *American Overture: Jewish Rights in Colonial Times.* Philadelphia, 1947.

Handy, Robert T. *The American Revolution and Religious Freedom.* The Sol Feinstone Lecture for 1979. The Jewish Theological Seminary, New York, 1979.

Katsh, Abraham I. *The Biblical Heritage of American Democracy.* New York, 1977.

Kohler, Max J. "Phases in the History of Religious Liberty in America with Special Reference to the Jews." Part 1. *Publications of the American Jewish Historical Society* 11 (1903).

Marcus, Jacob R. *The Colonial American Jew, 1492–1776.* Detroit, 1970.

Morris, Maxwell H. "Roger Williams and the Jews." *American Jewish Archives* 3 (1951): 24–27.

Morris, Richard B. "Civil Liberties and the Jewish Tradition in Early America." In *The Jewish Experience in America,* vol. 1, edited by Abraham J. Karp. Waltham, Mass., and New York, 1969.

Pratt, John W. *Religion, Politics, and Diversity: The Church-State Theme in New York History.* Ithaca, N.Y., 1967.

Sarna, Jonathan D. "The Impact of the American Revolution on American Jews." *Modern Judaism* 1 (September 1981): 149–160.

Sarna, Jonathan D., Benny Kraut, and Samuel K. Joseph. *Jews and the Founding of the Republic.* New York, 1985.
Schappes, Morris U., ed. *A Documentary History of the Jews in the United States, 1654–1875.* New York, 1971.
Schwartz, Bernard. *The Roots of the Bill of Rights.* New York, 1980.

II. The New Nation

Blau, Joseph L., and Salo W. Baron. *The Jews of the United States, 1790–1840: A Documentary History.* 3 vols. New York, 1963.
Borden, Morton. *Jews, Turks, and Infidels.* Chapel Hill, N.C., 1984.
Chyet, Stanley F. "The Political Rights of the Jews in the United States: 1776–1840." *American Jewish Archives* 10 (1958): 14–75.
Gaustad, Edwin Scott. "The Emergence of Religious Freedom in the Early Republic." In *Religion and the State: Essays in Honor of Leo Pfeffer,* edited by James E. Wood, Jr. Waco, Texas, 1985.
Handlin, Oscar, and Mary F. Handlin. "The Acquisition of Political and Social Rights by the Jews in the United States." *American Jewish Year Book* 56 (Philadelphia, 1955): 43–98.
Healey, Robert M. "Jefferson on Judaism and the Jews." *American Jewish History* 73 (1984): 359–374.
Tushnet, Mark. "Lawyers' History, Historians' Law: Original Intent, the Establishment Clause, and Minority Religions in the Era of the Framing of the Constitution." *American Jewish History* 78 (September 1988): 5–19.

III. In Search of Equal Footing

Altfeld, E. Milton. *The Jews' Struggle for Religious and Civil Liberty in Maryland.* Baltimore, 1924.
Eitches, Edward. "Maryland's Jew Bill." *American Jewish Historical Quarterly* 60 (March 1971): 258–279.
Huhner, Leon. "The Struggle for Religious Liberty in North Carolina with Special Reference to the Jews." In *The Jews in America after the American Revolution.* New York, 1959.

Sarna, Jonathan D. *Jacksonian Jew: The Two Worlds of Mordecai Noah.* New York, 1981.

IV. Christian America or Religious America?

Blau, Joseph L. *Cornerstones of Religious Freedom in America.* Boston, 1949.

Feldman, Egal. *Dual Destinies: The Jewish Encounter with Protestant America.* Urbana, Ill. and Chicago, 1990.

Handy, Robert T. "The Protestant Quest for a Christian America, 1830–1930." *Church History* 22 (March 1953): 8–20.

———. *A Christian America.* 2d ed. New York, 1984.

Kohler, Max J. "The Doctrine that 'Christianity is Part of the Common Law,' and Its Recent Judicial Overthrow in England with Particular Reference to Jewish Rights." *Publications of the American Jewish Historical Society* 31 (1928): 105–126.

Rohrer, James R. "Sunday Mails and the Church-State Theme in Jacksonian America." *Journal of the Early Republic* 7 (Spring 1987): 53–74.

Sarna, Jonathan D. "The Church-State Dilemma of American Jews." In *Jews in Unsecular America,* edited by Richard John Neuhaus. Grand Rapids, Mich., 1987.

———. "Jewish-Christian Hostility in the United States." In *Uncivil Religion: Interreligious Hostility in America,* edited by Robert Bellah and Frederick Greenspahn. New York, 1987.

Sussman, Lance J. *Isaac Leeser and the Making of American Judaism.* Detroit, 1995.

V. In Defense of Jewish Rights

Cohen, Naomi W. "Pioneers of American Jewish Defense." *American Jewish Archives* 19 (November 1977): 116–150.

———. *Encounter With Emancipation: The German Jews in the United States, 1830–1914.* Philadelphia, 1984.

Diner, Hasia. *A Time for Gathering: The Second Migration, 1820–1880.* The Jewish People in America, vol. 11. Baltimore, 1992.

Heller, James G. *Isaac M. Wise: His Life, Work and Thought.* New York, 1965.

Korn, Bertram W. *Eventful Years and Experiences: Studies in Nineteenth-Century American Jewish History.* Cincinnati, 1954.

———. *American Jewry and the Civil War.* New York, 1970.

Panitz, Esther L. *Simon Wolf: Private Conscience and Public Image.* Rutherford, N.J., 1987.

Tarshish, Allan. "The Board of Delegates of American Israelites (1859–1878)." In *The Jewish Experience in America,* vol. 3, edited by Abraham J. Karp. Waltham, Mass. and New York, 1969.

VI. Sunday Laws

Blakely, William. *American State Papers Bearing on Sunday Legislation.* New York and Washington, 1911.

Eshkenazi, Tamara, et al. *The Sabbath in Jewish and Christian Traditions.* Hoboken, N.J., 1991.

Friedenberg, Albert M. "Jews and the American Sunday Laws." *Publications of the American Jewish Historical Society* 11 (1903): 101–115.

———. "Sunday Laws of the United States and Leading Judicial Decisions Having Special Reference to the Jews." *American Jewish Year Book* 10 (1908–1909): 152–189.

Lightman, Jacob Ben. "The Status of Jews in American Sunday Laws." *Jewish Social Service Quarterly* 11 (1934–1935): 223–228, 269–276.

Pfeffer, Leo. "Sunday Laws and Sabbath Observance." *Congress Weekly* 17 (February 3, 1950): 9–11.

VII. The Shift to Separationism

Brewer, David J. *The United States—A Christian Nation.* Philadelphia, 1905.

Fink, Joseph. *Summary of C.C.A.R. Opinion on Church and State.* Philadelphia, 1948.

Hassler, Isaac. *A Reply to Justice Brewer's Lectures "The United States—A Christian Nation."* Philadelphia, 1908.

Kraut, Benny, "Frances E. Abbot: Perceptions of a Nineteenth-Century Religious Radical on Jews and Judaism." In *Studies in the American Jewish Experience,* edited by Jacob R. Marcus and Abraham J. Peck. Cincinnati, 1981.

Philipson, David. *Max Lilienthal.* New York, 1915.

———. *My Life as an American Jew.* Cincinnati, 1941.

Yahalom, Shlomith. "American Judaism and the Question of Separation Between Church and State." Unpublished Ph.D. dissertation in Hebrew, Hebrew University of Jerusalem, 1981.

VIII. Religion in the Public Schools

Brandon, Joseph R. "A Protest Against Sectarian Texts in California Schools in 1875." *Western States Jewish History* 20 (April 1988): 233–235.

Cohen, Naomi W. "Schools, Religion and Government: Recent American Jewish Opinions." *Michael* 3 (1975): 340–392.

Cohen, Seymour J. "Religious Freedom and the Constitution." *Conservative Judaism* 17 (1963): 13–38.

Freund, Paul, and Robert Ulich. *Religion and the Public Schools.* Cambridge, Mass., 1965.

Gartner, Lloyd P. *Jewish Education in the United States: A Documentary History.* New York, 1969.

———. "Temples of Liberty Unpolluted: American Jews and the Public Schools, 1840–1875." In *A Bicentennial Festschrift for Jacob Rader Marcus,* edited by Bertram W. Korn. Waltham, Mass. and New York, 1976.

Hertzberg, Arthur. "Church, State and the Jews." *Commentary* 35 (1963): 277–288.

Isaacs, Joakim. "The Struggle for the Soul: A Jewish Response to Bible Reading and Religion in American Public Schools, 1900–1915." *American Jewish Archives* 42 (Fall/Winter 1990): 119–132.

Lipman, Eugene. "The Conference Considers Relations between Religion and the State." In *Retrospect and Prospect: Essays in Commemoration of the Seventy-Fifth Anniversary of the Founding of the Central Conference of American Rabbis, 1889–1964,* ed. Bertram W. Korn. New York, 1965.

Muir, William K., Jr. *Prayer in the Public Schools: Law and Attitude Change.* Chicago, 1967.

Pfeffer, Leo. "The New York Regents' Prayer Case." *Journal of Church and State* 4 (November 1962): 150–159.

———. "The Schempp-Murray Decision on School Prayers and Bible Reading." *Journal of Church and State* 5 (1963): 165–175.

Sarna, Jonathan D. "Is Judaism Compatible with American Civil Religion? The Problem of Christmas and the National Faith." In *Religion in the Life of the Nation,* edited by Roland A. Sherrill. Urbana, Ill., and Chicago, 1990.

Schachner, Nathan. "Church, State and Education." *American Jewish Year Book* 49 (1947): 1–48.

Sussman, Lance J. "Rhetoric and Reality: The Central Conference of American Rabbis and the Church-State Debate, 1890–1940." In *In Celebration: An American Jewish Perspective on the Bicentennial of the United States Constitution,* edited by Kerry M. Olitzky. Lanham, Md., 1989.

IX. Religion and the State: The New Consensus

Cohen, Naomi W. *Not Free to Desist: A History of the American Jewish Committee, 1906–1966.* Philadelphia, 1972.

Cord, Robert L. *The Separation of Church and State: Historical Fact and Current Fiction.* New York, 1988.

Dalin, David G. "Leo Pfeffer and the Separationist Faith." *This World* 24 (Winter 1989): 136–140.

Friedman, Murray. *The Utopian Dilemma: American Judaism and Public Policy.* Washington, D.C., 1985.

Ivers, Gregg. "Organized Religion and the Supreme Court." *Journal of Church and State* 32 (1990): 775–793.

——. *To Build A Wall: American Jews and the Separation of Church and State.* Charlottesville, Va., 1995.

Pfeffer, Leo. "Amici in Church-State Litigation." *Law and Contemporary Problems* 44 (1981): 83–110.

——. "An Autobiographical Sketch." In *Religion in the State: Essays in Honor of Leo Pfeffer,* edited by James E. Wood, Jr. Waco, Tex., 1985.

Rabinove, Samuel. "How—and Why—American Jews Have Contended for Religious Freedom: The Requirements and Limits of Civility." *Journal of Law and Religion* 8 (1990): 131–152.

X. A Question of Priorities

Dalin, David G. *American Jews and the Separationist Faith: The New Debate on Religion in Public Life.* Washington, D.C., 1992.

——. "Will Herberg in Retrospect." *Commentary* 86 (July 1988): 38–43.

————, ed. *From Marxism to Judaism: The Collected Essays of Will Herberg.* New York, 1989.

Freund, Paul. "Public Aid to Parochial Schools." *Harvard Law Review* (1990): 1680–1692.

Herberg, Will. "The Sectarian Conflict Over Church and State." *Commentary* 14 (November 1952): 450–462.

Himmelfarb, Milton. "Church and State: How High a Wall." *Commentary* 42 (July 1966): 23–29.

Petuchowski, Jakob J. "A Rabbi's Christmas." *First Things* 18 (December 1991: 8–10.

Pickus, Noah. "Before I Built a Wall—Jews, Religion and American Public Life." *This World* 15 (Fall 1986): 28–43.

Schick, Marvin, ed. *Government Aid to Parochial Schools—How Far?* New York, 1967.

Siegel, Seymour. "Church and State." *Conservative Judaism* 17 (1963): 1–12.

————. "Church and State: A Reassessment." *Sh'ma* 1 (December 11, 1970). Reprinted in *Listening to American Jews,* edited by Carolyn T. Oppenheim (New York, 1986).

XI. Old Principles and New Rights: The Free Exercise Debate

Bleich, J. David. "Jewish Divorce: Judicial Misconceptions and Possible Means of Civil Enforcement." *Connecticut Law Journal* 16 (Winter 1984): 201–289.

Breitowitz, Irving A. *Between Civil and Religious Law: The Plight of the Agunah in American Society.* Hamden, Conn., 1993.

Chazin, Daniel D. "*Goldman v. Secretary of Defense:* A New Standard for Free Exercise Claims in the Military." *National Jewish Law Review* 1 (1986): 13–40.

Edelman, Martin. "Entangling Alliances: The 'Agunah' Problem in the Light of *Avitzur v. Avitzur.*" *The Jewish Law Annual* 8 (1990): 193–210.

————. "*Goldman v. Weinberger:* Yarmulkes, The Supreme Court and the Free Exercise of Religion." *The Jewish Law Annual* 8 (1990): 210–220.

Ellenson, David, and James S. Ellenson. "American Courts and the Enforceability of a Ketubah as a Private Contract: An Investigation of Recent U.S. Court Decisions." *Conservative Judaism* 35, no. 3 (Spring 1982): 35–42.

Garvey, John H. "Free Exercise and the Values of Religious Liberty." *Connecticut Law Review* 18 (Summer 1986): 779–802.

Haut, Irwin H. *Divorce in Jewish Law and Life.* New York, 1983.

Hoffman, Edward. *Despite All Odds: The Story of Lubavitch.* New York, 1991.
Lieberman, Joseph I. "The Future of the Establishment Clause in the Wake of Estate of Thornton v. Caldor, Inc." *Connecticut Law Review* 18 (Summer 1986): 845–853.
Meislin, Bernard J. "Civil Court Enforcement of Agreement to Obtain a 'Get.'" *The Jewish Law Annual* 1 (1978): 224–227.
———. "Jewish Law in America." In *Jewish Law in Legal History and the Modern World,* edited by Bernard S. Jackson (Leiden, 1980).
———. *Jewish Law in American Tribunals.* New York, 1976.
Riskin, Shlomo. *Women and Jewish Divorce.* Hoboken, N.J., 1989.
Sandel, Michael J. "Freedom of Conscience or Freedom of Choice?" In *Religious Liberty and the Supreme Court: The Cases That Define the Debate Over Church and State,* edited by Terry Eastland. Washington, D.C., 1993.
Stern, Marc. "Kosher Food and the Law." *Judaism* 39 (1990): 389–401.
Wurzberger, Walter. "Separation of Church and State Revisited." *Face to Face* 8 (Fall 1981): 8–10.

General Reading

Abraham, Henry J. *Freedom and the Court: Civil Rights and Liberties in the United States.* New York, 1982.
Alley, Robert S. *The Supreme Court on Church and State.* New York, 1988.
Eastland, Terry, ed. *Religious Liberty in the Supreme Court: The Cases That Define the Debate Over Church and State.* Washington, D.C., 1993.
Levy, Leonard W. *The Establishment Clause: Religion and the First Amendment.* 2d ed. Chapel Hill, N.C., 1994.
Maddox, Robert L. *Separation of Church and State.* New York, 1987.
McConnell, Michael W. "The Origins and Historical Understandings of Free Exercise of Religion." *Harvard Law Review* 103 (1990): 1410–1512.
Miller, Robert T., and Ronald B. Flowers. *Toward Benevolent Neutrality: Church, State, and the Supreme Court.* 4th ed. Waco, Tex., 1992.
Morgan, Richard E. *The Politics of Religious Conflict: Church and State in America.* New York, 1968.
Morgan, Richard E. *The Supreme Court and Religion.* New York, 1972.
Neuhaus, Richard John. *The Naked Public Square: Religion and Democracy in America.* Grand Rapids, Mich., 1984.
Noll, Mark A. *Religion and American Politics: From the Colonial Period to the 1980s.* New York, 1990.

Noonan, John T., Jr. *The Believers and the Powers That Are: Cases, History and Other Data Bearing on the Relation of Religion and Government.* New York, 1987.

Pfeffer, Leo. *Church, State, and Freedom.* Boston, 1967.

———. *God, Caesar, and the Constitution.* Boston, 1974.

———. *Religion, State, and the Burger Court.* Buffalo, 1985.

Reichley, A. James. *Religion in American Public Life.* Washington, D.C., 1985.

Sorauf, Frank J. *The Wall of Separation: The Constitutional Politics of Church and State.* Princeton, N.J., 1976.

Stokes, Anson Phelps. *Church and State in the United States.* 3 vols. New York, 1950.

Wilson, John E., and Donald L. Drakeman. *Church and State in American History.* 2d ed. Boston, 1987.

Sources and
Acknowledgments

◆ ❖ ◆

I. The Colonial Era

1. The Right to Settle and Trade

Petition to the West India Company on behalf of Jews in New Netherland, 1655; West India Company directive to New Netherland; Renewed petition to West India Company; Company's renewed directive to New Netherland.

    Publications of the American Jewish Historical Society 18 (1909): 8–11, 33, reprinted with the permission of the American Jewish Historical Society; and *American Jewish Archives* 7 (1955): 52–53, reprinted with the permission of the American Jewish Archives.

2. Religion and State in Colonial Law

First Charter of Virginia, 1606; Fundamental Orders of Connecticut, 1639; Maryland Act concerning Religion, 1649; Charter of Rhode Island and Providence Plantations, 1663; Fundamental Constitutions of Carolina, 1669; Pennsylvania Charter of Privileges, 1701.

    Bernard Schwartz, *The Roots of the Bill of Rights* (New York: Chelsea House, 1981), 55, 62–63, 91–94, 97–98, 121–123, 171–172.

3. Naturalization

British Naturalization Act, 1740.

    Publications of the American Jewish Historical Society 1 (1892): 94–98, reprinted with the permission of the American Jewish Historical Society.

4. The Lopez-Elizer Incident

Petition of Jews for naturalization, 1762; Petition dismissed by Rhode Island Court.
> Lee M. Friedman, *Pilgrims in a New Land* (Philadelphia: Jewish Publication Society, 1948), 34, 36, used by permission of The Jewish Publication Society.

II. The New Nation

1. Widening Religious Liberty in the States

Virginia Declaration of Rights, 1776; New Jersey Constitution, 1776; New York Constitution, 1777.
> Bernard Schwartz, *The Roots of the Bill of Rights* (New York: Chelsea House, 1981), 236, 260, 312.

2. The Battle over Religious Freedom in Virginia

Thomas Jefferson's bill for religious freedom in Virginia, 1779.
> *The Works of Thomas Jefferson,* ed. Paul L. Ford (New York, 1904), 2:438ff.

"To the Publick," a Christian's response to Jefferson.
> *The Virginia Gazette,* September 18, 1779, 1.

3. Jews Appeal for Religious Equality

Petition for equality by the Philadelphia Synagogue to Council of Censors of Pennsylvania, 1783; Letter from Jonas Phillips to the Federal Constitutional Convention, 1787.
> *A Documentary History of the Jews in the United States, 1654–1875,* ed. with notes and introductions by Morris U. Schappes, third edition (New York: Schocken Books, 1976), 64–66, 68–69, reprinted with permission of Morris U. Schappes.

4. The Federal Constitution and the Jews

Constitution of the United States of America, Art. VI, section 3; Amendment 1.

Debate of the North Carolina Convention, 1788.
> J. Elliot, ed., *The Debates in the Several State Conventions on the Adoption of the Federal Constitution* (Washington, D.C., 1888), 4:198–200.

5. "To Bigotry No Sanction, To Persecution No Assistance"

Letter from the Hebrew Congregation of Newport to President Washington, 1790; President Washington's reply.
Lewis Abraham, "Correspondence Between Washington and Jewish Citizens," *Publications of the American Jewish Historical Society* 3 (1895): 90–92, reprinted with the permission of the American Jewish Historical Society.

III. In Search of Equal Footing

1. Jacob Henry Demands the Right of Conscience

Jacob Henry's address to the North Carolina legislature, 1809.
J. Agar, *The American Orator's Own Book* (New York, 1859), 227–230.

2. Shearith Israel Seeks State Funds for Religious Education of the Poor

Petition of Congregation Shearith [Sheerith] Israel on state aid to religious schools, 1813.
Publications of the American Jewish Historical Society 27 (1920): 92–95, reprinted with the permission of the American Jewish Historical Society.

3. Mordecai Noah Protests His Recall from Tunis

Consul Mordecai Noah's dismissal based on religion, 1815.
M. M. Noah, *Travels in England, France, Spain and the Barbary States* (New York, 1819), 377–380.

4. "An Israelite" Condemns Christian Missions as Unconstitutional

On the state incorporation of a missionary society, 1820.
Israel Vindicated (New York, 1820), v-viii.

5. The Maryland Jew Bill

Plea to a Maryland legislator for civil equality, 1818.
E. Milton Altfeld, *The Jew's Struggle for Religious and Civil Liberty in Maryland* (Baltimore, 1924), 48–51.

IV. Christian America or Religious America?

1. The Case for Christian America

Supreme Court Justice Story on the Christian foundation of America, 1833.
  Joseph Story, *Commentaries on the Constitution of the United States* (1 volume edition, Boston and Philadelphia, 1833), 698–703.

Daniel Webster on Christianity as part of common law, 1844.
  Daniel Webster, "The Christian Ministry and the Religious Instruction of the Young," *The Works of Daniel Webster* (Boston, 1851), 176.

2. The Case for Religious Equality

Isaac Leeser, Christianity is not the state religion, 1850.
  Isaac Leeser, "The United States Not A Christian Nation," *Occident* 7 (1850): 564–566.

Nathaniel Levin on religious liberty, 1859.
  N. Levin, "Toast to Religious Liberty," *Occident* 16 (1859): 580–581.

3. New York Debates the Appointment of State Chaplains

New York committee opposes legislative chaplains, 1832.
  David Moulton and Mordecai Myers, "Report of the Select Committee of the New York State Assembly on the Several Memorials Against Appointing Chaplains to the Legislature" (1832). In Joseph L. Blau, *Cornerstones of Religious Freedom in America* (Boston: Beacon Press, 1949), 146–148, 154–156.

Solomon Southwick's response to the committee report, 1834.
  Solomon Southwick, *A Layman's Apology* ... (Albany, 1834), 283ff.

4. Thanksgiving Day Proclamations and Jewish Dissents

Exchange of letters on South Carolina Gov. Hammond's Thanksgiving proclamation of 1844, with a public protest.
  "Correspondence between the Jews of South Carolina and James H. Hammond," *Occident* 2 (1845): 500–510.

5. Reassurances from President Tyler

Letter from President Tyler on a national day of prayer; Letter from President Tyler on separation of church and state.
  Publications of the American Jewish Historical Society 9 (1901): 162; 11 (1903): 158–159. Reprinted with the permission of the American Jewish Historical Society.

V. In Defense of Jewish Rights

1. The Swiss Treaty

Protest by American Jews against the Swiss treaty of 1850.
Israelite, November 6, 1857, 142, as reprinted in *A Documentary History of the Jews in the United States, 1654–1875*, ed. with notes and introductions by Morris U. Schappes, third edition (New York: Schocken Books, 1976), 321–324. Reprinted with permission of Morris U. Schappes.

2. The Chaplaincy Bill

Statement submitted to the United States Senate Committee on Military Affairs by Arnold Fischel, 1861.
Jewish Messenger, December 27, 1861, 101.

3. General U. S. Grant's General Order No. 11

Proceedings of the Board of Delegates of American Israelites with respect to General Grant's General Order No. 11 of 1862.
Proceedings of the Board of Delegates of American Israelites . . . 5625 (New York, 1865), 20.

4. The Proposed Christian Amendment to the Constitution

Jewish memorial to Congress on a Christian amendment, 1865.
Proceedings of the Board of Delegates of American Israelites . . . 5625 (New York, 1865), 18–20.

VI. Sunday Laws

1. Petition for a Limited Exemption

Unsent petition to amend Pennsylvania Sunday law, 1838.
Isaac Leeser, *The Claims of the Jews to an Equality of Rights* (Philadelphia, 1841), 90–91.

2. The Case against Sunday Laws

Petition protesting Richmond's Sunday ordinance, 1845.
Occident 3 (1846): 564–567.

3. The Judicial Defense of Sunday Laws

Judge O'Neall's decision upholding Charleston's Sunday law, 1848.
Occident 5 (1848): 596–599.

"An Hebrew" condemns the judge's ruling, 1848.
Occident 6 (1848): 38–39.

Sunday Times and Noah's Weekly Messenger editorial sides with the court, 1848.
Sunday Times and Noah's Weekly Messenger, February 13, 1848, as reprinted
in *A Documentary History of the Jews in the United States, 1654–1875*, ed. with
notes and introductions by Morris U. Schappes, third edition (New York:
Schocken Books, 1976), 280–282. Reprinted with permission of Morris U.
Schappes.

4. The Limits of Sabbath Legislation

Rabbi Felsenthal on Sabbath legislation, 1893.
B. Felsenthal, "The Sabbath in Judaism," *Judaism at the World's Parliament of
Religions* (Cincinnati, 1894), 40–41.

5. Drafting an Exemption

Louis Marshall's bill to permit "secular business" on Sunday.
Charles Reznikoff, ed., *Louis Marshall: Champion of Liberty* (Philadelphia:
Jewish Publication Society, 1957), 923–925, used by permission of The
Jewish Publication Society.

6. The Call for Two Weekly Rest Days—
The Five-Day Week

Rabbi Drachman's address to Lord's Day Congress, 1915.
Bernard Drachman, "The Jewish Sabbath in its Relation to the General
Question of Sabbath Observance," *Sunday the World's Rest Day* (New York,
1916), 526–529.

7. The Supreme Court Rules

Supreme Court Justice Frankfurter's opinion upholding state Sunday laws,
1961.
McGowan v. Maryland, 366 U.S. 420 (1961), 496–522.

VII. The Shift to Separationism

1. Max Lilienthal Protests

Rabbi Lilienthal denounces the "Christian Amendment" movement, 1870; Rabbi Lilienthal on the folly of christianizing the nation, 1871.
David Philipson, *Max Lilienthal: American Rabbi* (New York, 1915), 113–114, 116–118.

2. For a Secular America

Rabbi Felsenthal, the non-Christian morality of the modern state, 1875.
Emma Felsenthal, *Bernhard Felsenthal, Teacher in Israel* (New York, 1924), 265–268.

3. Against Religious Legislation

The Union of American Hebrew Congregations commends the "Congress of Liberals," 1876.
Where We Stand: Social Action Resolutions Adopted by the Union of American Hebrew Congregations (New York, 1960), 14.

CCAR resolution protesting religious legislation, 1892.
Central Conference of American Rabbis Yearbook 3 (1893): 45.

4. Justice Brewer and the Jews

Isaac Hassler replies to Supreme Court Justice Brewer's lectures on the Christian state, 1908.
Isaac Hassler, *A Reply to Justice Brewer's Lectures* (Philadelphia, 1908).

VIII. Religion in the Public Schools

1. "Temples of Liberty Unpolluted": The Development of Jewish Attitudes toward the Public Schools

Isidor Busch in praise of public schools, 1855; Isaac Leeser's reply.
Occident 13 (1855): 85–89, as reprinted in Lloyd P. Gartner, *Jewish Education in the United States: A Documentary History*, Classics in Education no. 41 (New York: Teachers College, 1969), 68–75, used by permission of Lloyd P. Gartner.

2. The Nineteenth-Century Case for Nonsectarian Public Schools

Rabbi Wise for secular public schools, 1869.
The Israelite, October 8, 1869, 8.

Joseph Brandon on protecting public education from sectarianism, 1875.
Joseph R. Brandon, *A Reply to the Rev. Mr. Hemphill's Discourse on "Our Public Schools, Shall the Lord's Prayer Be Recited in Them?"* (San Francisco, 1875), as reprinted in Lloyd P. Gartner, *Jewish Education in the United States: A Documentary History*, Classics in Education no. 41 (New York: Teachers College, 1969), 91–93, used by permission of Lloyd P. Gartner.

3. Should the Bible Be Read in the Public Schools?

CCAR, "Why the Bible Should Not Be Read in the Public Schools," 1906.
Central Conference of American Rabbis Year Book 16 (1906): 156–166.

Louis Marshall for compromise on Bible reading, 1922.
Charles Reznikoff, ed., *Louis Marshall: Champion of Liberty* (Philadelphia: Jewish Publication Society, 1957), 967–970, used by permission of The Jewish Publication Society.

4. Nonsectarian Education in the Public Schools

Rabbi Felsenthal calls for public school instruction in "unsectarian ethics," 1882.
The Nation 34 (January 12, 1882): 34.

Rabbi Schanfarber proposes a CCAR resolution against ethical instruction in public schools, 1911; Rabbi Zielonka's dissent, 1911.
Central Conference of American Rabbis Year Book 21 (1911): 248–251, 257, 259–262.

5. The Debate over the Gary "Released Time" Plan

Isadore Levy's argument against the Gary Plan, 1915.
New York Times, November 5, 1915.

Rabbi Schulman in support of the Gary Plan, 1916.
Central Conference of American Rabbis Year Book 26 (1916): 445–446, 452–453.

6. Preserving the Rights of Nonpublic Schools

Louis Marshall defends the right to attend private and religious schools, 1925.
Charles Reznikoff, ed., *Louis Marshall: Champion of Liberty* (Philadelphia: Jewish Publication Society, 1957), 960–961, 965–967, used by permission of The Jewish Publication Society.

7. Prayer in the Public Schools—The Debate over *Engel v. Vitale*

Jewish agencies support the Supreme Court decision outlawing state-composed prayers, 1961; Letter from the Lubavitcher Rabbi on the need for public school prayer, 1964.
"Brief of Synagogue Council of America and National Community Relations Advisory Council as Amici Curiae . . . *Engel v. Vitale*" and "Letter from the Lubavitcher Rabbi," as reprinted in Naomi W. Cohen, "Schools, Religion and Government—Recent American Jewish Opinions," *Michael* 3 (1975): 352–356, 364–365, used by permission of Naomi W. Cohen.

8. Christmas in the Public Schools

CCAR resolution on religious celebrations in the public schools, 1937.
Joseph L. Fink, *Summary of C.C.A.R. Opinion on Church and State as Embodied in Resolutions Adopted at Conferences Through the Years* (New York: Central Conference of American Rabbis, 1948), 13–14.

"Statement of Principles on Religious Holiday Observances in Public Schools" (Joint Advisory Committee of the Synagogue Council of America and the National Community Relations Advisory Council, 1962).

Jakob J. Petuchowski, "A Rabbi's Christmas," *First Things* (December 1991): 8–10, reprinted with permission of *First Things*.

9. *Lee v. Weisman* and the Continuing Issue of Public School Prayer

Rabbi Gutterman on his commencement benediction, 1989.
Leslie Gutterman, "Still Unsettled Feelings on Public Prayer," reprinted with permission of Rabbi Leslie Gutterman.

IX. Religion and the State: The New Consensus

1. Jewish Legal Action through the Courts

Will Maslow on the strategy and tactics of the American Jewish Congress, 1972.
> Will Maslow, "The Legal Defense of Religious Liberty—The Strategy and Tactics of the American Jewish Congress," reprinted with the permission of the American Jewish Congress.

2. Leo Pfeffer: Apostle of Strict Separationism

Leo Pfeffer's autobiographical reflections, 1985.
> Leo Pfeffer, "An Autobiographical Sketch," originally published in *Religion and the State: Essays in Honor of Leo Pfeffer*, ed. James E. Wood, Jr. (Waco, Tex.: Baylor University Press, 1985), 487–488, 528–529; reprinted by permission.

3. Safeguarding Religious Liberty: The "Official" Jewish Position on Church-State Relationships

"Safeguarding Religious Liberty," a general guide, 1971.
> "Safeguarding Religious Liberty" (Joint Advisory Committee of the Synagogue Council of America and the National Community Relations Advisory Council, 1971), reprinted with the permission of Dr. Jerome Chanes, National Jewish Community Relations Advisory Council.

X. A Question of Priorities

1. Will Herberg and the Jewish Critique of Strict Separationism

Will Herberg's challenge to strict separationism, 1952; Herberg's support for religion in public life, 1963.
> Will Herberg, "The Sectarian Conflict Over Church and State" (1952) and "Religion and Public Life" (1963), as reprinted in *From Marxism to Judaism: Collected Essays of Will Herberg*, ed. David G. Dalin (New York: Markus Wiener, 1989), 203–213, 218–221. Reprinted by permission of Donald G. Jones, Professor of Social Ethics, Drew University, and Executor, Will Herberg Estate.

2. The Debate over State Aid to Parochial Schools

Leo Pfeffer on religion, the First Amendment, and the ESEA, 1966.
Leo Pfeffer, "Is the First Amendment Dead?" *Congress Bi-Weekly*, November 7, 1966.

Rabbi Sherer criticizes Jewish opposition to ESEA, 1965.
Morris Sherer, "The Great Society and Aid to Religious Schools," *Jewish Observer* 2 (January 1965): 3–5, as reprinted in Naomi W. Cohen, "Schools, Religion and Government—Recent American Jewish Opinions," *Michael* 3 (1975): 366–369, used by permission of Naomi W. Cohen.

3. The Rise of COLPA

Marvin Schick on the creation of COLPA, 1967.
Marvin Schick, "The National Jewish Commission on Law and Public Affairs: An Analytical Report," in *Government Aid to Parochial Schools–How Far?* ed. Marvin Schick (New York, 1967), 4–16, reprinted by permission of Marvin Schick, first president of COLPA.

4. The Breakdown of Consensus

Milton Himmelfarb on the wall of separation, 1966.
Milton Himmelfarb, "Church and State: How High a Wall," *Commentary* 42 (July 1966), as reprinted in *The Jews of Modernity* (New York: Basic Books, 1973), 164–178, reprinted with the permission of Milton Himmelfarb.

Seymour Siegel advocates state aid for all schools, 1970.
Seymour Siegel, "Church and State: A Reassessment," *Sh'ma* 1 (December 11, 1970), reprinted by permission of *Sh'ma: A Journal of Jewish Responsibility*.

XI. Old Principles and New Rights: The Free Exercise Debate

1. Do Jews Have the Legal Right to Observe the Sabbath?

Argument before the Supreme Court on Sabbath observance, 1985.
Brief for the American Jewish Congress and COLPA, Amicus Curiae, in *Estate of Donald E. Thornton v. Caldor Inc.*, 472 U.S. 703 (1984).

2. Do Jewish Prisoners Have the Legal Right to Kosher Food?

Attorney for Rabbi Kahane on prisoners' right to kosher food, 1975.
  United States of America v. Meir Kahane (71-CR-479); *Meir Kahane v. United States of America* (75-C-624), United States District Court, Eastern District of New York, Memorandum and Order.

3. Does a Jewish Soldier Have the Legal Right to Keep His Head Covered?

COLPA's defense of the right to wear a yarmulke, 1985.
  Brief for the Petitioner, *S. Simcha Goldman v. Casper W. Weinberger*, 84–1097 (1985), 11–12.

Defense Authorization Law amended to allow religious apparel.
  Defense Authorization Act, 10 *U.S. Code* § 774 (December 4, 1987).

4. Can a Secular Judge Compel a Religious Divorce?

New York Appeals Court rules that a ketubah is legally binding, 1983.
  "Opinion of the New York State Court of Appeals in *Avitzur v. Avitzur*," 58 N.Y. 2d 108; cert. denied, 464 U.S. 817 (1983).

New York law links civil and religious divorce, 1984.
  New York *Domestic Relations Law* § 253 (1987).

5. Do Jews Have the Legal Right to Light a Menorah in the Public Square?

Exchange of letters between Rabbi Joseph Glaser and Rabbi Menachem Schneerson on the menorah issue, 1978.
  Correspondence between Rabbi Joseph B. Glaser and Rabbi Menachem M. Schneerson, reprinted with the permission of Rabbi Simeon Glaser and with permission from The Estate of The Lubavitcher Rebbe, Rabbi Menachem M. Schneerson.

Nathan Lewin, "Making A Case for Menorahs on Public Property," *The Jewish Press*, November 22, 1991, 92, reprinted by permission of Nathan Lewin, Partner, Miller, Cassidy, Larroca and Lewin, Washington, D.C.

Allan Nadler, "Lubavitchers Setting Fire to Wall of Separation," Jewish Telegraphic Agency Release, week of November 28, 1991, reprinted with the permission of Allan Nadler of the YIVO Institute.

Index

❖

323